Lecture Notes in Computer Science 6916

Commenced Publication in 1973
Founding and Former Series Editors:
Gerhard Goos, Juris Hartmanis, and Jan van Leeuwen

Editorial Board

David Hutchison
Lancaster University, UK

Takeo Kanade
Carnegie Mellon University, Pittsburgh, PA, USA

Josef Kittler
University of Surrey, Guildford, UK

Jon M. Kleinberg
Cornell University, Ithaca, NY, USA

Alfred Kobsa
University of California, Irvine, CA, USA

Friedemann Mattern
ETH Zurich, Switzerland

John C. Mitchell
Stanford University, CA, USA

Moni Naor
Weizmann Institute of Science, Rehovot, Israel

Oscar Nierstrasz
University of Bern, Switzerland

C. Pandu Rangan
Indian Institute of Technology, Madras, India

Bernhard Steffen
TU Dortmund University, Germany

Madhu Sudan
Microsoft Research, Cambridge, MA, USA

Demetri Terzopoulos
University of California, Los Angeles, CA, USA

Doug Tygar
University of California, Berkeley, CA, USA

Gerhard Weikum
Max Planck Institute for Informatics, Saarbruecken, Germany

Antonio Cerone   Pekka Pihlajasaari (Eds.)

Theoretical Aspects of Computing – ICTAC 2011

8th International Colloquium
Johannesburg, South Africa
August 31 – September 2, 2011
Proceedings

 Springer

Volume Editors

Antonio Cerone
The United Nations University
International Institute for Software Technology
Casa Silva Mendes, Est. do Engenheiro Trigo No. 4
Macau, China
E-mail: antonio@iist.unu.edu

Pekka Pihlajasaari
Data Abstraction (Pty) Ltd
7 Saint David's Park, Saint David's Place
Parktown, Johannesburg, South Africa
E-mail: pekka@data.co.za

ISSN 0302-9743   e-ISSN 1611-3349
ISBN 978-3-642-23282-4   e-ISBN 978-3-642-23283-1
DOI 10.1007/978-3-642-23283-1
Springer Heidelberg Dordrecht London New York

Library of Congress Control Number: 2011934503

CR Subject Classification (1998): F.1, F.3, F.4, F.2, D.2.4, D.2-3

LNCS Sublibrary: SL 1 – Theoretical Computer Science and General Issues

Typesetting: Camera-ready by author, data conversion by Scientific Publishing Services, Chennai, India

Printed on acid-free paper

Springer is part of Springer Science+Business Media (www.springer.com)

Preface

The International Colloquia on Theoretical Aspects of Computing (ICTAC) bring together practitioners and researchers from academia, industry and government to present research results and exchange experience and ideas. An important aim of the colloquia is to promote cooperation in research and education between participants and their institutions, from developing and industrial countries, in accordance with the mandate of the United Nations University.

Research on theoretical aspects of computing has a direct impact on the practice of computer systems development as well as on the technologies associated with many disciplines other than computer science. The definition of effective theoretical frameworks for modelling and analyzing complex systems has resulted in the development of tools and methodologies for the verifications of software and hardware systems, before their actual construction, and for the simulation and analysis of natural systems, such as biological and ecological systems, supporting important predictions which otherwise would require expensive and difficult laboratory and field experiments, and the prevention of natural disasters. Moreover, research on theoretical aspects of computing has enabled the development of sophisticated techniques for mining and analyzing large amounts of data and support knowledge management in various application domains, such as education, health, economy and governance.

This volume contains the papers presented at the 8th International Colloquium on Theoretical Aspects of Computing (ICTAC 2011), which was held from August 31 to September 2, at Mabalingwe Nature Reserve, in the Waterberg mountains, two hours' travel from the center of Johannesburg, South Africa. There were 44 submissions by authors from 21 countries. Each submission was reviewed by at least two, and mostly three, Program Committee members and external reviewers. After extensive discussions, the Program Committee decided to accept the 14 papers included in this volume, with an acceptance rate of 32%. Authors of a selection of these papers will be invited to submit an extended version of their work to a special issue of the *Theoretical Computer Science* journal. The colloquium program also included three keynote talks. Jayadev Misra, from the University of Texas at Austin, USA, was the FME lecturer and presented a talk on "Virtual Time and Timeout in Client-Server Networks." David Lorge Parnas, Professor Emeritus at McMaster University, Canada, presented a talk on "The Use of Mathematics In Software Development." Willem Visser, from Stellenbosch University, South Africa, presented a talk on "Infinitely Often Testing."

Tutorials associated with ICTAC 2011 were held on August 29 and 30 at Mabalingwe Nature Reserve. During August 22–26 an International School on Software Engineering associated with ICTAC 2011 was hosted by the University of the Witwatersrand, Johannesburg, at its Braamfontein campus.

ICTAC 2011 and its associated events were organized jointly by the University of the Witwatersrand, Johannesburg, South Africa, and the International Institute for Software Technology of the United Nations University (UNU-IIST), Macau SAR China. Additional support was provided by Mircosoft Research, Formal Methods Europe (FME) and Data Abstraction (Pty) Ltd EasyChair was used to manage submissions, reviewing process and proceedings production. We are grateful to all members of the Program, Organizing and Steering Committees, and to all referees for their timely hard work. We are also grateful to Kyle Au and Kitty Chan, who contributed to the maintenance of the conference website, to the administrative staff at the School of Computational and Applied Mathematics of the University of the Witwatersrand, Johannesburg, and Data Abstraction for facilitating the event. Finally, we would like to thank all authors and all participants of the conference.

September 2011   Antonio Cerone
                                                    Pekka Pihlajasaari

Organization

Program Committee

Bernhard K. Aichernig	TU Graz, Austria
Junia Anacleto	Federal University of Sao Carlos, Brazil
Jonathan P. Bowen	Museophile Limited, UK
Christiano Braga	Universidade Federal Fluminense, Brazil
Vasco Brattka	University of Cape Town, South Africa
Andrew Butterfield	Trinity College Dublin, Ireland
Ana Cavalcanti	University of York, UK
Antonio Cerone	United Nations University, UNU-IIST, Macau SAR China
Van Hung Dang	Vietnam National University, Vietnam
Jim Davies	University of Oxford, UK
David Deharbe	Universidade Federal do Rio Grande do Norte, Brazil
Wan Fokkink	Vrije Universiteit Amsterdam, The Netherlands
Pascal Fontaine	Loria, INRIA, University of Nancy, France
Marcelo Frias	Universidad de Buenos Aires, Argentina
Lindsay Groves	Victoria University of Wellington, New Zealand
Stefan Gruner	University of Pretoria, South Africa
Michael R. Hansen	Technical University of Denmark, Denmark
Rob Hierons	Brunel University, UK
Lynne Hunt	University of Southern Queensland, Australia
Moonzoo Kim	KAIST, South Korea
Coenraad Labuschagne	University of the Witwatersrand, Johannesburg, South Africa
Martin Leucker	TU Munich, Germany
Zhiming Liu	United Nations University, UNU-IIST, Macau SAR China
Patricia Machado	Federal University of Campina Grande, Brazil
Mieke Massink	CNR-ISTI, Italy
Ali Mili	New Jersey Institute of Technology, USA
Marius Minea	"Politehnica" University of Timisoara, Romania
Tobias Nipkow	TU Munich, Germany
Odejobi Odetunji	Obafemi Awolowo University Ile-Ife, Nigeria
Mizuhito Ogawa	Japan Advanced Institute of Science and Technology, Japan
Jose Oliveira	Universidade do Minho, Portugal
Ekow Otoo	University of the Witwatersrand, Johannesburg, South Africa
Pekka Pihlajasaari	Data Abstraction (Pty) Ltd, South Africa

Francesca Pozzi	Istituto Tecnologie Didattiche - CNR, Italy
Anders Ravn	Aalborg University, Denmark
Markus Roggenbach	Swansea University, UK
Augusto Sampaio	Federal University of Pernambuco, Brazil
Bernhard Schaetz	TU Munich, Germany
Gerardo Schneider	Chalmers and University of Gothenburg, Sweden
Natarajan Shankar	SRI International, USA
Marjan Sirjani	Reykjavik University, Iceland
Fausto Spoto	University of Verona, Italy
Clint Van Alten	University of the Witwatersrand, Johannesburg, South Africa
Franck Van Breugel	York University, Canada
Govert van Drimmelen	University of Johannesburg, South Africa
Daniel Varro	Budapest University of Technology and Economics, Hungary
Herbert Wiklicky	Imperial College London, UK

Additional Reviewers

Andrade, Wilkerson L.
Bauer, Andreas
Bernardo, Marco
Beyer, Dirk
Bollig, Benedikt
Breuer, Peter
Carvalho, Gustavo
Chen, Chunqing
Chen, Haiming
Conradie, Willem
Damasceno, Adriana
De Wolf, Ronald
Ghassemi, Fatemeh
Hansen, Rene Rydhof
Holzer, Markus
Hong, Shin
Ishihara, Hajime
Khedri, Ridha
Kim, Youngjoo

Kim, Yunho
Kourie, Derrick
Liu, Wanwei
Mardare, Radu
Minamide, Yasuhiko
Mousavi, Mohammadreza
Nyman, Ulrik
Oliveira, Bruno
Phillips, Iain
Schäf, Martin
Shkatov, Dmitry
Silva, Paulo F.
Steedman, Mark
Steffen, Martin
Stoelinga, Marielle
Thomsen, Bent
Tiu, Alwen
Truong, Hoang
Van Raamsdonk, Femke

Table of Contents

Virtual Time and Timeout in Client-Server Networks
(Extended Abstract)

Jayadev Misra

The University of Texas at Austin, Austin, Texas, USA
misra@cs.utexas.edu

1 Introduction

This paper proposes that virtual time and virtual time-outs should be available as tools for programming distributed systems. Virtual time is already used for event ordering in distributed systems [4,3,5,1,9], though the numeric value of virtual time is irrelevant in this context (see Section 2). Virtual time-out has not been used in distributed systems. Virtual clock, i.e., virtual time and time-outs, is used in discrete event simulation applications though such applications are usually implemented on single machines using a single virtual clock, rather than on distributed systems.

Our proposal combines and extends both notions so that virtual clock may be used in full generality over a distributed set of machines. We argue that the benefits extend beyond mere ordering of events or simulations. We can show a solution to a combinatorial example, computing shortest path in a graph, that can be structured as a set of concurrent threads operating with virtual time-outs.

These concepts have been implemented in a concurrent programming language, Orc [7], designed by the author and his co-workers. We have used virtual clock for simplifying routine concurrent programming applications. A subset of distributed simulation [2,6] problems can be structured in this style. We expect virtual clock to simplify programming and remove a number of book-keeping operations from explicit consideration by the programmer.

2 Background

2.1 Causal Model of Virtual Time

In a classic paper [4], Lamport introduced the clock synchronization problem across a set of machines. Lamport argued that real-time clocks of different machines can not be perfectly synchronized; therefore, determining the order of events across machines is not a well-defined problem. However, it is possible to implement virtual clocks at different machines and synchronize them so that if an event at one machine causes an event at another machine (perhaps through a chain of intermediate events) then the preceding event happens earlier in *virtual*

A. Cerone and P. Pihlajasaari (Eds.): ICTAC 2011, LNCS 6916, pp. 1–3, 2011.

time[1]. The synchronization algorithm time-stamps each event with a natural number, its virtual time, so that an event that causally precedes another will be assigned a lower virtual time. Lamport's algorithm and some of its variations [3,5,1,9] have become fundamental in designs of practical distributed systems. Morgan [8] shows how to design several distributed algorithms using virtual clock.

The exact value of virtual time is irrelevant in the causal model because the time-stamps of different events are merely compared. Therefore, doubling all virtual times or increasing all by a fixed amount would not affect these comparisons.

2.2 Simulation Model of Virtual Time

Discrete event simulations of physical systems employ virtual time to mimic real time in the physical system. The numeric value of virtual time is important because entities in a physical system, e.g. persons waiting in a queue for service, wait for specific lengths of time. The computational steps in simulations consume no virtual time at all, and the passage of virtual time is dictated only by virtual time-outs.

Unlike the causal model, simulations are typically implemented on single processors; so, there is a single virtual clock under consideration in a simulation.

2.3 Contributions of This Work

We propose a general model that combines the causal and simulation models and generalizes them. We regard a distributed system as a client-server network; clients communicate with each other through the servers. Each client has a virtual clock. Each step of a client consumes an amount of virtual time between a lower and upper bound, as specified for that step. A client can request the current value of the virtual time (thus, obtaining the time-stamp for an event), and also wait for a certain amount of virtual time before starting its next step (thus, using virtual time-out). Causally dependent events obey the appropriate conditions on virtual times assigned to them.

Example. Consider a small example where the use of virtual time simplifies program design. A set of independent concurrent threads, numbered from 0 through n, are to be executed. It is required to start the threads sequentially, thread $i+1$ after thread i, $0 \leq i < n$. Since the threads are independent, there is no causal order among them. If each thread is executed on a separate machine, a causal order among their start events has to be imposed. One possibility is to have thread i send a token to thread $i+1$ after it starts, $0 \leq i < n$, and thread $i+1$ starts only after receiving the token. If all threads are executed on a single machine, a simpler strategy is applicable. Thread i waits for i units of time (real or virtual) before starting. Waiting for virtual time has the advantage

---

[1] Lamport used the term "logical time". We use "virtual time" to denote logical time whose magnitude is also relevant.

over waiting for real time in that (1) no real time is wasted, and (2) sequencing is guaranteed by the conditions imposed on virtual time, whereas threads may start out-of-order if the unit of real time is too small and the time-out mechanism is inexact. If the threads are implemented on two machines, say threads 0 through $k-1$ on machine 1 and k through n on machine 2, we can combine both strategies: thread i in machine 1, $0 \le i < k$, waits for i units of virtual time and then starts, machine 2 starts only after receiving a token from (thread $k - 1$ in) machine 1, and then thread j, $k \le j \le n$, waits for $j - k$ units of virtual time before starting.

We have exploited virtual time-out in this example, though not the exact values of the time outs. As a longer example, we can show how the single source shortest path problem in a weighted directed graph can be solved using virtual time; in that example, the lengths of edges determine values for the virtual time-outs.

In the full paper, we propose a set of conditions that the time-stamps must satisfy, and the machinery needed for synchronization of virtual clocks and time-stamping of events in a client-server network. The algorithm requires each client to maintain a virtual clock and the servers to help synchronize the virtual clocks of the clients.

References

1. Almeida, P.S., Baquero, C., Fonte, V.: Interval tree clocks. In: Baker, T.P., Bui, A., Tixeuil, S. (eds.) OPODIS 2008. LNCS, vol. 5401, pp. 259–274. Springer, Heidelberg (2008)
2. Bagrodia, R., Mani Chandy, K., Misra, J.: A message based approach to discrete event simulation. IEEE Transactions on Software Engineering SE-13(6) (1987)
3. Fidge, C.J.: Timestamps in message-passing systems that preserve the partial ordering. In: Raymond, K. (ed.) Proc. of the 11th Australian Computer Science Conference (ACSC 1988), pp. 56–66 (February 1988)
4. Lamport, L.: Time, clocks, and the ordering of events in a distributed system. Communications of the ACM 21(7), 558–565 (1978)
5. Mattern, F.: Virtual time and global states of distributed systems. In: Cosnard, M. (ed.) Proc. Workshop on Parallel and Distributed Algorithms, Chateau de Bonas, France, pp. 215–226. Elsevier, Amsterdam (1988)
6. Misra, J.: Distributed discrete event simulation. Computing Surveys 18(1), 39–65 (1986)
7. Misra, J., Cook, W.: Computation orchestration: A basis for wide-area computing. Software and Systems Modeling (SoSyM) 6(1), 83–110 (2007)
8. Morgan, C.: Global and logical time in distributed algorithms. Information Processing Letters 20(4), 189–194 (1985)
9. Torres-Rojas, F.J., Ahamad, M.: Plausible clocks: Constant size logical clocks for distributed systems (1996)

The Use of Mathematics in Software Development (Extended Abstract)

David Lorge Parnas

Middle Road Software, Ottawa, Ontario, Canada
parnas@mcmaster.ca

For many decades, computer science researchers have predicted that the "Formal Methods" that they develop and advocate would bring about a drastic improvement in the quality and cost of software. That improvement has never materialized. This talk explain the difference between the methods and notations that constitute "Formal Methods" and the mathematical methods and notation that are used successfully in other areas of Engineering. It discusses the reasons for the failure of Formal Methods to effect the desired changes in the practise of software. In traditional Engineering, mathematics plays three important roles:

- It is used in documentation of design decisions and product properties.
- It is used to compute the values of design parameters.
- It is used to verify that a proposed design has the properties required of it.

Mathematics can be used in the same way in software development. We can use mathematics to document system requirements and component interfaces [1], and to confirm important properties of documents and designs [2]. It has long been used to calculate parameters for numerical software. However, outside of numerical software, most programmers still consider mathematics to be irrelevant. One key to applying mathematics in software development is finding better representations for the piecewise-continuous mathematical functions that are approximated by software. Mathematical expressions in tabular form (also called tabular expressions or tables) have repeatedly been demonstrated to be useful for documenting and analyzing software systems. They are usually easier to read than conventional mathematical expressions but are no less precise. They can be used wherever mathematical expressions are used. To avoid misunderstandings, and to support users with trustworthy tools, the meaning of these expressions must be fully defined.The talk describes a new method for defining the meaning of tabular expressions. Each definition maps a well-formed tabular expression to a mathematical expression of a previously defined type. Since the meaning of conventional mathematical expressions is well known, describing an equivalent conventional expression fully defines the meaning of a tabular expression Mathematical definition of the meaning of software documentation makes it possible to develop a number of tools that can be of real help to software developers. The talk closes with a brief description of such tools.

A. Cerone and P. Pihlajasaari (Eds.): ICTAC 2011, LNCS 6916, pp. 4–5, 2011.
© Springer-Verlag Berlin Heidelberg 2011

References

1. Liu, Z., Parnas, D.L., Trancón y Widemann, B.: Documenting and verifying systems assembled from components. Frontiers of Computer Science in China 4(2), 151–161 (2010)
2. Parnas, D.L.: Precise documentation: The key to better software. In: Nanz, S. (ed.) The Future of Software Engineering, pp. 125–148. Springer, Heidelberg (2011)

Infinitely Often Testing
(Extended Abstract)

Willem Visser

Department of Computer Science, Stellenbosch University, South Africa
visserw@sun.ac.za

From the perspective of industry, formal methods over-promise and under-deliver. Theoretical computer scientists love the notion of proving programs correct, but have slowly come round to the realization that promises in grant proposals aren't the same as delivering in the real world. Essentially we started seeing a slow erosion of the importance of the notion of soundness; completeness was dropped long before. The ideal of showing that programs behave according to their specification, became the reality of finding situations where they don't. This maps perfectly onto an expensive activity well known to industry, namely software testing. This presentation looks at the happy marriage of techniques from formal methods and software testing. Software testing is expensive since it is time-consuming to derive tests to adequately cover the software's behavior. Techniques from formal methods allow one to generate tests automatically (hence reducing costs) and systematically (hence increasing the likelihood of discovering errors). We look at the use of software model checking to find errors in complex code, and specifically, consider the evolution of one of the world's most popular model checkers, JavaPathFinder (JPF). One of the core techniques in JPF is symbolic execution that, although introduced in the early seventies, has recently made a big comeback in the testing world. We discuss the reasons why it took this long for such a powerful technique to become popular (again) and how it is used within JPF. In addition we discuss some of the new advances in symbolic execution and how it is used for bug finding and test generation. Finally, we consider some of the new challenges facing the automated testing field and how formal techniques can be applied to address them.

A. Cerone and P. Pihlajasaari (Eds.): ICTAC 2011, LNCS 6916, p. 6, 2011.

Axiomatizing Weak Ready Simulation Semantics over BCCSP*

Luca Aceto[1,3], David de Frutos Escrig[2,3],
Carlos Gregorio-Rodríguez[2,3], and Anna Ingolfsdottir[1,3]

[1] ICE-TCS, School of Computer Science, Reykjavik University, Iceland
[2] Departamento de Sistemas Informáticos y Computación,
Universidad Complutense de Madrid, Spain
[3] Abel Extraordinary Chair, Universidad Complutense-Reykjavik University

Abstract. Ready simulation has proven to be one of the most significant semantics in process theory. It is at the heart of a number of general results that pave the way to a comprehensive understanding of the
spectrum of process semantics. Since its original definition by Bloom,
Istrail and Meyer in 1995, several authors have proposed generalizations
of ready simulation to deal with internal actions. However, a thorough
study of the (non-)existence of finite (in)equational bases for weak ready
simulation semantics is still missing in the literature. This paper presents
a complete account of positive and negative results on the axiomatizability of weak ready simulation semantics over the language BCCSP.
In addition, this study offers a thorough analysis of the axiomatizability
properties of weak simulation semantics.

1 Introduction

Process algebras, such as ACP [9,11], CCS [34] and CSP [29], are prototype
specification languages for reactive systems. Such languages offer a small, but
expressive, collection of operators that can be combined to form terms that
describe the behaviour of reactive systems.

Since the seminal work by Bergstra and Klop [11], and Hennessy and Milner [28], the search for (in)equational axiomatizations of notions of behavioural
semantics for fragments of process algebras has been one of the classic topics of investigation within concurrency theory. A complete axiomatization of a

---

* Luca Aceto and Anna Ingolfsdottir have been partially supported by the projects
'New Developments in Operational Semantics' (nr. 080039021) and 'Meta-theory of
Algebraic Process Theories' (nr. 100014021) of the Icelandic Research Fund. David de
Frutos Escrig and Carlos Gregorio-Rodríguez have been partially supported by the
Spanish projects TESIS (TIN2009-14312-C02-01), DESAFIOS10 (TIN2009-14599-
C03-01) and PROMETIDOS S2009/TIC-1465. The paper was begun when David
de Frutos Escrig and Carlos Gregorio-Rodríguez held Abel Extraordinary Chair po-
sitions at Reykjavik University, and finalized while Luca Aceto and Anna Ingolfsdottir held Abel Extraordinary Chairs at Universidad Complutense de Madrid, Spain,
supported by the NILS Mobility Project.

A. Cerone and P. Pihlajasaari (Eds.): ICTAC 2011, LNCS 6916, pp. 7–24, 2011.
© Springer-Verlag Berlin Heidelberg 2011

behavioural semantics yields a purely syntactic and model-independent characterization of the semantics of a process algebra, and paves the way to the application of theorem-proving techniques in establishing whether two process descriptions exhibit related behaviours.

There are three types of 'complete' axiomatizations that one meets in the literature on process algebras. An (in)equational axiomatization is called *ground-complete* if it can prove all the valid (in)equivalences relating closed terms, i.e. terms with no occurrences of variables, in the process algebra of interest. It is *complete* when it can be used to derive all the valid (in)equivalences. (A complete axiom system is also referred to as a *basis* for the algebra it axiomatizes.) These two notions of completeness relate the semantic notion of process, namely an equivalence class of terms, with the proof-theoretic notion of provability from an (in)equational axiom system. An axiomatization E is ω-*complete* when an inequation can be derived from E if, and only if, all of its closed instantiations can be derived from E. The notion of ω-completeness is therefore a proof-theoretic one. Its connections with completeness are well known, and are discussed in, e.g., [4].

In [23], van Glabbeek studied the semantics in his spectrum in the setting of the process algebra BCCSP, which is sufficiently powerful to express all finite synchronization trees [34]. In the aforementioned reference, van Glabbeek gave, amongst a wealth of other results, (in)equational ground-complete axiomatizations for the preorders and equivalences in the spectrum. In [17], two of the authors of this paper presented a unification of the axiomatizations of all the semantics in the linear time-branching time spectrum. This unification is achieved by means of conditional axioms that provide a simple and clear picture of the similarities and differences between all the semantics. In [26], Groote obtained ω-completeness results for most of the axiomatizations presented in [23], in case the alphabet of actions is infinite. The article [4] surveys results on the existence of finite, complete equational axiomatizations of equivalences over fragments of process algebras up to 2005. Some of the recent results on this topic may be found in [5,6,8].

In the setting of BCCSP, in a seminal journal paper that collects and unifies the results in a series of conference articles, Chen, Fokkink, Luttik and Nain have offered in [15] a definitive classification of the status of the finite basis problem— that is, the problem of determining whether a behavioural equivalence has a finite, complete, equational axiomatization over the chosen process algebra— for all the semantics in van Glabbeek's spectrum. Notable later results by Chen and Fokkink presented in [14] give the first example of a semantics—the so-called *impossible future semantics* from [40]—where the preorder defining the semantics can be finitely axiomatized over BCCSP, but its induced equivalence cannot. The authors of this paper have recently shown in [2] that complete simulation and ready simulation semantics do not afford a finite (in)equational axiomatization even when the set of actions is a singleton.

The collection of results mentioned in the previous paragraph gives a complete picture of the axiomatizability of behavioural semantics in van Glabbeek's spectrum over BCCSP. However, such notions of behavioural semantics are *concrete*, in the sense that they consider each action processes perform as being observable by their environment. Despite the fundamental role they play in the development of a theory of reactive systems, concrete semantics are not very useful from the point of view of applications. For this reason, notions of behavioural semantics that, in some well-defined way, abstract from externally unobservable steps of computation that processes perform have been proposed in the literature—see, e.g., the classic references [21,25,28], which offer, amongst many other results, ground-complete axiomatizations of the studied notion of behavioural semantics. Following Milner, such notions of behavioural semantics are usually called 'weak semantics' and the symbol τ is used to describe an unobservable action. However, to the best of our knowledge, no systematic study of the axiomatizability properties of variations on the classic notion of *simulation semantics* [32] that abstract away from internal steps of computation in the behaviour of processes has been presented in the literature. This is all the more surprising since simulation semantics is very natural and plays an important role in applications.

The aim of this paper is to offer a detailed study of the axiomatizability properties of the largest (pre)congruences over the language BCCSP induced by variations on the classic simulation preorder and equivalence that abstract from internal steps in process behaviours. We focus on the (pre)congruences associated with the weak simulation and the weak ready simulation [12,30] preorders. For each of these behavioural semantics, we present results on the (non)existence of finite (ground-)complete (in)equational axiomatizations. Following [17], we also discuss the axiomatization of those semantics using conditional equations in some detail.

We begin our study of the weak simulation semantics over BCCSP in Section 3 by focusing on the natural extension of the classic simulation preorder to a setting with the internal action τ. We show how to lift all the known results on the (non)existence of finite (ground-)complete axiomatizations from the setting of the classic simulation semantics to its weak counterpart using, for instance, the approach developed in [6].

In Section 4, we study the notion of *weak ready simulation*, namely a weak simulation that can only relate states that afford the same sets of observable actions. The finite axiomatizability of this semantics depends crucially on the presence of an infinite set of observable actions. Indeed, if the set of actions is infinite, we offer finite (un)conditional (ground-)complete axiomatizations for the weak ready simulation precongruence. In sharp contrast to this positive result, we prove that, when the set of observable actions A is finite and non-empty, the (in)equational theory of the weak ready simulation precongruence over BCCSP does not have a finite (in)equational basis.

2 Preliminaries

To set the stage for the developments offered in the rest of the paper, we present the syntax and the operational semantics for the language BCCSP, some background on (in)equational logic, and classic axiom systems for strong bisimulation equivalence and observational congruence [34].

Syntax of BCCSP. $BCCSP(A_\tau)$ is a basic process algebra for expressing finite process behaviour. Its syntax consists of closed (process) terms p, q, r that are constructed from a constant $\mathbf{0}$, a binary operator $\_ + \_$ called *alternative composition*, or *choice*, and unary *prefix* operators $\alpha\_$, where α ranges over some set A_τ of *actions* of the form $A \cup \{\tau\}$, where τ is a distinguished action symbol that is not contained in A. Following Milner, we use τ to denote an internal, unobservable action of a reactive system, and we let a, b, c denote typical elements of A and α range over A_τ. The set of closed terms is named $T(BCCSP(A_\tau))$, in short $T(A_\tau)$. We write $|A|$ for the cardinality of the set of observable actions.

Open terms t, u, v can moreover contain occurrences of variables from a countably infinite set V (with typical elements x, y, z). We use $\mathbb{T}(BCCSP(A_\tau))$, in short $\mathbb{T}(A_\tau)$, to denote the set of open terms. The *depth* of a term t is the maximum nesting of prefix operators in t.

In what follows, for each non-negative integer n and term t, we use $a^n t$ to stand for t when $n = 0$, and for $a(a^{n-1}t)$ otherwise. As usual, trailing occurrences of $\mathbf{0}$ are omitted; for example, we shall usually write α in lieu of $\alpha\mathbf{0}$.

A (closed) substitution maps variables in V to (closed) terms. For every term t and substitution σ, the term $\sigma(t)$ is obtained by replacing every occurrence of a variable x in t by $\sigma(x)$. Note that $\sigma(t)$ is closed if σ is a closed substitution.

Transitions and Their Defining Rules. Intuitively, closed $BCCSP(A_\tau)$ terms represent finite process behaviours, where $\mathbf{0}$ does not exhibit any behaviour, $p + q$ is the nondeterministic choice between the behaviours of p and q, and αp executes action α to transform into p. This intuition is captured, in the style of Plotkin [37], by the simple transition rules below, which give rise to A_τ-labelled transitions between closed terms.

$$\frac{}{\alpha x \xrightarrow{\alpha} x} \qquad \frac{x \xrightarrow{\alpha} x'}{x + y \xrightarrow{\alpha} x'} \qquad \frac{y \xrightarrow{\alpha} y'}{x + y \xrightarrow{\alpha} y'}$$

The operational semantics is extended to open terms by assuming that variables do not exhibit any behaviour.

The so-called *weak transition relations* $\xRightarrow{\alpha}$ ($\alpha \in A_\tau$) are defined over $\mathbb{T}(A_\tau)$ in the standard fashion as follows.

– We use $\xRightarrow{\tau}$ for the reflexive and transitive closure of $\xrightarrow{\tau}$.
– For each $a \in A$ and for all terms $t, u \in \mathbb{T}(A_\tau)$, we have that $t \xRightarrow{a} u$ if, and only if, there are $t_1, t_2 \in \mathbb{T}(A_\tau)$ such that $t \xRightarrow{\tau} t_1 \xrightarrow{a} t_2 \xRightarrow{\tau} u$.

For each term t, we define $I^*(t) = \{a \mid a \in A \text{ and } t \xRightarrow{a} t' \text{ for some } t'\}$.

Preorders and Their Kernels. We recall that a *preorder* $\precsim$ is a reflexive and transitive relation. In what follows, any preorder $\precsim$ we consider will first be defined over the set of closed terms $\mathrm{T}(A_\tau)$. For terms $t, u \in \mathbb{T}(A_\tau)$, we define $t \precsim u$ if, and only if, $\sigma(t) \precsim \sigma(u)$ for each closed substitution σ.

The *kernel* $\approx$ of a preorder $\precsim$ is the equivalence relation it induces, and is defined thus: $t \approx u$ if, and only if, $(t \precsim u$ and $u \precsim t)$. It is easy to see that the kernel of a preorder $\precsim$ is the largest symmetric relation included in $\precsim$.

Inequational Logic. An *inequation* (respectively, an *equation*) over the language $\mathrm{BCCSP}(A_\tau)$ is a formula of the form $t \leq u$ (respectively, $t = u$), where t and u are terms in $\mathbb{T}(A_\tau)$. An *(in)equational axiom system* is a set of (in)equations over the language $\mathrm{BCCSP}(A_\tau)$. An equation $t = u$ is derivable from an equational axiom system E, written $E \vdash t = u$, if it can be proven from the axioms in E using the rules of equational logic (viz. reflexivity, symmetry, transitivity, substitution and closure under $\mathrm{BCCSP}(A_\tau)$ contexts).

$$t = t \qquad \frac{t = u}{u = t} \qquad \frac{t = u \quad u = v}{t = v} \qquad \frac{t = u}{\sigma(t) = \sigma(u)} \qquad \frac{t = u}{\alpha t = \alpha u} \qquad \frac{t = u \quad t' = u'}{t + t' = u + u'}$$

For the derivation of an inequation $t \leq u$ from an inequational axiom system E, the rule for symmetry—that is, the second rule above—is omitted. We write $E \vdash t \leq u$ if the inequation $t \leq u$ can be derived from E.

It is well known that, without loss of generality, one may assume that substitutions happen first in (in)equational proofs, i.e., that the fourth rule may only be used when its premise is one of the (in)equations in E. Moreover, by postulating that for each equation in E also its symmetric counterpart is present in E, one may assume that applications of symmetry happen first in equational proofs, i.e., that the second rule is never used in equational proofs. (See, e.g., [15, page 497] for a thorough discussion of this notion of 'normalized equational proof.') In the remainder of this paper, we shall always tacitly assume that equational axiom systems are closed with respect to symmetry. Note that, with this assumption, there is no difference between the rules of inference of equational and inequational logic. In what follows, we shall consider an equation $t = u$ as a shorthand for the pair of inequations $t \leq u$ and $u \leq t$.

The depth of $t \leq u$ and $t = u$ is the maximum of the depths of t and u. The depth of a collection of (in)equations is the supremum of the depths of its elements. So, the depth of a finite axiom system E is zero, if E is empty, and it is the largest depth of its (in)equations otherwise.

An inequation $t \leq u$ is *sound* with respect to a given preorder relation $\precsim$ if $t \precsim u$ holds. An (in)equational axiom system E is sound with respect to $\precsim$ if so is each (in)equation in E.

Classic Axiomatizations for Notions of Bisimilarity. The well-known axioms B_1–B_4 for $\mathrm{BCCSP}(A_\tau)$ given below stem from [28]. They are ω-complete [36], and sound and ground-complete [28,34], over $\mathrm{BCCSP}(A_\tau)$ (over any nonempty set of actions) modulo bisimulation equivalence, which is the finest semantics in van Glabbeek's spectrum [23].

$$
\begin{aligned}
B_1 & \quad x + y = y + x \\
B_2 & \quad (x + y) + z = x + (y + z) \\
B_3 & \quad x + x = x \\
B_4 & \quad x + \mathbf{0} = x
\end{aligned}
$$

In what follows, for notational convenience, we consider terms up to the least congruence generated by axioms B_1–B_4, that is, up to bisimulation equivalence. We use *summation* $\sum_{i=1}^{n} t_i$ (with $n \geq 0$) to denote $t_1 + \cdots + t_n$, where the empty sum denotes $\mathbf{0}$. Modulo the equations B_1–B_4 each term $t \in \mathbb{T}(A_\tau)$ can be written in the form $\sum_{i=1}^{n} t_i$, where each t_i is either a variable or is of the form $\alpha t'$, for some action α and term t'.

In a setting with internal transitions, the classic work of Hennessy and Milner on *weak bisimulation equivalence* and on the largest congruence included in it, *observational congruence*, shows that the axioms B_1–B_4 together with the axioms W_1–W_3 below are sound and complete over BCCSP(A_τ) modulo observational equivalence. (See [28,34,35].)

$$
\begin{aligned}
W_1 & \quad \alpha x = \alpha \tau x \\
W_2 & \quad \tau x = \tau x + x \\
W_3 & \quad \alpha(\tau x + y) = \alpha(\tau x + y) + \alpha y
\end{aligned}
$$

The above axioms are often referred to as the τ-*laws*. For ease of reference, we write

$$
BW = \{B_1, B_2, B_3, B_4, W_1, W_2, W_3\}.
$$

3 Weak Simulation

We begin our study of the equational theory of weak simulation semantics by considering the natural, τ-abstracting version of the classic simulation preorder [32]. We start by defining the notion of weak simulation preorder and the equivalence relation it induces. We then argue that all the known positive and negative results on the existence of (ground-)complete (in)equational axiomatizations for the concrete simulation semantics over the language BCCSP(A_τ) can be lifted to the corresponding weak semantics.

Definition 1. *The* weak simulation preorder, *denoted by* $\precsim_S$, *is the largest relation over terms in* $\mathrm{T}(A_\tau)$ *satisfying the following condition whenever $p \precsim_S q$ and $\alpha \in A_\tau$:*

– *if $p \xrightarrow{\alpha} p'$ then there exists some q' such that $q \xRightarrow{\alpha} q'$ and $p' \precsim_S q'$.*

We say that $p, q \in \mathrm{T}(A_\tau)$ are weak simulation equivalent, *written $p \approx_S q$, iff p and q are related by the kernel of $\precsim_S$, that is when both $p \precsim_S q$ and $q \precsim_S p$ hold.*

Unlike many other notions of behavioural relations that abstract away from internal steps in the behaviour of processes, see [25,34] for classic examples, the weak simulation preorder is a precongruence over the language we consider in this study.

Proposition 1. *The preorder $\precsim_S$ is a precongruence over* $T(A_\tau)$. *Hence* $\approx_S$ *is a congruence over* $T(A_\tau)$. *Moreover, the axiom*

$$(\tau e) \quad \tau x = x$$

holds over $T(A_\tau)$ *modulo* $\approx_S$.

The soundness of equation τe is the key to all the results on the equational theory of the weak simulation semantics we present in the remainder of this section. In establishing the negative results, we shall make use of the reduction technique from the paper [6].

3.1 Ground-Completeness for Weak Simulation

Besides the equation τe previously stated in Proposition 1, there will be another important equation to consider in order to achieve an axiomatic characterization of the weak simulation preorder, namely

$$(S) \quad x \leq x + y.$$

This equation also plays an essential role in the axiomatization of the simulation preorder in the concrete case [18,23].

Proposition 2. *The set of equations*

$$E_{S\leq} = \{B_1, B_2, B_3, B_4, S, \tau e\}$$

is sound and ground-complete for $BCCSP(A_\tau)$ *modulo* $\precsim_S$.[1]

Note that the equations W_1–W_3, even if sound for $\precsim_S$, are not needed in order to obtain a ground-complete axiomatization of $\precsim_S$ over $BCCSP(A_\tau)$. Those equations can easily be derived from the axiom system in Proposition 2.

To obtain an axiomatization for the weak simulation equivalence, we need the equation

$$(SE) \quad a(x + y) = a(x + y) + ay \qquad (a \in A).$$

This equation is well known from the setting of standard simulation equivalence, where it is known to be the key to a ground-complete axiomatization [23].

Proposition 3. *The set of equations*

$$E_{S=} = \{B_1, B_2, B_3, B_4, SE, \tau e\}$$

is sound and ground-complete for $BCCSP(A_\tau)$ *modulo* $\approx_S$.

---

[1] This completeness result was announced in [24] by van Glabbeek.

3.2   ω-Completeness for Weak Simulation

Propositions 2 and 3 offer ground-complete axiomatizations for the weak simulation preorder and its kernel over BCCSP(A_τ). The inequational axiomatization
of the weak simulation preorder is finite, and so is the one for its kernel if the
set of actions A is finite. In the presence of an infinite collection of actions, the
axiom system in Proposition 3 is finite if we consider a to be an action variable. It is natural to wonder whether the weak simulation semantics afford finite
(in)equational axiomatizations that are complete over $\mathbb{T}(A_\tau)$. The following results answer this question.

Proposition 4. *If the set of actions is infinite, then the axiom system*

$$E_{S^\le} = \{B_1, B_2, B_3, B_4, S, \tau e\}$$

is both ω-complete and complete over BCCSP(A_τ) *modulo* $\precsim_S$.

So the weak simulation preorder can be finitely axiomatized over $\mathbb{T}(A_\tau)$ when A
is infinite. This state of affairs changes dramatically when A is a finite collection
of actions of cardinality at least two.

Theorem 1. *If $1 < |A| < \infty$, then the weak simulation equivalence does not
afford a finite equational axiomatization over $\mathbb{T}(A_\tau)$. In particular, no finite
axiom system over $\mathbb{T}(A_\tau)$ that is sound modulo weak simulation equivalence can
prove all the (valid) equations in the family on page 511 of [15].*

Table 1. Axiomatizations for the weak simulation semantics

Weak Simulation	Ground-complete		Complete	
Finite Equations	Order	Equiv.	Order	Equiv.
$\|A\| = \infty$	$E_{S^\le}$	$E_{S^=}$	$E_{S^\le}$	$E_{S^=}$
$1 < \|A\| < \infty$	$E_{S^\le}$	$E_{S^=}$	Do not exist	
$\|A\| = 1$	$E_{S_1^\le}$	$E_{S_1^=}$	$E_{S_1^\le}$	$E_{S_1^=}$

Table 2. Axioms for the weak simulation semantics

$E_{S^\le} = \{B_1\text{–}B_4, \tau e, S\}$ $E_{S^=} = \{B_1\text{–}B_4, \tau e, SE\}$ $E_{S_1^\le} = \{B_1\text{–}B_4, \tau e, S, TE, Sg_\le\}$ $E_{S_1^=} = \{B_1\text{–}B_4, \tau e, TE, Sg\}$	$(\tau e)\quad \tau x = x$ $(S)\quad x \le x + y$ $(Sg_\le)\quad x \le ax$ $(SE)\quad a(x + y) =$ $\qquad\qquad a(x + y) + ay$ $(TE)\quad a(x + y) = ax + ay$ $(Sg)\quad ax = ax + x$

Corollary 1. *If* $1 < |A| < \infty$, *then the weak simulation preorder does not afford a finite inequational axiomatization over* $\mathbb{T}(A_\tau)$.

Remark 1. If A is a singleton then the simulation preorder coincides with trace inclusion. In that case, the simulation preorder is finitely based over $\mathbb{T}(A)$, as is simulation equivalence —see, e.g., [4]. Those axiomatizations can be lifted to the setting of weak simulation semantics simply by adding the equation τe to any complete axiomatization of the simulation preorder or equivalence.

Tables 1 and 2 summarize the positive and negative results on the existence of finite axiomatizations for weak simulation semantics. On Table 1, and in subsequent ones, 'Do not exist' indicates that there is no *finite* (in)equational axiomatization for the corresponding semantic relation.

4   Weak Ready Simulation

In this section, we shall study the equational theory of the largest precongruence included in the weak ready simulation preorder. We first define the notion of weak ready simulation that will be the cornerstone in subsequent developments. We then proceed to study its induced precongruence, first in the case in which the set of actions A is infinite and then in case that A is finite.

In order to define the weak ready simulation semantics we recall the definition of the function I^*, presented in Section 2, that returns the set of initial visible actions of a term: $I^*(t) = \{a \mid a \in A \text{ and } t \xrightarrow{a} t' \text{ for some } t'\}$.

Definition 2. *The* weak ready simulation preorder, *which we denote by* $\precsim_{RS}$, *is the largest relation over terms in* $T(A_\tau)$ *satisfying the following conditions whenever* $p \precsim_{RS} q$ *and* $\alpha \in A_\tau$:

- *if* $p \xrightarrow{\alpha} p'$ *then there exists some term* q' *such that* $q \xRightarrow{\alpha} q'$ *and* $p' \precsim_{RS} q'$, *and*
- $I^*(p) = I^*(q)$.

We say that $p, q \in T(A_\tau)$ *are* weak ready simulation equivalent, *written* $p \approx_{RS} q$, *iff* p *and* q *are related by the kernel of* $\precsim_{RS}$, *that is when both* $p \precsim_{RS} q$ *and* $q \precsim_{RS} p$ *hold.*

Remark 2. $\precsim_{RS}$ is not a precongruence with respect to the choice operator of BCCSP(A_τ). It is immediate to show that $\tau a \precsim_{RS} a$. However, $\tau a + b \not\precsim_{RS} a + b$.

There are many possible ways to define a weak ready simulation semantics (see, for instance, [22]). The preorder defined above is based on a natural 'weak counterpart' of the constraint used in capturing ready simulation as a constrained simulation [18]. This design criterion was important for us, because we aim at extending the general and natural results we obtained for this family of semantics from the strong to the weak setting.

There are, of course, other guiding principles that could lead to alternative definitions. For instance, the inequation $\alpha x \leq \alpha x + \alpha y$ $(\alpha \in A_\tau)$ appears in [16] as a benchmark for characterizing weak preorders. Although the authors of [16] do not claim to define weak ready simulation semantics, from an algebraic viewpoint it would be appealing to have a weak ready simulation preorder satisfying this inequation. Unfortunately, so far we have failed to obtain a simple operational characterization of a weak simulation satisfying the previous inequation, even allowing for the addition of some other (simple and reasonable) axioms. Another reasonable requirement one might want to impose on a notion of weak ready simulation preorder is that it be preserved by hiding. As our readers can easily check, the preorder in Definition 2 does not meet this requirement. The study of the (in)equational theory of the largest precongruence with respect to hiding included in the weak ready simulation preorder defined above is an interesting topic for future research.

Summing up, we do not claim that our weak ready simulation is 'the right one', but, after a thorough study of the question, we postulate that it is the simplest notion of weak ready simulation that affords both a simple operational definition, as we have seen above, and good algebraic properties over BCCSP, as we will see below. Much more on the subject can be found in the extended version of the paper.

Definition 3. *We denote by $\sqsubseteq_{RS}$ the largest precongruence included in $\precsim_{RS}$. Formally, $p \sqsubseteq_{RS} q$ iff*

- *$p \precsim_{RS} q$,*
- *$p \precsim_{RS} q \Rightarrow \forall \alpha \in A_\tau \quad \alpha p \precsim_{RS} \alpha q$, and*
- *$p \precsim_{RS} q \Rightarrow \forall r \in \mathrm{T}(A_\tau) \quad p + r \precsim_{RS} q + r$.*

The behavioural characterization of the relation $\sqsubseteq_{RS}$ and its axiomatic properties will depend crucially on whether the set of visible actions A is finite or infinite.

4.1 Axiomatizing $\sqsubseteq_{RS}$ When A Is Infinite

If the set of actions A is infinite, then we can obtain a behavioural characterization of the largest precongruence included in the weak ready simulation preorder using a standard construction due to Milner.

Definition 4. *The preorder relation $\precsim_{RS}$ between processes is defined as follows: We say that $p \precsim_{RS} q$ iff*

- *for any $\alpha \in A_\tau$ such that $p \xrightarrow{\alpha} p'$, there exists some q' such that $q \overset{\tau}{\Longrightarrow}\xrightarrow{\alpha}\overset{\tau}{\Longrightarrow} q'$ with $p' \precsim_{RS} q'$, and*
- *$I^*(p) = I^*(q)$.*

We denote the kernel of $\precsim_{RS}$ by $\approx_{RS}$.

Proposition 5 (Behavioural Characterization of $\sqsubseteq_{RS}$). *If A is infinite then $p \precsim_{RS} q$ if, and only if, $p \sqsubseteq_{RS} q$, for all $p, q \in \mathrm{T}(A_\tau)$. Therefore, $\approx_{RS}$ coincides with the kernel of the preorder $\sqsubseteq_{RS}$.*

Ground-completeness. We shall now provide ground-complete (conditional) axiomatizations of the relations $\lesssim_{RS}$ and $\approx_{RS}$.

To axiomatize $\lesssim_{RS}$ using conditional inequations, the key axiom is

$$(RS_\tau) \quad I^*(x) = I^*(y) \Rightarrow x \leq x + y.$$

This axiom mirrors the one used in the concrete setting in [17,23].

Proposition 6. *The set of equations*

$$E^c_{RS\leq} = BW \cup \{RS_\tau\},$$

in which RS_τ is conditional, is sound and ground-complete for $\lesssim_{RS}$ over the language BCCSP(A_τ).

We now give a ground-complete and unconditional axiomatization for the weak ready simulation preorder. For that we will consider the equations

$$\begin{aligned} (RS) & \quad ax \leq ax + ay \\ (\tau g) & \quad x \leq \tau x. \end{aligned}$$

Equation RS is a well known and important one in the study of process semantics. RS appears as a necessary condition for process semantics in many general results in process theory—see, e.g. [3,19,20,31].

As for equation τg, this is indeed a simple and natural one that is satisfied by any 'natural' precongruence on processes with silent moves.

Theorem 2. *The set of non-conditional equations defined by*

$$E_{RS\leq} = BW \cup \{RS, \tau g\}$$

is sound and ground-complete for BCCSP(A_τ) *modulo* $\lesssim_{RS}$.

To obtain a ground-complete axiomatization of the largest congruence included in weak ready simulation equivalence, it would be desirable to use a general 'ready-to-preorder result' [3,20] as the one we have for the concrete case. There is indeed a similar result for weak semantics by Chen, Fokkink and van Glabbeek, see [16], but unfortunately it is not general enough to cover the case of the weak ready simulation congruence in Definition 4.

We now provide a ground-completeness result in which a key role is played by the equation

$$(RSE_\tau) \quad I^*(x) = I^*(y) \Rightarrow \alpha(x+y) = \alpha(x+y) + \alpha y,$$

which is quite similar to the equation needed for the concrete case.

Proposition 7. *The set of equations*

$$E^c_{RS=} = BW \cup \{RSE_\tau\},$$

in which RSE_τ is conditional, is sound and ground-complete for $\approx_{RS}$ over the language BCCSP(A_τ).

In order to give an unconditional axiomatization of $\simeq_{RS}$, we consider the following equations:

$$(RSE) \qquad \alpha(bx + z + by) = \alpha(bx + z + by) + \alpha(bx + z)$$
$$(RSE_{\tau e}) \qquad \alpha(x + \tau y) = \alpha(x + \tau y) + \alpha(x + y).$$

Theorem 3. *The set of equations*

$$E_{RS^=} = BW \cup \{RSE, RSE_{\tau e}\}$$

is sound and ground-complete for BCCSP(A_τ) *modulo* $\simeq_{RS}$.

ω-**Completeness.** We shall now provide an axiomatization for the relation $\lesssim_{RS}$ that is (ω-)complete.

Theorem 4. *If the set of actions A is infinite, then the axiom system*

$$E_{RS^\leq} = BW \cup \{RS, \tau g\}$$

is both ω-complete and complete for BCCSP(A_τ) *modulo* $\lesssim_{RS}$.

4.2   Axiomatizing $\sqsubseteq_{RS}$ When A Is Finite

Proposition 5 gives an explicit characterization of the largest precongruence included in the weak ready simulation preorder when the collection of actions is infinite. In this section, we shall study the (in)equational theory of $\sqsubseteq_{RS}$ when the set of observable actions A is finite and non-empty.

First of all, note that if A is finite then the relation $\lesssim_{RS}$ defined in Definition 4 is *not* the largest precongruence included in the weak ready simulation preorder. To see this, consider the terms

$$p = \tau \sum_{a \in A} a \text{ and } q = \sum_{a \in A} a. \tag{1}$$

Observe that, for each $r \in$ BCCSP(A_τ), the following statements hold:

1. $p \lesssim_{RS} q + r$ and
2. $p + r \lesssim_{RS} q + r$.

From these statements if follows that $p \leq q$ is valid modulo the largest precongruence included in $\lesssim_{RS}$.

Definition 5. *The relation $\lesssim_{RS}^F$ is defined as follows: We say that $p \lesssim_{RS}^F q$ iff*

- *for each $a \in A$ and p' such that $p \xrightarrow{a} p'$, there exists some q' such that $q \xRightarrow{a} q'$ with $p' \lesssim_{RS} q'$;*
- *for each p' such that $p \xrightarrow{\tau} p'$,*
  - *either there exists some q' such that $q(\xrightarrow{\tau})^+ q'$ with $p' \lesssim_{RS} q'$,*
  - *or $I^*(p') = A$ and $p' \lesssim_{RS} q$; and*
- *$I^*(q) \subseteq I^*(p)$.*

Note that $p \lesssim_{RS}^F q$, for the processes p and q defined in (1). Indeed, since $I^*(q) = A$, process q can match the initial τ-labelled transition from p by remaining idle.

Proposition 8 (Behavioural Characterization of $\sqsubseteq_{RS}$). *If A is finite then $p \lesssim_{RS}^F q$ if, and only if, $p \sqsubseteq_{RS} q$, for all $p, q \in$ T(A_τ).*

Ground-completeness. In order to give a ground-complete axiomatization of the relation $\lesssim_{RS}^F$, we consider the equation

$$(RS_\Sigma) \quad \tau(\sum_{a\in A} ax_a + y) = \sum_{a\in A} ax_a + y$$

Proposition 9. *The set of equations $E_{RS\le}^{Fc} = BW \cup \{RS_\tau, RS_\Sigma\}$, in which RS_τ is conditional, is sound and ground-complete for $\lesssim_{RS}^F$ over the language* BCCSP(A_τ).

Theorem 5. *The set of equations*

$$E_{RS\le}^F = BW \cup \{RS, \tau g, RS_\Sigma\}$$

is sound and ground-complete for BCCSP(A_τ) *modulo $\lesssim_{RS}^F$.*

We now proceed to offer (un)conditional axiomatizations of $\approx_{RS}^F$, the kernel of the preorder $\lesssim_{RS}^F$.

Proposition 10. *The set of equations $E_{RS=}^{Fc} = BW \cup \{RSE_\tau, RS_\Sigma\}$, in which RSE_τ is conditional, is sound and ground-complete for* BCCSP(A_τ) *modulo $\approx_{RS}^F$.*

Theorem 6. *The set of equations*

$$E_{RS=}^F = BW \cup \{RSE, RS_{\tau e}, RS_\Sigma\}$$

is sound and ground-complete for BCCSP(A_τ) *modulo $\approx_{RS}^F$.*

Remark 3. Since, in the case $|A| < \infty$, the preorder $\lesssim_{RS}^F$ is the largest precongruence included in $\precsim_{RS}$, all the axiomatizations above are also sound and ground-complete for $\sqsubseteq_{RS}$ and its kernel, in this case.

Nonexistence of Finite Complete Axiomatizations. We shall now prove that, if the set of actions A is finite, then neither $\lesssim_{RS}^F$ nor its kernel afford a finite (in)equational axiomatization. The following proposition was shown in [15].

Proposition 11. *For each $n \ge 0$, the equation*

$$a^n x + a^n \mathbf{0} + \sum_{b\in A} a^n(x+b) = a^n\mathbf{0} + \sum_{b\in A} a^n(x+b) \quad (2)$$

is sound modulo ready simulation equivalence, and therefore modulo the kernel of $\lesssim_{RS}^F$.

The family of equations (2) plays a crucial role in the proof of Theorem 36 in [15], to the effect that the equational theory of ready simulation equivalence is not finitely based over BCCSP(A_τ) when the set of actions is finite and contains at least two distinct actions. (In fact, as we showed in [2], ready simulation semantics is not finitely based, even when the set of actions is a singleton.)

Theorem 7. *If $|A| \ge 1$ then the (in)equational theory of $\lesssim_{RS}^F$ over* BCCSP(A_τ) *does not have a finite (in)equational basis. In particular, the following statements hold true.*

Table 3. Axiomatizations for the largest (pre)congruence included in the weak ready simulation semantics

Weak Ready Simulation	Ground-complete		Complete	
Finite Equations	Order	Equiv.	Order	Equiv.
$|A| = \infty$	$E_{RS\le}$	$E_{RS=}$	$E_{RS\le}$	$E_{RS=}$
$1 \le |A| < \infty$	$E_{RS\le}^F$	$E_{RS=}^F$	Do not exist	

Table 4. Axioms for the largest (pre)congruence included in the weak ready simulation semantics

Unconditional	
$E_{RS\le} = BW \cup \{RS, \tau g\}$ $E_{RS=} = BW \cup \{RSE, RS_{\tau e}\}$ $E_{RS\le}^F = BW \cup \{RS, \tau g, RS_\Sigma\}$ $E_{RS=}^F = BW \cup$ $\qquad \{RSE, RS_{\tau e}, RS_\Sigma\}$	$(RS) \quad ax \le ax + ay$ $(\tau g) \quad x \le \tau x$ $(RSE) \quad \alpha(bx + z + by) =$ $\qquad \alpha(bx + z + by) + \alpha(bx + z)$ $(RS_{\tau e}) \quad \alpha(x + \tau y) =$ $\qquad \alpha(x + \tau y) + \alpha(x + y)$ $(RS_\Sigma) \quad \tau(\sum_A ax_a + y) = \sum_A ax_a + y$
Conditional	
$E_{RS\le}^c = BW \cup \{RS_\tau\}$ $E_{CS=}^c = BW \cup \{RSE_\tau\}$	$(RS_\tau) \quad (I^*(x) \Leftrightarrow I^*(y)) \Rightarrow$ $\qquad x \le x + y$ $(RSE_\tau) \quad (I^*(x) \Leftrightarrow I^*(y)) \Rightarrow$ $\qquad \alpha(x + y) = \alpha(x + y) + \alpha x$

1. *No finite set of sound inequations over* $\mathrm{BCCSP}(A_\tau)$ *modulo* $\lesssim_{RS}^F$ *can prove all of the sound inequations in the family*

$$a^n x \le a^n \mathbf{0} + \sum_{b \in A} a^n(x + b) \qquad (n \ge 1).$$

2. *No finite set of sound (in)equations over* $\mathrm{BCCSP}(A_\tau)$ *modulo* $\lesssim_{RS}^F$ *can prove all of the sound equations in the family (2).*

Theorem 7 is a corollary of the following result. As usual, we consider processes up to strong bisimilarity.

Proposition 12. *Assume that* $|A| \ge 1$. *Let* E *be a collection of inequations whose elements are sound modulo* $\lesssim_{RS}^F$ *and have depth smaller than* n. *Suppose furthermore that the inequation* $t \le u$ *is derivable from* E *and that* $u \lesssim_{RS}^F$ $a^n \mathbf{0} + \sum_{b \in A} a^n(x + b)$. *Then* $t \xrightarrow{a^n} x$ *implies* $u \xrightarrow{a^n} x$.

Corollary 2. *If* $1 \leq |A| < \infty$ *then the collection of (in)equations in at most one variable that hold over* BCCSP(A_τ) *modulo* $\lesssim^F_{RS}$ *does not have a finite (in)equational basis. Moreover, for each* n, *the collection of all sound (in)equations of depth at most* n *cannot prove all the valid (in)equations in at most one variable that hold in weak ready simulation semantics over* BCCSP(A_τ).

Tables 3 and 4 summarize the positive and negative results on the existence of finite axiomatizations for weak ready simulation semantics.

5 Conclusion

In this paper, we have offered a detailed study of the axiomatizability properties of the largest (pre)congruences over the language BCCSP induced by the 'weak' versions of the classic simulation and ready simulation preorders and equivalences. For each of these notions of behavioural semantics, we have presented results related to the (non)existence of finite (ground-)complete (in)equational axiomatizations. As in [15], the finite axiomatizability of the studied notions of semantics depends crucially on the cardinality of the set of observable actions. Following [17], we have also discussed ground-complete axiomatizations of those semantics using conditional (in)equations in some detail. In particular, we have shown how to prove ground-completeness results for (in)equational axiom systems from similar results for conditional axiomatizations in a fairly systematic fashion.

The results presented in this article paint a rather complete picture of the axiomatic properties of the above-mentioned weak simulation semantics over BCCSP. We have also obtained similar results for the intermediate case of the *weak complete simulation* semantics, to be presented in a forthcoming paper. Moreover, in the cases in which the studied notions of semantics do not afford finite complete axiomatizations, it would be interesting to obtain infinite, but finitely described, complete axiomatizations. This is a topic that we leave for future research.

The results presented in this study complement those offered in, e.g., [7,38,39,41], where notions of divergence-sensitive preorders based on variations on prebisimilarity [27,33] or on the refusal simulation preorder have been given ground-complete inequational axiomatizations. They are just a first step in the study of the equational logic for notions of behavioural semantics in the extension of van Glabbeek's spectrum to behavioural semantics that abstract from internal steps in computation [22].

A natural avenue for future research is to investigate the equational logic of weak versions of semantics in van Glabbeek's spectrum that are based on notions of decorated traces. We have already started working on this topic and we plan to report on our results in a forthcoming article.

Following the developments in [1,10,38], it would also be interesting to study rule formats for operational semantics that provide congruence formats for the semantics considered in this paper, and to give procedures for generating ground-complete axiomatizations for them for process languages in the given formats.

In [16], Chen, Fokkink and van Glabbeek have provided an extension to weak process semantics of the 'ready to preorder' procedure for generating axiomatizations of process equivalences from those of their underlying preorders, first studied in [3,20]. It would be worthwhile to study whether the scope of the algorithm presented in [16] can be extended to cover the case of the weak ready simulation congruence in Definition 4 and related semantics. The doctoral dissertation [13] also presents an algorithm to turn an axiomatization of a semantics for concrete processes into one for 'its induced weak semantics.' An extension of the scope of applicability of that algorithm would also be a significant advance on the state of the art in the study of axiomatizability results for process semantics over process algebras.

References

1. Aceto, L., Bloom, B., Vaandrager, F.W.: Turning SOS rules into equations. Information and Compututation 111(1), 1–52 (1994)
2. Aceto, L., de Frutos Escrig, D., Gregorio-Rodríguez, C., Ingólfsdóttir, A.: Complete and ready simulation semantics are not finitely based over BCCSP, even with a singleton alphabet. Information Processing Letters 111(9), 408–413 (2011)
3. Aceto, L., Fokkink, W.J., Ingólfsdóttir, A.: Ready to preorder: Get your BCCSP axiomatization for free! In: Mossakowski, T., Montanari, U., Haveraaen, M. (eds.) CALCO 2007. LNCS, vol. 4624, pp. 65–79. Springer, Heidelberg (2007)
4. Aceto, L., Fokkink, W.J., Ingólfsdóttir, A., Luttik, B.: Finite equational bases in process algebra: Results and open questions. In: Middeldorp, A., van Oostrom, V., van Raamsdonk, F., de Vrijer, R. (eds.) Processes, Terms and Cycles: Steps on the Road to Infinity. LNCS, vol. 3838, pp. 338–367. Springer, Heidelberg (2005)
5. Aceto, L., Fokkink, W., Ingolfsdottir, A., Luttik, B.: A finite equational base for CCS with left merge and communication merge. ACM Trans. Comput. Log. 10(1) (2009)
6. Aceto, L., Fokkink, W., Ingólfsdóttir, A., Mousavi, M.R.: Lifting non-finite axiomatizability results to extensions of process algebras. Acta Informatica 47(3), 147–177 (2010)
7. Aceto, L., Hennessy, M.: Termination, deadlock and divergence. Journal of the ACM 39(1), 147–187 (1992)
8. Aceto, L., Ingolfsdottir, A., Luttik, B., van Tilburg, P.: Finite equational bases for fragments of CCS with restriction and relabelling. In: 5th IFIP International Conference on Theoretical Computer Science. IFIP, vol. 273, pp. 317–332. Springer, Heidelberg (2008)
9. Baeten, J., Basten, T., Reniers, M.: Process Algebra: Equational Theories of Communicating Processes. Cambridge Tracts in Theoretical Computer Science, vol. 50. Cambridge University Press, Cambridge (2009)
10. Baeten, J.C.M., de Vink, E.P.: Axiomatizing GSOS with termination. Journal of Logic and Algebraic Programming 60-61, 323–351 (2004)
11. Bergstra, J.A., Klop, J.W.: Process algebra for synchronous communication. Information and Control 60(1-3), 109–137 (1984)
12. Bloom, B., Istrail, S., Meyer, A.R.: Bisimulation can't be traced. Journal of the ACM 42(1), 232–268 (1995)

13. Chen, T.: Clocks, Dice and Processes. PhD thesis, Centrum voor Wiskunde en Informatica (CWI), Vrije Universiteit, Amsterdam (2009)
14. Chen, T., Fokkink, W.: On the axiomatizability of impossible futures: Preorder versus equivalence. In: LICS, pp. 156–165. IEEE Computer Society, Los Alamitos (2008)
15. Chen, T., Fokkink, W., Luttik, B., Nain, S.: On finite alphabets and infinite bases. Information and Computation 206(5), 492–519 (2008)
16. Chen, T., Fokkink, W., van Glabbeek, R.J.: Ready to preorder: The case of weak process semantics. Information Processing Letters 109(2), 104–111 (2008)
17. de Frutos-Escrig, D., Gregorio-Rodríguez, C., Palomino, M.: On the unification of process semantics: Equational semantics. Electronic Notes in Theoretical Computer Science 249, 243–267 (2009)
18. de Frutos-Escrig, D., Gregorio-Rodríguez, C.: Universal coinductive characterizations of process semantics. In: 5th IFIP International Conference on Theoretical Computer Science. IFIP, vol. 273, pp. 397–412. Springer, Heidelberg (2008)
19. de Frutos-Escrig, D., Gregorio-Rodríguez, C.: (Bi)simulations up-to characterise process semantics. Information and Computation 207(2), 146–170 (2009)
20. de Frutos-Escrig, D., Gregorio-Rodríguez, C., Palomino, M.: Ready to preorder: an algebraic and general proof. Journal of Logic and Algebraic Programming 78(7), 539–551 (2009)
21. De Nicola, R., Hennessy, M.: Testing equivalences for processes. Theoretical Computer Science 34, 83–133 (1984)
22. van Glabbeek, R.J.: The linear time - branching time spectrum II. In: Best, E. (ed.) CONCUR 1993. LNCS, vol. 715, pp. 66–81. Springer, Heidelberg (1993)
23. van Glabbeek, R.J.: The linear time – branching time spectrum I; the semantics of concrete, sequential processes. In: Handbook of Process Algebra, ch. 1, pp. 3–99. Elsevier, Amsterdam (2001)
24. van Glabbeek, R.J.: A characterisation of weak bisimulation congruence. In: Middeldorp, A., van Oostrom, V., van Raamsdonk, F., de Vrijer, R. (eds.) Processes, Terms and Cycles: Steps on the Road to Infinity. LNCS, vol. 3838, pp. 26–39. Springer, Heidelberg (2005)
25. van Glabbeek, R.J., Weijland, P.: Branching time and abstraction in bisimulation semantics. Journal of the ACM 43(3), 555–600 (1996)
26. Groote, J.F.: A new strategy for proving omega-completeness applied to process algebra. In: Baeten, J.C.M., Klop, J.W. (eds.) CONCUR 1990. LNCS, vol. 458, pp. 314–331. Springer, Heidelberg (1990)
27. Hennessy, M.: A term model for synchronous processes. Informationa and Control 51(1), 58–75 (1981)
28. Hennessy, M., Milner, R.: Algebraic laws for nondeterminism and concurrency. Journal of the ACM 32, 137–161 (1985)
29. Hoare, C.: Communicating Sequential Processes. Prentice-Hall, Englewood Cliffs (1985)
30. Larsen, K.G., Skou, A.: Bisimulation through probabilistic testing. Information and Computation, 94(1):1–28 (1991)
31. Lüttgen, G., Vogler, W.: Ready simulation for concurrency: It's logical! Information and Computation 208(7), 845–867 (2010)
32. Milner, R.: An algebraic definition of simulation between programs. In: Proceedings 2nd Joint Conference on Artificial Intelligence, pp. 481–489. BCS (1971); Also available as Report No. CS-205, Computer Science Department, Stanford University

33. Milner, R.: A modal characterisation of observable machine behaviour. In: Aste-siano, E., Böhm, C. (eds.) CAAP 1981. LNCS, vol. 112, pp. 25–34. Springer, Heidelberg (1981)
34. Milner, R.: Communication and Concurrency. Prentice-Hall, Englewood Cliffs (1989)
35. Milner, R.: A complete axiomatisation for observational congruence of finite-state behaviors. Information and Computation 81(2), 227–247 (1989)
36. Moller, F.: Axioms for Concurrency. PhD thesis, Report CST-59-89, Department of Computer Science, University of Edinburgh (1989)
37. Plotkin, G.D.: A structural approach to operational semantics. Journal of Logic and Algebraic Programming 60-61, 17–139 (2004)
38. Ulidowski, I.: Axiomatisations of weak equivalences for De Simone languages. In: Lee, I., Smolka, S.A. (eds.) CONCUR 1995. LNCS, vol. 962, pp. 219–233. Springer, Heidelberg (1995)
39. Ulidowski, I.: Refusal simulation and interactive games. In: Kirchner, H., Ringeissen, C. (eds.) AMAST 2002. LNCS, vol. 2422, pp. 208–222. Springer, Heidelberg (2002)
40. Voorhoeve, M., Mauw, S.: Impossible futures and determinism. Information Processing Letters 80(1), 51–58 (2001)
41. Walker, D.: Bisimulation and divergence. Information and Computation 85(2), 202–241 (1990)

Symbolic Worst Case Execution Times*

Ernst Althaus[1], Sebastian Altmeyer[2], and Rouven Naujoks[3]

[1] Johannes-Gutenberg-Universität Mainz and Max-Planck-Institut für Informatik
ernst.althaus@uni-mainz.de
[2] Saarland University
altmeyer@cs.uni-saarland.de
[3] Max-Planck-Institut für Informatik
naujoks@mpi-inf.mpg.de

Abstract. In *immediate* or *hard real-time systems* the correctness of an operation depends not only upon its logical correctness, but also on the time in which it is is computed. In such systems, it is imperative that operations are performed within a given deadline because missing this deadline constitutes the failure of the complete system. Such systems include medical systems, flight control systems and other systems whose failure in responding punctually results in a high economical loss or even in the loss of human lives.

These systems are usually analyzed in a sequence of steps in which first, a so-called control flow graph (CFG) is constructed that represents possible program flows. Furthermore, bounds on the time necessary to execute small code blocks are computed along with bounds on the number of possible executions of the program loops. Depending on the type of the analysis, these loop bounds can either be numerical values or symbolic variables, corresponding to inputs given for instance by a user or by sensors. In the last step, in such a CFG the weight of a longest path with respect to the loop bounds is computed, reflecting a bound on the worst case execution time.

In this paper, we will show how to compute such symbolic longest path weights in CFGs of software with a rather regular structure like software developed for hard real-time systems. We will present the first algorithm that is capable of computing such paths in time polynomial in the size of both the input *and* the output. Our approach replaces the application of integer linear programming solvers in the case of purely numerical loop bounds. Furthermore, it improves upon the speed and accuracy of existing approaches in the case of symbolic bounds.

1 Introduction

Immediate real-time systems require tasks to finish in time. To guarantee the timeliness of such systems, upper bounds on the worst case execution times of the their tasks have to be computed. To be useful in practice, such an analysis must be *sound* to ensure the reliability of the guarantee, *precise* to increase the chance of proving the satisfiability of the timing requirements, and *efficient*, to make them useful in industrial practice.

---

* This work was partly supported by the German Research Council (DFG) as part of the Transregional Collaborative Research Center "Automatic Verification and Analysis of Complex Systems" (SFB/TR 14 AVACS, www.avacs.org).

A. Cerone and P. Pihlajasaari (Eds.): ICTAC 2011, LNCS 6916, pp. 25–44, 2011.

The high complexity of modern processors and modern embedded software hampers the analysis to achieve all three properties at once. Exhaustive measurement, for instance, may be sound and precise but is infeasible for realistically sized programs. Simple end-to-end measurements are easy to derive, but are possibly unsound. We refer to [12] for a general overview of methods for the worst-case execution-time problem and to [10],[7] presenting the results of challenges in which state-of-the-art tools are compared. A general approach to achieve all three properties is to represent a program P that has to be analyzed as a so-called *control flow graph* in which a node corresponds to a *basic code block* B of P, i.e. to a maximal sequence of consecutive operations of P such that only B's first operation is the target of a jump operation in P and such that the last operation in B is a jump directive. The edges in such a graph represent the source/target relationship of the jumps in P. In a set of analyses, upper bounds on the running times of the basic blocks and upper bounds on the number of loop iterations are determined. The execution time bound of the program is then given by the weight of a longest path P in the CFG that respects the given loop bounds. The step of the timing analysis that computes such a path is usually referred to as *path analysis*.

Timing analyses treating bounds on the maximal number of loop iterations as numerical values are referred to as *numeric* or *traditional timing analyses*. The drawback of such an analysis is that bounds on loop iterations must be known statically, i.e. during design time. Some systems need guarantees for timely reactions which are not absolute, but dependent on inputs of for example a user or a sensor. In such cases, traditional timing analysis offers only two possibilities. Either one provides constant bounds for the unknown variables or one starts a new analysis each time the task is used with different inputs. While the first option endangers precision, the second may be an unacceptable increase in the analysis time. *Parametric timing analyses* circumvents this problem. Instead of computing numeric bounds valid for specific variable assignments only, parametric analysis derives symbolic formulas representing upper bounds on the task's execution times.

Traditionally, the computation of a longest path in a CFG is done by formulating the problem as an integer program. While in the case of numeric timing analyses, the corresponding integer program is linear and can be solved by an ILP-solver, the integer program in the presence of symbolic bounds on the loop iterations is in general nonlinear, which makes it necessary to relax the non-linear constraints, leading to a loss of accuracy (see 2.2 for a more detailed discussion).

Even the traditional path analysis is NP-hard since by setting all loop bounds to one, the problem reduces to the longest path problem in graphs. In this paper, we discuss a new and purely combinatorial approach for the symbolic path analysis and for arbitrary loop bounds, exploiting the rather regular structure of software written for such time critical systems. Such software must be clearly structured, avoiding for instance constructs like gotos, to make the code verifiable. For CFGs arising from such code, we present an approach for the path analysis, which solves two major problems of the previous approaches: in stark contrast to the exponential running time of the ILP approach, our algorithm has a running time that is polynomial in the size of both the input and the output. Note that in case of numeric path analysis, only one path is reported. Furthermore, in the case of symbolic analyses, our algorithm avoids any relaxation of non-linear constraints, leading to potentially better bounds. We also show that for a certain type of CFGs the size of the output is minimal.

2 Related Work

In this section we briefly discuss two state-of-the-art approaches for path analysis which make use of an ILP formulation. For a detailed discussion we refer to [3,8,11]. Note, that in some cases it is convenient to assign the runtime of a basic blocks to the outgoing edges of the corresponding node in the CFG. We also restrict the discussion to the computation of a longest path from a source node s with in-degree 0 to some sink node t with out-degree 0.

2.1 Numeric Path Analysis

For the longest path computation usually a technique called *implicit path enumeration* (see [8,11]) is used. Each edge e_i is assigned a variable n_i called the *traversal count* denoting how often e_i is traversed by a control flow. Since a control flow enters a nodes v exactly as often as it leaves it, the sum of the traversal counts of edges entering v must equal the sum of the counts of the edges leaving v. For the source node and the target node we have the special rule, that the sum of traversal counts of incident edges must equal 1 since each program flow enters s and leaves t exactly once. In a third class of inequalities, the number of times a loop is traversed is limited to the number of times it is entered multiplied by its loop bound. The objective function of this ILP is then to maximize the sum over the costs of the basic blocks times the traversal counts of edges entering them (see 1 for an example).

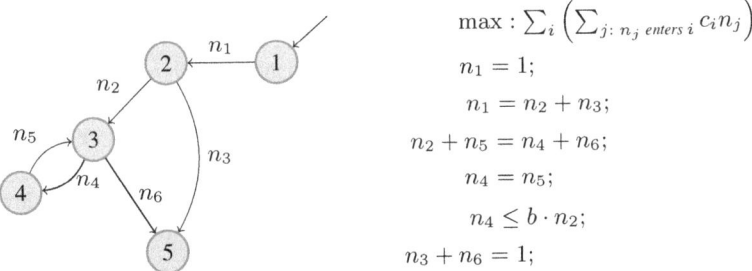

$$\max : \sum_i \left(\sum_{j:\, n_j \text{ enters } i} c_i n_j \right)$$

$$n_1 = 1;$$

$$n_1 = n_2 + n_3;$$

$$n_2 + n_5 = n_4 + n_6;$$

$$n_4 = n_5;$$

$$n_4 \leq b \cdot n_2;$$

$$n_3 + n_6 = 1;$$

Fig. 1. A control flow graph and the corresponding ILP formulation. The running time of the basic block i is denoted as c_i. It is transfered to the incoming edges of i. b denotes the loop bound of the loop $\{3, 4\}$. Equalities ensure the flow-balance, i.e. a node is entered exactly as many times as it is left. The inequality $n_4 \leq b \cdot n_2$ ensures that the loop is traversed (i.e. edge n_4 is used) only b times the number of times it is entered (i.e. edge n_2 is used). In case of numberic loop bounds, the inequality is linear. If the loop bound is symbolic, i.e. b is a variable and we are seeking for all paths which are longest of at least one b, the inequality is non-linear and has to be relaxed by finding an upper bound on n_2.

2.2   Parametric Path Analysis

In the approach given in [9] and [3] for the parametric path analysis basically the same ILP construction as in the previous discussion is used. The difference is now that the loop bounds used in this formulation are now variables, yielding non-linear constraints – in the example 1, there is for instance the non-linear constraint $n_4 \leq b \cdot n_2$ if the loop bound b is symbolic. In order to solve such an integer program, these non-linearities must be relaxed by bounding the variables in the ILP by constants. For instance, is it easy to verify that in our example, the constraint $n_4 \leq b \cdot n_2$ can be replaced by the constraint $n_4 \leq b$, since $n_2 \leq 1$. Once, all non-linear constraints are relaxed we are left with a parametric ILP, i.e. with an ILP containing symbolic constants, which can be solved by a parametric ILP-solver as proposed by Feautrier [5] using symbolic versions of the simplex [4] and the cutting plane algorithm [6]. The two big disadvantages of this approach are that such parametric ILP-solvers are much slower than existing ILP solvers and that the method yields a loss in accuracy by the relaxation of the constraints.

3   Longest Paths in Singleton-Loop-Graphs

So far we have treated the concept of a program loop as given. But to discuss our algorithm we have to formally define what a program loop corresponds to in the CFG. Considering nested loops in a piece of code, one can observe, that any two points can be reached from each other by a possible control flow, leading to the definition that a loop is a strongly connected component in the CFG. The sub-loops of a loop L are then just the strongly connected components of L after removing the node over which L is entered. Note that this also means that the sub-loops of a loop depend on the node over which L is entered.

Assuming wlog. that such a program was written in a high level language like c, the constructs causing the control flow to branch are *for*, *repeat-until*, and *while-do* loops with *continue* and *break* statements, *if-then-else* constructs, *function calls* and *goto* directives. Recall that we want to compute upper bounds on the worst case execution times of programs developed for immediate real-time systems. As discussed before such programs typically have a rather regular structure. That is, usually the use of directives like *goto*, *break* and *continue* is avoided. If a program now does not contain *goto* directives, our definition of a loop coincides with the intuitive concept of a loop. Moreover, there is a unique node over which the loop is entered, which we call the entry node of the loop, and thus, each loop must have uniquely defined sub-loops. The same holds recursively for all sub-loops. We call graphs with this property singleton-loop graphs. Beside a CFG and upper bounds for the runtime of the basic blocks, we assume that we are given loop bounds for all induced sub-loops of the CFG, which can either be explicit numerical values or symbols. In this section we will first describe the algorithm for singleton-loop graphs, achieving a polynomial running time in the size of the input and the output. In the following section, we will describe a slight variation of this algorithm for certain graphs, which we call *while-loop-graphs* in which we additionally disallow break statements. For this type of graph, we will show that we can even guarantee, that the output is of minimal size.

3.1   Preliminaries

Definition 1 (Loop). *Given a directed graph $G = (V, E)$, we call a strongly connected component $S = (V_S, E_S)$ in G with $|E_S| > 0$, a* loop *of G. We denote by* loops(G), *the set of all loops of G.*

Definition 2 (Entry Node). *Given a directed graph $G = (V, E)$ and a loop $L = (V_L, E_L)$ of G, we call $e \in V_L$ such that there exists an edge (u, e) in $\delta_G^+(V \setminus V_L)$ an* entry node *of L.*

Definition 3 (Singleton-Loop). *A loop L in a graph G is called a* singleton-loop *if L has exactly one entry node e. For the unique entry node of a singleton loop L, we write $\mathscr{E}(L)$.*

Definition 4 (Sub-loops). *Given a loop $L = (V_L, E_L)$, we define*

$$\text{sloops}(L) := \bigcup_{v \text{ is entry node of } V_L} \text{loops}(G_v)$$

where G_v is the subgraph induced by $V_L \setminus \{v\}$.

Definition 5 (Induced Sub-loops). *Given a loop $L = (V, E)$, we call the recursively defined set*

$$\text{iloops}(L) := \{L\} \cup \Big(\bigcup_{L_s \in \text{sloops}(L)} \text{iloops}(L_s) \Big)$$

the set of induced sub-loops *of L. For a graph G, we extend the definition of* iloops *to graphs:*

$$\text{iloops}(G) := \bigcup_{L_s \in \text{loops}(G)} \text{iloops}(L_s)$$

We call a graph G a *singleton-loop graph* if each induced sub-loop of G is a singleton-loop. For such a graph, we write $\mathscr{E}(G) := \{\mathscr{E}(L) \mid L \in \text{iloops}(G)\}$ to denote the set of entry nodes of all induced sub-loops in G.

Definition 6 (Portal Nodes, Transit Edges). *Given a directed graph $G = (V, E)$ and a loop $L = (V_L, E_L)$ in G, we call $\mathcal{T}(L) := \delta_G^+(V_L)$ the set of* transit edges *of L, i.e. the edges, leaving the loop L, and $\mathcal{P}(L) := \{p \in V_L \mid \exists (p, v) \in \mathcal{T}(L)\}$ the set of* portal nodes *of L. A portal node is thus a source node of a transit edge.*

Note that there is a one-to-one correspondence between singleton-loops and their entry nodes, which justifies the following definition.

Definition 7 (Loop-Bound Function). *Given a singleton-loop graph $G = (V, E)$, we call a function* $b \colon \mathscr{E}(G) \to \mathbb{N} \cup \{+\infty\}$ *a loop-bound function for G.*

Now we have to classify the valid paths, i.e. the paths that respect the loop-bound conditions. If for a loop L, a loop-bound of $b(\mathscr{E}(L))$ is given, we say that an execution path is not allowed to enter L and iterate on L more than $b(\mathscr{E}(L))$ times, before the path leaves L again.

Definition 8 (Valid Path). *Given a singleton-loop graph* $G = (V, E)$, *two nodes* $s, t \in V$ *and a loop-bound function* b *for* G, *we call a path* $P := s \rightsquigarrow t$ *a* valid path *if for all* $L := (V_L, E_L) \in \mathrm{iloops}(G)$ *and for all sub-paths* $(\mathscr{E}(L), v_0, v_1, \ldots, v_k)$ *of* P *with* $v_i \in V_L$, *the sub-path* $(\mathscr{E}(L), v_0, v_1, \ldots, v_{k-1})$ *contains at most* $b(\mathscr{E}(L))$ *times the node* $\mathscr{E}(L)$.

In the following, we write $\mathrm{lps}(G, s, t)$ for a longest valid path from a node s to a node t and for a $\overline{\mathrm{lps}}(G, s, t)$ to denote the longest valid path from s to t, that contains t exactly once. Most of the times, we will limit the discussion to the task of computing just the path weights for sake of simplicity. Note, that this is not a real limitation, as the algorithm can easily be extended to also cope with the problem of reporting the paths as well. Furthermore, we will assume that for each $v \in V$ there is a path from s to t containing v. All other nodes can be removed by a preprocessing step in time $O(|V| + |E|)$. Note that the resulting graph has at least $|V| - 1$ edges.

3.2 The Algorithm

Let us recall that a problem instance is given by a singleton-loop graph $G = (V, E)$, a source node $s \in V$, an edge weight function $w: E \mapsto \mathbb{N}$ and a loop-bound function $b: \mathscr{E}(G) \to \mathbb{N} \cup \{+\infty\}$. As we implicitly compute the single source all destination problem we do not specify t in the algorithm. Since from now on, we will only talk about singleton-loop graphs, we will only write loops instead of singleton-loops.

The algorithm uses the following observation. Assume the longest path traverses a loop L. It does so by traversing the longest cycle starting at the entry node in L for $b(\mathscr{E}(L)) - 1$ times and then traversing via a longest path to one of its portal nodes. Hence, our algorithm first computes for each loop L its longest loop and the longest paths to its portals in a recursive manner. This is done by splitting the entry node into one having the outgoing edge, the other having the incoming edges. The longest paths to the portal nodes do not change and the longest cycle is the longest path from the copy of the entry node with the outgoing edges to the one with the incoming edges. Then we contract the loops to single nodes where the transit edges (v, w) over portal node v, are assigned the weight that corresponds to the longest path that cycles through the entry node $b(\mathscr{E}(L)) - 1$ times, then goes to v and uses the transit edge (v, w). Finally, notice that in order to return the path itself, we have to store the path that we used to reach the entry node, denoted by $\overline{\mathrm{lps}}(G, s, \mathscr{E}(L))$, which is not the longest path to $\mathscr{E}(L)$ as this is allowed to traverse a cycle in L $b(\mathscr{E}(L)) - 1$ times. In pseudo-code our algorithm looks as follows.

$LPS(G, s) :=$

1. Identify the loops $(L_j)_{j \in \{1, \ldots, l\}}$ of G by computing the strongly connected components.
2. For each $L_j = (V_{L_j}, E_{L_j})$:
   (a) modify L_j by replacing $\mathscr{E}(L_j)$ by two nodes $\mathscr{E}_{\mathrm{out}}$ and $\mathscr{E}_{\mathrm{in}}$ and by replacing all incoming edges $(v, \mathscr{E}(L_j))$ by edges $(v, \mathscr{E}_{\mathrm{in}})$ and all outgoing edges $(\mathscr{E}(L), v)$ by edges $(\mathscr{E}_{\mathrm{out}}, v)$
   (b) call $LPS(L_j, \mathscr{E}_{\mathrm{out}})$

(c) For all $v \in V_{L_j}$ we set

$$\mathrm{lps}(G, \mathscr{E}(L_j), v) := (\mathrm{b}(\mathscr{E}(L_j)) - 1) \cdot \mathrm{lps}(L_j, \mathscr{E}_{\mathrm{out}}, \mathscr{E}_{\mathrm{in}}) + \mathrm{lps}(L_j, \mathscr{E}_{\mathrm{out}}, v),$$

(d) replace L_j in G by a single node r_j and add an edge (r_j, x) for each $(p, x) \in \mathcal{T}(L_j)$ with appropriate weights, namely: $w(r_j, x) := lps(G, \mathscr{E}(L_j), p) + w(p, x)$. Add an edge (v, r_j) for each $(v, \mathscr{E}(L_j)) \in E$ and set $w(v, r_j) := w(v, \mathscr{E}(L_j))$

3. We call the altered graph the condensed graph G'. It is a DAG, thus we can easily determine the longest paths.

4. Compute the longest path weights to nodes within the loops: Replace the nodes r_j again by the corresponding loops and set for each $L_j = (V_{L_j}, E_{V_j})$ and for all $v \in V_{L_j}$:

$$\mathrm{lps}(G, s, v) := \overline{\mathrm{lps}}(G, s, \mathscr{E}(L_j)) + \mathrm{lps}(L_j, \mathscr{E}(L_j), v)$$

So far, we haven't discussed, how the $\overline{\mathrm{lps}}(G, s, \mathscr{E}(L_j))$ in step 4 are computed. Note, that $\mathscr{E}(L_j)$ corresponds to a contraction node c in the condensed graph G'. When we compute the longest path weight from s to c, we set $\overline{\mathrm{lps}}(G', s, c) := \max_{v \in \mathrm{inc}(c)} \mathrm{lps}(G', s, v) + w(v, c)$, where $inc(c)$ denotes the set of nodes v such that there is an edge (v, c) from v to c.

Running Time - Numeric Bounds. Let us first analyze the algorithm's running time $T(|V|, |E|)$ for the case in which all loop-bounds are numeric values. In step 1), the strongly connected components of G are computed, which can be done in $O(|V| + |E|)$ time by depth-first search. Step 2a) can be computed in $O(\deg(\mathscr{E}(L_j)))$ time. In step 2b), the algorithm is called recursively which takes $T(|V_{L_j}| + 1, |E_{L_j}|)$ time. The weight updates in 2c) can be performed in $O(|V_{L_j}|)$ and the updates in 2d) in $O(|\mathcal{T}(L_j)|)$ time. It is folklore, that the computation of longest path weights in a DAG, as done in step 3), takes no more than $O(|V| + |E|)$ time. Finally, step 4 can be done in $O(|V|)$. Thus, without the recursive calls, we have a linear running time of $O(|V| + |E|)$. Note that the recursion depth of our algorithm is bounded by $|V|$, as each node is split at most once. Furthermore, the edge sets of the sub-loops are disjoint. Although nodes are split, we can argue that the total number of nodes in a certain recursion depth is bounded by $2|V|$ as follows: Let $V^{out} = \{v \in V \mid v \text{ has at least 1 outgoing edge}\}$ and $V^{in} = \{v \in V \mid v \text{ has at least 1 incoming edge}\}$. Then $\sum_{L \in \mathrm{sloops}(G)} |V_{\bar{L}}^{out}| \leq |V^{out}|$ and $\sum_{L \in \mathrm{sloops}(G)} |V_{\bar{L}}^{in}| \leq |V^{in}|$, where $V_{\bar{L}}$ is the set of nodes of L after splitting the entry node. Thus, in total we have

$$T(|V|, |E|) = O(|V| \cdot (|V^{out}| + |V^{in}| + |E|)) = O(|V| \cdot |E|)$$

Running Time - Symbolic Bounds. In the presence of symbolic loop-bounds we have to change our algorithm slightly. Notice, that an ordinary longest path algorithm starts with a lower bound on the length of the longest path and iteratively increases the path length if a longer path is found. In the presence of symbolic loop bounds, paths may become incomparable, i.e. if one path has length 4, the other $2 \cdot b$ for a symbolic loop bound b. Hence, instead of a unique longest path, we now have to consider for each target node a set of paths to that node, that may be longest for a particular choice of the symbolic loop bounds (see Figure 2 for an example). When concatenating two paths we now have to concatenate all pairs of paths. Since the operations on the path weights include multiplications and additions, they can be represented as polynomials over the symbolic loop-bounds. Clearly, we aim at getting all possible path weights that are maximal for at least one choice for the symbolic loop-bound parameters. On the down side, testing whether a path weight is maximum for some choice (or instantiation) of the parameters seems to be non trivial. A compromise is to keep all paths with weights that are not dominated by another weight (i.e. all coefficients in the weight polynomial are at least as big as the coefficients in the other weight polynomial) to keep the solution set sparse in practice, which can be implemented very efficiently. Furthermore, as we will see later, for a some certain class of CFGs this step is necessary and sufficient to compute a minimal number of paths. For a problem instance $I = (G, s, t)$, consisting of a graph, a source node s and a destination node t, we denote by $\mathcal{D}(I)$ (or short $\mathcal{D}(s, t)$, if G can be deduced from the context) the set of longest path weights from s to t computed by our algorithm. The property of $\mathcal{D}(I)$, that its elements are pairwise non-dominating can be achieved by eliminating dominated elements after the execution of step 2c. We write $\mathrm{slbs}(I)$ for the number of symbolic loop-bounds of a problem instance $I = (G, s, t)$ and $\mathrm{lbs}(I) := \mathrm{lbs}(G) := |\mathrm{iloops}(G)|$ for the number of induced loops of G.

Theorem 1. *The algorithm's running time is polynomial in the input size and in the size of the output.*

Proof. First note that the running time only changes for the parts of the algorithm in which calculations on path weights are performed, namely the parts 2c), 2d) and 4). We will restrict this proof to the operations involved in step 2c), since the number of operations involved in 2c) is certainly not smaller than the ones in 2d) and 4).

Let us first count the number of operations on weight polynomials. Consider a longest path P from the source node s to the destination node t. Let $\mathrm{lps}(u, v)$ denote the longest path weights, computed by the algorithm for the longest paths from node u to node v, then for each loop $L = (V_L, E_L) \in \mathrm{loops}(G)$ that is traversed by P, we have $|\mathrm{lps}(\mathscr{E}(L), p_L)| \leq |\mathrm{lps}(s, p_L)|$ for $p_L \in \mathcal{P}(L)$ over which P leaves L again. Furthermore, for each $p_L \in portals(L)$ we have $O(|\mathrm{lps}(\mathscr{E}(L), \mathscr{E}(L))| \cdot |\mathrm{lps}(\mathscr{E}(L), p_L)|)$ operations, since the addition involves the addition of all pairs of weights in $\mathrm{lps}(\mathscr{E}(L), \mathscr{E}(L))$ and in $\mathrm{lps}(\mathscr{E}(L), p_L)$. Since L is strongly connected, $|\mathrm{lps}(\mathscr{E}(L), \mathscr{E}(L))| \leq |\mathrm{lps}(\mathscr{E}(L), p_L)|$. Thus the number of operations is bounded by $|\mathrm{lps}(\mathscr{E}(L), p_L)|^2 \leq |\mathrm{lps}(s, p_L)|^2$. Since each node in V_L can be a portal node of L, the total number of operations on polynomials occurring on the first recursion level is bounded by $\sum_{v \in V} |lps(s, v)|^2 \leq \left(\sum_{v \in V} |lps(s, v)| \right)^2$. But, since $\sum_{v \in V} |lps(s, v)|$ is just the number of path weights, reported by the algorithm, the number of operations on polynomials is polynomial in the number of reported path weights. Note that each weight has a unique representation and that all operations on the weight polynomials can be carried out in time polynomial in the size of these polynomials.

What is left to show is, that the weight polynomials computed for the nodes in the input graph have a size polynomially bounded by the size of the weight polynomials that are reported by our algorithm, that is the weight polynomials of the longest paths from the source node s to the sink node t. We will use a structural induction over the input graph G to prove so. If G contains no loops, the claim is true since G must be a DAG and therefore, all computed longest path weights are just constants. So, let us assume that G contains loops. By induction hypothesis, the claim holds now for each problem instance $(L, \mathscr{E}_{\text{out}}, p)$ where L is a loop of G, where the entry node of L is split into the nodes $\mathscr{E}_{\text{out}}$ and $\mathscr{E}_{\text{in}}$ and where p is an arbitrary portal node of L. But then the claim is also true for $(L, \mathscr{E}(L), p)$ what can be seen as follows: Recall that a longest path weight from $\mathscr{E}(L)$ to p is given by the equation

$$\text{lps}(G, \mathscr{E}(L), p) = (\text{b}(\mathscr{E}(L)) - 1) \cdot \text{lps}(L, \mathscr{E}_{\text{out}}, \mathscr{E}_{\text{in}}) + \text{lps}(L, \mathscr{E}_{\text{out}}, p)$$

for some path weights $\text{lps}(L, \mathscr{E}_{\text{out}}, \mathscr{E}_{\text{in}})$ and $\text{lps}(L, \mathscr{E}_{\text{out}}, p)$. But then, $\text{lps}(G, \mathscr{E}(L), p)$ is as least as large as the maximum of the sizes of $\text{lps}(L, \mathscr{E}_{\text{out}}, \mathscr{E}_{\text{in}})$ and of $\text{lps}(L, \mathscr{E}_{\text{out}}, p)$ as each term in $\text{lps}(L, \mathscr{E}_{\text{out}}, \mathscr{E}_{\text{in}})$ appears with a multiple of $\text{b}(\mathscr{E}(L))$, $\text{lps}(L, \mathscr{E}_{\text{out}}, p)$ does not contain $\text{b}(\mathscr{E}(L))$ and each term in $\text{lps}(L, \mathscr{E}_{\text{out}}, p)$ can eliminate only terms that are not multiplied with $\text{b}(\mathscr{E}(L))$. The last thing we have to show now is, that the claim holds for (G', s, t), where again G' denotes the condensed graph. We compute the longest path weights in the directed acyclic graph G' by the recurrence $\text{lps}(G, s, u) = \max_{v \in \text{inc}(u)} (\text{lps}(G, s, v) + w(v, u))$ starting with $u := t$. Consider now a weight polynomial $P = \text{lps}(G, s, v) + w(v, u)$. Since we consider the condensed graph G', $w(v, u)$ is a polynomial containing only variables associated with the loop that in turn is associated with the node v (in the case that v is not a condensed node, $w(v, u)$ is just a constant). Thus, except for the constant terms, P contains at least as many terms as there are in $\text{lps}(G, s, v)$ or in $w(v, u)$, which completes the proof.

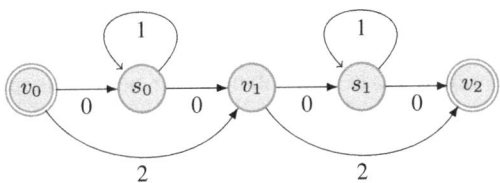

Fig. 2. The different weights for the longest paths from v_0 to v_2 are $4, 2 + \text{b}(s_0), 2 + \text{b}(s_1)$ and $\text{b}(s_0) + \text{b}(s_1)$

Correctness. Now, we will show, that our algorithm indeed computes the weight of a longest valid path $\text{lps}(G, s, t)$ from a source vertex s to a destination vertex t. In the following, when talking about paths we always mean valid paths. Again we will assume that G is a singleton-loop graph with weight function $w \colon E \mapsto \mathbb{N}$ and that we are given a loop-bound function $\text{b} \colon \mathscr{E}(G) \to \mathbb{N} \cup \{+\infty\}$. We will show the claim by induction over the recursion-level of the algorithm. If we assume that G contains no loops, G must be a directed acyclic graph and thus, our algorithm is correct. So, now assume that G contains loops. The induction hypothesis tells us now that for all recursive calls of our algorithm, we obtain correct results. Let $p := s \rightsquigarrow t$ be a longest path in G. Let us assume w.l.o.g. that p shares at least one node with a sub-loop of G, i.e. for some

$L := (V_L, E_L) \in \text{sloops}(G)$: $\mathscr{E}(L) \in V_L$. Thus p can be written as $p = s \rightsquigarrow p' \rightsquigarrow t$ with $p' = (\mathscr{E}(L) = v_0, v_1, \ldots, v_k)$ such that $v_i \in V_L$ and k is maximal. Since any sub-path of a longest path must be again a longest path between its starting- and end-node (with respect to the validity), we have that $w(p') = \text{lps}(G, \mathscr{E}(L), v_k)$. Consider now the condensed graph G' obtained by replacing loop L by a node r as described in the algorithm. Then the path $s \rightsquigarrow r \rightarrow v_k \rightsquigarrow t$ is valid and has weight $w(p)$. Therefore, $w(\text{lps}(G, s, t)) \leq w(\text{lps}(G', s, t))$. On the other hand, $w(\text{lps}(G, s, t))$ cannot be strictly less than $w(\text{lps}(G', s, t))$, because otherwise there would be a path in G' with weight strictly greater than a longest path in G, which also would not traverse L, since the weights of these paths are unequal. But this would mean, that there is also a path in G – just bypassing L – with the weight $w(\text{lps}(G', s, t))$, which leads to a contradiction.

What is left to show is, that our algorithm computes correct values for $\text{lps}(G, \mathscr{E}(L), v_k)$. Let $p = (\mathscr{E}(L) =: v_0, v_1, \ldots, v_k)$ with $v_i \in V_L$ be a longest path. We can assume that p contains exactly $\text{b}(\mathscr{E}(L))$ (respectively $\text{b}(\mathscr{E}(L))+1$ if $v_k = \mathscr{E}(L)$) times the node $\mathscr{E}(L)$, otherwise we could extend the path by the path $v_k \rightsquigarrow \mathscr{E}(L) \rightsquigarrow v_k$ without violating validity. Now each sub-path p' of p with $p' = \mathscr{E}(L) \rightsquigarrow \mathscr{E}(L)$ must have the same weight, since otherwise, by replacing the lower weight sub-path by the corresponding higher weight sub-path, we could obtain a path with higher weights. Thus, we can assume that there exists a longest path $\mathscr{E}(L) \overset{p'}{\rightsquigarrow} \mathscr{E}(L) \overset{p'}{\rightsquigarrow} \ldots \overset{p'}{\rightsquigarrow} \mathscr{E}(L) \overset{p''}{\rightsquigarrow} v_k$ with weight $(\text{b}(\mathscr{E}(L))-1) \cdot w(p') + w(p'')$. Since p' and p'' must be longest paths, we are left to show that our algorithm computes the weights $\overline{\text{lps}}(G, \mathscr{E}(L), \mathscr{E}(L))$ and $\overline{\text{lps}}(G, \mathscr{E}(L), v_k)$ correctly. But this follows directly by the way we alter the loop L, i.e. by splitting the entry node of L into the two nodes $\mathscr{E}_{\text{out}}$ and $\mathscr{E}_{\text{in}}$. Since L was a loop, every node in L is reachable from $\mathscr{E}_{\text{out}}$. by induction hypothesis the algorithm now computes recursively the right values, where obviously $w(\text{lps}(\overline{L}, \mathscr{E}_{\text{out}}, \mathscr{E}_{\text{in}})) = w(\overline{\text{lps}}(G, e, e))$.

3.3 While-Loop-Graphs

Even though our algorithm runs in time polynomial in both the input size and the output size, we haven't discussed so far, how large the output size can get. One can show that there is a problem instance such that the number of paths that any correct algorithm has to report is $2^{\text{slbs}(G)}$. Unfortunately, we can only show that our algorithm produces outputs such that the number of reported paths is not larger than $2^{2^{\text{lbs}(G)}}$ and even worse, there is a problem instance such that the minimal output size is 2 while our algorithm reports $2^{2^{\text{lbs}(G)-1}}$ paths. On the other hand, experiments have shown that in practice the number of reported paths is quite small. For proofs of these claims and for some experimental results we want to refer to Appendix A, respectively to [1]. Unfortunately, a precise discussion of the conducted experiments goes beyond the scope of this paper.

In this section we will discuss our algorithm on a certain type of graphs with the additional property that each induced sub-loop has exactly one portal node which coincides with the entry node of the loop. The motivation for considering such CFGs is that if additionaly to goto directives we also avoid break statements, the CFG corresponds to a while-program. Since a while–loop is entered and left only via its loop header, we can assume wlog. that the corresponding CFG exhibits this special property. The reason why we haven't considered this case before is of practical nature. Converting a program into a while–program can change its worst case running time. On the other hand, most of the CFGs that we have considered in experiments, consisted mostly of such loops. Thus, the ideas presented in this section, can also lead to a significant reduction in the output size in practice.

Thus, we assume for now that the CFG, has the additional property that $\forall L \in$ iloops(G): $\mathcal{P}(L) = \{\mathcal{E}(L)\}$. We now modify our algorithm as follows. Since the entry node of a loop always coincides with its only portal node, we have in step 2c): lps$(G, \mathcal{E}(L_j), \mathcal{E}(L_j)) = b(\mathcal{E}(L_j)) \cdot$ lps$(L_j, \mathcal{E}_{\text{out}}, \mathcal{E}_{\text{in}})$ and can thus avoid the addition operation. In Lemma 1 we will show, that for this class of graphs, the reported path weight polynomials are small. Then we will state in Lemma 2 that also the worst case number of distinct longest paths is significantly smaller in such graphs. Finally, we show in Theorem 2 that the modified algorithm reports a minimal number of path weights.

Lemma 1. *For any problem instance I, $\mathcal{D}(I)$ contains only weights with at most* slbs$(G) + 1$ *terms with non-zero coefficients.*

Proof. First observe that by the construction of our algorithm, all weights are indeed polynomials over the symbolic loop-bounds. We will now show, that any such polynomial consists of at most slbs $+ 1$ terms, by first proving several claims about the possible structure of such terms and by concluding from that, that there cannot be more than slbs $+ 1$ such terms in the polynomial. The claims to show are:

1. Any path in G enters the loops of G in a unique order, i.e. there don't exist two paths P_1, P_2 in G, such that there exist loops L_1, L_2 of G such that the paths P_1 and P_2 can be written as $P_1 = (\ldots, \mathcal{E}(L_1), \ldots, \mathcal{E}(L_2), \ldots)$ and $P_2 = (\ldots, \mathcal{E}(L_2), \ldots, \mathcal{E}(L_1), \ldots)$.
2. Any term in the weight polynomial contains only variables associated with the induced sub-loops of one $L \in$ loops(G).
3. Let $L \in$ loops(G) and $L' \in$ iloops(L). Furthermore, let $(L_i)_{i=1\ldots k}$ be the sequence of induced sub-loops of L such that $L = L_1$, $L' = L_k$ and such that L_{i+1} is a sub-loop of L_i for all $i \in \{1, \ldots, k-1\}$. If a term T in the weight polynomial contains the variable associated with L', then T also contains all variables associated with the loops L_i.

We now prove the first claim, by assuming that such two paths P_1 and P_2 exist. This implies that there are two paths (sub-paths of P_1 and P_2) from $\mathcal{E}(L_1)$ to $\mathcal{E}(L_2)$ and vice versa. Since L_1 and L_2 are loops of G, L_1 and L_2 are strongly connected. But we have just seen that the two nodes $\mathcal{E}(L_1)$, $\mathcal{E}(L_2)$ are also connected, which directly implies that L_1 and L_2 can't be strongly connected components of G, which leads to a contradiction.

For the second claim, suppose there exists a term, containing variables associated with induced sub-loops of two different loops L_1 and L_2 of G. By construction of our algorithm, multiplication (and thus, addition of a variable to a term) only occurs, if $L_1 \in$ iloops(L_2) or if $L_2 \in$ iloops(L_1). Thus, L_1 must be a subgraph of L_2 or vice versa, and hence, L_1 and L_2 can only be both loops of G, if $L_1 = L_2$.

For the last claim, let us assume otherwise, and let there be a $j \in \{1, \ldots, k - 1\}$ such that the associated variable of L_j is not contained in T but also such that

L_{j+1} contributes its variable to T. By the construction of our algorithm, the variable associated with L_{j+1} was added to T, after splitting $\mathscr{E}(L_j)$ and identifying L_{j+1} as a strongly connected component of this altered graph. But splitting the node $\mathscr{E}(L_j)$ also involves the multiplication of the weight polynomial with the variable associated with L_j, which contradicts the fact, that this variable is not contained in T.

Now let us count the number of possible terms in a longest path weight, that contain at least one loop-bound variable. For each loop L of G we have a possible set of terms. For each term in such a set, we know that only variables associated with induced sub-loops of the corresponding loop of G are contained in it. Since a variable must be contained in such a term whenever the variable of a sub-loop is contained in the term, there are exactly $\mathrm{slbs}(L)$ possible terms per set. Thus in total, the number of possible terms, that contain at least one variable is bounded by $\sum_{L \in \mathrm{loops}(G)} \mathrm{slbs}(L) = \mathrm{slbs}(G)$. Together with the fact, that there is only one term, containing no variables, this completes the proof.

Lemma 2. *For any problem instance* $I = (G, s, t)$, *there are at most* 2^{slbs} *distinct longest path weights.*

Proof. We will give only the idea of the proof and assume for sake of simplicity that all loop bounds are symbolic. A detailed proof can be found in [1]. Basically, we prove the claim by structural induction. If G is a DAG, we are done. Thus, assume that G contains loops. Note that in the following we will implicitly assume that all mentioned paths have maximal length. The main insight is, that two paths with distinct weights must traverse the induced sub-loops of G in a different way. Consider now an s-t path P in G. Since the condensed graph G' is a DAG, there cannot be an s-t path, traversing the same loops but in a different order. Thus all paths can be classified by the loops they traverse. Applying this insight recursively to all induced sub-loops of G, a path (respectively its weights) is uniquely defined by the set of induced sub-loops of G it traverses, yielding in total 2^{slbs} possible paths.

Theorem 2. *The modified algorithm reports a minimal number of longest paths.*

Proof. We want to prove the following claim by induction over $|\mathrm{iloops}(G)|$: For all $w_P \in \mathcal{D}(G, s, t)$, there exists an instantiation I such that under I (written: $w_P[I]$), for all weights $w_Q \in \mathcal{D}(G, s, t)$ such that $w_Q \neq w_P$ we have $w_P[I] > w_Q[I]$.

In the base case $|\mathrm{iloops}(G)| = 0$, G is a directed acyclic graph and the claim trivially holds, since $|\mathcal{D}(G, s, t)| = 1$. For the induction step, consider the condensed graph G' as constructed by the algorithm by replacing all loops $(L_i)_{1 \leq i \leq |\mathrm{loops}(G)|}$ in G by nodes $(c_i)_{1 \leq i \leq |\mathrm{loops}(G)|}$. We denote by $C := \{c_i \mid 1 \leq i \leq |\mathrm{loops}(G)|\}$ the set of all contraction nodes and for a path Q, we write $C_Q := \{c_i \in C \mid Q \text{ traverses } L_i\}$. Additionally, we write $w_{c_i}^Q$ for the weight polynomials corresponding to the loop L_i for a path Q.

In the following we will show that the claim holds for a particular instantiation: For all $c_i \in C \setminus C_P$ and for all $L \in \mathrm{iloops}(L_i)$ we set $I(\mathrm{b}(\mathscr{E}(L))) := 0$ if $\mathrm{b}(\mathscr{E}(L))$ is symbolic. For all $c_i \in C_P$ and for all $L \in \mathrm{iloops}(L_i)$ such that $\mathrm{b}(\mathscr{E}(L))$ is symbolic we will choose values that dependent on the weights in $\mathcal{D}(G, s, t) \setminus \{w_P\}$. For a moment, we will consider these weights in $\mathcal{D}(G, s, t)$ independent of each other. We will show at the end of the proof, that we can do so as long as we only increase symbolic loop bounds occurring in w_P.

First note, that either w_P or w_Q must contain symbolic loop bound variables since otherwise both would just be constants and since w_P and w_Q are mutually non-dominating, this would lead to the contradiction that both are distinct longest path weights. If w_P is now a constant and w_Q not, then w_P must be larger than the constant term c in w_Q, because otherwise w_Q would dominate w_P and w_P would not have been reported by our algorithm. Since all symbolic loop bounds not occurring in w_P, i.e. all variables in this case, are set to 0, we have that $w_P = w_P[I] > w_Q[I] = c$. Thus, we can assume that w_P is not a constant. If now w_Q is a constant, any symbolic loop bound occurring in a term t in w_P can just be chosen such large, that t becomes larger than w_Q, which can be done, because – by construction of the weights – all coefficients in the weight polynomials must be positive. Thus, we can assume that both paths P and Q traverse loops of G.

Assume now, that the sets of loops traversed by P and by Q are disjoint. Because $w_Q[I]$ is a constant – recall that all variables corresponding to loops that are not traversed by P are set to 0 – and because w_P contains a variable b not contained in w_Q, we can make $w_P[I]$ larger than $w_Q[I]$ by choosing b large enough. Hence, we can assume now that there are loops that are traversed by both P and Q. Then, we can write P and Q as paths in the condensed graph G' in the following way. Let L_i be some loop that is traversed by P and by Q. Then $P = s \overset{P_1}{\rightsquigarrow} c_i \overset{P_2}{\rightsquigarrow} t$ and $Q = s \overset{Q_1}{\rightsquigarrow} c_i \overset{Q_2}{\rightsquigarrow} t$ for suitable sub-paths P_1 and P_2 of P, and for Q_1 and Q_2 of Q. Let $(v_1, v_2, \ldots, v_k, c_i, v_{k+1}, v_{k+2}, \ldots, v_l)$ (we assume here wlog. that $v_1 = s$ and $v_l = t$) be a topological ordering of the nodes of G' (note that this can be done, since G' is directed and acyclic). Consider now the two sub-graphs G_1 and G_2 of G, induced by the node sets $\{v_1, v_2, \ldots, v_k, \mathscr{E}(L_i)\}$ and $\{\mathscr{E}(L_i), v_{k+1}, v_{k+2}, \ldots, v_l\}$. Since any sub-path of a longest path must also be a longest path (with respect to validity), we know that $\{w_{P_1}, w_{Q_1}\} \subseteq \mathcal{D}(G_1, s, \mathscr{E}(L_i))$, $\{w_{P_2}, w_{Q_2}\} \subseteq \mathcal{D}(G_2, \mathscr{E}(L_i), t)$. Because G_1 and G_2 have less induced sub-loops than G, by induction hypothesis I can be chosen such that $w_{P_1}[I] \geq w_{Q_1}[I]$ and $w_{P_2}[I] \geq w_{Q_2}[I]$ – note that we have to allow equality here, since it is possible that the weights of the sub-paths are equal. Furthermore, we know for the same reason that $w_{c_i}^P[I] \geq w_{c_i}^Q[I]$, since after splitting the entry node of L_i, the loop also has less induced sub-loops than G. The crucial observation now is that at least one of these three inequalities has to be strict, because by induction hypothesis the inequalities can only be equalities if the corresponding weight polynomials are equal. So, if all of them would be equal, this would also mean that $w_P = w_Q$ which would be a contradiction to our assumption. Thus, $w_P[I] = w_{P_1}[I] + w_{L_i}^P[I] + w_{P_2}[I] > w_{Q_1}[I] + w_{L_i}^Q[I] + w_{Q_2}[I] = w_Q$. What is left to show is that we can indeed consider the weights in $\mathcal{D}(G, s, t)$ independently. We will show that given an instantiation I as constructed above for the two weights w_P and w_Q, for all instantiations I' with the properties that $I'(s) \geq I(s)$ for all symbolic loop bounds s and $I'(s) = 0$ if s is not contained in w_P, we have $w_P[I'] > w_Q[I']$. We will prove the claim by structural induction over G. If G is a directed acyclic graph, nothing has to be shown. Thus, we can assume that G contains loops. Consider the paths P and Q as paths in the condensed graph G'. By the construction of I we know that

$w_{c_i}^P[I] > w_{c_i}^Q[I]$ for $c_i \in C_P \cap C_Q$ if $w_{c_i}^P \neq w_{c_i}^Q$ and thus, by induction hypothesis, $w_{c_i}^P[I'] > w_{c_i}^Q[I']$. We now have

$$w_P[I'] = \sum_{e \in P} w(e) + \sum_{c_i \in C_P \cap C_Q} I'(L_i)w_{c_i}^P[I'] + \sum_{c_i \in C_P \backslash C_Q} I'(L_i)w_{c_i}^P[I']$$

$$\overset{(I)}{>} \sum_{e \in P} w(e) + \sum_{c_i \in C_P \cap C_Q} I'(L_i)w_{c_i}^Q[I'] + \sum_{c_i \in C_P \backslash C_Q} I'(L_i)w_{c_i}^P[I']$$

$$\overset{(II)}{\geq} \sum_{e \in Q} w(e) + \sum_{c_i \in C_P \cap C_Q} I'(L_i)w_{c_i}^Q[I'] + \sum_{c_i \in C_Q \backslash C_P} I'(L_i)w_{c_i}^Q[I'] = w_Q[I']$$

where inequality (I) follows by induction hypothesis (to simplify the discussion we assume wlog. that there is at least one common loop that is traversed differently by P and Q). Inequality (II) clearly holds if

$$\sum_{e \in P} w(e) + \sum_{c_i \in C_P \backslash C_Q} I'(L_i)w_{c_i}^P[I'] \geq \sum_{e \in Q} w(e) + \sum_{c_i \in C_Q \backslash C_P} I'(L_i)w_{c_i}^Q[I']$$

But this must be true, for two reasons: First, $\sum_{c_i \in C_Q \backslash C_P} I'(L_i)w_{c_i}^Q[I'] = \sum_{c_i \in C_Q \backslash C_P} I(L_i)w_{c_i}^Q[I]$ because all variables not contained in w_P are set to 0 in I and in I' and second, $\sum_{c_i \in C_P \backslash C_Q} I'(L_i)w_{c_i}^P[I'] \geq \sum_{c_i \in C_P \backslash C_Q} I(L_i)w_{c_i}^P[I]$ by induction hypothesis and the property that $I'(L_i) \geq I(L_i)$.

4   Conclusion

We presented an algorithm to compute longest path in control flow graphs. In earlier work [2], we performed experiments that demonstrate that our algorithm is the first algorithm that allows us to analyze the worst case execution times of programs with several symbolic loop bounds. In this paper, we give the theoretical foundation. We analyzed running time and the output size of our algorithm for the case of programs avoiding goto-constructs. We tailored the analysis of the output size, if one additionally avoids break and continue statements. This explains the observed small output sizes that are in contrast to the worst case doubly exponential output size that is possible for general control flow graphs.

In future work, we plan to investigate on the difference between the upper and the lower bound on the minimal output size and the difference of the output size of our algorithm and the minimal possible output size for programs avoiding goto-constructs but allowing break and continue statements.

References

1. Althaus, E., Altmeyer, S., Naujoks, R.: A new combinatorial approach to parametric path analysis. Reports of SFB/TR 14 AVACS 58, SFB/TR 14 AVACS (June 2010), http://www.avacs.org, ISSN: 1860-9821
2. Althaus, E., Altmeyer, S., Naujoks, R.: Precise and efficient parametric path analysis. In: Proceedings of the ACM SIGPLAN/SIGBED 2011 Conference on Languages, Compilers, and Tools for Embedded Systems, LCTES, pp. 141–150 (2011)

3. Altmeyer, S., Hümbert, C., Lisper, B., Wilhelm, R.: Parametric timing analyis for complex architectures. In: Procedeedings of the 14th IEEE International Conference on Embedded and Real-Time Computing Systems and Applications (RTCSA 2008), Kaohsiung, Taiwan, pp. 367–376. IEEE Computer Society, Los Alamitos (2008)
4. Dantzig, G.B.: Linear Programming and Extensions. Princeton University Press, Princeton (1963)
5. Feautrier, P.: The parametric integer programming's home, http://www.piplib.org
6. Gomory, R.E.: An algorithm for integer solutions to linear programming. In: Graves, R.L., Wolfe, P. (eds.) Recent Advances in Mathematical Programming, pp. 269–302. McGraw-Hill, New York (1969)
7. Holsti, N., Gustafsson, J., Bernat, G., Ballabriga, C., Bonenfant, A., Bourgade, R., Cassé, H., Cordes, D., Kadlec, A., Kirner, R., Knoop, J., Lokuciejewski, P., Merriam, N., de Michiel, M., Prantl, A., Rieder, B., Rochange, C., Sainrat, P., Schordan, M.: Wcet 2008 – report from the tool challenge 2008 – 8th intl. workshop on worst-case execution time (wcet) analysis. In: Kirner, R. (ed.) 8th Intl. Workshop on Worst-Case Execution Time (WCET) Analysis, Dagstuhl, Germany, Schloss Dagstuhl - Leibniz-Zentrum fuer Informatik, Germany (2008); also published in print by Austrian Computer Society (OCG) under ISBN 978-3-85403-237-3
8. Li, Y.-T.S., Malik, S.: Performance analysis of embedded software using implicit path enumeration. In: DAC 1995: Proceedings of the 32nd Annual ACM/IEEE Design Automation Conference, pp. 456–461. ACM, New York (1995)
9. Lisper, B.: Fully automatic, parametric worst-case execution time analysis. In: Third Internation Workshop on Worst-Case Execution Time Analysis, pp. 77–80 (July 2003)
10. Tan, L.: The worst case execution time tool challenge 2006: Technical report for the external test. In: Proc. 2nd International Symposium on Leveraging Applications of Formal Methods, ISOLA 2006 (2006)
11. Theiling, H.: ILP-based Interprocedural Path Analysis. In: Proceedings of the Workshop on Embedded Software, Grenoble, France (October 2002)
12. Wilhelm, R., Engblom, J., Ermedahl, A., Holsti, N., Thesing, S., Whalley, D., Bernat, G., Ferdinand, C., Heckmann, R., Mitra, T., Mueller, F., Puaut, I., Puschner, P., Staschulat, J., Stenström, P.: The worst-case execution-time problem—overview of methods and survey of tools. ACM Trans. Embed. Comput. Syst. 7(3), 1–53 (2008)

A Appendix

Lemma 3. *For any problem instance* $I = (G, s, t)$ $|\mathcal{D}(I)| \leq 2^{2^{\text{lbs}(G)}}$.

Proof. Let P be a path reported by our algorithm. We recursively define the loop-pattern $\mathcal{L}(P, G)$ of a path P in G as follows. If G is a DAG, the loop-pattern of any path is empty. To define a loop-pattern in the general case, we shortly recall some facts of the algorithm. We compute P as a longest path in the condensed graph (for which we have contracted each loop of G into a single node), which is known to be an acyclic graph, since the loops are the strongly connected components of G. Let $L_1, \ldots, L_k$ be the subloops of G that are entered by P. Each loop L_i is entered exactly once (as the condensed graph is a DAG). Within the loop, P traverses a unique subpath P_i' for $b_{L_i} - 1$ times and then a path P_i'' to a portal node. The loop pattern of P is then defined as the sequence

$$\mathcal{L}(P) := (L_1(\mathcal{L}(P_1', L_1'), \mathcal{L}(P_1'', L_1')), L_2(\mathcal{L}(P_2', L_2'), \mathcal{L}(P_2'', L_2')), \ldots,$$
$$L_k(\mathcal{L}(P_k', L_k'), \mathcal{L}(P_k'', L_K'))),$$

where L_i' is the graph obtained by splitting $\mathscr{E}(L_i)$.

We proof the following claims:

1. Any two paths with the same loop-pattern (not necessarily with same source and target node) computed by the algorithm have the same cost up to a constant term.
2. Any two $s - t$-paths reported by the algorithm have different loop-patterns.
3. Let $T(\text{lbs}(G))$ be the maximum possible number of loop patterns of a graph G, then T can be bounded by the recurrence $T(0) = 1$, $T(\text{lbs}(G)) \leq T(\text{lbs}(G) - 1)^2 + 1$.

We will prove the points in turn. We proof the first point by structural induction over G. If G is a DAG, all path weights are constants (as there are no symbolic loop-bounds). Hence, there is nothing to show. Now consider two paths P and Q in a graph G constructed by our algorithm with $\mathcal{L}(P, G) = \mathcal{L}(Q, G)$. Let $L_1, \ldots, L_k$ be the subloops of G contained in $\mathcal{L}(P, G)$. Decompose P into $(\bar{P}_0, (P_1')^{b_{L_1} - 1}, P_1'', \bar{P}_1, \ldots, (P_k')^{b_{L_k} - 1}, P_k'', \bar{P}_k)$, where $\bar{P}_i$ is the path from the portal of L_i used by P (respectively from the source of P if $i = 0$) to $\mathscr{E}(L_{i+1})$ (respectively to the target of P for $i = k$), P_i' is the path used for cycling within L_i and P_i'' if the path from the entering node of L_i to the portal-node used by P. Analogously decompose Q. The cost of P can then be written as

$$w(\bar{P}_0) + \sum_{i=1}^{k} [(b_L - 1)w(P_i') + w(P_i'') + w(\bar{P}_i)],$$

the cost of Q as

$$w(\bar{Q}_0) + \sum_{i=1}^{k} [(b_L - 1)w(Q_i') + w(Q_i'') + w(\bar{Q}_i)].$$

The costs of $\bar{P}_i$ and $\bar{Q}_i$ are some constants. By induction hypothesis, the costs of P_i' and Q_i' only differ by a constant. The same holds for the cost of P_i'' and Q_i''. Hence the difference of $w(P)$ and $w(Q)$ is a sum of constants and thus constant.

The second point immediately follows from the first, as our algorithm won't report two paths whose weights only differ in a constant.

For the third point, we argue as follows: Let $L_1, \ldots, L_k$ be the subloops of G given in topologial order. Each loop pattern can be constructed by chosing for each subloop L_i either that it is not entered, or we use some loop pattern of L_i for the cycling path and one loop pattern for the path to the portal. Hence, we get $T(\text{lbs}(G)) \le \prod_i T(\text{lbs}(L_i'))^2 + 1$. Notice that $\sum_i \text{lbs}(L_i) = \text{lbs}(G)$ and $\text{lbs}(L_i') = \text{lbs}(L_i) - 1$ and hence $\sum_i \text{lbs}(L_i') = \text{lbs}(G) - k$. A simple calculation shows that $T(\text{lbs}(G))$ is maximized, if each induced subloop of G containts exactly one subloop. Hence we get $T(\text{lbs}(G)) \le T(\text{lbs}(G) - 1)^2 + 1$.

Note that if L_i as a numeric loop-bound, the length of a path that does not enter L_i and the length of a path that enteres L_i but no subloop of L_i differ only in a constant. Hence, in this case we can drop the addition of one in the recursive formula. Finally for $T(\text{lbs}(G)) = T(\text{lbs}(G) - 1)^2 + 1$, $T(0) = 1$ holds $T(\text{lbs}(G)) \le 2^{2^{\text{lbs}(G)}}$ and for $T'(\text{lbs}(G)) = T'(\text{lbs}(G) - 1)^2$, $T'(1) = 2$ holds $T'(\text{lbs}(G)) \ge 2^{2^{\text{lbs}(G)-1}}$.

Lemma 4. *There exists a problem instance* $I = (G, s, t)$, *such that* $|\mathcal{D}(I)| = 2^{2^{\text{lbs}(G)-1}}$ *and* $\text{slbs}(G) = 1$.

Proof. We will first prove a slightly different claim, namely we proof the bound using symbolic loop-bounds for all loops. More precisely, we show that there exists a problem instance I such that

- a) $\mathcal{D}(I) = 2^{2^{\text{slbs}(G)-1}}$
- b) there is an element in $\mathcal{D}(I)$ containing a positive constant
- c) there is an element in $\mathcal{D}(I)$ containing the constant 0

where x is the number of symbolic loop-bounds.

We construct a graph G in the following way: we start with the left graph G_l in Figure 3 and repeatedly replace the selfloop of G by the loop of G_l. Note, that after k iterations, the resulting graph consists of $k + 2$ induced subloops. We will show the claim by induction over the recursive structure of G, i.e. over the number $\text{slbs}(G)$ of induced subloops of G.

For the base case ($\text{slbs}(G) = 2$), in which G corresponds to the graph G_l, it is easy to verify that

$$\mathcal{D}(v_0, v_2) = \{b(v_0), b(v_0)b(v_1), -1 + b(v_0) + b(v_1), 1 - b(v_1) + b(v_0)b(v_1)\}$$

and that one of these weight polynomials contains a positive constant.

Now let us consider the induction step. Recall that we want to compute $\mathcal{D}(v_0, v_2)$. In the first step of our algorithm, the node v_0 is split into two nodes v_{in} and v_{out} and recursively the sets $\mathcal{D}(v_1, v_1)$, $\mathcal{D}(v_{out}, v_{in})$ and $\mathcal{D}(v_{out}, v_2)$ are computed. Then, the set $\text{lps}(v_0, v_2)$ is computed as the set of polynomials given by $(b(v_0) - 1) \cdot l_{ee} + l_{ep}$ for all $l_{ee} \in \mathcal{D}(v_{out}, v_{in})$ and for all $l_{ep} \in \mathcal{D}(v_{out}, v_2)$.

By the way, we have chosen the edge weights, we have that $\mathcal{D}(v_{out}, v_{in}) = \mathcal{D}(v_{out}, v_2) = \mathcal{D}(G, v_1, v_1)$. In particular, note that the constant polynomial 1 is not in contained in $\mathcal{D}(v_{out}, v_{in})$, since by induction hypothesis, $\mathcal{D}(v_1, v_1)$ contains a polynomial with a positive constant (which must be greater or equal to 1), dominating 1.

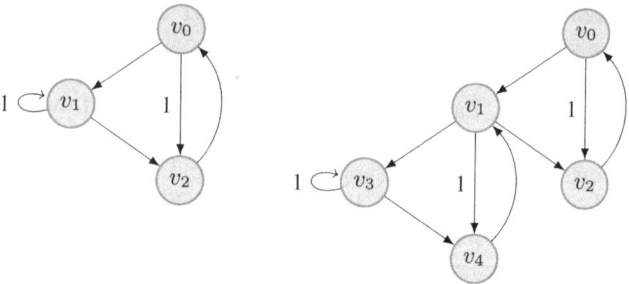

Fig. 3. Suppose the edge weights are 0 if not stated otherwise, then the longest path weights from v_0 to v_2 constructed by our algorithm for the left graph are $b(v_0)$, $b(v_0)b(v_1)$, $-1+b(v_0)+b(v_1)$ and $1 - b(v_1) + b(v_0)b(v_1)$. The right graph was constructed from the left one by replacing the selfloop $\{v_1\}$ by the loop $\{v_0, v_1, v_2\}$. For the right graph, the algorithm computes 16 non-dominant longest path weights. In general, graphs obtained by repeatedly replacing the selfloop by the loop of the left graph, yield $2^{2^{\mathrm{slbs}(G)-1}}$ non-dominant longest path weights and furthermore, one can show that there is a longest path weight that consists of $2^{\mathrm{slbs}(G)} - 1$ terms where $\mathrm{slbs}(G)$ is the number of symbolic loop-bounds.

This in turn, means that $|\mathrm{lps}(v_0, v_2)| = |\mathcal{D}(v_1, v_1)|^2$. We now have to show, that the elements in $\mathrm{lps}(v_0, v_2)$ are pairwise non-dominating. Let $l_1, l_2 \in \mathrm{lps}(v_0, v_2)$, given as $l_1 = (b(v_0) - 1) \cdot l_{ee} + l_{ep}$ and $l_2 = (b(v_0) - 1) \cdot l'_{ee} + l'_{ep}$ for weights $l_{ee}, l'_{ee} \in \mathcal{D}(v_{out}, v_{in})$ and $l_{ep}, l'_{ep} \in \mathcal{D}(v_{out}, v_{in})$, l_1. We distinguish two cases. In the first one, we assume that $l_{ee} \neq l'_{ee}$. Since by induction hypothesis, l_{ee} and l'_{ee} are pairwise non-dominant, the terms in l_1 and l_2 containing variable $b(v_0)$, namely $b(v_0) \cdot l_{ee}$ and $b(v_0) \cdot l'_{ee}$ - and thus also l_1 and l_2 - must be pairwise non-dominant. Now we assume that $l_{ee} = l'_{ee}$. In this case, the terms, not containing the variable $b(v_0)$, are $l_{ep} - l_{ee}$ and $l'_{ep} - l_{ee}$. Since by induction hypothesis l_{ee} and l'_{ee} are pairwise non-dominant, l_1 and l_2 must also be pairwise non-dominant.

Thus, $|\mathcal{D}(v_0, v_2)| = |\mathcal{D}(v_1, v_1)|^2$. Since by induction hypothesis $|\mathcal{D}(v_1, v_1)| = 2^{2^{x-2}}$, $|\mathcal{D}(v_0, v_2)| = 2^{2^{x-1}}$, which establishes the first part of the claim. For the second part, note that by induction hypothesis, there is a weight in $l_1 \in \mathcal{D}(v_1, v_1)$ with a positive constant and there is a weight in $l_2 \in \mathcal{D}(v_1, v_1)$ with zero constant. Thus the weight $l \in \mathcal{D}(v_0, v_2)$ with $l = (b(v_0) - 1) \cdot l_2 + l_1 = b(v_0) \cdot l_2 + l_1 - l_2$ has again a postive constant as a term. On the other hand, the weight $l \in \mathcal{D}(v_0, v_2)$ with $l = (b(v_0) - 1) \cdot l_2 + l_2 = b(v_0) - 1) \cdot l_2$ has a zero as constant term.

So far, we have assumed that all loop-bounds are symbolic. Now we will examine an instance in which all but one loop-bounds are numeric. For this, we use the same graph G as constructed above, but we assume that only the bound for the selfloop is symbolic. Then we can show by the very same induction as above, that by choosing the right numeric values for the loop-bounds, $|\mathcal{D}(v_0, v_2)| = 2^{2^{\mathrm{iloops}(G)-1}}$. For the base case, we choose $b(v_0) := 3$ and obtain $\mathcal{D}(v_0, v_2) = \{3, 2 + b(v_1), 1 + 2b(v_1), 3b(v_1)\}$ which clearly satisfies the induction properties.

The only difference occurs now in the induction step, when arguing, that no two path weights l_1, l_2 exist, such that the first one dominates the other. Since there is just one symbolic loop-bound, all path weight polynomials consist of only two terms, i.e. $\mathcal{D}(v_1, v_1)$ consists of polynomials $c_i + c'_i \cdot a$ where a is the symbolic loop-bound in G. It is easy to see that these polynomials are non-dominated if and only if they can be ordered in such a way, that the constants c_i are appear in increasing order while the c'_i appear in decreasing order.

The idea of proof is now to show, that the numeric bound $\mathrm{b}(v_0)$ can recursively be chosen in such a way, that the constructed weights in $\mathcal{D}(v_0, v_2)$ can be ordered in the same way. To see this, suppose we are given two weights in $\mathcal{D}(v_0, v_2)$, namely $p_1 := (\mathrm{b}(v_0)-1)\cdot d_1 + d'_1$ and $p_2 := (\mathrm{b}(v_0)-1)\cdot d_2 + d'_2$ for $d_1, d_2, d'_1, d'_2 \in \mathcal{D}(v_0, v_2)$. Clearly by choosing $\mathrm{b}(v_0)$ big enough, it is possible to put p_1 and p_2 into the same relative order as d_1 and d_2. We will now show, that there is such a value for $\mathrm{b}(v_0)$ for all pairs of weights in $\mathcal{D}(v_0, v_2)$ that is not too big.

Consider again the pair p_1, p_2. Let us denote by $c(p)$ the constant term of such a weight p and by $v(p)$ the coefficient of the variable term. Without loss of generality, let us restrict our discussion to the case $c(d_1) \geq c(d_2)$. It is easy to verify that for $\mathrm{b}(v_0) :=$ $\left\lceil \max\left\{ \frac{c(d'_2)-c(d'_1)}{c(d_1)-c(d_2)}, \frac{v(d'_1)-v(d'_2)}{v(d_2)-v(d_1)} \right\} \right\rceil + 1$ we have $c(p_1) \geq c(p_2)$ and $v(p_1) \leq v(p_2)$.

Choosing $\mathrm{b}(v_0)$ as the maximum of all possible choices of $p_1, p_2 \in \mathcal{D}(v_0, v_2)$ we can establish the same relative order as for the d_i, completing the proof.

Lemma 5. *There exists a problem instance I, such that any correct algorithm must report $2^{\mathrm{slbs}(G)}$ longest paths.*

Proof. Consider the graph G_f in Figure 2. By repeated concatenation of the subgraph of G_f induced by the nodes $\{v_0, s_1, v_1\}$, we obtain a weighted graph $G = (V, E, w)$ that consists of nodes $V = \{v_0, \ldots, v_{\mathrm{slbs}(G)}, s_0, \ldots s_{\mathrm{slbs}(G)-1}\}$, edges

$$E = \{(v_i, s_i), (s_i, v_i), (s_i, s_i), (v_i, v_{i+1}) \mid$$
$$i \in \{0, \ldots, \mathrm{slbs}(G) - 1\} \cup \{(s_{\mathrm{slbs}(G)-1}, v_{\mathrm{slbs}(G)})\}\}$$

and of edge weights as given in the graph G_f.

Then there are exactly $2^{\mathrm{slbs}(G)}$ different paths from v_0 to $v_{\mathrm{slbs}(G)}$, namely one for each choice of bypassing a selfloop $\{s_i\}$ via the edge (v_i, v_{i+1}) or not. For these paths we have the set of corresponding weights

$$\left\{ \sum_{p_i \in p} p_i \cdot \mathrm{b}(s_i) + 2 \cdot \sum_{p_i \in p} (1 - p_i) \mid p \in \{0, 1\}^{\mathrm{slbs}(G)} \right\}$$

The claim now is, that for each weight in this set, there is an instantiation I of its symbolic loop-bounds, such that this weight dominates all other weights. To see this, consider a weight w. For each loop-bound variable s_i contained in w, set $I(\mathrm{b}(s_i)) :=$ $2\mathrm{slbs}(G) + 1$ and for all other bounds to 0. Now consider any other weight w' and let n (n') be the number of variables in w (in w') and k be the number of variables that w and w' share. Then $w[I] = n(2\mathrm{slbs}(G) + 1) + 2(\mathrm{slbs}(G) - n)$ and $w'[I] = k(2\mathrm{slbs}(G) + 1) + 2(\mathrm{slbs}(G) - n')$. If now $k = n$, then there must be a variable in w' which is not in w, since $w \neq w'$. Thus, $n' > n$ and therefore $w[I] = n(2\mathrm{slbs}(G)+1) + 2(\mathrm{slbs}(G) - n) >$ $n(2\mathrm{slbs}(G) + 1) + 2(\mathrm{slbs}(G) - n') = w'[I]$. Since $k \leq n$, let us now assume that $k < n$. Then $w[I] - w'[I] = (n - k)(2\mathrm{slbs}(G) + 1) + 2(n' - n)$ can only be negative if $n' < n$, but on the other hand $n' - n \geq -\mathrm{slbs}(G)$, which implies that in this case $w[I] - w'[I] \geq (n-k)(2\mathrm{slbs}(G)+1) - 2\mathrm{slbs}(G) = 2\mathrm{slbs}(G)(n-k-1)+n-k > 0$. Hence any algorithm has to report w.

Thus any correct algorithm must report all the $2^{\mathrm{slbs}(G)}$ paths.

Lemma 6. *There exists a problem instance I, such that $\mathcal{D}(I)$ contains a weight with $2^{\mathrm{slbs}(G)} - 1$ terms with non-zero coefficients.*

Proof. Consider the same graph construction as in Lemma 4. We again prove a slightly stricter claim, namely that there is

- a weight polynomial in $\mathcal{D}(G, v_0, v_2)$ such that all terms have non-zero coefficients except the term consisting of all loop-bound variables
- a weight polynomial in $\mathcal{D}(G, v_0, v_2)$ such that all terms have zero coefficients except the term consisting of all loop-bound variables.

We again proof the claim by induction. As stated in the proof of this lemma, in the base case $(\mathrm{slbs}(G) = 2)$, the set of computed path weights is $\mathcal{D}(v_0, v_2) = \{b(v_0), b(v_0)b(v_1), -1 + b(v_0) + b(v_1), 1 - b(v_1) + b(v_0)b(v_1)\}$. Clearly the claim holds in this case. For the induction step, consider the weights $l, l' \in \mathcal{D}(v_1, v_1)$ such that l corresponds to the weight in the first part of the claim and l' corresponds to the weight in the second part of the claim. Recall from the discussion in the proof of Lemma 4, that $\mathcal{D}(v_0, v_2)$ consists of weights build by evaluating the expression $(b(v_0) - 1) \cdot l_1 + l_2$ for $l_1, l_2 \in \mathcal{D}(v_1, v_1)$. Since $l \in \mathcal{D}(v_1, v_1)$, $(b(v_0) - 1) \cdot l + l = b(v_0) \cdot l$ is in $\mathcal{D}(v_0, v_2)$ and thus the first part of the claim also holds for G. But also the weight $(b(v_0) - 1) \cdot l + l' = b(v_0) \cdot l + (l' - l)$ is in $\mathcal{D}(v_0, v_2)$. Since l and l' have distinct terms with non-zero coefficients and by induction hypothesis, l has $2^{\mathrm{slbs}(G)-1} - 1$ terms with non-zero coefficients, the number of terms in $(b(v_0) - 1) \cdot l + l'$ with non-zero coefficients must be $2(2^{\mathrm{slbs}(G)-1} - 1) + 1 = 2^{\mathrm{slbs}(G)} - 1$, which finishes the proof.

Lemma 7. *There is a problem instance $I = (G, s, t)$, such that the minimal output size is 2 but $|\mathcal{D}(I)| = 2^{2^{\mathrm{lbs}(G)-1}}$.*

Proof. Reconsider again the example given in Figure 3 and the graph G as constructed in the proof of Lemma 4. We have argued in this proof, that the set $\mathrm{lps}(v_0, v_2)$ of path weights consists of all weights $(b(v_0) - 1) \cdot l_{ee} + l_{ep}$ for $l_{ee}, l_{ep} \in \mathcal{D}(v_1, v_1)$, since $\mathcal{D}(v_{out}, v_{in}) = \mathcal{D}(v_{out}, v_2) = \mathcal{D}(G, v_1, v_1)$. But one could do better, since it can be assumed wlog. that a longest path from v_0 to v_2 just corresponds to $b(v_0)$ times a path in $\mathcal{D}(v_1, v_1)$. Thus, instead creating a set $\mathrm{lps}(v_0, v_2)$ of cardinality $|\mathcal{D}(v_1, v_1)|^2$, we create one of cardinality $|\mathcal{D}(v_1, v_1)|$. But this leads by an inductive argument to a set of weights of the base case, namely 4 path weights. You could also apply this idea to the base case and get just the two path weights $b(v_0)$ and $b(v_0)b(v_1)$, but then the induction step in the proof of Lemma 4 would not work out in the same way, as there would be no path weight in $\mathcal{D}(v_1, v_1)$ with a positive constant (even though, it is possible to modify G slightly to make it work). So, we end up with four (respectivally 2) longest path weights which still is in stark contrast to the set of $2^{2^{\mathrm{lbs}(G)-1}}$ weights, constructed by our algorithm.

Selecting Good *a Priori* Sequences for Vehicle Routing Problem with Stochastic Demand

Ei Ando[1], Binay Bhattacharya[2,*], Yuzhuang Hu[2],
Tsunehiko Kameda[2,*], Qiaosheng Shi[2]

[1] Sojo University, Kumamoto, Japan
ando-ei@cis.sojo-u.ac.jp
[2] School of Computing Science, Simon Fraser University, Burnaby, Canada, V5A 1S6
{binay,yhu1,tiko,qshi1}@sfu.ca

Abstract. In the vehicle routing problem with stochastic demand, the customers' demands vary from one collection/delivery period to the next. Under the assumption that they become known only upon arrival of the vehicle at their sites, our objective is to find a fixed *a priori* sequence that is used in every period. We present *a priori* sequences that achieve 2-, 2-, 3- and 5-approximation in the worst case on trees, cycles, cactus graphs, and general graphs, respectively, in the case where the demand of a customer must be serviced all at once. These approximation ratios are with respect to the optimal distance computed off-line, when all demands are non-zero and are known in advance. If the demand of a customer can be serviced in parts, we present a linear time algorithm to find an optimal solution for cycles.

1 Introduction

In the classical *capacitated vehicle routing problem* (*CVRP* for short), a vehicle with a finite capacity Q (integer) is available to collect/deliver known numbers of units from/to a set of geographically scattered customers. The vehicle starts from a central *depot*, services customers, and returns to the depot if it cannot accommodate the total demand of the current customer, before resuming service at that customer. The objective is to find an optimal *schedule*, consisting of a set of *routes* with the smallest total distance to service all customers in one collection/delivery period. Each route starts from and ends at the depot, and at most Q units of demand are collected on it [11].

In this paper we consider a stochastic variation of the classical CVRP, named *vehicle routing problem with stochastic demand* (*VRPSD* for short) [9], where customers' demands fluctuate from one period to the next. Moreover, we assume that a customer's demand becomes known only upon arrival of the vehicle at the customer site. This situation arises naturally in real-world collection/delivery systems [4,11]. We concentrate on collection systems, but our results are equally

---

* This work was supported partially by a MITACS grant to Bhattacharya and NSERC Discovery Grants to Bhattacharya and Kameda.

A. Cerone and P. Pihlajasaari (Eds.): ICTAC 2011, LNCS 6916, pp. 45–61, 2011.
© Springer-Verlag Berlin Heidelberg 2011

applicable to delivery systems. Examples include the collection of money from bank branches [9], the delivery of some products/commodities such as petroleum products and industrial gases [10], route design before customer demands are known [4], and the pickup and delivery of mail [17], etc.

1.1 The *a Priori* Strategy for VRPSD

There are two standard strategies to deal with unpredictable, fluctuating demands [4]. The *re-optimization* strategy computes a schedule, after all the customer demands are known. It may not be practical due to lack of information, time constraints or computing cost. In this paper we adopt the other strategy, named the *a priori* strategy, which selects an *a priori* sequence of all the customer nodes beforehand. The vehicle always visits customer sites in this sequence, returning to the depot from time to time to empty its load. A review of the *a priori* strategy can be found in [5,15]. Bertsimas [4] presents both practical and analytical evidences that the *a priori* strategy is a strong contender to the re-optimization strategy.

In the *non-split* model of CVRP and VRPSD, the entire demand by a customer must be serviced in one shot; therefore the maximum amount of demand at each customer site must be at most Q (the vehicle capacity). In the *split* model, on the other hand, the vehicle can load from the same customer site more than once in the same period.[1] We sometimes use the adjective split (or non-split) when we refer to a solution or schedule of the split (or non-split) model.

1.2 Previous Results

In the literature on vehicle routing, algorithms designed for CVRP are often used for VRPSD. The split CVRP is NP-hard for trees [13], and the non-split CVRP is NP-hard even for paths [16]. Therefore, researchers have investigated polynomial-time approximation algorithms with performance guarantees. A few approximation algorithms are known for the split CVRP. For example, Asano et al. [2] designed a 1.35078-approximation algorithm on trees, and Haimovich et al. [12] proposed a 2.5-approximation algorithm, called the *cyclic heuristic*, on general graphs. For the non-split CVRP, Labbé et al. [16] gave a 2-approximation algorithm on trees, and Altinkemer et al. [1] presented a $(3.5 - 3/Q)$-approximation algorithm on general graphs.

The first practical example of VRPSD was given by Tillman in 1969 [19]. Papers on the re-optimization strategy often investigate methods of making the decision on the next customer site to visit dynamically, and model the problem as a Markov decision process [11]. The *a priori* strategy was first proposed by Jaillet et al. [14] for the probabilistic version of the *traveling salesman problem* (*TSP*), and by Bertsimas [4] for VRPSD. Let α be the ratio of a polynomial-time

---

[1] If a customer is completely serviced, his/her site will not be visited again in the current period. The customer's demand may change between successive visits to his site in the same period, as long as it is not reduced to 0.

heuristic solution to the TSP over the optimal solution. Such a solution is called an α-*approximate TSP tour*.[2]

Bertsimas proposed an *a priori* algorithm [4] for the split VRPSD, which is based on the cyclic heuristic. If it is started with the 1.5-approximate TSP tour in [8], it achieves a $(2.5+O(1/n))$-approximation in the expected distance, where n is the number of customer nodes, under the assumption that the demand distributions of the customer nodes are all identical. Berman et al. [3] gave a randomized algorithm that achieves an approximation ratio of $1+\alpha$ in expected distance, and also presented an *a priori* sequence and an analysis showing that it achieves a $(1+2\alpha)$-approximation in the worst case for the split VRPSD on general graphs. Viswanath [20]'s randomized algorithm achieves an approximation ratio of $2+\alpha$ in expected distances for the non-split VRPSD on general graphs. Throughout this paper, we adopt the deterministic approach, and we conduct the worst-case analyses.

1.3   Our Model

We represent the demands and distances by an undirected graph $G = (V, E)$, where $V = \{v_0, v_1, \ldots, v_{n-1}\}$ consists of the nodes representing the customer sites and the depot v_0, which is sometimes denoted by o. Each edge $e \in E$ has a nonnegative distance (also called a *cost*) $c(e)$ satisfying the triangle inequality. For a path P, $c(P)$ will denote the total distance of the edges on P. In an *instance* $\mathcal{I}$ of VRPSD, each node $v \in V$ is associated with a discrete, random demand variable X_v that is distributed over the integers in the range $[1, Q]$. In this paper, we do not need to know the actual distribution, other than its range. In a *realization*, on the other hand, each customer node $v \in V - \{v_0\}$ has a concrete demand $d(v)$, satisfying $0 < d(v) \leq Q$. We denote a VRPSD realization by $R(G, d)$. If we assume that function d is known in advance, then we can consider $R(G, d)$ as an instance of CVRP, and denote it by $\mathcal{I}_{\mathrm{cvrp}}(G, d)$.

We select an *a priori* sequence σ of customer nodes to be visited (with the depot node o attached at the end), based solely on the graph topology and the edge distances. Our collection procedure for the non-split model proceeds according to the following very simple rule:

Procedure Non-Split(G, o, σ)
Input: graph G; depot node o in G; *a priori* service sequence σ.
Initialize: $\ell = 0$ (vehicle load); $u =$ the first node in σ.

1 **if** $u = o$ **then** dump the current load and **stop**
2   **else** visit u via the shortest path **endif**
3 **if** $\ell + d(u) \leq Q$ **then** service u ($\ell \leftarrow \ell + d(u)$); **goto** step 6
4   **else** return to the depot and dump the current load; service u ($\ell \leftarrow d(u)$)
5 **endif**
6 set u to the next node in σ, and **goto** step 1   □

---

[2] It is known that $\alpha \leq 1.5$ [8].

The distance traveled by the vehicle is clearly affected not only by σ but also by the particular set of demands in a realization, because the vehicle's occasional trips (called *recourses*) back to the depot are dictated by the actual demands. Our objective function is the total distance traveled by the vehicle following a given *a priori* sequence for realization $R(G, d)$, divided by the optimal solution to $I_{\text{cvrp}}(G, d)$.

1.4   Our Results

We propose *a priori* sequences for the split and non-split VRPSD on some special classes of graphs and general graphs, and compute the worst-case approximation ratio in each case. The approximation ratios are relative to the optimal distances when all demands are known in advance. However, since the optimal distance is hard to compute, we use a lower bound on it when we compute the approximation ratio. Therefore, the approximation ratios we compute are simply just upper bounds, and the actual performance is likely much better.

Throughout the paper, we adopt the simple greedy collection approach given by `Non-Split(G, o, σ)`. We always assume that the demands at all customer sites are non-zero in each collection period.[3] Our results can be summarized as follows:

(1) If the pre-order or post-order is used as the *a priori* sequence for the non-split VRPSD on trees, then it achieves a 2-approximation. (Section 2)
(2) An *a priori* sequence for the non-split VRPSD on cycles that achieves a 2-approximation. (Section 3)
(3) A linear time algorithm to find an optimal solution to the split CVRP on cycles. (Appendix)
(4) An *a priori* sequence for the split and non-split VRPSD on *cactus graphs*[4] that achieves a 3-approximation. (Section 4)
(5) If an α-approximate TSP tour is used as the *a priori* sequence for the non-split VRPSD on general graphs, then it achieves a $(2+2\alpha)$-approximation. (Section 5) Since $\alpha \leq 1.5$ [8], this is at worst a 5-approximation.

2   Non-split VRPSD on Trees

Consider a VRPSD realization $R(T, d)$ on a rooted tree T, where the depot o is located at the root. For a node u in T, we denote the subtree rooted at u by $T(u)$, and the parent of u by $p(u)$, where $p(u)$ is null if u is the root of T. Let $D(T(u))$ denote the total demand of the nodes in $T(u)$. We pay special attention to edge $e = (p(u), u)$ and tree $T(u)$. For tree T, we use either the pre-order or the post-order for the customer nodes in T as σ (with o attached at the end). During the execution of `Non-Split(T, o, σ)`, the vehicle in general may have a

---

[3] In the conclusion section of the paper, we discuss the case where demand can be 0.
[4] A cactus graph is one in which every edge belongs to at most one simple cycle. See Fig. 2 for an example.

load $\ell > 0$ before traversing $e = (p(u), u)$ into $T(u)$ for the first time. Therefore, in the worst case the vehicle may collect no unit from $T(u)$ on its first visit, as we discuss in the proof of Theorem 1.

As we commented earlier, the optimal distance is hard to compute. So we first establish a lower bound for $I_{\text{cvrp}}(T, d)$ as a benchmark, against which we later compare the performance of Non-Split(T, o, σ). Let us introduce the *flow bound* for edge $e = (p(u), u)$, defined by

$$B_T(e) = \lceil D(T(u))/Q \rceil. \tag{1}$$

Note that $B_T(e) \geq 1$ since $D(T(u)) \geq 1$. It is easy to see that $B_T(e)$ is a lower bound on the number of times e needs to be traversed in one direction in any optimal solution to $I_{\text{cvrp}}(T, d)$. Similar flow bounds were used for the k-delivery TSP [6], the Dial-a-Ride problem [7], and CVRP on trees [16].

Lemma 1. *The approximation ratio of* Non-Split(T, o, σ) *is no more than 2 for* $R(T, d)$, *where* σ *is the pre-order or the post-order for* T.

Proof. Let $r_1, r_2, \ldots, r_t$ be all the routes passing through edge e that are traversed in this order by Non-Split(T, o, σ). We claim that $t \leq 2B_T(e)$. Since each of the t routes traverses e twice, the total number of traversals, $2t$, is at most $4B_T(e)$. Clearly, the optimal schedule must traverse e at least $2B_T(e)$ times. Therefore, the approximation ratio $2t/2B_T(e) \leq 2$, proving the lemma. Because the above claim is trivially true if $t = 1$ or 2 since $B_T(e) \geq 1$, we assume that $t \geq 3$ in what follows. Let the vehicle have a load of $\ell > 0$ just before entering $T(u)$ in r_1. In $R(T, d)$, the vehicle still needs to visit the next node v in sequence σ in $T(u)$, even if it may turn out that $\ell + d(v) > Q$, and the vehicle may not collect any unit from $T(u)$ in r_1. However, it is clear that, for $k = 1, 2, \ldots (2k+1 \leq t)$, Non-Split$(T, o, \sigma)$ makes the vehicle carry a total of at least $Q+1$ units from $T(u)$ in any two consecutive routes, r_{2k} and r_{2k+1}, when crossing e from u to $p(u)$.

If t is even, excluding r_1 and r_t, we can see that the total amount carried back across e from $T(u)$ is at least $(t-2)(Q+1)/2$. If t is odd, this bound is also valid because r_t need not be excluded. Since $(t-2)(Q+1)/2 \geq (t-2)Q/2+1/2$, we have

$$B_T(e) = \lceil D(T(u))/Q \rceil \geq (t-2)/2 + 1. \tag{2}$$

We obtain an upper bound on t from (2): $t \leq 2B_T(e)$.   □

Since Lemma 1 is valid for any realization $R(T, d)$, we have

Theorem 1. *The a priori sequence corresponding to the pre-order or the post-order achieves a 2-approximation in the worst case for the non-split VRPSD on trees.*   □

3   Non-split VRPSD on Cycles

Consider a cycle C consisting of depot $v_0(=o)$ and n customer nodes, $v_1, \ldots, v_n$ in the clockwise order. (See Fig. 1).

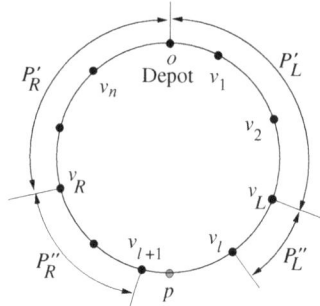

Fig. 1. A cycle. Point p is the midpoint.

We first determine the midpoint p on C such that $c(C[o,p]) = c(C[p,o])$, where $C[a,b]$ denotes the part of cycle C clockwise from point a to point b. Note that p may not be unique if some edges have 0 cost. Let p lie on the edge $e_l = (v_l, v_{l+1})$ of the cycle. We assume $1 \leq l \leq n-1$.[5] The main result of this section is the proof that Non-Split$(C\backslash\{e_l\}, o, \sigma)$ with sequence $\sigma = \langle v_l, v_{l-1}, \ldots, v_1, v_{l+1}, v_{l+2}, \ldots, v_n, o \rangle$ yields a 2-approximation for any VRPSD realization $R(C, d)$.

Define two paths, $P_L = C[o, v_l]$ and $P_R = C[v_{l+1}, o]$.[6] To first find a lower bound on the optimal solution, the following two lemmas consider split solutions to $I_{\text{cvrp}}(C, d)$. Let r_a and r_b be two routes in a split solution to $I_{\text{cvrp}}(C, d)$. Routes r_a and r_b are said to *intersect* if they share at least one edge. Route r_a is said to *contain* route r_b, if all the edges of r_b are also in r_a.

Lemma 2. *In an optimal split solution to $I_{\text{cvrp}}(C, d)$, if two routes intersect, then they can be replaced by two routes such that one contains the other.*

Proof. If both routes are contained in P_L or P_R then the assertion already holds. It also holds if one of the routes is the entire cycle C. So suppose that one of the routes crosses middle point p but returns to o across p (this can happen in an optimal solution if some edges near p have 0 cost). Then we can make it proceed in the same direction to return to o without increasing the total distance.   □

Lemma 3. *Let route r_a contain route r_b in an optimal split solution to $I_{\text{cvrp}}(C, d)$, in which the total demand is more than Q. Then the following hold.*

(a) There exists an optimal schedule in which exactly Q units are collected from the nodes on r_a, and each node serviced on r_b has a subscript that is not larger (or not smaller) than those serviced on r_a.
(b) If r_a crosses the mid-edge e_l, then r_b need not cross it.   □

Proof. (a) Let V_a (V_b) denote the set of nodes serviced on r_a (r_b). Since they are routes in an optimal solution, the total number of units collected on those

---

[5] If p were on the interior of e_n, for example, then the optimal schedule would not traverse e_l at all, and the problem would become easier. Note that $p = v_l$ is possible.
[6] L(eft) and R(ight) are from the perspective of the depot node o.

routes are at least $Q+1$. Since this is a split solution, we can assume that Q units are collected from V_a. We can now reorganize the composition of V_a and V_b, if necessary, to satisfy the conditions of the lemma.

If r_b is within path P_L (resp. P_R), then we can make the reorganized V_a consist of the minimum number of the highest-indexed (resp. lowest-indexed) nodes from $V_a \cup V_b$ whose total demand is at least Q. Now suppose that both r_a and r_b cross p. Then as argued in the proof of Lemma 2, we can assume that both routes are the entire C. In this case, let V_a consist of the minimum number of either the highest-indexed or lowest-indexed nodes from $V_a \cup V_b$ whose total demand is at least Q.

(b) We can assume that, after the adjustment was made, V_a contains vertices from both P_L and P_R, since otherwise there is no need for r_a to cross p. It is clear that r_b need not cross p. □

Let r be the route, if any, that crosses e_l in an optimal split solution to $I_{\text{cvrp}}(C, d)$. By Lemma 3(b), we may assume that at most one such route exists. If r exists, then by Lemma 3(a), we may further assume that the vehicle collects exactly Q units on r from nodes that are consecutive "around" midpoint p.[7] We compute the cost of r and the other routes, separately. In a (not necessarily optimal) solution, let x $(0 < x < Q)$ be the number of units collected on r from nodes on P_L. Then $Q-x$ units are collected on r from nodes on P_R. We can compute the flow bound on any edge $e \in P_L \cup P_R$, excluding the units collected on route r, as follows:

$$f_L(e, x) = \lceil \{D(C[v_{i+1}, v_l]) - x\}/Q \rceil \text{ for } e = (v_i, v_{i+1}) \in P_L \tag{3}$$

$$f_R(e, x) = \lceil \{D(C[v_{l+1}, v_i]) - (Q-x)\}/Q \rceil \text{ for } e = (v_i, v_{i+1}) \in P_R. \tag{4}$$

Let us sum them for all $e \in P_L \cup P_R$ and add the cost of r.

$$F(x) = \sum_{e \in P_L} f_L(e, x) \cdot c(e) + \sum_{e \in P_R} f_R(e, x) \cdot c(e) + c(C). \tag{5}$$

Setting aside the problem of minimizing $F(x)$, which is discussed in the Appendix, suppose $x = x^*$ minimizes it. Then clearly $F(x^*)$ is a lower bound on the total cost. Let L be the largest subscript such that $\sum_{L \leq i \leq l} d(v_i) > x^*$, and R be the smallest subscript such that $\sum_{l+1 \leq i \leq R} d(v_i) > Q - x^*$. Define paths $P'_L = C[o, v_L]$, $P'_R = C[v_R, o]$, $P''_L = C[v_L, v_l]$, and $P''_R = C[v_{l+1}, v_R]$. If r exists, the optimal solution collects Q units on r from the nodes on $P''_L \cup P''_R$.

Theorem 2. Non-Split$(C \backslash \{e_l\}, o, \sigma)$ *with* $\sigma = \langle v_l, \ldots, v_1, v_{l+1}, \ldots, v_n, o \rangle$ *achieves a 2-approximation for the non-split VRPSD on cycles.*

Proof. If e_l is not crossed in the optimal solution, then $\sigma = \langle v_l, \ldots, v_1, v_{l+1}, \ldots, v_n, o \rangle$ is the post-order for the tree $C \backslash \{e_l\}$. Therefore, the theorem follows from Theorem 1 in this case.

---

[7] Assuming, of course, that the total demand by the customer nodes is at least Q.

So assume that one route r of the optimal solution crosses it. (Lemma 3(b).) Let $r_1, r_2, \ldots, r_t$ be the routes used by $\texttt{Non-Split}(C\backslash\{e_l\}, o, \sigma)$. Since there are at most Q units of demand from the nodes on $C[v_{L+1}, v_l]$, $\texttt{Non-Split}(C\backslash\{e_l\}, o, \sigma)$ will traverse every edge on path $e \in P''_L$ exactly twice in r_1, once towards v_l and the second time on return from it, which is twice the optimum. Let us now examine an edge $e = (v_i, v_{i+1}) \in P'_L$. Note that the vehicle is empty when it starts out from the depot on each of the t routes. Thus, as in the proof of Lemma 1, the vehicle collects a total of at least $Q+1$ units on any pair of routes $\{r_k, r_{k+1}\}$. Therefore, we get an upper bound on t: $t \leq 2B_{C\backslash\{e_l\}}(e) - 1$, where $B_{C\backslash\{e_l\}}(e)$ is the flow bound for edge e in tree $B_{C\backslash\{e_l\}}$. (See the proof of Lemma 1.) Let us define a unified flow bound for $e \in P_L \cup P_R$, excluding the x^* (resp. $Q - x^*$) units of demand from the nodes on P''_L (resp. P''_R), by

$$B^*_{C\backslash\{e_l\}}(e) = \begin{cases} f_L(e, x^*) & \text{for } e \in P_L \\ f_R(e, x^*) & \text{for } e \in P_R. \end{cases} \tag{6}$$

Since $B_{C\backslash\{e_l\}}(e) - 1 \leq B^*_{C\backslash\{e_l\}}(e)$ by definition, we get $t \leq 2B^*_{C\backslash\{e_l\}}(e) + 1$ from $t \leq 2B_{C\backslash\{e_l\}}(e) - 1$. Thus the number of traversals across e is no more than

$$2t \leq 2\{2B^*_{C\backslash\{e_l\}}(e) + 1\}. \tag{7}$$

Note that $2B^*_{C\backslash\{e_l\}}(e) + 1$ is a lower bound on the number of times that e is traversed in the optimal solution, including the one traversal on route r. This means that the right hand side of (7) is twice the lower bound on the optimum. Similar analysis applies to each edge $e = (v_i, v_{i+1}) \in P'_R$. This completes the proof. $\qquad\square$

4 VRPSD on Cactus Graphs

A cactus graph is defined to be one in which every edge belongs to at most one simple cycle. See Fig. 2, for an example. We shall present a node sequence σ for a given cactus graph G such that $\texttt{Non-Split}(\tau(G), o, \sigma)$ achieves a 3-approximation, where tree $\tau(G)$ is derived from G, as we explain below. It is based on the observation that removing the edge on which the midpoint of each

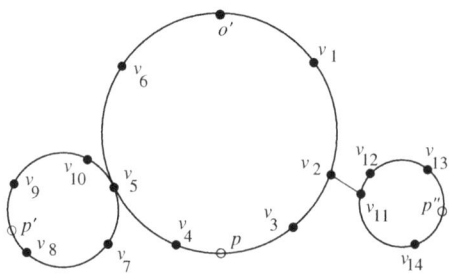

Fig. 2. A cactus graph

cycle lies (e.g., points p, p' and p'' in Fig. 2) results in a tree, and we can use the pre-order or post order on it.

Our first task is to transform the original graph G into a tree G' as follows. Starting with $G' = G$, we pick a simple cycle C in G' arbitrarily. As in Section 3, let e_l be the edge on which the middle point of C lies. We now set $G' = G \backslash \{e_l\}$. We repeat this process until no cycle exists in G', and let $\tau(G)$ be the resulting G'. We can now invoke $\texttt{Non-Split}(\tau(G), o, \sigma)$, where σ is a depth first sequence on $\tau(G)$ that mixes the pre-order and post-order, as we illustrate below.

Assume that the vehicle reaches node o'^8 belonging to a simple cycle C in the original graph G for the first time. We use a sequence σ that services one of the subtrees rooted at o' that contains one half of C in the pre-order and then the subtree that contains the other half in the post-order. As for node o', when it is visited is determined by the visiting order in the cycle to which o' belongs and is closer to the depot o, if any, or by that for the entire tree rooted at o, if not.[9] For example, in Fig. 2, $T(v_1)$ will be serviced in the pre-order and $T(v_6)$ will be serviced in the post-order. The entire visiting sequence for the cactus graph in Fig. 2 is
$$\langle v_1, v_2, v_{11}, v_{12}, v_{13}, v_{14}, v_3, v_4, v_7, v_8, v_9, v_{10}, v_5, v_6 \rangle.$$

We shall use the notation defined in Section 3. Let C be a simple cycle in G as described in Section 3. Consider an edge $e = (v_i, v_{i+1})$ on the path $P_L = C[o', v_l]$. We now derive a lower bound on the number of traversals on e. Consider a maximal subtree $\hat{T}(v_{i+1})$ of $T(v_{i+1})$ such that $\hat{T}(v_{i+1}) \cap C = \{v_j\}$, where $i + 1 \leq j \leq l$. As e is on the shortest paths to the depot for the nodes in $\hat{T}(v_{i+1}$, the most cost effective way to service every Q units of demand from the nodes in $\hat{T}(v_{i+1}$ is to traverse e from v_i to v_{i+1} to gather these units, and traverse e backwards to carry them to the depot. Therefore, there must be an optimal schedule that works this way, and $2\lfloor D(\hat{T}(v_{i+1})/Q \rfloor$ is a lower bound on the number of times e is traversed.

Let $D(\hat{T}(v_{i+1})) = (k{-}1)Q{+}d$, where $k \geq 1$. We thus have $d = D(\hat{T}(v_{i+1}))$ mod Q. We make k copies of node v_j, tentatively named $u_1, \ldots, u_k$, such that $d(u_h) = Q$ for $h = 1, \ldots, k{-}1$ and $d(u_k) = d$, and connect u_h to u_{h+1} by a zero-distance edge. Remove $\hat{T}(v_{i+1}) - \{v_j\}$ from G' and replace v_j by those k copies, and connect u_1 to v_{j-1} (resp. u_k to v_{j+1}) with an edge of the original cost $c(v_{j-1}, v_j)$ (resp. $c(v_j, v_{j+1})$). After processing the rest of $T(v_{i+1})$ in a similar way, we obtain a new CVRP instance $I_{\text{cvrp}}(C', d)$ defined on the modified cycle C'. In what follows, we assume that all the nodes are renumbered and named as $u_1, u_2, \ldots, u_{n'}$ along C' clockwise from o'. We replace node names $\{v_i\}$ used in Section 3 by $\{u_j\}$ and redefine the mid edge e_l accordingly. We also redefine L, R, P_L, P_L', P_L'', P_R, P_R', and P_R'', and x^* in the new context. For example, we have $P_L = C'[o', u_l]$ and $P_L' = C'[o', u_L]$.

If the middle edge e_l is traversed in the optimal split schedule, then to achieve an approximation ratio of 3, we can afford to traverse the edges on $P_L'' \cup P_R''$ up to

---

[8] Node o' may or may not be depot o.

[9] There is some freedom here, but we adopt this particular sequence for the sake of concreteness.

three times. We claim that if $\texttt{Non-Split}(\tau(G), o, \sigma)$ traverses some edge $e \in P_L''$ in two routes (i.e., e is crossed four times), then it traverses each edge $e' \in P_R''$ only in one route (i.e., e' is crossed twice) and vice versa.

Lemma 4. *(a) If* $\texttt{Non-Split}(\tau(G), o, \sigma)$ *traverses some edge on* P_L'' *more than twice, then the total cost for traversing the edges on* $P_L'' \cup P_R''$ *is bounded by*

$$4c(P_L'') + 2c(P_R'').$$

(b) If $\texttt{Non-Split}(\tau(G), o, \sigma)$ *traverses all edges on* P_L'' *exactly twice, then the total cost for traversing the edges on* $P_L'' \cup P_R''$ *is bounded by*

$$4c(P_R'') + 2c(P_L'').$$

Proof. (a) If an edge $e \in P_L''$ is traversed four times by $\texttt{Non-Split}(\tau(G), o, \sigma)$, then the vehicle will have a load $\ell < x^*$ when the vehicle finishes servicing the nodes in $T(u_1)$. This is because, when e is traversed for the third time (away from u_1), the vehicle will carry no load. $\texttt{Non-Split}(\tau(G), o, \sigma)$ will continue to service the nodes in $T(u_{n'})$ in the post-order. As $\ell < x^*$, the vehicle will traverse every edge $e' \in P_R''$ exactly twice, because the nodes on P_R'', excluding u_R, has a total demand of no more than $Q - x^*$.

(b) In this case, the vehicle may have a load $\ell > x^*$ when it finishes servicing the nodes in $T(u_1)$. If so, it cannot service all $Q - x^*$ units from the nodes on $P_R'' - \{u_R\}$, which means that some edges on P_R'' must be traversed four times. □

Theorem 3. *Procedure* $\texttt{Non-Split}(\tau(G), o, \sigma)$ *achieves a 3-approximation for any realization* $R(G, d)$ *of the non-split VRPSD on cactus graphs.*

Proof. Note first that the optimal solution may traverse e_l at most once, but $\texttt{Non-Split}(G', o, \sigma)$ does not.

Case 1. $[e \in P_L' \cup P_R']$: Consider edge $e \in P_L'$. The case $e \in P_R'$ is symmetric. Applying the analysis in the proof of Lemma 1, we see that $\texttt{Non-Split}(\tau(G), o, \sigma)$ traverses e at most $4B_{C' \backslash \{e_l\}}(e)$ times, where $B_{C' \backslash \{e_l\}}(e)$ is the flow bound defined on $C' \backslash \{e_l\}$. We have

$$B_{C' \backslash \{e_l\}}(e) = \lceil D(C'[u_{i+1}, u_l]) / Q \rceil \leq B_{C' \backslash \{e_l\}}^*(e) + 1,$$

because $0 < x^* < Q$. In the optimal split solution, e is traversed at least $2B_{C' \backslash \{e_l\}}^*(e)$ +1 times. The difference between three times this amount and the cost of $\texttt{Non-Split}(\tau(G), o, \sigma)$ is

$$3(2B_{C' \backslash \{e_l\}}^*(e) + 1) - 4B_{C' \backslash \{e_l\}}(e) \geq 3(2B_{C' \backslash \{e_l\}}^*(e) + 1) - 4(B_{C' \backslash \{e_l\}}^*(e) + 1)$$
$$= 2B_{C' \backslash \{e_l\}}^*(e) - 1 \geq 1. \qquad (8)$$

This implies that every edge $e \in P_L'$ could be traversed one more time without exceeding the upper bound of three times the optimum. Namely we have an "excess capacity" of $c(P_L')$ (and $c(P_R')$), which will be utilized in the cost analysis for Case 2.

Case 2. $[e \in P_L'' \cup P_R'']$: By Lemma 4 the total cost for traversing the edges on $P_L'' \cup P_R''$ is bounded by the larger of $4c(P_L'') + 2c(P_R'')$ and $4c(P_R'') + 2c(P_L'')$.

Summing three times the cost of traversing the path $P_L'' \cup P_R'' \cup \{e_l\}$ (in the optimal schedule) and the "excess capacity", we get

$$3[c(P_L'') + c(P_R'') + c(e_l)] + c(P_L') + c(P_R').$$

Subtracting $4c(P_L'') + 2c(P_R'')$ from this, we get the difference,

$$c(P_R'') + 3c(e_l) + c(P_L') + c(P_R') - c(P_L'') \geq 2c(e_l) + c(C)/2 + c(P_L') - c(P_L'')$$
$$\geq 2c(e_l) + 2c(P_L') \geq 0. \tag{9}$$

If we subtract $4c(P_R'') + 2c(P_L'')$, the difference is $2c(e_l) + 2c(P_R') \geq 0$. We can thus conclude that in this case the cost of the solution generated by $\texttt{Non-Split}(\tau(G),$ $o, \sigma)$ is no more than three times the optimum.   □

Note that the above theorem is valid for the split solution as well, since the performance was computed relative to the optimal split solution.

5 Non-split VRPSD on General Graphs

In this section we use an α-approximate TSP tour as the *a priori* sequence and analyze its performance. The following result [12] plays an important role in our analysis.

Lemma 5. *Given a VRPSD realization $R(G, d)$ for a general graph $G = (V, E)$, we have*

$$\sum_{v \in V} c(v, o) \leq \frac{Q}{2} \cdot OPT(I_{\text{cvrp}}(G, d)). \tag{10}$$

□

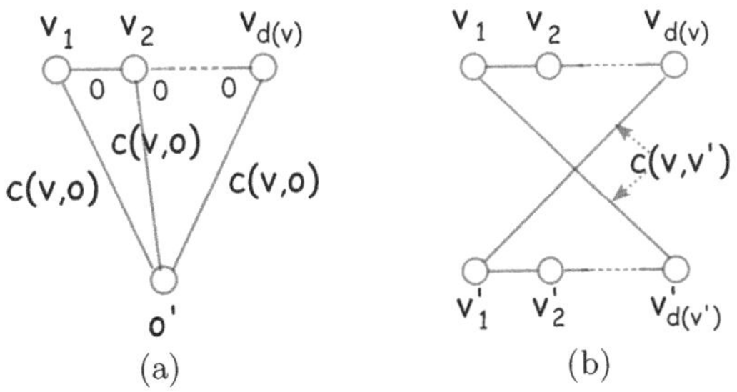

Fig. 3. (a) A node chain in G' corresponding to $v \in V \setminus \{o\}$; (b) Two edges $(v_1, v_{d(v')}')$, $(v_1', v_{d(v)}) \in E'$ for each pair $v, v' \in V \setminus \{o\}$

To facilitate our analysis, we transform a given general VRPSD realization $R(G, d)$ into another VRPSD realization $R(G', d')$ such that each customer node in $G' = (V', E')$ has exactly one unit of demand. We do this by introducing the depot node $o' \in V'$ and a chain of $d(v)$ nodes, $v_1, v_2, \ldots, v_{d(v)}$, which are chained by 0 cost edges, for each node $v \in V \setminus \{o\}$. We now introduce an edge $(v_i, o') \in E'$

with cost $c(v, o)$ for $i = 1, \ldots, d(v)$. See Fig. 3(a). Finally, for each pair of nodes in $v, v' \in V \backslash \{o\}$, we introduce two edges $(v_1, v'_{d(v')})$, $(v'_1, v_{d(v)}) \in E'$ with cost $c(v, v')$, as shown in Fig. 3(b). If $d(v) = d(v') = 1$ then only one edge with cost $c(v, v')$ is introduced.

Find an α-approximate TSP tour τ (from depot o back to itself) in G, and map it to tour τ' in G'. Tour τ' starts at o' and when τ visits node v, τ' visits $v_1, v_2, \ldots, v_{d(v)}$ in this order. We clearly have $c'(\tau') = c(\tau)$, where $c'(\ )$ is the cost function for G'. We now partition τ', excluding its first and last edges incident on o', into a sequence of paths $P_1, P_2, \ldots, P_m$, each consisting of exactly Q nodes,[10] as shown in Fig. 4. We name the nodes along τ', except o', $u_1, u_2, \ldots, u_{|V'|-1}$, so that P_i consists of $\{u_k \mid (i-1)Q+1 \leq k \leq iQ\}$.

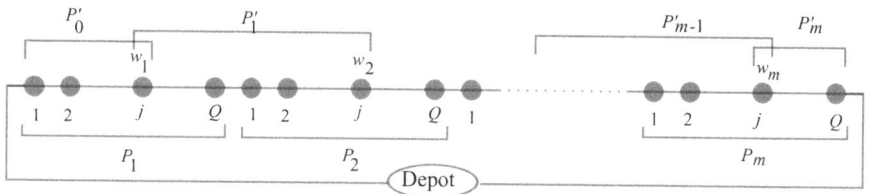

Fig. 4. Illustration for P_i, P'_i, w_i, etc

Lemma 6. *For $h = 1, \ldots, Q$, select one node from every path P_i $(i = 1, \ldots, m)$ and put them in set S_h. Then there exists an index j $(1 \leq j \leq Q)$ such that*

$$\sum_{u \in S_j} c'(u, o') \leq OPT(I_{\text{cvrp}}(G, d))/2. \tag{11}$$

Proof. As $S_1 \cup S_2 \cup \cdots \cup S_Q$ contains all the customer nodes in $G'(V', E')$, we have

$$\sum_{u \in S_1 \cup \cdots \cup S_Q} c'(u, o') \leq (Q/2) OPT(I_{\text{cvrp}}(G, d))$$

from (10) . Thus there must be an S_j satisfying the lemma. $\square$

Theorem 4. *The a priori strategy achieves a $(2 + 2\alpha)$-approximation for the non-split VRPSD on general graphs.*

Proof. In Lemma 6, for $h = 1, \ldots, Q$, let us select the nodes to put in S_h as follows. Let τ' and P_i be as defined above. From each path P_i, select one node, $u_{(i-1)Q+h}$, and put it in S_h. Thus we have $|S_h| = Q$ and the indices of the nodes in S_h selected from P_i and P_{i+1} are Q apart. Let $S_j = \{w_1, \ldots, w_m\}$ be the set defined in Lemma 6, where $w_i = u_{(i-1)Q+j} \in P_i$. For $i = 1, \ldots, m-1$, define path $P'_i = \tau'[w_i, w_{i+1}]$, where $\tau'[u, u']$ denotes the subpath of τ' from node u to u'.

---

[10] If P_m consists of fewer than Q nodes, then we insert the required number of fictitious nodes just before its last node. Each of these fictitious nodes is connected with 0 cost edges to its neighbors and the depot node.

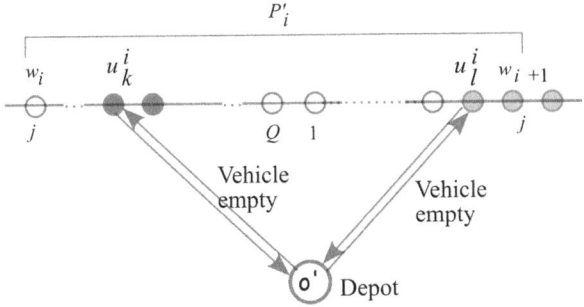

Fig. 5. The nodes (of G') of the same shade type correspond to a single node in G

See the top part of Fig. 4. We also define $P'_0 = \tau'[u_1, w_1]$ and $P'_m = \tau'[w_m, u_{n'-1}]$. Note that P'_i and P'_{i+1} share one node, w_{i+1}, in common.

For $i = 1, \ldots, m-1$, the total demand from the nodes on P'_i is exactly $Q+1$ units, and it is clear that there can be at most two recourses from within P'_i for $i = 1, \ldots, m-1$, and at most one recourse each from within P'_0 and P'_m. We consider the worst case, where those upper bounds on the number of recourses actually happen. In our analysis, we assume that the vehicle goes back to the same node once more after a recourse, even if no more unserviced demand remains there. This is done to compute the upper bound on the distance traveled more easily. Let the first (second) recourse from P'_i be from u^i_k (u^i_ℓ) back to itself via o', as illustrated in Fig. 5.

They can be mapped back to two recourses in the original graph G. It is easy to see that $c'(u^i_\ell, o') = c'(w_{i+1}, o')$ holds, since u^i_ℓ and w_{i+1} correspond to the same node in G. See Fig. 6, where the nodes (of G') of the same shade type correspond to a single node in G, just as in Fig. 5. The cost of the second recourse is thus $2c'(u^i_\ell, o') = 2c'(w_{i+1}, o')$. Using Fig. 6, let us now bound the cost of the first recourse. By the triangle inequality, we have $c'(u^i_k, o') \le a + c(w_i, o')$ and $c'(u^i_k, o') \le b + c(w_{i+1}, o')$. Adding these two inequalities, we obtain

$$2c'(u^i_k, o') \le c(w_i, o') + c(w_{i+1}, o') + c'(P'_i). \tag{12}$$

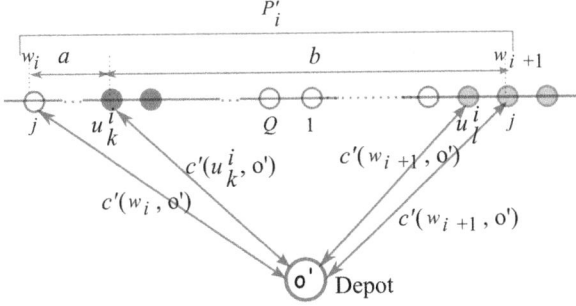

Fig. 6. Bounding $c'(u^i_k, o')$

Therefore, the total cost of the two recourses is bounded by $c'(w_i, o')$ $+3c'(w_{i+1}, o')+c'(P_i')$. As for paths P_0' and P_m', the cost of the very first (and only) recourse from P_0' is clearly bounded by $c'(u_1, o')+c'(w_1, o')+c'(P_0')$, and the cost of the very last (and only) recourse from P_m' is bounded by $c'(u_{n'-1}, o')+c'(w_m, o')+$ $c'(P_m')$. Adding the costs of all other recourses from (12) for $i = 1, \ldots, m-1$, we find the sum is no more than $4 \sum_{w \in S_j} c'(w, o') + c'(\tau')$. Finally, including the cost of the TSP tour $c'(\tau')$, the total distance traveled is bounded by $4 \sum_{w \in S_j} c'(w, o') + 2c'(\tau')$. The first term is bounded by $2OPT(I_{\text{cvrp}}(G, d))$ by (11), and the second term is bounded by $2\alpha OPT(I_{\text{cvrp}}(G, d))$ since $c'(\tau') = c(\tau)$ for TSP tour τ of G. It follows that

$$4 \sum_{w \in S_j} c'(w, o') + 2c'(\tau') \leq (2 + 2\alpha) OPT(I_{\text{cvrp}}(G, d)).$$

This completes the proof.   □

6   Discussion

It is conceivable that tighter upper bounds can be obtained by comparing our solutions with the VRPSD optima under the *a priori* strategy, instead of the VRPSD optima under re-optimization, as was done in this paper.

We made a general assumption that each node had non-zero demand and must be visited. Suppose we discard this assumption, and adopt the policy that the vehicle visits only the nodes with a non-zero demand. This is called Strategy **b** in [4]. For this modified model to make practical sense, we need to assume that those nodes with zero demands are known in advance. This is the case in parcel delivery service, and we may not want to change the visiting sequence for reasons, such as cost and predictability of the collection/delivery time. Or it may be the case that whether a site has a non-zero demand is communicated to the driver beforehand, but the exact demand is not known until the vehicle reaches the site. We think this modified model is worth investigating.

7   Conclusion

We considered the *a priori* strategy for VRPSD. We proposed *a priori* sequences for different classes of graphs, and showed that they achieve approximation ratios of 2, 2, and 3 for trees, cycles and cacti, respectively, under the non-split constraint. We also demonstrated that an α-optimal TSP route achieves a $(2+2\alpha)$-approximation for general graphs under the non-split constraint. We feel that the analysis techniques that we introduced in this paper will be useful in analyzing other problems related to vehicle routing.

References

1. Altinkemer, K., Gavish, B.: Heuristics for unequal weight delivery problems with a fixed error guarantee. Operations Research Letters 6(4), 149–158 (1987)
2. Asano, T., Katoh, N., Kawashima, K.: A new approximation algorithm for the capacitated vehicle routing problem on a tree. J. of Combinatorial Optimization 5(2), 213–231 (2004)
3. Berman, P., Das, S.K.: On the vehicle routing problem. In: Proc. Workshop on Algorithms and Data Structures, pp. 360–371 (2005)
4. Bertsimas, D.J.: A vehicle routing problem with stochastic demand. Operations Research 40(3), 574–585 (1992)
5. Bertsimas, D.J., Simchi-Levi, D.: A new generation of vehicle routing research: Robust algorithms, addressing uncertainty. Operations Research 44, 216–304 (1996)
6. Charikar, M., Khuller, S., Raghavachari, B.: Algorithms for capacitated vehicle routing. SIAM J. on Computing 31(3), 665–682 (2002)
7. Charikar, M., Raghavachari, B.: The finite capacity Dial-a-Ride problem. In: Proc. 39th Annual Symp. on Foundations of Computer Science, pp. 458–467 (1998)
8. Christofides, N.: The traveling salesman problem. In: Christofides, N., Mingozzi, A., Toth, P., Sandi, C. (eds.) Combinatorial Optimization, pp. 315–318 (1979)
9. Dror, M., Laporte, G., Trudeau, P.: Vehicle routing with stochastic demands: Properties and solution frameworks. Transportation Science 23(3), 166–176 (1989)
10. Dror, M., Ball, M., Golden, B.: A computational comparison of algorithms for the inventory routing problem. Annals of Operations Research 6, 3–23 (1985)
11. Golden, B.L., Raghavan, S., Wasil, E.A. (eds.): The Vehicle Routing Problem: Latest Advances and New Challenges. Operations Research Computer Science Interfaces Series, vol. 43. Springer, Heidelberg (2008)
12. Haimovich, A., Kan, A.R.: Bounds and heuristics for capacitated routing problems. Mathematics of Operations Research 10, 527–542 (1985)
13. Hamaguchi, S.-y., Katoh, N.: A capacitated vehicle routing problem on a tree. In: Chwa, K.-Y., Ibarra, O.H. (eds.) ISAAC 1998. LNCS, vol. 1533, pp. 397–406. Springer, Heidelberg (1998)
14. Jaillet, P., Odoni, A.: The probabilistic vehicle routing problem. In: Golden, B.L., Assad, A.A. (eds.) Vehicle Routing: Methods and Studies. North Holland, Amsterdam (1988)
15. Kenyon, A., Morton, D.P.: A survey on stochastic location and routing problems. Central European J. of Operations Research 9, 277–328 (2002)
16. Labbé, M., Laporte, G., Mercure, H.: Capacitated vehicle routing on trees. Operations Research 39(4), 616–622 (1991)
17. Marković, L., Ćavar, I., Carić, T.: Using data mining to forecast uncertain demands in stochastic vehicle routing problem. In: Proc. 13th Intn'l Symp. on Electronics in Transport (ISEP), Slovenia, pp. 1–6 (2005)
18. Novoa, C.: Static and dynamic approaches for solving the vehicle routing problem with stochastic demands. Ph.D. dissertation, Industrial and Systems Engineering Dept., Lehigh University (2005)
19. Tillman, F.: The multiple terminal delivery problem with probabilistic demands. Transportation Science 3, 192–204 (1969)
20. Viswanath, N.: Approximation Algorithms for Sequencing Problems. Ph.D. dissertation, Tepper School of Business, Carnegie Mellon University University (2009)

Appendix: Split CVRP on Cycles

In the main body of this paper, we discussed the non-split VRPSD. Here we shall discuss the split CVRP for cycles, using the notation developed in Section 3. The main result is an algorithm that finds the optimal solution in linear time.

Lemma 7. *For any split solution to $I_{\text{cvrp}}(C, d)$, the total distance is lower-bounded by the smaller of the following two quantities:*

$$B_1 = \sum_{e \in P_L \cup P_R} 2B_{C \setminus \{e_l\}}(e) \cdot c(e), \tag{13}$$

$$B_2 = \sum_{e \in P_L \cup P_R} \{2B^*_{C \setminus \{e_l\}}(e)\} \cdot c(e) + c(C), \tag{14}$$

where $B_{C \setminus \{e_l\}}(e)$ and $B^*_{C \setminus \{e_l\}}(e)$ were defined for tree $C \setminus \{e_l\}$ by (1) and (6), respectively.

Proof. Lemma 3 implies that at most one route crosses the mid-edge e_l in the optimal solution. If no route crosses e_l, then we need only consider tree $C \setminus \{e_l\}$, and the total cost is at least B_1.

Suppose now a route r of the optimal schedule crosses e_l. In the proof of Theorem 2 we saw that $2B^*_{C \setminus \{e_l\}}(e)$ is a lower bound on the number of times that e is traversed in the optimal solution to $I_{\text{cvrp}}(C, d)$, minus the one traversal on r. Since the cost (distance) of r is $c(C)$, the total cost is given by B_2. Note that $B^*_{C \setminus \{e_l\}}(e) = 0$ for $e \in P''_L \cup P''_R$.   □

Since we are discussing the split CVRP, we can assume without loss of generality that $d(v) = 1$ for every $v \in V \setminus \{o\}$. Let l, P_L, P_R be as defined in Section 3. We now show that the bound given by Lemma 7 can be achieved in the sense that the optimal schedule can be computed in polynomial time.

Case 1. [edge $e_l = (v_l, v_{l+1})$ is not crossed] In this case, the lower bound B_1 in Lemma 7 can be achieved using service sequence $\sigma = \langle v_l, \ldots, v_1, v_{l+1}, \ldots, v_n, o \rangle$.

Case 2. [e_l is crossed] According to Lemma 3(b), in the optimal solution the edges on the path $C[v_L, v_R]$ will be traversed only once. The remaining problem is how to compute x^*. Function $f_L(e, x)$ defined in (3) is clearly nonincreasing in x. Note that $f_L(e, x)$ can take at most two different values for $x \in [1, Q-1]$. In fact it decreases by 1 at $x = x_e = D(C[v_{i+1}, v_l])$ mod Q, which we call the *critical value* for e. It is a constant function over its domain $[1, Q-1]$ when $x_e = 0$.

Recall from (5) that

$$F_L(x) = \sum_{e \in P_L} f_L(e, x) \cdot c(e), \tag{15}$$

is the total cost for all the edges on P_L, excluding the cost of route r. We can classify the edges on P_L into Q equivalence classes, based on their critical values. It is easy to compute $F_L(1) = \sum_{e \in P_L} f_L(e, 1) \cdot c(e)$ in time linear in the number of edges on P_L. To compute $F_L(x)$ for $x = 2, 3, \ldots, Q-1$, we subtract $2c(e)$ from $F_L(x-1)$ for every e such that $x_e = x$. Since each edge only has one critical value (i.e., belongs to one equivalence class), the above computation can be carried out in linear time.

Function $f_R(e, x)$ defined in (4) is clearly nondecreasing in x, and

$$F_R(x) = \sum_{e \in P_R} f_R(e, x) \cdot c(e)$$

is the counterpart for $F_L(x)$ in (15). We finally determine $x = x^*$ that minimizes $F_L(x) + F_R(x)$, i.e, the total cost excluding $c(C)$. In route r that crosses e_l, the vehicle collects x^* (resp. $Q - x^*$) units from nodes of P_L'' (resp. P_R''). In the remaining routes, the vehicle uses the post-order sequence σ adopted in Case 1. If $F(x^*) = F_L(x^*) + F_R(x^*) + c(C) \geq B_1$ holds, then we have Case 1. See (5). Otherwise, we have Case 2. We have proved the following theorem.

Theorem 5. *The split CVRP on cycles with n customer nodes can be optimally solved in $O(n)$ time.* □

On Characterization, Definability and ω-Saturated Models

Facundo Carreiro*

Dto. de Computación, FCEyN, Universidad de Buenos Aires
fcarreiro@dc.uba.ar

Abstract. Two important classic results about modal expressivity are the Characterization and Definability theorems. We develop a general theory for modal logics below first order (in terms of expressivity) which exposes the following result: Characterization and Definability theorems hold for every (reasonable) modal logic whose ω-saturated models have the Hennessy-Milner property. The results are presented in a general version which is relativized to classes of models.

1 Introduction

Syntactically, *modal languages* [1] are propositional languages extended with *modal operators*. Indeed, the basic modal language is defined as the extension of the propositional language with the unary operator $\square$. Although these languages have a very simple syntax, they are extremely useful to describe and reason about *relational structures*.

A relational structure is a nonempty set together with a family of relations. Given the generality of this definition it is not surprising that modal logics are used in a wide range of disciplines: mathematics, philosophy, computer science, computational linguistics, etc. For example, theoretical computer science uses labeled transition systems (which are nothing but relational structures) to model the execution of a program.

An important observation that might have gone unnoticed in the above paragraph is that there are *many different modal logics*. There is, nowadays, a wide variety of modal languages and an extensive menu of modal operators to choose from (e.g. *Since* and *Until* [2], universal modality [3], difference modality [4], fix-point operators [5], etc.), enabling the design of a particular logic for each specific application.

It is in this context that the notion of *bisimulation* [6] becomes fundamental. Intuitively, a bisimulation characterizes, from a structural point of view, when a state in a model is indistinguishable from a state in another model. Bisimulations are a crucial tool in the process of studying relational structures and they open the way to formally analyze the exact expressive power of modal languages.

If we comprehend in detail the notion of bisimulation, we can measure and try to balance expressiveness and complexity, and thus obtain a logic appropriate

---
* F. Carreiro was partially supported by a grant by CONICET Argentina.

A. Cerone and P. Pihlajasaari (Eds.): ICTAC 2011, LNCS 6916, pp. 62–76, 2011.

to the context of use with the minimum possible computational complexity. However, deciding which is the correct notion of bisimulation for a given logic is not an easy task.

In this paper we investigate Characterization and Definability, two model-theoretical results intimately related with the notion of bisimulation. We pursue a general study of these properties without referring to a particular modal logic. In general, the validity of these theorems is a good indicator that the underlying notion of bisimulation for a given logic is indeed the correct one.

Characterization results for modal logics identify them as fragments of a better known logic. This type of characterizations allows for the transfer of results and a better understanding of the modal logic. The first work in this direction was done by van Benthem [7] who used bisimulations to characterize the basic modal logic (BML) as the bisimulation invariant fragment of first order logic.

Theorem (J. van Benthem). *A first order formula α is equivalent to the translation of a* BML *formula iff α is invariant under bisimulations.*

For example, as a corollary of this theorem, we know that the first order formula $\varphi(x) = R(x,x)$ is not expressable in BML because we can construct a model with a reflexive element which is bisimilar to a non-reflexive element. Observe that in this case the notion of bisimulation is that of BML. As we have said before, every modal logic has a, potentially different, notion of bisimulation.

A theorem of this kind would identify which first order properties can be captured with each particular modal logic. But —as the syntax, semantics of the logic and the definition of bisimulation involved have changed— each such theorem needs a new ad-hoc proof.

Let us now discuss definability. Given a logic $\mathcal{L}$, definability results identify the properties that a class of $\mathcal{L}$-models K should satisfy in order to guarantee the existence of an $\mathcal{L}$-formula (or a set of $\mathcal{L}$-formulas) safisfied exactly by the models in K.[1] This question has already been addressed for first order logic [8], BML [1] and many others logics [9,10]. Whereas the answer for first order logic is presented in terms of *potential isomorphisms* [8], in the case of modal logics, the notion of bisimulation plays a fundamental role.

Theorem (M. de Rijke). *A class of Kripke models K is definable by means of a single* BML *formula iff both K and its complement are closed under bisimulations and ultraproducts.*

As a corollary of this theorem we get, for example, that the class of finite models is not definable in BML (because it is not closed under bisimulations). As with the characterization theorem, definability results similar to the one presented here also hold for a vast number of modal logics. However, every logic requires a different proof.

In this article we undertake a study of the proof techniques used for Characterization and Definability results. Our objective is to find sufficient conditions that an arbitrary logic has to fulfill to validate these theorems. Such conditions are captured in the notion of an *adequate pair* (introduced in Section 2).

---

[1] We consider definability of classes of models; we will not discuss frame definability.

If a given modal logic $\mathfrak{L}$ —together with its syntax, semantics and its notion of bisimulation— is compatible with our general theory, we guarantee the validity of Characterization and Definability theorems for $\mathfrak{L}$. We prove a more general version of these theorems were we allow a relativization to different classes of models.

The article is organized as follows. In Section 2 we give the set of basic definitions needed to state our main results. In Sections 3 and 4 we prove a generalization of the Characterization and Definability theorems and finally in Section 5 we draw some conclusions and propose further lines of research. Most of the proofs are presented in the main body of the article while the most technical ones can be found in the Appendix.

2   Basic Definitions

The theorems discussed in this article deal with two logics: one less expressive than the other. Different modal logics play the part of the former while we will always take first order logic (with or without equality) as the latter.

Definition 1 (Languages). *We denote the modal language as $\mathfrak{L}$ and the first order language as $\mathfrak{F}$. We consider languages $\mathfrak{L}$ extending $\mathfrak{P} = \langle (p_i)_{i \in \mathbb{N}}, \wedge, \vee, \top, \bot \rangle$ with the usual interpretations. $\mathfrak{F}$ is a countable first order language which may contain equality. For any language $\mathfrak{A}$, we call $\mathrm{FORM}(\mathfrak{A})$ to the set of formulas of the language $\mathfrak{A}$ and $\mathrm{FORM}_1(\mathfrak{F})$ to the subset of $\mathrm{FORM}(\mathfrak{F})$ with at most one free variable x.*

We do not impose any restrictions on the structures over which the language $\mathfrak{L}$ is interpreted. We only assume that every $\mathfrak{L}$-model $\mathcal{M}$ has a set of elements (also called worlds) which is called the domain or universe of $\mathcal{M}$ (notated $|\mathcal{M}|$).

Definition 2 (Models). *We define $\mathrm{MODS}(\mathfrak{L})$ to be the class of $\mathfrak{L}$-models under study (not necessarily the class of all models of the signature of $\mathfrak{L}$), and $\mathrm{MODS}(\mathfrak{F})$ to be the class of all $\mathfrak{F}$-models. We use $\overline{\mathsf{K}}$ to denote the complement of the class K.*

An $\mathfrak{L}$-pointed model is pair $\langle \mathcal{M}, w \rangle$ where $\mathcal{M}$ is an $\mathfrak{L}$-model and $w \in |\mathcal{M}|$. We define the class of $\mathfrak{L}$-pointed models corresponding to $\mathrm{MODS}(\mathfrak{L})$ as

$$\mathrm{PMODS}(\mathfrak{L}) = \{\langle \mathcal{M}, w \rangle : \mathcal{M} \in \mathrm{MODS}(\mathfrak{L}) \text{ and } w \in |\mathcal{M}|\}.$$

An $\mathfrak{F}$-pointed model is a pair $\langle \mathcal{M}, g \rangle$ where $\mathcal{M}$ is an $\mathfrak{F}$-model and $g : \{x\} \to |\mathcal{M}|$. The class of $\mathfrak{F}$-pointed models corresponding to $\mathrm{MODS}(\mathfrak{F})$ is defined as

$$\mathrm{PMODS}(\mathfrak{F}) = \{\langle \mathcal{M}, g \rangle : \mathcal{M} \in \mathrm{MODS}(\mathfrak{F}) \text{ and } g : \{x\} \to |\mathcal{M}|\}.$$

Definition 3. *We use $\mathcal{M}, w \models \varphi$ to denote that an $\mathfrak{L}$-formula φ is true in the point w of the $\mathfrak{L}$-model $\mathcal{M}$. Similarly, we use $\mathcal{M}, g \models \varphi$ to denote that a $\mathfrak{F}$-formula φ is true in the $\mathfrak{F}$-model $\mathcal{M}$ under the assignment g.*

If Γ is a set of first order formulas, we write $\Gamma \models_{\mathsf{K}} \beta$ to mean that the entailment is valid within the class K. We say that the first order formulas α and β are K-equivalent when $\models_{\mathsf{K}} \alpha \leftrightarrow \beta$.

Let $\langle \mathcal{M}, w \rangle, \langle \mathcal{N}, v \rangle \in \mathrm{PMODS}(\mathfrak{L})$. We write $\mathcal{M}, w \leadsto_{\mathfrak{L}} \mathcal{N}, v$ to mean that for every $\mathfrak{L}$-formula φ, if $\mathcal{M}, w \models \varphi$ then $\mathcal{N}, v \models \varphi$. We write $\mathcal{M}, w \leftrightsquigarrow_{\mathfrak{L}} \mathcal{N}, v$ when $\mathcal{M}, w \leadsto_{\mathfrak{L}} \mathcal{N}, v$ and $\mathcal{N}, v \leadsto_{\mathfrak{L}} \mathcal{M}, w$. This notation extends analogously to $\mathrm{PMODS}(\mathfrak{F})$. We drop the subscript when the logic involved is clear from context.

During the article, we will use and adapt some classical first order notions (such as potential isomorphism, ω-saturation and definability) to the context of our framework; see [8] for reference on these classical definitions. We start by adapting the notion of closure under potential isomorphisms to make it relative to a class of models.

Definition 4 (C-closure under potential isomorphisms). *Let* $\langle \mathcal{M}, g \rangle$ *and* $\langle \mathcal{N}, h \rangle \in \mathrm{PMODS}(\mathfrak{F})$ *we write* $\mathcal{M}, g \cong \mathcal{N}, h$ *to mean that there exists a potential isomorphism* I *between* $\mathcal{M}$ *and* $\mathcal{N}$ *such that* $\langle g(x) \rangle I \langle h(x) \rangle$.
A class $\mathsf{K} \subseteq \mathsf{C} \subseteq \mathrm{PMODS}(\mathfrak{F})$ *is* C-closed under potential isomorphisms *if for every* $\langle \mathcal{M}, g \rangle \in \mathsf{K}$ *and* $\langle \mathcal{N}, h \rangle \in \mathsf{C}$ *such that* $\mathcal{M}, g \cong \mathcal{N}, h$ *then* $\langle \mathcal{N}, h \rangle \in \mathsf{K}$.

We can see a model as an information repository. We need to define a way to access this information from the perspective of both the $\mathfrak{L}$ and the $\mathfrak{F}$ language.

Definition 5 (Truth preserving translations). *A formula translation is a function* $\mathsf{Tf}_x : \mathrm{FORM}(\mathfrak{L}) \to \mathrm{FORM}_1(\mathfrak{F})$ *such that* $\mathsf{Tf}_x(\varphi \wedge \psi) = \mathsf{Tf}_x(\varphi) \wedge \mathsf{Tf}_x(\psi)$ *and* $\mathsf{Tf}_x(\varphi \vee \psi) = \mathsf{Tf}_x(\varphi) \vee \mathsf{Tf}_x(\psi)$. *Given a class of models* $\mathsf{K} \subseteq \mathrm{PMODS}(\mathfrak{F})$, *a* model translation *is a bijective function* $\mathsf{T} : \mathrm{PMODS}(\mathfrak{L}) \to \mathsf{K}$.
A pair of translations $(\mathsf{Tf}_x, \mathsf{T})$ *is* truth-preserving *if for all* $\varphi \in \mathrm{FORM}(\mathfrak{L})$ *and all* $\langle \mathcal{M}, w \rangle \in \mathrm{PMODS}(\mathfrak{L})$ *they satisfy* $\mathcal{M}, w \models \varphi$ *iff* $\mathsf{T}(\mathcal{M}, w) \models \mathsf{Tf}_x(\varphi)$. *As an abuse of notation we use* $\mathsf{T}(\mathcal{M})$ *when we are not interested in the associated point of evaluation.*

For the rest of the article, we fix $(\mathsf{Tf}_x, \mathsf{T})$ to be an arbitrary pair of truth-preserving translations. We will also need to translate formulas from $\mathfrak{L}$ to $\mathfrak{F}$ and then go back to $\mathfrak{L}$-formulas. A priori, as we are not requiring Tf_x to be injective this could lead to a problem but it can be easily solved.

Notice that, for any α, β such that $\mathsf{Tf}_x(\alpha) = \mathsf{Tf}_x(\beta)$ we have $\alpha \models \beta$ and $\beta \models \alpha$. Hence, without loss of generality, we can work with equivalence classes of $\mathfrak{L}$-formulas (modulo $\mathfrak{L}$-equivalence) and assume that the formula translation Tf_x is injective. In the following definition we recall the classical notion of definability adapted to the context of $\mathfrak{L}$-models.

Definition 6. *A class* $\mathsf{M} \subseteq \mathrm{PMODS}(\mathfrak{L})$ *is* defined *by a set of* $\mathfrak{L}$-formulas Γ *(resp. a formula* φ*) when* $\langle \mathcal{M}, w \rangle \in \mathsf{M}$ *iff* $\mathcal{M}, w \models \Gamma$ *(resp.* $\mathcal{M}, w \models \varphi$*).*

In Section 1 we talked about bisimulations. This notion is usually used in the context of logics with negation where the relation is symmetrical. In the case of negation-free logics the analogous notion is not symmetrical and it is called *simulation*. For the framework developed in this article we take a broader approach and define an abstract notion of $\mathfrak{L}$-*simulation* which generalizes it.

Definition 7 ($\mathfrak{L}$-simulation). *An* $\mathfrak{L}$-simulation *is a non-empty relation* $Z \subseteq \mathrm{PMODS}(\mathfrak{L}) \times \mathrm{PMODS}(\mathfrak{L})$ *such that if* $\langle \mathcal{M}, w \rangle Z \langle \mathcal{N}, v \rangle$ *then* $\mathcal{M}, w \leadsto \mathcal{N}, v$.

We write $\mathcal{M}, w \rightrightarrows_\mathfrak{L} \mathcal{N}, v$ *to indicate that there exists an* $\mathfrak{L}$-*simulation* Z *such that* $\langle \mathcal{M}, w \rangle Z \langle \mathcal{N}, v \rangle$. *We drop the subscript when the logic is clear from context.*

It is worth mentioning that we do not assume any particular 'structural' property for the notion of $\mathfrak{L}$-simulation (e.g., the *zig* or *zag* condition for the basic modal logic). We only require it to be defined as a non-empty binary relation between $\mathfrak{L}$-pointed models and to preserve the truth of formulas (in one direction). This is something that any reasonable observational equivalence notion should satisfy.

It is known that, in general, $\mathcal{M}, w \rightsquigarrow \mathcal{N}, v$ does not imply $\mathcal{M}, w \rightrightarrows \mathcal{N}, v$. The classes of models where this property holds are called *Hennessy-Milner classes* [1]. An important class which is closely related to this property is the class of ω-saturated models.

Definition 8 (ω-**saturation**). *A first order model* $\mathcal{M}$ *is* ω-*saturated if for every finite* $A \subseteq |\mathcal{M}|$ *the expansion* $\mathcal{M}_A$ *with new constants* $\bar{a}$ *for every* $a \in A$ *satisfies: Let* $\Gamma(x)$ *be a set of formulas such that every finite subset is satisfiable in* $\mathcal{M}_A$ *then* $\Gamma(x)$ *should also be satisfied in* $\mathcal{M}_A$.

Informally, it resembles a kind of 'intra-model' compactness. That is, given a set $\Gamma(x)$ if every finite subset is satisfied in (possibly different) elements in $\mathcal{M}$ then there is *a single element* in $\mathcal{M}$ which satisfies the whole set.

The notion of ω-saturation [8] is defined for first order models, but it also applies to $\mathfrak{L}$-models using the model translation introduced in Definition 5: we define an $\mathfrak{L}$-model $\mathcal{M}$ to be ω-saturated if $\mathsf{T}(\mathcal{M})$ is so.

Not all models are ω-saturated but it is a known result that every first order model has an ω-saturated extension with the same first order theory (i.e., an elementarily equivalent extension). The ω-saturated extension $\mathcal{M}^+$ can be constructed by taking the ultrapower of $\mathcal{M}$ with a special kind of ultrafilter.[2] Observe that, in our setting, this extension will also have the same $\mathfrak{L}$-theory (via Tf_x and T as in Definition 5).

The following definition is central in this article. It makes explicit the requirements for our main theorems of Sections 3 and 4 to hold. From now on, we fix an arbitrary modal logic $\mathfrak{L}$ and a class of models K with the following properties.

Definition 9 (Adequate pair). *A logic* $\mathfrak{L}$ *and a class* $\mathsf{K} \subseteq \mathrm{PMODS}(\mathfrak{F})$ *are said to be an* adequate pair *if they fulfill the following requirements:*

1. K *is closed under ultraproducts.*
2. *There exist truth-preserving translations* Tf_x, T *(c.f. Definition 5).*
3. *There exists an* $\mathfrak{L}$-*simulation notion (c.f. Definition 7).*
4. *The class of* ω-*saturated* $\mathfrak{L}$-*models has the Hennessy-Milner property with respect to* $\mathfrak{L}$-*simulations (c.f. Definition 8).*

As we will show in the rest of the paper, we will be able to establish Characterization and Definability results for any arbitrary adequate pair. The crucial condition in the definition is item 4, which will usually be the hardest property to establish when defining an adequate pair. The other conditions should be naturally satisfied by any modal logic whose expressivity is below first order.

---

[2] We assume that the reader is familiar with the definition of *ultraproducts*, *ultrapowers* and *ultrafilters*; for details, see [11].

3   Characterization

One of the central notions of the Characterization theorem stated in Section 1 was that of bisimulation invariance. In the following definition we restate this notion in terms of $\mathfrak{L}$ and K.

Definition 10 ($\mathfrak{L}$-simulation K-invariance). *Let $\langle \mathfrak{L}, \mathsf{K} \rangle$ be an adequate pair. A formula $\alpha(x) \in \mathrm{FORM}_1(\mathfrak{F})$ is K-invariant for $\mathfrak{L}$-simulations if for all $\mathfrak{L}$-pointed models $\mathcal{M}, w$ and $\mathcal{N}, v$, such that $\mathcal{M}, w \rightrightarrows \mathcal{N}, v$, if $\mathsf{T}(\mathcal{M}, w) \models \alpha(x)$ then $\mathsf{T}(\mathcal{N}, v) \models \alpha(x)$.*

This property is defined for first order formulas but $\mathfrak{L}$-simulations are defined between $\mathfrak{L}$-models. When trying to generalize the notion of invariance, at least two options come up naturally.

The first one is to call a first order formula $\alpha(x)$ 'invariant for $\mathfrak{L}$-simulations' if, for every two $\mathfrak{L}$-pointed models $\mathcal{M}, w$ and $\mathcal{N}, v$ such that $\mathcal{M}, w \rightrightarrows_{\mathfrak{L}} \mathcal{N}, v$ whenever $\alpha(x)$ is true in $\mathsf{T}(\mathcal{M}, w)$ then it is also true in $\mathsf{T}(\mathcal{N}, v)$. In this case we would be checking simulation in $\mathfrak{L}$ and satisfaction in $\mathfrak{F}$.

The second option is to define a simulation relation $\rightrightarrows_{\mathfrak{F}}$ for $\mathfrak{F}$-models (e.g. as done in [12]). In this case we could just say that a first order formula $\alpha(x)$ is 'invariant for $\mathfrak{L}$-simulations' if for every two $\mathfrak{F}$-models $\mathcal{M}, g$ and $\mathcal{N}, h$ such that $\mathcal{M}, g \rightrightarrows_{\mathfrak{F}} \mathcal{N}, h$ whenever $\alpha(x)$ is true in $\mathcal{M}, g$, then it is also true $\mathcal{N}, h$.

In this article we will use the first option because it is simpler and requires no new definitions.

Theorem 11 (Characterization). *Let $\langle \mathfrak{L}, \mathsf{K} \rangle$ be an adequate pair. A formula $\alpha(x) \in \mathrm{FORM}_1(\mathfrak{F})$ is K-equivalent to the translation of an $\mathfrak{L}$-formula iff $\alpha(x)$ is K-invariant for $\mathfrak{L}$-simulations.*

The proof of this theorem will be the guide in the next few pages but the reader should be aware that, in order to do it, we will prove some propositions and lemmas which will allow us to conclude the desired result.

Proof. The claim from left to right is a consequence of the invariance of $\mathfrak{L}$-formulas over $\mathfrak{L}$-simulations. The implication from the right to left, suppose that $\alpha(x)$ is K-invariant for $\mathfrak{L}$-simulations, we want to see that it is K-equivalent to the translation of an $\mathfrak{L}$-formula. Consider the set of $\mathfrak{L}$-consequences of α:

$$\mathrm{SLC}(\alpha) = \{ \mathsf{Tf}_x(\varphi) : \varphi \text{ is an } \mathfrak{L}\text{-formula and } \alpha(x) \models_{\mathsf{K}} \mathsf{Tf}_x(\varphi) \}.$$

The following Proposition shows that it suffices to prove that $\mathrm{SLC}(\alpha) \models_{\mathsf{K}} \alpha(x)$.

Proposition 12. *If $\mathrm{SLC}(\alpha) \models_{\mathsf{K}} \alpha(x)$ then $\alpha(x)$ is K-equivalent to the translation of an $\mathfrak{L}$-formula.*

Proof. Suppose $\mathrm{SLC}(\alpha) \models_{\mathsf{K}} \alpha(x)$, by relative compactness (see Theorem 20 in the Appendix) there is a finite set $\Delta \subseteq \mathrm{SLC}(\alpha)$ such that $\Delta \models_{\mathsf{K}} \alpha(x)$, therefore $\models_{\mathsf{K}} \bigwedge \Delta \to \alpha(x)$. Trivially (by definition) we have that $\models_{\mathsf{K}} \alpha(x) \to \bigwedge \Delta$ so we conclude $\models_{\mathsf{K}} \alpha(x) \leftrightarrow \bigwedge \Delta$. As every $\beta \in \Delta$ is the translation of an $\mathfrak{L}$-formula and the translation preserves conjunctions then $\bigwedge \Delta$ is also the translation of some modal formula. □

Hence, the proof reduces to show that $\mathrm{SLC}(\alpha) \models_K \alpha(x)$. Let us suppose that $\mathsf{T}(\mathcal{M}, w) \models \mathrm{SLC}(\alpha)$. We show that $\mathsf{T}(\mathcal{M}, w) \models \alpha(x)$. Define $\mathsf{NTh}^w(x)$ as

$$\mathsf{NTh}^w(x) = \{\neg \mathsf{Tf}_x(\varphi) : \varphi \text{ is an } \mathfrak{L}\text{-formula and } \mathcal{M}, w \not\models \varphi\}$$

Observe that if $\mathfrak{L}$ has negation then $\mathsf{NTh}^w(x)$ will be the translation of w's modal theory and every model of $\mathsf{NTh}^w(x)$ will be modally equivalent to w. If $\mathfrak{L}$ does not have negation we will only preserve formulas that are not true in w. The above definition works in both cases. Let

$$\Sigma(x) = \{\alpha(x)\} \cup \mathsf{NTh}^w(x).$$

Proposition 13. $\Sigma(x)$ *has a model in* K.

Proof. Let us suppose that there is no model in K for $\Sigma(x)$ and use the contrapositive of Theorem 20. Then there is a finite subset $\{\alpha(x), \neg \delta_1, \dots, \neg \delta_n\} \subseteq \Sigma(x)$ with $\neg \delta_i \in \mathsf{NTh}^w(x)$ which does not have a model in K. Notice that this finite set should include $\alpha(x)$, otherwise it would have a had model, namely $\mathsf{T}(\mathcal{M}, w)$.

Observe that for every model $\mathcal{A}^f \in K$, as $\mathcal{A}^f \not\models \{\alpha(x), \neg \delta_1, \dots, \neg \delta_n\}$ then $\mathcal{A}^f \models \alpha(x) \to \neg(\neg \delta_1 \wedge \cdots \wedge \neg \delta_n)$. This means that $\alpha(x) \to (\delta_1 \vee \cdots \vee \delta_n)$ is valid in K, therefore $\alpha(x) \models_K \delta_1 \vee \cdots \vee \delta_n$. If $\delta_1 \vee \cdots \vee \delta_n$ is a K-consequence of $\alpha(x)$ then, as the formula translation preserves disjunction, $\delta_1 \vee \cdots \vee \delta_n \in \mathrm{SLC}(\alpha)$. But, as $\mathsf{T}(\mathcal{M}, w) \models \mathrm{SLC}(\alpha)$ then $\mathsf{T}(\mathcal{M}, w) \models \delta_1 \vee \cdots \vee \delta_n$. This is a contradiction, since $\mathsf{T}(\mathcal{M}, w) \not\models \delta_i$ for every i. $\square$

As $\Sigma(x)$ is satisfiable in K we have a model $\mathcal{N}$ and an element v such that $\langle \mathcal{N}, v \rangle \in K$ and $\mathsf{T}(\mathcal{N}, v) \models \Sigma(x)$. We make the following proposition.

Proposition 14. $\mathcal{N}, v \leadsto_{\mathfrak{L}} \mathcal{M}, w.$

Proof. Take the contrapositive. Suppose that $\mathcal{M}, w \not\models \varphi$ then $\neg \mathsf{Tf}_x(\varphi) \in \mathsf{NTh}^w(x)$ and because $\mathsf{NTh}^w(x) \subseteq \Sigma(x)$ we can state that $\mathsf{T}(\mathcal{N}, v) \models \neg \mathsf{Tf}_x(\varphi)$ which implies that $\mathsf{T}(\mathcal{N}, v) \not\models \mathsf{Tf}_x(\varphi)$. By truth-preservation of the translations we get $\mathcal{N}, v \not\models \varphi$. $\square$

Now we link $\mathsf{T}(\mathcal{N}, v)$ and $\mathsf{T}(\mathcal{M}, w)$ in a way that lets us transfer the validity of $\alpha(x)$ from the first model to the second. The next lemma, which makes a detour through the class of ω-saturated models, will be useful for this matter.

Lemma 15 (Big Detour Lemma). *Let* $\alpha(x) \in \mathrm{FORM}_1(\mathfrak{F})$ *be* $\mathfrak{L}$-*simulation* K-*invariant. If* $\mathcal{N}, v \leadsto_{\mathfrak{L}} \mathcal{M}, w$ *and* $\mathsf{T}(\mathcal{N}, v) \models \alpha(x)$ *then* $\mathsf{T}(\mathcal{M}, w) \models \alpha(x)$.

Proof. We define some terminology to avoid cumbersome notation. We add a subscript f to the first order translations of $\mathfrak{L}$-models, e.g. $\mathcal{M}_f = \mathsf{T}(\mathcal{M})$. We also add a superscript $+$ to first order saturated models and a superscript $*$ to modal saturated models.

Applying Theorem 21 to $\mathcal{M}, w$ and $\mathcal{N}, v$ (with $M_1 = M_2 = \mathrm{MODS}(\mathfrak{L})$) we build up new models. The theorem explicitly states the relationship among them, we will use this result to prove this lemma. Hereafter we will use the same

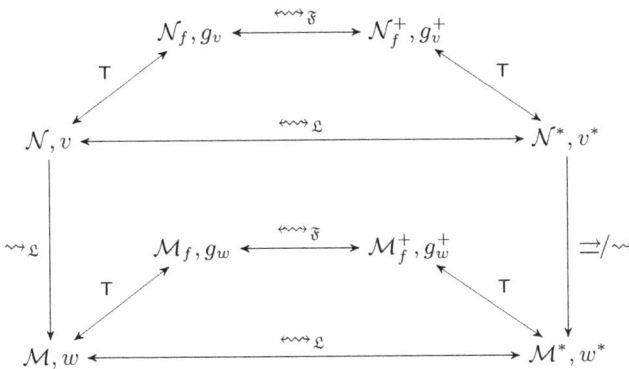

Fig. 1. Directions for the detour

notation as in Theorem 21. The diagram in Fig. 1 helps to illustrate the current situation along with the relationship between the various models. Think of it as a cube. The front face represents the $\mathcal{L}$-models and the back face has the $\mathfrak{F}$-models.

With this new notation the lemma can be restated as follows: Let $\alpha(x)$ be an $\mathcal{L}$-simulation K-invariant $\mathfrak{F}$-formula, if $\mathcal{N}, v \leadsto_{\mathcal{L}} \mathcal{M}, w$ and $\mathcal{N}_f, g_v \models \alpha(x)$ then $\mathcal{M}_f, g_w \models \alpha(x)$.

We can see that, as $\mathcal{N}_f, g_v \models \alpha(x)$ and $\mathcal{N}_f^+, g_v^+$ is elementarily equivalent to $\mathcal{N}_f, g_v$, then $\mathcal{N}_f^+, g_v^+ \models \alpha(x)$. Because $\alpha(x)$ is invariant under $\mathcal{L}$-simulations and $\mathcal{N}^*, v^* \rightleftharpoons_{\mathcal{L}} \mathcal{M}^*, w^*$ we know that $\mathcal{M}_f^+, g_w^+ \models \alpha(x)$. Again by elementary equivalence we finally conclude that $\mathcal{M}_f, g_w \models \alpha(x)$. □

Since $\alpha(x) \in \Sigma(x)$ and $\mathsf{T}(\mathcal{N}, v) \models \Sigma(x)$, aplying this lemma to $\mathcal{M}, w$ and $\mathcal{N}, v$ yields $\mathsf{T}(\mathcal{M}, w) \models \alpha(x)$, and this concludes the proof of the characterization theorem.

We have proved that a $\mathfrak{F}$-formula $\alpha(x)$ is K-equivalent to the translation of an $\mathcal{L}$-formula iff $\alpha(x)$ is K-invariant for $\mathcal{L}$-simulations. We did it by showing that $\alpha(x)$ was equivalent to the translation of the modal consequences of $\alpha(x)$. This was accomplished by taking a detour through the class of ω-saturated *first order* models (Lemma 15).

It is worth noting that the handling of ω-saturated models has been isolated in Theorem 21. After invoking the theorem, we only used the relationships among the models named by it. Also, the requirements for the adequate pair (Definition 9) were used during the proof, e.g., closure under ultraproducts was used for compactness in Theorem 20 and the Hennessy-Milner property of the ω-saturated models was critically used in Theorem 21.

This result can already be applied to many logics, for example, ranging from sub-boolean logics to hybrid or temporal logics. It is important to notice that it allows for a relativization of the first order class of models (called K in the definition of adequate pair). This particular point will be revisited in Section 5 when we draw conclusions over the developed framework.

4 Definability

Definability theorems address the question of which properties of models are definable by means of formulas of a given logic. In this section we answer the question of Definability for $\mathfrak{L}$, our arbitrary logic under study. We present two results in this direction: one considers sets of $\mathfrak{L}$-formulas, and the other a single $\mathfrak{L}$-formula. We begin with definability by a set of $\mathfrak{L}$-formulas.

Theorem 16 (Definability by a set). *Let* $\langle \mathfrak{L}, \mathsf{K} \rangle$ *be an adequate pair and let* $\mathsf{M} \subseteq \mathrm{PMODS}(\mathfrak{L})$. *Then* M *is definable by a set of* $\mathfrak{L}$-*formulas iff* M *is closed under* $\mathfrak{L}$-*simulations*, $\mathsf{T}(\mathsf{M})$ *is closed under ultraproducts and* $\mathsf{T}(\overline{\mathsf{M}})$ *is closed under ultrapowers.*

Proof. From left to right, suppose that M is defined by the set Γ of $\mathfrak{L}$-formulas and there is a model $\langle \mathcal{M}, w \rangle \in \mathsf{M}$ such that $\mathcal{M}, w \rightrightarrows \mathcal{N}, v$ for some pointed model $\mathcal{N}, v$. Since $\langle \mathcal{M}, w \rangle \in \mathsf{M}$, we have $\mathcal{M}, w \models \Gamma$. By simulation preservation we have $\mathcal{N}, v \models \Gamma$ and therefore $\langle \mathcal{N}, v \rangle \in \mathsf{M}$. Hence M is closed under $\mathfrak{L}$-simulations.

To see that $\mathsf{T}(\mathsf{M})$ is closed under ultraproducts we take a family of models $\langle \mathcal{M}_i^f, g_i \rangle \in \mathsf{T}(\mathsf{M})$. As $\mathcal{M}_i^f \models \mathsf{Tf}_x(\Gamma)$ for all i then, by [8, Theorem 4.1.9], the ultraproduct $\prod_D \mathcal{M}_i^f \models \mathsf{Tf}_x(\Gamma)$. We conclude that $\prod_D \mathcal{M}_i^f \in \mathsf{T}(\mathsf{M})$. We still have to check that $\mathsf{T}(\overline{\mathsf{M}})$ is closed under ultrapowers. Take $\langle \mathcal{M}^f, g \rangle \in \mathsf{T}(\overline{\mathsf{M}})$. By definition $\mathcal{M}^f, g \not\models \mathsf{Tf}_x(\Gamma)$. Let $\mathcal{M}_*^f = \prod_D \mathcal{M}^f$ be an ultrapower of $\mathcal{M}^f$. By [8, Corollary 4.1.10], the ultrapower is elementarily equivalent to the original model. Hence, for the canonical mapping $h(x) = \lambda z.g(x)$, we have $\mathcal{M}_*^f, h \not\models \mathsf{Tf}_x(\Gamma)$. This means that $\langle \mathcal{M}_*^f, h \rangle \in \mathsf{T}(\overline{\mathsf{M}})$, therefore $\mathsf{T}(\overline{\mathsf{M}})$ is closed under ultrapowers.

For the right to left direction we proceed as follows: Define the set $\Gamma = \mathsf{Th}(\mathsf{M})$, i.e. Γ is the set of all $\mathfrak{L}$-formulas which are valid in the class M. Trivially $\mathsf{M} \models \Gamma$, and it remains to show that if $\mathcal{M}, w \models \Gamma$ then $\langle \mathcal{M}, w \rangle \in \mathsf{M}$. We define the following set:

$$\mathsf{NTh}^w(x) = \{ \neg \mathsf{Tf}_x(\varphi) : \varphi \text{ is an } \mathfrak{L}\text{-formula and } \mathcal{M}, w \not\models \varphi \}.$$

Using a compactness argument it can be shown that $\mathsf{NTh}^w(x)$ is satisfiable in $\mathsf{T}(\mathsf{M})$. Suppose not, then by Theorem 20, there exists a finite $\Gamma_0 \subseteq \Gamma$ such that $\Gamma_0 = \{ \neg\sigma_1, \ldots, \neg\sigma_n \}$ is not satisfiable in $\mathsf{T}(\mathsf{M})$. This means that the formula $\psi = \mathsf{Tf}_x^{-1}(\sigma_1 \vee \cdots \vee \sigma_n)$ is valid in M therefore $\psi \in \Gamma$. This is absurd because $\mathcal{M}, w \not\models \sigma_i$ for any i and by hypothesis $\mathcal{M}, w \models \Gamma$. We conclude that there is a model $\langle \mathcal{N}, v \rangle \in \mathsf{M}$ such that $\mathsf{T}(\mathcal{N}, v) \models \mathsf{NTh}^w(x)$. Observe that $\mathcal{N}, v \rightsquigarrow \mathcal{M}, w$.

Let $\mathcal{M}, w \models \Gamma$ and suppose by contradiction that $\langle \mathcal{M}, w \rangle \in \overline{\mathsf{M}}$. Using Theorem 21 (with $\mathsf{M}_1 = \overline{\mathsf{M}}, \mathsf{M}_2 = \mathsf{M}$) we conclude that there exist ω-saturated extensions $\langle \mathcal{N}^*, v^* \rangle \in \mathsf{M}$ and $\langle \mathcal{M}^*, w^* \rangle \in \overline{\mathsf{M}}$ such that $\mathcal{N}^*, v^* \rightrightarrows \mathcal{M}^*, w^*$. As M is closed under $\mathfrak{L}$-simulations then $\langle \mathcal{M}, w \rangle \in \mathsf{M}$ and this is a contradiction. □

The above result gives sufficient and necessary conditions for a class of $\mathfrak{L}$-models to be definable by a set of $\mathfrak{L}$-formulas. It is worth noting most of the work is done in the first order side and therefore detached from $\mathfrak{L}$. In the last part of the theorem we make use of Theorem 21 which connects both logics through the class of ω-saturated models. This gives us another hint that this theorem isolates the very core of characterization and definability results.

Our second result considers classes of models definable by a *single* formula. To prove the result we first need the following lemmas:

Lemma 17. *Let* $\mathsf{M} \subseteq \mathrm{PMODS}(\mathcal{L})$. *If* M *is closed under* $\mathcal{L}$-*simulations and both* $\mathsf{T}(\mathsf{M})$ *and* $\mathsf{T}(\overline{\mathsf{M}})$ *are closed under ultrapowers then* $\mathsf{T}(\mathsf{M})$ *and* $\mathsf{T}(\overline{\mathsf{M}})$ *are* K-*closed under potential isomorphisms.*

The proof of this lemma can be found in the Appendix. Intuitively, as the notion of $\mathcal{L}$-simulation is at most as strong as that of potential isomorphism then closure under $\mathcal{L}$-simulations should imply closure under partial isomorphisms.

Lemma 18. *Let* $\mathsf{M} \subseteq \mathrm{PMODS}(\mathcal{L})$. *If* M *is closed under* $\mathcal{L}$-*simulations and both* $\mathsf{T}(\mathsf{M})$ *and* $\mathsf{T}(\overline{\mathsf{M}})$ *are closed under ultraproducts then there exists an* $\mathfrak{F}$-*formula* $\alpha(x)$ *such that for every* $\langle \mathcal{M}, g \rangle \in \mathsf{K}$ *we have* $\mathcal{M}, g \models \alpha(x)$ *iff* $\langle \mathcal{M}, g \rangle \in \mathsf{T}(\mathsf{M})$.

Proof. The proof is a combination of Lemma 17 and [13, Theorem A.2]. This last result uses a relativized version of the first order definability theorem (see [13] for details).

Theorem 19 (Definability by a Single Formula). *Let* $\langle \mathcal{L}, \mathsf{K} \rangle$ *be an adequate pair and let* $\mathsf{M} \subseteq \mathrm{PMODS}(\mathcal{L})$. *Then* M *is definable by a single* $\mathcal{L}$-*formula iff* M *is closed under* $\mathcal{L}$-*simulations and both* $\mathsf{T}(\mathsf{M})$ *and* $\mathsf{T}(\overline{\mathsf{M}})$ *are closed under ultraproducts.*

Proof. From left to right, suppose M is definable by a single $\mathcal{L}$-formula φ. Using Theorem 16, as M is defined by the singleton set $T = \{\varphi\}$ we conclude that M is closed under $\mathcal{L}$-simulations and $\mathsf{T}(\mathsf{M})$ is closed under ultraproducts.

To see that $\mathsf{T}(\overline{\mathsf{M}})$ is closed under ultraproducts proceed as follows. Observe that $\mathsf{T}(\overline{\mathsf{M}}) = \mathsf{N} \cap \mathsf{K}$. where $\mathsf{N} = \{\langle \mathcal{M}^f, g \rangle : \mathcal{M}^f, g \models \neg \mathsf{Tf}_x(\varphi)\}$. Observe that the class N is defined by the first order formula $\neg \mathsf{Tf}_x(\varphi)$, thus it is closed under ultraproducts [8]. It is easy to check that the intersection of ultraproduct-closed classes is also closed under ultraproducts. With this final observation we conclude that $\mathsf{T}(\overline{\mathsf{M}})$ is closed under ultraproducts.

For the right to left direction, because M is closed under $\mathcal{L}$-simulations and both $\mathsf{T}(\mathsf{M})$ and $\mathsf{T}(\overline{\mathsf{M}})$ are closed under ultraproducts then, by Lemma 18, there is a first order formula $\alpha(x)$ such that for every $\langle \mathcal{M}^f, g \rangle \in \mathsf{K}$ we have $\mathcal{M}^f, g \models \alpha(x)$ iff $\langle \mathcal{M}^f, g \rangle \in \mathsf{T}(\mathsf{M})$. As M is closed under $\mathcal{L}$-simulations then α is K-invariant for $\mathcal{L}$-simulations. Using Theorem 11 we conclude that $\alpha(x)$ is K-equivalent to the translation of an $\mathcal{L}$-formula φ, which defines M. □

In this result we give necessary and sufficient conditions for a class of $\mathcal{L}$-models to be definable by a single $\mathcal{L}$-formula. The most interesting part is the right to left direction where we use Lemma 18. For this step, standard proofs such as those found in [1,9,10] use *structural* properties of the notion of $\mathcal{L}$-simulation. Namely, symmetry in the case of BML-bisimulation and that $\underline{\leftrightarrow} \subseteq \underline{\rightarrow}_{\mathcal{L}}$ when $\mathcal{L}$ is the negation free basic modal logic and $\underline{\leftrightarrow}$ is the BML-bisimulation relation.

In our case we get, as a corollary of Lemma 17, that in our setting $\cong \subseteq \ \underline{\leftrightarrow}_{\mathfrak{L}}$ for any notion of $\mathfrak{L}$-simulation regardless of its structural definition. Using this fact, the proof goes smoothly.

5 Conclusions and Further Work

We can usually think of many different notions of simulation for a given logic $\mathfrak{L}$ but, which is the correct one? At least, the following property should hold:

$$\text{If } \mathcal{M}, w \ \underline{\leftrightarrow}_{\mathfrak{L}} \ \mathcal{N}, v \text{ then } \mathcal{M}, w \rightsquigarrow_{\mathfrak{L}} \mathcal{N}, v \tag{1}$$

But this is not enough. Suppose that we claim that the right notion of simulation $\underline{\leftrightarrow}_{\mathfrak{L}}$ for the basic modal logic is the equivalence notion for first order (namely, partial isomorphisms). It is clear that we will be able to prove (1) but still $\underline{\leftrightarrow}_{\mathfrak{L}}$ would be too strong.

In the process of finding the right simulation notion, candidates are often checked against finite models, or against image finite models. In those cases, one expects to be able to prove the converse of (1). These classes of models are special cases of ω-saturated models. The main results of this article show that proving the converse of (1) for the class of ω-saturated models is enough to develop the basic model theory for that logic, at least in what respects to Characterization and Definability. This observation stresses the crucial relationship between ω-saturated models and the suitability of a simulation notion for a given logic.

The general framework presented in this work can also be used to give new and unifying proofs of Characterization and Definability for logics where these theorems are well-known to hold, e.g. hybrid logics [13] and temporal logic with *Since* and *Until*. It is worth noting that it can even be used to prove results for non-classical modal logics such as monotonic neighbourhood logics where the models are *not* Kripke models [12]. It also establishes these theorems for logics that have not been investigated so far (e.g., *Memory Logics* [14,15]). In all cases, we only need to check that the requirements in Definition 9 are met.

In general, characterization and definability results are stated with respect to the class of *all models*. For example, BML is the fragment of first order formulas which are bisimulation invariant in the class of *all first models*. The relativization introduced in this framework (the K class in Definition 9) allows a new technique to prove this kind of results. Think of the following motivational example.

The 'Basic Temporal Logic' is a modal logic which has two modalities F and P. The classical perspective on this logic interprets it over Kripke models defined as a tuple $\langle W, R, V \rangle$ such that

$$\mathcal{M}, w \models F\varphi \text{ iff there is a } v \text{ such that } wRv \text{ and } \mathcal{M}, v \models \varphi$$
$$\mathcal{M}, w \models P\varphi \text{ iff there is a } v \text{ such that } vRw \text{ and } \mathcal{M}, v \models \varphi$$

Observe that the F modality can be thought as a normal 'diamond' over the relation R but that is not possible with the P modality. An alternative is to interpret it over Kripke models with two relations R_1, R_2 where K are the models such that $R_2 = R_1^{-1}$. In this case, both modalities can be interpreted as simple 'diamonds' (which have been given fancy names F and P) over R_1 and R_2 respectively. Our framework can be used to obtain characterization and definability results for this perspective. In fact, formulas of this logic are exactly the BML-bisimulation K-invariant fragment of first order.

Although our results cover a big family of logics, they cannot be used to prove Characterization or Definability results for the class of *finite* models. This is an important class which lays beyond our framework, since it is *not* closed under ultraproducts. Many Characterization or Definability theorems are known to hold in the class of finite models [16]. Other logics outside of the scope of this paper are those without *disjuction*. For example, several description logics are known to satisfy preservation theorems but they do not have disjunction in the language (see [17]).

We think that our results can be generalized, without much difficulty, to cover the case without disjunction. On the other hand, the problem found in the class of finite models is much more difficult to avoid. Our result requires K to be closed under ultraproducts because that implies compactness and because we use ultraproducts to get ω-saturated models. Although finite models are ω-saturated, they are not closed under ultraproducts. Further study of proofs that do not use these properties [7,18] may yield a result which would be able to handle more cases uniformly.

Generalizations in this same line of thought have been pursued in the work of Hollenberg, for instance. In [19] relativized versions of the characterization and definability theorems for the so-called *normal* first order definable modalities are stated —though without proof. Those modalities are defined by Σ_1^0-formulas and, therefore, they cannot be used to define the *Since* and *Until* operators of temporal logics. Also, the results obtained in [19] do not take into account sub-boolean logics. Our proofs work for any modality with a first order translation and both boolean and sub-boolean logics. Therefore, they would subsume previous generalizations that we are aware of.

The work done by Areces and Gorín in [20] gives a uniform way to define many modalities by using the standard semantics over a restricted class of models. From our perspective, the most important point of their work is that we get a *unique* notion of model equivalence for every logic that fits in their framework. The right simulation notion turns to be the same as BML's bisimulation.

Not every modality can be expressed within their framework (e.g., the Since and Until operators [21]). Nevertheless, we think that an interesting way to continue the work in this article is to try to expand the framework developed in [20] to support more types of operators. This would allow us to give a 'canonical' simulation notion for a broader set of logics and therefore be able to easily prove the Hennessy-Milner property for them. This line of work definitely looks as a promising path to give an automatic derivation of the Characterization and Definability theorems for a greater set of modal logics.

References

1. Blackburn, P., de Rijke, M., Venema, Y.: Modal Logic. Cambridge University Press, Cambridge (2001)
2. Kamp, H.: Tense Logic and the Theory of Linear Order. PhD thesis, University of Califormia, Los Angeles (1968)
3. Goranko, V., Passy, S.: Using the universal modality: Gains and questions. Journal of Logic and Computation 2(1), 5–30 (1992)
4. de Rijke, M.: The modal logic of inequality. Journal of Symbolic Logic 57, 566–584 (1992)
5. Kozen, D.: Results on the propositional μ-calculus. Theoretical Computer Science 27(3), 333–354 (1983)
6. Sangiorgi, D.: On the origins of bisimulation and coinduction. ACM Trans. Program. Lang. Syst. 31(4), 1–41 (2009)
7. van Benthem, J.: Modal Correspondence Theory. PhD thesis, Universiteit van Amsterdam, Instituut voor Logica en Grondslagenonderzoek van Exacte Wetenschappen (1976)
8. Chang, C.C., Keisler, H.J.: Model Theory. Studies in Logic and the Foundations of Mathematics, vol. 73. Elsevier Science B.V., Amsterdam (1973)
9. Kurtonina, N., de Rijke, M.: Simulating without negation. Journal of Logic and Computation 7, 503–524 (1997)
10. Kurtonina, N., de Rijke, M.: Bisimulations for temporal logic. Journal of Logic, Language and Information 6, 403–425 (1997)
11. Keisler, H.J.: The ultraproduct construction. In: Proceedings of the Ultramath Conference, Pisa, Italy (2008)
12. Hansen, H.H.: Monotonic modal logics. Master's thesis, ILLC, University of Amsterdam (2003)
13. Carreiro, F.: Characterization and definability in modal first-order fragments. Master's thesis, Universidad de Buenos Aires (2010), arXiv:1011.4718
14. Areces, C., Figueira, D., Figueira, S., Mera, S.: Expressive power and decidability for memory logics. In: Hodges, W., de Queiroz, R. (eds.) Logic, Language, Information and Computation. LNCS (LNAI), vol. 5110, pp. 56–68. Springer, Heidelberg (2008)
15. Areces, C., Figueira, D., Figueira, S., Mera, S.: The expressive power of memory logics. Review of Symbolic Logic (to appear)
16. Rosen, E.: Modal logic over finite structures. Journal of Logic, Language and Information 6, 95–27 (1995)
17. Kurtonina, N., de Rijke, M.: Classifying description logics. In: Brachman, R.J., Donini, F.M., Franconi, E., Horrocks, I., Levy, A.Y., Rousset, M.C. (eds.) Description Logics. URA-CNRS, vol. 410 (1997)
18. Otto, M.: Elementary proof of the van Benthem-Rosen characterisation theorem. Technical Report 2342, Department of Mathematics, Technische Universität Darmstadt (2004)
19. Hollenberg, M.: Logic and Bisimulation. PhD thesis, Philosophical Institute, Utrecht University (1998)
20. Areces, C., Gorín, D.: Coinductive models and normal forms for modal logics. Journal of Applied Logic (2010) (to appear)
21. Blackburn, P., van Benthem, J., Wolter, F.: Handbook of Modal Logic. Studies in Logic and Practical Reasoning, vol. 3. Elsevier Science Inc., New York (2006)

Appendix

Theorem 20 (First order compactness relative to a class of models).
Let C *be a class of first order models which is closed under ultraproducts and let* Σ *be a set of first order formulas. If every finite set* $\Delta \subseteq \Sigma$ *has a model in* C *then there is a model in* C *for* Σ.

Proof. Let $\mathcal{M}_i^f$ be a model for each finite subset $\Delta_i \subseteq \Sigma$, algebraic proofs of the compactness theorem [11, Theorem 4.3] show that the ultraproduct of the models $\mathcal{M} = \prod_U \mathcal{M}_i^f$ satisfies $\mathcal{M} \models \Sigma$ (with a suitable ultrafilter U). As each $\mathcal{M}_i^f$ is in C and C is closed under ultraproducts we conclude that $\mathcal{M} \in$ C.

The above argument proves the theorem for the case where Σ is a set of sentences. If Σ has some formulas with free variables $x_1, x_2, \dots$ we proceed as follows. We extend the original first order language with constants $\overline{x}_1, \overline{x}_2, \dots$ and use the above result with a new set Σ' where each free appearance of x_i has been replaced by $\overline{x}_i$. It is left to the reader to check that this transformation preserves satisfiability. $\square$

Theorem 21. *Let* $\langle \mathfrak{L}, \mathsf{K} \rangle$ *be an adequate pair and let* $\mathsf{M}_1, \mathsf{M}_2 \subseteq \mathrm{MODS}(\mathfrak{L})$ *be two classes such that* $\mathsf{T}(\mathsf{M}_1)$ *and* $\mathsf{T}(\mathsf{M}_2)$ *are closed under ultrapowers. Let* $\mathcal{M} \in \mathsf{M}_1$ *and* $\mathcal{N} \in \mathsf{M}_2$ *be two* $\mathfrak{L}$-*models such that for some* $w \in |\mathcal{M}|$, $v \in |\mathcal{N}|$ *they satisfy* $\mathcal{N}, v \rightsquigarrow_{\mathfrak{L}} \mathcal{M}, w$. *Then there exist models* $\mathcal{M}^* \in \mathsf{M}_1$ *and* $\mathcal{N}^* \in \mathsf{M}_2$ *and elements* $w^* \in |\mathcal{M}^*|$, $v^* \in |\mathcal{N}^*|$ *such that*

1. $\mathsf{T}(\mathcal{M}, w) \leftrightsquigarrow_{\mathfrak{F}} \mathsf{T}(\mathcal{M}^*, w^*)$ *and* $\mathsf{T}(\mathcal{N}, v) \leftrightsquigarrow_{\mathfrak{F}} \mathsf{T}(\mathcal{N}^*, v^*)$
   Their translations are pairwise elementarily equivalent.
2. $\mathcal{M}, w \leftrightsquigarrow_{\mathfrak{L}} \mathcal{M}^*, w^*$ *and* $\mathcal{N}, v \leftrightsquigarrow_{\mathfrak{L}} \mathcal{N}^*, v^*$
   They are pairwise $\mathfrak{L}$-*equivalent.*
3. $\mathcal{N}^*, v^* \rightleftarrows_{\mathfrak{L}} \mathcal{M}^*, w^*$
   There is a simulation from $\mathcal{N}^*, v^*$ *to* $\mathcal{M}^*, w^*$.

Proof. We define some terminology for the models with which we will be working on before starting with the proof. Call $\mathcal{M}_f, g_w = \mathsf{T}(\mathcal{M}, w)$ and $\mathcal{N}_f, g_v = \mathsf{T}(\mathcal{N}, v)$. Take $\mathcal{M}_f^+, \mathcal{N}_f^+$ to be ω-saturated ultrapowers of $\mathcal{M}_f$ and $\mathcal{N}_f$. As the classes are closed under ultrapowers, the saturated models lay in the same class as the original models.

By [8, Corollary 4.1.13] we have an elementary embedding $d : |\mathcal{M}_f| \to |\mathcal{M}_f^+|$. Let g_w^+ be an assignment for $\mathcal{M}_f^+$ such that $g_w^+(x) = d(g_w(x))$. Take the modal preimage of $\mathcal{M}_f^+, g_w^+$ and call it $\mathcal{M}^*, w^* = \mathsf{T}^{-1}(\mathcal{M}_f^+, g_w^+)$. We repeat the same process and assign similar names to models and points deriving from $\mathcal{N}$.

1. As a consequence of [8, Corollary 4.1.13], since there is an elementary embedding, we have that $\mathcal{M}_f, g_w \leftrightsquigarrow_{\mathfrak{F}} \mathcal{M}_f^+, g_w^+$. The same argument works with $\mathcal{N}_f$ and $\mathcal{N}_f^+$.
2. Following the last point, we can conclude, through the truth-preserving translations, that $\mathcal{M}, w \leftrightsquigarrow_{\mathfrak{L}} \mathcal{M}^*, w^*$. The same proof works with $\mathcal{N}, v$ and $\mathcal{N}^*, v^*$. Corollary: $\mathcal{N}^*, v^* \rightsquigarrow_{\mathfrak{L}} \mathcal{M}^*, w^*$.

3. As both $\mathcal{M}_f^+$ and $\mathcal{N}_f^+$ are ω-saturated, by definition of adequate pair, that implies that they have the Hennesy-Milner property. Therefore, because we proved that $\mathcal{N}^*, v^* \rightsquigarrow_{\mathfrak{L}} \mathcal{M}^*, w^*$ we conclude that $\mathcal{N}^*, v^* \rightleftharpoons_{\mathfrak{L}} \mathcal{M}^*, w^*$. □

Lemma 17. *Let* M $\subseteq$ PMODS($\mathfrak{L}$). *If* M *is closed under $\mathfrak{L}$-simulations and both* T(M) *and* T($\overline{\text{M}}$) *are closed under ultrapowers then* T(M) *and* T($\overline{\text{M}}$) *are* K-*closed under potential isomorphisms.*

Proof. Suppose that T(M) is not K-closed under potential isomorphisms. This means that there exist models $\langle \mathcal{M}^f, g \rangle \in$ T(M) and $\langle \mathcal{N}^f, h \rangle \in$ T($\overline{\text{M}}$) such that $\mathcal{M}^f, g \cong \mathcal{N}^f, h$. Recall that K $\setminus$ T(M) = T($\overline{\text{M}}$). For a smoother proof, call their modal counterparts $\mathcal{M}, w$ and $\mathcal{N}, v$ respectively. Therefore $\langle \mathcal{M}, w \rangle \in$ M and $\langle \mathcal{N}, v \rangle \notin$ M.

As $\mathcal{M}^f, g \cong \mathcal{N}^f, h$ we know by [8, Proposition 2.4.4] that $\mathcal{M}^f, g \models \varphi(x)$ if and only if $\mathcal{N}^f, h \models \varphi(x)$. In particular they have the same modal theory, $\mathcal{M}, w \leftrightsquigarrow_{\mathfrak{L}} \mathcal{N}, v$. As this implies that $\mathcal{M}, w \rightsquigarrow_{\mathfrak{L}} \mathcal{N}, v$ we can use Theorem 21 (instantiating with $K_1 =$ T(M), $K_2 =$ T($\overline{\text{M}}$) and $\mathcal{M}, \mathcal{N}$ interchanged) and get models $\langle \mathcal{M}^*, w^* \rangle \in$ M and $\langle \mathcal{N}^*, v^* \rangle \in \overline{\text{M}}$ such that $\mathcal{M}^*, w^* \rightleftharpoons_{\mathfrak{L}} \mathcal{N}^*, v^*$.

Knowing that $\mathcal{M}^*, w^* \rightleftharpoons_{\mathfrak{L}} \mathcal{N}^*, v^*$ and that M is closed under simulations we conclude that $\langle \mathcal{N}^*, v^* \rangle \in$ M. This is absurd because it contradicts $\langle \mathcal{N}^*, v^* \rangle \in \overline{\text{M}}$. Hence $T_K(\text{M})$ is K-closed under potential isomorphisms.

To see that T($\overline{\text{M}}$) is K-closed under potential isomorphisms we argue by contradicction. Suppose it is not the case, then there exist $\langle \mathcal{M}^f, g \rangle \in$ T($\overline{\text{M}}$) and $\langle \mathcal{N}^f, h \rangle \in$ K $\setminus$ T($\overline{\text{M}}$) such that $\mathcal{M}^f, g \cong \mathcal{N}^f, h$. As $\langle \mathcal{N}^f, h \rangle \in$ K $\setminus$ T($\overline{\text{M}}$) this means that $\langle \mathcal{N}^f, h \rangle \in$ T(M). We have just proved that T(M) is K-closed under potential isomorphism then, as $\mathcal{M}^f, g \cong \mathcal{N}^f, h$ (and because of the symmetry of the potential isomorphism relation), we conclude that $\langle \mathcal{M}^f, g \rangle \in$ T(M) which contradicts our hypothesis. Absurd. □

On the Complexity of Szilard Languages of Regulated Grammars

Liliana Cojocaru and Erkki Mäkinen

University of Tampere
School of Information Sciences, Computer Science
Kanslerinrinne 1, Tampere, FIN-33014, Finland
cslico@uta.fi, em@cs.uta.fi

Abstract. We investigate computational resources used by alternating Turing machines (ATMs) to accept Szilard languages (SZLs) of regulated rewriting grammars. The main goal is to relate these languages to low-level complexity classes such as $\mathcal{NC}^1$ and $\mathcal{NC}^2$. We focus on the derivation process in random context grammars (RCGs) with context-free rules. We prove that unrestricted SZLs and leftmost-1 SZLs of RCGs can be accepted by ATMs in logarithmic time and space. Hence, these languages belong to the U_{E^*}-uniform $\mathcal{NC}^1$ class. Leftmost-i SZLs, $i \in \{2,3\}$, of RCGs can be accepted by ATMs in logarithmic space and square logarithmic time. Consequently, these languages belong to $\mathcal{NC}^2$. Moreover, we give results on SZLs of RCGs with phrase-structure rules and present several applications on SZLs of other regulated rewriting grammars.

Keywords: regulated rewriting grammars, Szilard languages, alternating Turing machines, $\mathcal{NC}^1$ and $\mathcal{NC}^2$ complexity classes.

1 Introduction

A *Szilard language* (SZL) provides information concerning the derivational structures in a formal grammar. If labels are associated with productions in one-to-one correspondence, then each terminal derivation can be expressed as a word over the set of labels, such that labels in this word are concatenated in the same order they have been used during the derivation. Informally, the SZL associated with a generative device is the set of all words obtained in this way. If restrictions are imposed on the derivation order then particular classes of SZLs, such as *leftmost Szilard languages* [12], [20] are obtained. Consequently, SZLs have been used to study closure, decidability, and complexity properties of derivations in several types of grammars, such as Chomsky grammars [11], [13], [15], [16], [21], or regulated rewriting grammars [5], [6], [14], [20], [21].

Characterizations of (leftmost) SZLs of CFGs and phrase-structure (unrestricted) grammars (PSGs) in terms of Turing machine resources are provided in [11] and [16]. In [16] it is proved that unrestricted SZLs and leftmost SZLs of CFGs can be recognized by a linear bounded (realtime) multicounter machine. Since each realtime multicounter machine can be simulated by a deterministic

A. Cerone and P. Pihlajasaari (Eds.): ICTAC 2011, LNCS 6916, pp. 77–94, 2011.

off-line[1] Turing machine with logarithmic space, in terms of the length of the input string [8], it follows that the classes of unrestricted SZLs and leftmost SZLs associated with CFGs are contained[2] in DSPACE($\log n$). In [3] we strengthened this result by proving that these classes of SZLs can be accepted by an indexing alternating Turing machine (ATM) in logarithmic time and space. Since the class of languages recognizable by an indexing ATM in logarithmic time equals the U_{E^*}-uniform $\mathcal{NC}^1$ class [19], we obtain that the above classes of SZLs are strictly contained in $\mathcal{NC}^1$. In [11] it is proved that $\log n$ is the optimal space bound for an *on-line*[3] deterministic Turing machine to recognize (leftmost) SZLs of CFGs. It is also an optimal bound for an off-line deterministic Turing machine to recognize leftmost SZLs of PSGs. However, the optimal bound for an on-line deterministic Turing machine to recognize leftmost SZLs of CFGs and PSGs is n, where n is the length of the input word. Since leftmost SZLs of PSGs are off-line recognizable by a deterministic Turing machine that uses only logarithmic space, in terms of the length of the input string, it follows that the class of leftmost SZLs of PSGs is contained in DSPACE($\log n$). In [3] we proved that this class is strictly included in $\mathcal{NC}^1$ under the U_{E^*}-uniformity restriction.

For formal definitions and results on computational models, such as (realtime) multicounter machines, (off-line and on-line) Turing machines, and (indexing) ATMs the reader is referred to [1], [2], [8], and [10].

Regulated rewriting grammars are classes of Chomsky grammars with restricted use of productions. The regulated rewriting mechanism in these grammars obeys several filters and controlling constraints that allow or prohibit the use of the rules during the generative process. There exists a wide variety of regulated rewriting mechanisms [5], which enriches the Chomsky hierarchy with various language classes. They are useful because each of them uses totally different regulating restrictions, providing thus structures to handle problems in formal language theory, programming languages, computational linguistics, grammatical inference, learning theory, and graph grammars [5].

In this paper we focus on the derivation mechanism in *random context grammars* (RCGs) with context-free rules by studying their SZLs. The main aim is to relate classes of SZLs of RCGs to parallel complexity classes, such as ALOGTIME, $\mathcal{NC}^1$ and $\mathcal{NC}^2$. We recall that $ALOGTIME$ is the class of languages recognizable by an indexing (random-access) ATM in logarithmic time [2]. For each integer i, the $\mathcal{NC}^i$ class is the class of Boolean functions computable by polynomial size Boolean circuits with depth $\mathcal{O}(\log^i n)$ and fan-in two. $ALOGTIME$ is equal to U_{E^*}-uniform $\mathcal{NC}^1$ [19]. For $i \geq 2$, $\mathcal{NC}^i = ATIME\text{-}SPACE(\log^i n, \log n)$ [19]. For more results, relationships and hierarchies on

---

[1] An *off-line* Turing machine is a Turing machine equipped with a read-only input tape and a read-write working tape. It is allowed to shift both heads on both directions. Otherwise, it works similar to a Turing machine.

[2] DSPACE($\log n$) is the class of languages recognizable by a deterministic (off-line) Turing machine using logarithmic space.

[3] An *on-line* Turing machine is an off-line Turing machine with the restriction that the input head cannot be shifted to the left.

complexity classes, such as DSPACE($\log n$), ALOGTIME, and $\mathcal{NC}^i$, $i \geq 1$, the reader is referred to [1], [19], and [22].

The methods presented for SZLs of RCGs are afterward applied for other regulated rewriting grammars. Approaching classes of SZLs of regulated rewriting grammars to low-level complexity classes is the most natural way to relate SZLs to circuit complexity classes. This may bring new insights in finding fast parallel algorithms to recognize languages generated by regulated rewriting grammars.

Our contribution. We prove that unrestricted SZLs and leftmost-1 SZLs of RCGs with CF rules can be accepted by indexing ATMs in logarithmic time and space (Sections 3). According to [19] these languages belong also to the U_{E^*}-uniform $\mathcal{NC}^1$ class. Leftmost-i SZLs [5], $i \in \{2, 3\}$, of RCGs with CF rules can be accepted by indexing ATMs in logarithmic space and square logarithmic time (Section 3). Hence, these classes of languages belong to $\mathcal{NC}^2$ [19]. The results presented for SZLs of RCGs with CF rules are then generalized for RCGs with PS rules (Section 4). The methods used for SZLs of RCGs are extended for other regulated rewriting grammars such as programmed grammars, matrix grammars, regularly controlled grammars, valence grammars and conditional RCGs (Section 5).

2   SZLs of RCGs - Prerequisites

The aim of this section is to introduce the main concepts concerning SZLs of RCGs. We assume the reader to be familiar with the basic notions of formal language theory [10]. For an alphabet X, X^* denotes the free monoid generated by X. By $|x|_a$ we denote the number of occurrences of letter a in the string x.

RCGs are regulated rewriting grammars in which the application of a rule is enabled by the existence in the current sentential form of some nonterminals that provides the *context* under which the rule can be applied. The use of a rule may be disabled by the existence in the sentential form of some nonterminals that provide the *forbidden context* under which the rule in question cannot be applied. RCGs with CF rules have been introduced in [23] to cover the gap existing between the classes of context-free languages and context-sensitive languages. A generalization of RCGs for PS rules can be found in [5]. The generative capacity and several descriptional properties of these regulated rewriting grammars can be found in [4], [5], [7], [23], and [24].

Definition 1. A *random context grammar* is a quadruple $G = (N, T, S, P)$ where S is the axiom, N and T, $N \cap T = \emptyset$, are finite sets of *nonterminals* and *terminals*, respectively. P is a finite set of *triplets* (random context rules) of the form $r = (p_r, Q_r, R_r)$, where p_r is an unrestricted Chomsky rule, Q_r and R_r are subsets of N, called the *permitting* and *forbidding context* of r, respectively. If $R_r = \emptyset$, for any $r \in P$, then G is a *permitting* RCG. If $Q_r = \emptyset$, for any $r \in P$, then G is a *forbidding* RCG.

A permitting RCG is a RCG without appearance checking. If $R \neq \emptyset$, then the grammar is called a RCG with appearance checking (henceforth RCG^{ac}).

80   L. Cojocaru and E. Mäkinen

Definition 2. Let $G = (N, T, S, P)$ be a RCG^{ac} and $V = N \cup T$. The language $L(G)$ generated by G is defined as the set of all words $w \in T^*$ such that there is a derivation D: $S = w_0 \Rightarrow_{r_{i_1}} w_1 \Rightarrow_{r_{i_2}} w_2 \Rightarrow_{r_{i_3}} \ldots \Rightarrow_{r_{i_s}} w_s = w$, $s \geq 1$, where $r_{i_j} = (\alpha_{i_j} \to \beta_{i_j}, Q_{i_j}, R_{i_j})$, $1 \leq j \leq s-1$, $w_{j-1} = w'_{j-1}\alpha_{i_j}w''_{j-1}$, $w_j = w'_{j-1}\beta_{i_j}w''_{j-1}$ for some $w'_{j-1}, w''_{j-1} \in V^*$, all symbols in Q_{i_j} occur in $w'_{j-1}w''_{j-1}$, and no symbol of R_{i_j} occur in $w'_{j-1}w''_{j-1}$.

If labels are associated with triplets $r = (p_r, Q_r, R_r)$, in one-to-one correspondence, then the SZL of a RCG^{ac} is defined as follows.

Definition 3. Let $G = (N, T, S, P)$ be a RCG^{ac}, $P = \{r_1, r_2, ..., r_k\}$ the set of productions, $L(G)$ the language generated by G, and $w \in L(G)$. The *Szilard word* of w associated with derivation D: $S = w_0 \Rightarrow_{r_{i_1}} w_1 \Rightarrow_{r_{i_2}} w_2 \Rightarrow_{r_{i_3}} \ldots \Rightarrow_{r_{i_s}} w_s = w$, $s \geq 1$, is defined as $Sz_D(w) = r_{i_1}r_{i_2}...r_{i_s}$, $r_{i_j} \in P$, $1 \leq j \leq s$. The *Szilard language* of G is $Sz(G) = \{Sz_D(w) | w \in L(G), D$ is a derivation of $w\}$.

Hence, the productions and their unique labels are used identically.

To reduce the nondeterminism in RCGs^{ac} three types of leftmost derivations have been defined for RCGs^{ac} with CF rules [4], [5].

Definition 4. Let $G = (N, T, S, P)$ be a RCGs^{ac}. A derivation in G is called

- *leftmost-1* if each rule used in the derivation rewrites the leftmost nonterminal occurring in the current sentential form,
- *leftmost-2* if at each step of derivation, the leftmost occurrence of a nonterminal which can be rewritten has to be rewritten[4],
- *leftmost-3* if each rule used in the derivation rewrites the leftmost occurrence of its left-hand side in the current sentential form.

SZLs associated with leftmost-i, $i \in \{1, 2, 3\}$, derivations are defined in the same way as in Definition 3, with the specification that D is a leftmost-i derivation of w. We denote by $SZRC^{ac}(CF)$ and $SZRCL_i^{ac}(CF)$ the classes of SZLs and leftmost-i SZLs of RCGs^{ac} with CF rules, respectively.

Henceforth, in any reference to a RCG, $G = (N, T, A_1, P)$, A_1 is considered to be the axiom, $N = \{A_1, ..., A_m\}$ the ordered finite set of nonterminals, and $P = \{r_1, r_2, ..., r_k\}$ the ordered finite set of labels associated with triplets in P. Unless otherwise specified (as in Section 4), each rule p_r of a triplet $r \in P$ is a CF rule of the form $\alpha_{p_r} \to \beta_{p_r}$, $\alpha_{p_r} \in N$, and $\beta_{p_r} \in (N \cup T)^*$. If $\beta_{p_r} \in T^*$, then p_r is called *terminal* rule. Otherwise, p_r is called *non-terminal* rule.

For each RC rule $r = (p_r, Q_r, R_r) \in P$ the *net effect* or rule p_r with respect to each nonterminal $A_l \in N$, $1 \leq l \leq m$, is given by $df_{A_l}(p_r) = |\beta_{p_r}|_{A_l} - |\alpha_{p_r}|_{A_l}$. To each rule r we associate a vector $V(r) \in \mathbf{Z}^m$ defined by $V(r) = (df_{A_1}(p_r),$

---

[4] In other words, the RC rule $r = (p_r, Q_r, R_r)$ can be applied in leftmost-2 derivation manner if p_r rewrites the leftmost nonterminal X that can be rewritten by any rule eligible to be applied on the current sentential form, in the sense that if any other RC rule $\bar{r} = (p_{\bar{r}}, Q_{\bar{r}}, R_{\bar{r}}) \in P$ can be applied on the sentential form, because it contains all nonterminals in $Q_{\bar{r}}$ and no nonterminal in $R_{\bar{r}}$, without counting one occurrence of X', then the nonterminal X' rewritten by $\bar{r}$ is either equal to X, case in which the rule is nondeterministically chosen, or X' follows X in this sentential form.

$df_{A_2}(p_r), ..., df_{A_m}(p_r))$, where $\mathbf{Z}$ is the set of integers. The value of $V(r)$ taken at the lth place, $1 \le l \le m$, is denoted by $V_l(r)$.

3   On the Complexity of SZLs of RCGs

In this section we focus on the complexity of SZLs of RCGs^{ac} with CF rules. All results presented for RCGs^{ac} hold also for RCGs without appearance checking.

We recall that an indexing ATM is an ATM that is allowed to write any binary number on a special tape, called *index* tape. This number is interpreted as an address of a location on the input tape. With i, written in binary on the index tape, the machine can read the symbol placed on the ith cell of the input tape. In terms of indexing ATM resources, for SZLs associated with unrestricted derivations in RCGs^{ac} with CF rules, we have the next result.

Theorem 1. *Each language $L \in SZRC^{ac}(CF)$ can be recognized by an indexing ATM in $\mathcal{O}(\log n)$ time and space $(SZRC^{ac}(CF) \subseteq ALOGTIME)$.*

Proof. Let $G = (N, T, P, A_1)$ be an arbitrary RCG^{ac} with CF rules. We describe an indexing ATM that decides in logarithmic time and space whether an input word $\gamma = \gamma_1\gamma_2...\gamma_n \in P^*$ of length n, belongs to $Sz(G)$. Let $\mathcal{A}$ be an indexing ATM composed of an input tape that stores γ, an index tape, and a working tape composed of three tracks. Here and throughout this paper, each label γ_i corresponds to a triplet in P of the form $(p_{\gamma_i}, Q_{\gamma_i}, R_{\gamma_i})$, where p_{γ_i} is a CF rule of the form $\alpha_{\gamma_i} \to \beta_{\gamma_i}$, $\alpha_{\gamma_i} \in N$, and $\beta_{\gamma_i} \in (N \cup T)^*$, $1 \le i \le n$.

At the beginning of the computation the first track stores $k + 1$ vectors, V^0 corresponding to the axiom, i.e, $V_1^0 = 1$ and $V_l^0 = 0$, $2 \le l \le m$, and $V(r_i)$, $1 \le i \le k$. The other two tracks are initially empty.

Level 1 (*Existential*). In an existential state $\mathcal{A}$ guesses the length of γ, i.e., writes on the index tape n, and checks whether the nth cell of the input tape contains a terminal symbol and the cell $n + 1$ contains no symbol. The correct value of n is recorded in binary on the second track of the working tape.

Level 2 (*Universal*). $\mathcal{A}$ spawns n universal processes $\wp_i$, $1 \le i \le n$.

- On $\wp_1$, $\mathcal{A}$ checks whether $\alpha_{\gamma_1} = A_1$. Process $\wp_1$ returns 1 if this equality holds.
- For each $\wp_i$, $2 \le i \le n$, $\mathcal{A}$ counts the number of occurrences of each rule $r_j \in P$, $1 \le j \le k$, in $\gamma^{(i)} = \gamma_1\gamma_2...\gamma_{i-1}$. Suppose that each r_j occurs $c_j^{(i)}$ times, $0 \le c_j^{(i)} \le i-1$, in $\gamma^{(i)}$. $\mathcal{A}$ computes $s_{A_l}^{(i)} = V_l^0 + \sum_{j=1}^{k} c_j^{(i)} V_l(r_j)$, i.e., the number of times each nonterminal A_l, $1 \le l \le m$, occurs in the sentential form obtained at the ith step of derivation. Besides, for $\wp_n$, for each $1 \le l \le m$, $\mathcal{A}$ computes $s_{A_l}^{(n,out)} = V_l^0 + \sum_{j=1}^{k} c_j^{(n)} V_l(r_j) + V_l(\gamma_n)$. Each $\wp_i$, $2 \le i \le n-1$, returns 1 if only one of the conditions $1-3$ holds. Process $\wp_n$ returns 1, if one of the conditions $1-3$ holds, and besides $s_{A_l}^{(n,out)} = 0$, for each $1 \le l \le m$.

1. $s_{\alpha_{\gamma_i}}^{(i)} \ge 1$, $\alpha_{\gamma_i} \notin Q_{\gamma_i} \cup R_{\gamma_i}$, $s_X^{(i)} \ge 1$, for each $X \in Q_{\gamma_i}$, and $s_Y^{(i)} = 0$ for each $Y \in R_{\gamma_i}$,

2. $s_{\alpha_{\gamma_i}}^{(i)} \geq 2$ if $\alpha_{\gamma_i} \in Q_{\gamma_i} - R_{\gamma_i}$, $s_X^{(i)} \geq 1$, for each $X \in Q_{\gamma_i}$, $X \neq \alpha_{\gamma_i}$, and $s_Y^{(i)} = 0$ for each $Y \in R_{\gamma_i}$,

3. $s_{\alpha_{\gamma_i}}^{(i)} = 1$ if $\alpha_{\gamma_i} \in R_{\gamma_i} - Q_{\gamma_i}$, $s_X^{(i)} \geq 1$, for each $X \in Q_{\gamma_i}$, and $s_Y^{(i)} = 0$ for each $Y \in R_{\gamma_i}$, $Y \neq \alpha_{\gamma_i}$.

The computation tree of $\mathcal{A}$ has only two levels, in which each node has unbounded out-degree. By using a divide and conquer algorithm each of these levels can be converted into a binary tree of height $\mathcal{O}(\log n)$. All functions used in the algorithm, such as counting and addition, are in $\mathcal{NC}^1$, which is equal to ALOG-TIME under the U_{E^*}-uniformity restriction [19]. In order to store, on the third track of the working tape, the binary value of $c_j^{(i)}$, and to compute in binary $s_{A_l}^{(i)}$ and $s_{A_l}^{(n,out)}$, $1 \leq i \leq n$, $1 \leq j \leq k$, $1 \leq l \leq m$, $\mathcal{A}$ needs $\mathcal{O}(\log n)$ space. Hence, for the whole computation $\mathcal{A}$ uses $\mathcal{O}(\log n)$ time and space. $\qquad\square$

Corollary 1. $SZRC^{ac}(CF) \subset \mathcal{NC}^1$.

Proof. The claim is a direct consequence of Theorem 1 and results in [19]. The inclusion is strict since there exists $L = \{p^n | n \geq 0\} \in \mathcal{NC}^1 - SZRC^{ac}(CF)$. $\quad\square$

Corollary 2. $SZRC^{ac}(CF) \subset DSPACE(\log n)$.

Theorem 2. *Each language $L \in SZRCL_1^{ac}(CF)$ can be recognized by an indexing ATM in $\mathcal{O}(\log n)$ time and space ($SZRCL_1^{ac}(CF) \subseteq ALOGTIME$).*

Proof. Let $G = (N, T, P, A_1)$ be a RCG^{ac} with CF rules working in leftmost-1 derivation manner. Consider an indexing ATM $\mathcal{A}$ having a similar structure as in the proof of Theorem 1. Let $\gamma \in P^*$, $\gamma = \gamma_1 \gamma_2 ... \gamma_n$, be an input word of length n. In order to guess the length of γ, $\mathcal{A}$ proceeds with the procedure described at Level 1-*Existential*, Theorem 1. Then $\mathcal{A}$ spawns (Level 2-*Universal*) n universal processes $\wp_i$, $1 \leq i \leq n$, and (briefly) proceeds as follows.

For each $\wp_i$, $1 \leq i \leq n$, $\mathcal{A}$ checks as in Theorem 1, whether each triplet γ_i can be applied on $\gamma^{(i)} = \gamma_1 \gamma_2 ... \gamma_{i-1}$ according to Definition 2. Then $\mathcal{A}$ checks whether rule p_{γ_i} can be applied in a leftmost-1 derivation manner on $\gamma^{(i)}$. To do so, $\mathcal{A}$ spawns at most $i - 1$ existential branches (Level 3-*Existential*) each branch corresponding to a label γ_v, $1 \leq v \leq i - 1$, such that p_{γ_v} in $(p_{\gamma_v}, Q_{\gamma_v}, R_{\gamma_v})$ is a non-terminal rule. Denote by q the number of non-terminal rules used in γ between γ_{v+1} and γ_{i-1} (including γ_{v+1} and γ_{i-1}), and by s_q the total number of nonterminals produced by these rules, and let $s = i - v - s_q$. $\mathcal{A}$ checks whether α_{γ_i} is the sth nonterminal occurring on the right-hand side[5] of rule p_{γ_v}.

---

[5] If p_{γ_v} is the rule that produces the nonterminal rewritten by rule p_{γ_i}, and this is the sth nonterminal occurring on the right-hand side of p_{γ_v}, then for the case of leftmost-1 derivation order, we must have $s + s_q = i - v$. This is because each nonterminal produced in the sentential form by rules used in a leftmost-1 derivation manner, between p_{γ_v} and p_{γ_i} (including nonterminals existing up to the sth nonterminal on the right-hand side of p_{γ_v}), must be fully rewritten by these rules. The nonterminals existing in the sentential form before p_{γ_v} has been applied, will be rewritten only after the new nonterminals produced between p_{γ_v} and p_{γ_i} are fully rewritten.

An existential branch spawned at Level 3, is labeled by 1 if p_{γ_v} satisfies these properties. For each existential branch labeled by 1 at Level 3, $\mathcal{A}$ checks whether the sth nonterminal occurring in β_{γ_v} is indeed the α_{γ_i} nonterminal rewritten by rule p_{γ_i}, i.e., no other rule used between rule p_{γ_v} of γ_v and rule p_{γ_i} of γ_i rewrites the sth nonterminal, equal to α_{γ_i}, in β_{γ_v} (for which a relation of type "$s+s_q = i-v$" may also hold). Hence, $\mathcal{A}$ universally branches (Level 4- *Universal*) all symbols occurring between rules γ_{v+1} and γ_{i-1}. On each branch holding a triplet $\gamma_l = (p_{\gamma_l}, Q_{\gamma_l}, R_{\gamma_l})$, $v < l < i$, $\mathcal{A}$ checks whether

1. α_{γ_l} equals α_{γ_i},
2. $s + \bar{s}_q = l - v$, providing that α_{γ_i} is the sth nonterminal occurring on the right-hand side of rule p_{γ_v} (found at Level 3) and $\bar{s}_q$ is the number of nonterminals produced between rules p_{γ_v} and p_{γ_l},
3. the number of nonterminals α_{γ_i} rewritten between p_{γ_v} and p_{γ_l} is equal to the number of nonterminals α_{γ_i} produced between these rules, up to the sth nonterminal occurring on the right-hand side of rule p_{γ_v}.

On each universal branch (Level 4) $\mathcal{A}$ returns 0 if conditions $1 - 3$ hold. Otherwise, it returns 1. Note that, for each $\wp_i$, $1 \leq i \leq n$, $\mathcal{A}$ does not have to check whether γ_v and γ_l, can be applied in leftmost-1 derivation manner. This condition is checked by each of the processes $\wp_v$ and $\wp_l$, since all of them are universally considered. It is easy to estimate that $\mathcal{A}$ performs the whole computation in logarithmic time and space.   □

Corollary 3. $SZRCL_1^{ac}(CF) \subset \mathcal{NC}^1$.

Corollary 4. $SZRCL_1^{ac}(CF) \subset DSPACE(\log n)$.

In order to simulate letfmost-i derivations, $i \in \{2, 3\}$, and to check whether $\gamma = \gamma_1 \gamma_2 ... \gamma_n \in P^*$ belongs to $SZRCL_i^{ac}(CF)$, for each triplet γ_i, $1 \leq i \leq n$, an ATM must have information concerning the order in which the first occurrence of each nonterminal $A_l \in N$, $1 \leq l \leq m$, occurs in the sentential form at any step of derivation. In this respect we introduce the notion of *ranging vector*.

Definition 5. Let $G = (N, T, P, A_1)$ be a RCG^{ac} with CF rules, where $P = \{r_1, r_2, ..., r_k\}$ is the ordered finite set of triplets in P. Let SF_{r_j} be the sentential form obtained after the triplet $r_j = (p_j, Q_j, R_j)$, $1 \leq j \leq k$, has been applied at a certain step of derivation in G. The *ranging vector* associated with SF_{r_j}, denoted by $S(r_j)$, $1 \leq j \leq k$, is a vector in $\mathbf{N}^m$ defined as

$$S_l(r_j) = \begin{cases} 0, & \text{if } A_l \in N \text{ does not occur in } SF_{r_j}, \text{ i.e., } |SF_{r_j}|_{A_l} = 0, \\ i, & \text{if the first occurrence of } A_l \text{ in } SF_{r_j} \text{ is the } i^{th} \text{ element in the order of first occurrences of nonterminals from } N \text{ in } SF_{r_j}. \end{cases}$$

Depending on the context, the value of $S(r_j)$ taken at the lth place, $1 \leq l \leq m$, i.e., $S_l(r_j)$, is also denoted by $S_{\alpha_{p_j}}(r_j)$ if p_j in $r_j = (p_j, Q_j, R_j)$ is a CF rule of the form $\alpha_{p_j} \to \beta_{p_j}$ and $\alpha_{p_j} = A_l$.

Note that, if $r_{j'} = (p_{j'}, Q_{j'}, R_{j'})$ is applied in the Szilard word before $r_j = (p_j, Q_j, R_j)$ then the ranging vector $S(r_j)$ can be computed knowing $S(r_{j'})$. This observation holds for both leftmost-2 and leftmost-3 derivations (Example 1).

Example 1. Consider $S(r_{j'}) = (3, 0, 2, 1, 0) \in \mathbf{N}^5$ the ranging vector associated with the sentential form $SF_{r_{j'}}$, obtained after rule $r_{j'}$ has been applied, at the ith step of derivation. Suppose that $SF_{r_{j'}}$ contains one occurrence of A_1, three occurrences of A_3, and arbitrary number of A_4. According to Definition 5, $SF_{r_{j'}}$ looks like $SF_{r_{j'}} = tA_4X_4A_3X_{3,4}A_1\bar{X}_{3,4}$, where $t \in T^*$, $X_4 \in (\{A_4\} \cup T)^*$, $X_{3,4}, \bar{X}_{3,4} \in (\{A_3, A_4\} \cup T)^*$. If in $r_j = (p_j, Q_j, R_j)$, p_j is the rule $A_3 \rightarrow tA_5$, $Q_j = \{A_3, A_4\}$ and $R_j = \{A_5\}$, then r_j can be applied in leftmost-2 derivation manner after $r_{j'}$, if there is no other RC rule $r_{j''} = (p_{j''}, Q_{j''}, R_{j''}) \in P$, able to be applied on $SF_{r_{j'}}$ according to Definition 2, such that $p_{j''}$ rewrites A_4. Depending on the position of the second occurrence of A_3 in $SF_{r_{j'}}$, the sentential form obtained after p_j has been applied on $SF_{r_{j'}}$ may look like

- $SF_{r_j} = tA_4X_4A_5A_3X_{3,4}A_1\bar{X}_{3,4}$ or $SF_{r_j} = tA_4X_4A_5\bar{X}_4A_3X_{3,4}A_1\bar{X}_{3,4}$, $t \in T^*$, $X_4, \bar{X}_4 \in (\{A_4\} \cup T)^*$, $X_{3,4}, \bar{X}_{3,4} \in (\{A_3, A_4\} \cup T)^*$, i.e., $S(r_j) = (4, 0, 3, 1, 2)$, or like
- $SF_{r_j} = tA_4X_4A_5\bar{X}_4A_1A_3X_{3,4}$, or $SF_{r_j} = tA_4X_4A_5\bar{X}_4A_1\tilde{X}_4A_3X_{3,4}$, $t \in T^*$, $X_4, \bar{X}_4, \tilde{X}_4 \in (\{A_4\} \cup T)^*$, $X_{3,4} \in (\{A_1, A_3, A_4\} \cup T)^*$, i.e., $S(r_j) = (3, 0, 4, 1, 2)$.

For the case of leftmost-3 derivation, rule r_j can be applied in leftmost-3 manner after $r_{j'}$, by rewriting the leftmost occurrence of A_3 in $S(r_{j'})$, even if there exists a RC rule $r_{j''} \in P$ able to rewrite A_4.

Next we sketch an ATM $\mathcal{A}$ that decides whether an input word $\gamma = \gamma_1\gamma_2...\gamma_n$ belongs to $SZRCL_i^{ac}(CF)$, $i \in \{2, 3\}$.

Let $\mathcal{Q}_1$ be the quotient, and $\mathcal{R}_1$ be the remainder of n divided[6] by $[\log n]$. Dividing $\mathcal{Q}_1$ by $[\log n]$ a new quotient $\mathcal{Q}_2$ and remainder $\mathcal{R}_2$ are obtained. If this "iterated" division is performed until the resulted quotient, denoted by $\mathcal{Q}_\ell$, can be no longer divided by $[\log n]$, then n (written in the base $[\log n]$) is $n = ((...((\mathcal{Q}_\ell[\log n] + \mathcal{R}_\ell)[\log n] + \mathcal{R}_{\ell-1})[\log n] + ...)[\log n] + \mathcal{R}_2)[\log n] + \mathcal{R}_1$, $1 \leq \mathcal{Q}_\ell < \log n$, $0 \leq \mathcal{R}_l < \log n$, $l \in \{1, ..., \ell\}$, and $\ell < \log n$.

Knowing $\mathcal{R}_1$, $\mathcal{A}$ guesses an $\mathcal{R}_1$-tuple of ranging vectors associated with the first $\mathcal{R}_1$ triplets (RC rules) occurring in γ and checks whether $\gamma_1\gamma_2...\gamma_{\mathcal{R}_1}$ is valid, according to the leftmost-i derivation manner, $i \in \{2, 3\}$. Then $\mathcal{A}$ guesses a $[\log n]$-tuple of ranging vectors associated with triplets placed at the $[\log n]$ cutting points in γ obtained by dividing $[\mathcal{R}_1 + 1...n]$ in $[\log n]$ intervals of length $\mathcal{Q}_1$. $\mathcal{A}$ continues with this routine for each interval of length $\mathcal{Q}_1$ as follows. First $\mathcal{A}$ checks, in parallel, whether the first $\mathcal{R}_2$ triplets in each $\mathcal{Q}_1$-interval form a valid substring of a leftmost-i, $i \in \{2, 3\}$, Szilard word. Then, in parallel for each $\mathcal{Q}_1$-interval, $\mathcal{A}$ guesses another $[\log n]$-tuple of ranging vectors associated with triplets placed at the $[\log n]$ cutting points in γ obtained by dividing each interval of length $\mathcal{Q}_1 - \mathcal{R}_2$ into $[\log n]$ intervals of length $\mathcal{Q}_2$. This procedure is repeated until intervals of length $\mathcal{Q}_\ell < \log n$ are obtained. At this point, $\mathcal{A}$ checks whether the substrings of γ corresponding to the $\mathcal{Q}_\ell$-intervals are valid according to the leftmost-i derivation order, $i \in \{2, 3\}$. It can be proved that all cutting points

---

[6] By $[a]$ we denote the largest integer not greater than a, where a is a real number.

are right edges of these intervals. If correct ranging vectors can be found for all intervals and all cutting points, then γ is a correct leftmost-i, $i \in \{2,3\}$, Szilard word. Hence, we have

Theorem 3. *Each language* $L \in SZRCL_i^{ac}(CF)$, $i \in \{2,3\}$, *can be recognized by an indexing ATM in* $\mathcal{O}(\log n)$ *space and* $\mathcal{O}(\log^2 n)$ *time.*

Proof. We prove the claim for the leftmost-2 derivation. For the leftmost-3 case the proof is almost the same. Let $G = (N, T, P, A_1)$ be an arbitrary RCG^{ac} working in leftmost-2 derivation manner, and $\mathcal{A}$ be an indexing ATM with a similar configuration as in the proof of Theorem 1. Let $\gamma = \gamma_1 \gamma_2 ... \gamma_n \in P^*$, be an input of length n. To guess the length of γ, $\mathcal{A}$ proceeds with the procedure described at Level 1 (*Existential*), Theorem 1.

Level 2 (*Existential*). Consider the quotient $\mathcal{Q}_1$ and the remainder $\mathcal{R}_1$ of the division of n by $[\log n]$, where $0 \leq \mathcal{R}_1 < [\log n]$. $\mathcal{A}$ spawns $\mathcal{O}(c^{\log n})$ existential branches, each branch holding an $\mathcal{R}_1$-tuple $\Re_{\mathcal{R}_1} = (S(\gamma_1), S(\gamma_2), ..., S(\gamma_{\mathcal{R}_1}))$ of ranging vectors, where[7] $c = \mathcal{O}(\sum_{s=1}^{m-1}(m-s+1)^m)$ and $S(\gamma_v)$ is the ranging vector associated with γ_v, $2 \leq v \leq \mathcal{R}_1$. $\mathcal{A}$ checks (Levels 3) in $\mathcal{O}(\log n)$ time and space, whether all vectors in $\Re_{\mathcal{R}_1}$ are correct, in the sense that $S(\gamma_v)$ can be obtained from $S(\gamma_{v-1})$ by applying rule γ_v in leftmost-2 derivation manner on the sentential form built from $S(\gamma_{v-1})$.

Level 3 (*Universal*). $\mathcal{A}$ spawns $\mathcal{R}_1$ universal processes $\wp_v^{(\mathcal{R}_1)}$, $1 \leq v \leq \mathcal{R}_1$.

- Process $\wp_1^{(\mathcal{R}_1)}$ reads $\gamma_1 = (p_{\gamma_1}, Q_{\gamma_1}, R_{\gamma_1})$ and it checks whether γ_1 can be applied on A_1, i.e., $\alpha_{\gamma_1} = A_1$, and whether $S(\gamma_1)$ is the ranging vector associated with β_{γ_1}. If these conditions hold, $\wp_1^{(\mathcal{R}_1)}$ returns 1. Otherwise, it returns 0.

- For each $\wp_v^{(\mathcal{R}_1)}$, $2 \leq v \leq \mathcal{R}_1$, $\mathcal{A}$ counts the number of occurrences of each RC rule $r_j \in P$, $1 \leq j \leq k$, in $\gamma^{(v)} = \gamma_1 \gamma_2 ... \gamma_{v-1}$. Suppose that each r_j occurs $c_j^{(v)}$ times in $\gamma^{(v)}$, $0 \leq c_j^{(v)} \leq v - 1$. For each $1 \leq l \leq m$, $\mathcal{A}$ computes $s_{A_l}^{(v)} = V_l^0 + \sum_{j=1}^k c_j^{(v)} V_l(r_j)$, i.e., the number of times nonterminal A_l occurs in the sentential form obtained at the vth step of derivation. Each $\wp_v^{(\mathcal{R}_1)}$, $2 \leq v \leq \mathcal{R}_1$, returns 1 if only one of the conditions in $\mathbf{I}_1^{(v)}$ and all conditions in $\mathbf{I}_2^{(v)}$ hold.

$$\mathbf{I}_1^{(v)} \begin{cases} 1.\ s_{\alpha_{\gamma_v}}^{(v)} \geq 1,\ \alpha_{\gamma_v} \notin Q_{\gamma_v} \cup R_{\gamma_v},\ s_X^{(v)} \geq 1,\ \text{for each } X \in Q_{\gamma_v},\ \text{and } s_Y^{(v)} = 0 \\ \quad \text{for each } Y \in R_{\gamma_v}, \\ 2.\ s_{\alpha_{\gamma_v}}^{(v)} \geq 2 \text{ if } \alpha_{\gamma_v} \in Q_{\gamma_v} - R_{\gamma_v},\ s_X^{(v)} \geq 1,\ \text{for each } X \in Q_{\gamma_v},\ X \neq \alpha_{\gamma_v}, \\ \quad \text{and } s_Y^{(v)} = 0 \text{ for each } Y \in R_{\gamma_v}, \\ 3.\ s_{\alpha_{\gamma_v}}^{(v)} = 1 \text{ if } \alpha_{\gamma_v} \in R_{\gamma_v} - Q_{\gamma_v},\ s_X^{(v)} \geq 1,\ \text{for each } X \in Q_{\gamma_v},\ \text{and } s_Y^{(v)} = 0 \\ \quad \text{for each } Y \in R_{\gamma_v},\ Y \neq \alpha_{\gamma_v}. \end{cases}$$

---

[7] The constant c depends on the number of vectors in $\mathbf{N}^m$ that can be built upon the set $\{0, 1, ..., m\}$. If a certain sentential form has only $m - s$ distinct nonterminals, then there are $(m - s + 1)^m$ guesses that provide the ranging vector associated with this sentential form. Hence, here and throughout the paper, $c = \mathcal{O}(\sum_{s=1}^{m-1}(m-s+1)^m)$.

$\mathbf{I}_2^{(v)}$ $\begin{cases}\end{cases}$

1. $S(\gamma_{v-1})$ is a possible ranging vector on which γ_{v-1} ends the $(v-1)^{th}$ step of derivation, i.e., $S_l(\gamma_{v-1}) = 0$ if $s_{A_l}^{(v)} = 0$, and $S_l(\gamma_{v-1}) \neq 0$ if $s_{A_l}^{(v)} > 0$, for each $1 \leq l \leq m$,

2. for any RC rule $r = (p, Q, R) \in P$, p of the form $\alpha_p \to \beta_p$, $\alpha_p \neq \alpha_{\gamma_v}$, that can be applied on $\gamma^{(v)}$ (because it satisfies one of the conditions of type $1 - 3$ in $\mathbf{I}_1$) we have $S_{\alpha_{\gamma_v}}(\gamma_{v-1}) < S_{\alpha_p}(\gamma_{v-1})$, i.e., p_{γ_v} can be applied in leftmost-2 manner on $\gamma^{(v)}$ with the ranging vector $S(\gamma_{v-1})$,

3. $S(\gamma_v)$ is a possible ranging vector with which γ_v ends the vth step of derivation, i.e., $S_l(\gamma_v) = 0$ if $s_{A_l}^{(v)} + V_l(\gamma_v) = 0$, and $S_l(\gamma_v) \neq 0$ if $s_{A_l}^{(v)} + V_l(\gamma_v) > 0$, for each $1 \leq l \leq m$.

If all $\wp_v^{(\mathcal{R}_1)}$, $1 \leq v \leq \mathcal{R}_1$, return 1 then $\Re_{\mathcal{R}_1}$ is a correct guess and the existential branch holding the $[\log n]$-tuple, spawned at Level 2, is labeled by 1.

Level 4 (*Existential*). Let $\mathcal{Q}_2$ be the quotient and $\mathcal{R}_2$ the remainder of $\mathcal{Q}_1$ divided by $[\log n]$, $0 \leq \mathcal{R}_2 < [\log n]$. $\mathcal{A}$ spawns $\mathcal{O}(c^{\log n})$ existential branches, each branch holding a $2[\log n]$-tuple $\Re_{\mathcal{R}_2}^c = (S(\gamma_{\mathcal{R}_1}), S(\gamma_{\mathcal{R}_1 + \mathcal{R}_2}), S(\gamma_{\mathcal{R}_1 + \mathcal{Q}_1}),$ $S(\gamma_{\mathcal{R}_1 + \mathcal{Q}_1 + \mathcal{R}_2}), ..., S(\gamma_{\mathcal{R}_1 + ([\log n]-1)\mathcal{Q}_1}), S(\gamma_{\mathcal{R}_1 + ([\log n]-1)\mathcal{Q}_1 + \mathcal{R}_2}))$, where $S(\gamma_{\mathcal{R}_1})$ is the ranging vector belonging to the $\mathcal{R}_1$-tuple found correct at Level 3. Because the tuple $\Re_{\mathcal{R}_1}$ is not useful anymore, the space used by $\mathcal{A}$ to record $\Re_{\mathcal{R}_1}$ is allocated now to record $\Re_{\mathcal{R}_2}^c$.

Level 5 (*Universal*). On each existential branch from Level 4, $\mathcal{A}$ spawns $[\log n]$ universal processes $\wp_{i_1}^{(\mathcal{Q}_1)}$, $0 \leq i_1 \leq [\log n] - 1$. Each process $\wp_{i_1}^{(\mathcal{Q}_1)}$ takes the interval $[\mathcal{R}_1 + i_1\mathcal{Q}_1...\mathcal{R}_1 + i_1\mathcal{Q}_1 + \mathcal{R}_2]$, and checks whether the ranging vectors $S(\gamma_{\mathcal{R}_1 + i_1\mathcal{Q}_1})$ and $S(\gamma_{\mathcal{R}_1 + i_1\mathcal{Q}_1 + \mathcal{R}_2})$, $0 \leq i_1 \leq [\log n] - 1$, provide a correct order in which the leftmost-2 derivation can be performed between $\gamma_{\mathcal{R}_1 + i_1\mathcal{Q}_1}$ and $\gamma_{\mathcal{R}_1 + i_1\mathcal{Q}_1 + \mathcal{R}_2}$. Besides $S(\gamma_{\mathcal{R}_1 + i_1\mathcal{Q}_1})$ and $S(\gamma_{\mathcal{R}_1 + i_1\mathcal{Q}_1 + \mathcal{R}_2})$, each $\wp_{i_1}^{(\mathcal{Q}_1)}$ also keeps, from the previous level, the ranging vector $S(\gamma_{\mathcal{R}_1 + (i_1+1)\mathcal{Q}_1})$. In this way each ranging vector $S(\gamma_{\mathcal{R}_1 + i_1\mathcal{Q}_1})$, $1 \leq i_1 \leq [\log n] - 1$, guessed at Level 4, is redirected to only one process, i.e., $\wp_{i_1-1}^{(\mathcal{Q}_1)}$. Denote by $x_{i_1} = \mathcal{R}_1 + i_1\mathcal{Q}_1$, $0 \leq i_1 \leq [\log n] - 1$.

Level 6 (*Existential*). For each universal process $\wp_{i_1}^{(\mathcal{Q}_1)}$, $0 \leq i_1 \leq [\log n] - 1$, $\mathcal{A}$ spawns $\mathcal{O}(c^{\log n})$ existential branches, each branch holding an $(\mathcal{R}_2 + 1)$-tuple of ranging vectors $\Re_{\mathcal{R}_2} = (S(\gamma_{x_{i_1}}), S(\gamma_{x_{i_1}+1}), ..., S(\gamma_{x_{i_1}+\mathcal{R}_2-1}), S(\gamma_{x_{i_1}+\mathcal{R}_2}))$. Then $\mathcal{A}$ checks whether all vectors in $\Re_{\mathcal{R}_2}$ are correct ranging vectors according to the leftmost-2 derivation requirements. This can be done, for each process $\wp_{i_1}^{(\mathcal{Q}_1)}$ in $\mathcal{O}(\log n)$ time and space, through Level 7 as follows.

Level 7 (*Universal*). For each existential branch spawned at Level 6, $\mathcal{A}$ spawns $\mathcal{R}_2$ universal processes $\wp_v^{(\mathcal{R}_2)}$, $1 \leq v \leq \mathcal{R}_2$. On each $\wp_v^{(\mathcal{R}_2)}$, $\mathcal{A}$ checks whether each substring $\gamma_{x_{i_1}} \gamma_{x_{i_1}+1} ... \gamma_{x_{i_1}+v}$ is correct according to the leftmost-2 derivation order. In this respect, for each $\wp_v^{(\mathcal{R}_2)}$, $1 \leq v \leq \mathcal{R}_2$, $\mathcal{A}$ counts the number of occurrences of each RC rule $r_j \in P$, $1 \leq j \leq k$, in $\gamma^{(i_1,v)} = \gamma_1\gamma_2...\gamma_{x_{i_1}+v-1}$. Suppose that each r_j occurs $c_j^{(i_1,v)}$ times, $0 \leq c_j^{(i_1,v)} \leq x_{i_1} + v - 1$, in $\gamma^{(i_1,v)}$. For each $1 \leq l \leq m$, $\mathcal{A}$ computes $s_{A_l}^{(i_1,v)} = V_l^0 + \sum_{j=1}^k c_j^{(i_1,v)} V_l(r_j)$, i.e., the number of times A_l occurs in the sentential form obtained at the $(x_{i_1} + v)^{th}$ step of derivation. Then $\mathcal{A}$ checks conditions of type $\mathbf{I}_1^{(v)}$ and $\mathbf{I}_2^{(v)}$ (Level 3) for the RC rule $\gamma_{x_{i_1}+v}$, i.e., instead of v, $x_{i_1} + v$ is considered. Denote by $\mathbf{I}_1^{(i_1,v)}$ and $\mathbf{I}_2^{(i_1,v)}$ these conditions.

Each $\wp_v^{(\mathcal{R}_2)}$, $1 \leq v \leq \mathcal{R}_2$, is said *partially correct* if one of the conditions in $\mathbf{I}_1^{(i_1,v)}$ and all conditions in $\mathbf{I}_2^{(i_1,v)}$ hold. If $\wp_v^{(\mathcal{R}_2)}$ is not partially correct, it is labeled by 0. Note that, at this moment we cannot decide whether $\wp_v^{(\mathcal{R}_2)}$ can be labeled by 1, since we do not know whether $S(\gamma_{x_{i_1}})$ is valid, i.e., whether $\gamma_{x_{i_1}}$ indeed ends the $x_{i_1}^{th}$ step of derivation with the ranging vector $S(\gamma_{x_{i_1}})$, and whether $\gamma_{x_{i_1}}$ can be applied in the leftmost-2 derivation manner upon the ranging vector $S(\gamma_{x_{i_1}}-1)$ (which is not yet guessed[8]). The logical value of each $\wp_v^{(\mathcal{R}_2)}$ will be decided at the end of computation, when it will be known whether $S(\gamma_{x_{i_1}})$ is a valid ranging vector with respect to the rules that compose the subword $\gamma_{\mathcal{R}_1+(i_1-1)\mathcal{Q}_1} \cdots \gamma_{\mathcal{R}_1+i_1\mathcal{Q}_1-1} = \gamma_{x_{i_1}-1} \cdots \gamma_{x_{i_1}-1}$. A partially correct process $\wp_v^{(\mathcal{R}_2)}$ is labeled by $\diamond$. If all $\wp_v^{(\mathcal{R}_2)}$'s are labeled by $\diamond$, then the existential branch holding the tuple $\Re_{\mathcal{R}_2}$, provided at Level 6, is labeled by $\diamond$. Otherwise, this branch is labeled by 0. $\wp_{i_1}^{(\mathcal{Q}_1)}$, yielded at Level 5, will be labeled by $\diamond$ if there exists at least one existential branch labeled by $\diamond$ at Level 6. Otherwise, $\wp_{i_1}^{(\mathcal{Q}_1)}$ returns 0.

Suppose that we have run the algorithm up to the $(\ell-1)^{th}$ "iterated" division of n by $[\log n]$, i.e., we know the quotient $\mathcal{Q}_{\ell-1}$ and the remainder $\mathcal{R}_{\ell-1}$ of $\mathcal{Q}_{\ell-2}$ divided by $[\log n]$. More precisely, $\mathcal{Q}_{\ell-2} = \mathcal{Q}_{\ell-1}[\log n] + \mathcal{R}_{\ell-1}$ and $n = ((...((\mathcal{Q}_{\ell-1}[\log n] + \mathcal{R}_{\ell-1})[\log n] + \mathcal{R}_{\ell-2})[\log n] + ...)[\log n] + \mathcal{R}_2)[\log n] + \mathcal{R}_1$, with $\mathcal{Q}_{\ell-1} > [\log n]$, $0 \leq \mathcal{R}_l < [\log n]$, $l \in \{1, 2, ..., \ell-1\}$, and $\ell \leq [\log n]$.

Level $4(\ell-1)$ (*Existential*). Let $\mathcal{Q}_\ell$ be the quotient and $\mathcal{R}_\ell$ the remainder of $\mathcal{Q}_{\ell-1}$ divided by $[\log n]$, $0 \leq \mathcal{Q}_\ell, \mathcal{R}_\ell < [\log n]$. Since $\mathcal{Q}_{\ell-2}$, $\mathcal{R}_{\ell-2}$ and $\mathcal{R}_{\ell-1}$ are no more needed, the space used to record them is now used to record $\mathcal{Q}_\ell$ and $\mathcal{R}_\ell$ in binary, still keeping $\mathcal{Q}_{\ell-1}$. Denote by $x_{i_{\ell-2}} = \sum_{l=1}^{\ell-1} \mathcal{R}_l + \sum_{l=1}^{\ell-2} i_l \mathcal{Q}_l$. For each existential branch labeled by $\diamond$ at Level $4\ell-6$, $\mathcal{A}$ spawns $\mathcal{O}(c^{\log n})$ existential branches, each branch holding a $2[\log n]$-tuple $\Re_{\mathcal{R}_\ell}^c = (S(\gamma_{x_{i_{\ell-2}}}), S(\gamma_{x_{i_{\ell-2}}+\mathcal{R}_\ell}),$ $S(\gamma_{x_{i_{\ell-2}}+\mathcal{Q}_{\ell-1}}), S(\gamma_{x_{i_{\ell-2}}+\mathcal{Q}_{\ell-1}+\mathcal{R}_\ell}), ..., S(\gamma_{x_{i_{\ell-2}}+([\log n]-1)\mathcal{Q}_{\ell-1}}),$ $S(\gamma_{x_{i_{\ell-2}}+([\log n]-1)\mathcal{Q}_{\ell-1}+\mathcal{R}_\ell}))$, where $S(\gamma_{x_{i_{\ell-2}}})$ is the ranging vector belonging to tuple $\Re_{\mathcal{R}_{\ell-1}}$ found correct at Level $4\ell-5$. Because $\Re_{\mathcal{R}_{\ell-1}}$ is no more needed the space used to record $\Re_{\mathcal{R}_{\ell-1}}$ is allocated now to record $\Re_{\mathcal{R}_\ell}^c$. Then $\mathcal{A}$ proceeds with Level $4\ell-3$, similar to Levels $5,..., 4\ell-7$.

Level $4\ell-3$ (*Universal*). On each existential branch spawned at Level $4(\ell-1)$, $\mathcal{A}$ spawns $[\log n]$ universal processes $\wp_{i_{\ell-1}}^{(\mathcal{Q}_{\ell-1})}$, $0 \leq i_{\ell-1} \leq [\log n]-1$. Denote by

---

[8] $S(\gamma_{x_{i_1}-1})$ will be guessed at the last level of the computation tree of $\mathcal{A}$, when all the remainders of the "iterated" division of n by $[\log n]$ will be spent, and when $\gamma_{x_{i_1}-1}$ will be the last rule occurring in the suffix of length $\mathcal{Q}_\ell$ of the substring $\gamma_{\mathcal{R}_1+(i_1-1)\mathcal{Q}_1} \cdots \gamma_{\mathcal{R}_1+i_1\mathcal{Q}_1-1} = \gamma_{x_{i_1}-1} \cdots \gamma_{x_{i_1}-1}$ of γ.

$x_{i_{\ell-1}} = \sum_{l=1}^{\ell-1} \mathcal{R}_l + \sum_{l=1}^{\ell-1} i_l \mathcal{Q}_l = x_{i_{\ell-2}} + i_{\ell-1} \mathcal{Q}_{\ell-1}$, $0 \leq i_{\ell-1} \leq [\log n] - 1$. Each process $\wp_{i_{\ell-1}}^{(\mathcal{Q}_{\ell-1})}$ takes the interval $[x_{i_{\ell-1}} ... x_{i_{\ell-1}} + \mathcal{R}_\ell]$, and it checks whether the ranging vectors (guessed at Level $4(\ell-1)$) $S(\gamma_{x_{i_{\ell-1}}})$ and $S(\gamma_{x_{i_{\ell-1}}+\mathcal{R}_\ell})$, $0 \leq i_{\ell-1} \leq [\log n] - 1$, provide a correct order in which the leftmost-2 derivation can be performed between $\gamma_{x_{i_{\ell-1}}}$ and $\gamma_{x_{i_{\ell-1}}+\mathcal{R}_\ell}$. Besides $S(\gamma_{x_{i_{\ell-1}}})$ and $S(\gamma_{x_{i_{\ell-1}}+\mathcal{R}_\ell})$, each $\wp_{i_{\ell-1}}^{(\mathcal{Q}_{\ell-1})}$, also keeps from the previous level $S(\gamma_{x_{i_{\ell-2}}+(i_{\ell-1}+1)\mathcal{Q}_{\ell-1}})$. Then $\mathcal{A}$ continues with Level $4\ell - 2$, similar to Levels 6, ..., $4\ell - 6$.

Level $4\ell-2$ (*Existential*). For each universal process $\wp_{i_{\ell-1}}^{(\mathcal{Q}_{\ell-1})}$, $0 \leq i_{\ell-1} \leq [\log n] - 1$, $\mathcal{A}$ spawns $\mathcal{O}(c^{\log n})$ existential branches, each branch holding an $(\mathcal{R}_\ell+1)$-tuple of ranging vectors $\Re_{\mathcal{R}_\ell}=(S(\gamma_{x_{i_{\ell-1}}}), S(\gamma_{x_{i_{\ell-1}}+1}), ..., S(\gamma_{x_{i_{\ell-1}}+\mathcal{R}_\ell-1}), S(\gamma_{x_{i_{\ell-1}}+\mathcal{R}_\ell}))$. Then $\mathcal{A}$ checks whether all vectors composing $\Re_{\mathcal{R}_\ell}$ are correct. This can be done, for each process $\wp_{i_{\ell-1}}^{(\mathcal{Q}_{\ell-1})}$, $0 \leq i_{\ell-1} \leq [\log n] - 1$, in $\mathcal{O}(\log n)$ time and space, through Level $4\ell - 1$ similar to Levels 3, 7, ..., $4\ell - 5$.

Level $4\ell - 1$ (*Universal*). For each existential branch spawned at Level $4\ell - 2$, $\mathcal{A}$ spawns $\mathcal{R}_\ell$ universal processes $\wp_v^{(\mathcal{R}_\ell)}$, $1 \leq v \leq \mathcal{R}_\ell$. On each $\wp_v^{(\mathcal{R}_\ell)}$, $\mathcal{A}$ checks whether each substring $\gamma_{x_{i_{\ell-1}}} ... \gamma_{x_{i_{\ell-1}}+v}$ and each ranging vector in $\Re_{\mathcal{R}_\ell}$ is correct according to the leftmost-2 derivation order. In this respect $\mathcal{A}$ checks conditions of type $\mathbf{I}_1^{(v)}$ and $\mathbf{I}_2^{(v)}$ (Level 3) for the RC rule $\gamma_{x_{i_{\ell-1}}+v}$, i.e., instead of v, $x_{i_{\ell-1}} + v$ is considered. Denote by $\mathbf{I}_1^{(i_{\ell-1},v)}$ and $\mathbf{I}_2^{(i_{\ell-1},v)}$ these conditions.

Each process $\wp_v^{(\mathcal{R}_\ell)}$, $1 \leq v \leq \mathcal{R}_\ell$, that satisfies only one of the conditions in $\mathbf{I}_1^{(i_{\ell-1},v)}$ and all conditions in $\mathbf{I}_2^{(i_{\ell-1},v)}$ is partially correct, and it is labeled by a $\diamond$. Otherwise, $\wp_v^{(\mathcal{R}_\ell)}$ is labeled by 0. If all $\wp_v^{(\mathcal{R}_\ell)}$'s are labeled by $\diamond$, then the existential branch holding the tuple $\Re_{\mathcal{R}_\ell}$, provided at Level $4\ell - 2$, is labeled by $\diamond$. Otherwise, this branch is labeled by 0. Process $\wp_{i_{\ell-1}}^{(\mathcal{Q}_{\ell-1})}$, yielded at Level $4\ell - 1$ is labeled by $\diamond$ if there exists at least one existential branch labeled by $\diamond$ at Level $4\ell - 2$. Otherwise, $\wp_{i_{\ell-1}}^{(\mathcal{Q}_{\ell-1})}$ is labeled by 0.

At this level the only substrings of γ left unchecked are those substrings that corresponds to the intervals of the form $I_{\mathcal{Q}_{\ell-1}} = [\sum_{l=1}^{\ell-1} \mathcal{R}_l + \sum_{l=1}^{\ell-2} i_l \mathcal{Q}_l + i_{\ell-1} \mathcal{Q}_{\ell-1} + \mathcal{R}_\ell ... \sum_{l=1}^{\ell-1} \mathcal{R}_l + \sum_{l=1}^{\ell-2} i_l \mathcal{Q}_l + (i_{\ell-1}+1)\mathcal{Q}_{\ell-1}]$, $0 \leq i_l \leq [\log n] - 1$, $1 \leq l \leq \ell - 1$, and besides the cutting points $P_\ell^u = \sum_{l=1}^{u} \mathcal{R}_l + \sum_{l=1}^{u-1} i_l \mathcal{Q}_l + (i_u+1)\mathcal{Q}_u$, $1 \leq u \leq \ell - 1$. On each interval of type $I_{\mathcal{Q}_{\ell-1}}$, $\mathcal{A}$ proceeds with Level 4ℓ.

Level 4ℓ (*Existential*). Each interval $I_{\mathcal{Q}_{\ell-1}}$ can be divided into $[\log n]$ subintervals of length $1 \leq \mathcal{Q}_\ell < [\log n]$. Hence, $\mathcal{A}$ spawns $\mathcal{O}(c^{\log n})$ existential branches (guess-es) each of which holds a $[\log n]$-tuple $\Re_{\mathcal{Q}_\ell}^c = (S(\gamma_{x_{i_{\ell-1}}+\mathcal{R}_\ell}), S(\gamma_{x_{i_{\ell-1}}+\mathcal{R}_\ell+\mathcal{Q}_\ell}), ..., S(\gamma_{x_{i_{\ell-1}}+\mathcal{R}_\ell+([\log n]-1)\mathcal{Q}_\ell}))$, where $S(\gamma_{x_{i_{\ell-1}}+\mathcal{R}_\ell})$ is the ranging vector found valid at Level $4\ell - 1$.

Level $4\ell + 1$ (*Universal*). For each existential branch spawned at Level 4ℓ, $\mathcal{A}$ spawns $[\log n]$ universal processes $\wp_{i_\ell}^{(\mathcal{Q}_\ell)}$, $0 \leq i_\ell \leq [\log n] - 1$. Each process $\wp_{i_\ell}^{(\mathcal{Q}_\ell)}$ takes an interval of length $\mathcal{Q}_\ell$ of the form $[\sum_{l=1}^{\ell} \mathcal{R}_l + \sum_{l=1}^{\ell-1} i_l \mathcal{Q}_l + i_\ell \mathcal{Q}_\ell ... \sum_{l=1}^{\ell} \mathcal{R}_l +$

$\sum_{l=1}^{\ell-1} i_l \mathcal{Q}_l + (i_\ell + 1)\mathcal{Q}_\ell]$. Denote by $x_{i_\ell} = \sum_{l=1}^{\ell} \mathcal{R}_l + \sum_{l=1}^{\ell-1} i_l \mathcal{Q}_l + i_\ell \mathcal{Q}_\ell$, $0 \le i_\ell \le \lceil \log n \rceil - 1$. For each interval $[x_{i_\ell} \dots x_{i_\ell+1}]$, $\mathcal{A}$ checks whether the substring $\gamma_{x_{i_\ell}} \dots$ $\gamma_{x_{i_\ell+1}}$ is valid according to the leftmost-2 derivation order (Level $4\ell + 2$).

Level $4\ell+2$ (*Existential*). For each $\wp_{i_\ell}^{(\mathcal{Q}_\ell)}$, $0 \le i_\ell \le \lceil \log n \rceil - 1$, $\mathcal{A}$ spawns $\mathcal{O}(c^{\log n})$ existential branches, each branch holding an $(\mathcal{Q}_\ell + 1)$-tuple of ranging vectors $\mathfrak{R}_{\mathcal{Q}_\ell} = (S(\gamma_{x_{i_\ell}}), S(\gamma_{x_{i_\ell}+1}), ..., S(\gamma_{x_{i_\ell}+\mathcal{Q}_\ell-1}), S(\gamma_{x_{i_\ell+1}}))$. In each $\mathfrak{R}_{\mathcal{Q}_\ell}$ the vectors $S(\gamma_{x_{i_\ell}})$ and $S(\gamma_{x_{i_\ell+1}})$ have been guessed at Level 4ℓ. They are ranging vectors associated with triplets placed in cutting points, i.e., edges of intervals of length $\lceil \log n \rceil$. They are also overlapping points of two consecutive intervals of type $[x_{i_\ell} \dots x_{i_\ell+1}]$. Hence, each ranging vector $S(\gamma_{x_{i_\ell}})$ is checked two times. Once if it is a valid vector on which $\gamma_{x_{i_\ell}+1}$ can be applied in leftmost-2 derivation manner (checked by process $\wp_{i_\ell}^{(\mathcal{Q}_\ell)}$). Then, if by applying $\gamma_{x_{i_\ell}}$ on the sentential form built upon the ranging vector $S(\gamma_{x_{i_\ell}-1})$ a sentential form with an associated ranging vector equal to $S(\gamma_{x_{i_\ell}})$ is obtained (which is checked by $\wp_{i_\ell-1}^{(\mathcal{Q}_\ell)}$).

As all intervals of type $[x_{i_\ell} \dots x_{i_\ell+1}]$ are universally checked by processes $\wp_{i_\ell}^{(\mathcal{Q}_\ell)}$, the tuple $\mathfrak{R}_{\mathcal{Q}_\ell}^c$ spawned at Level 4ℓ is labeled by 1, if all ranging vectors $S(\gamma_{x_{i_\ell}})$ and all vectors in $\mathfrak{R}_{\mathcal{Q}_\ell}$ are correct. To check whether all ranging vectors in $\mathfrak{R}_{\mathcal{Q}_\ell}$ are correct, for each $\wp_{i_\ell}^{(\mathcal{Q}_\ell)}$, $0 \le i_\ell \le \lceil \log n \rceil - 1$, $\mathcal{A}$ follows the same procedure, that requires $\mathcal{O}(\log n)$ time and space, described at Levels 3, 7, ..., $4\ell - 1$ (Universals). For the last substring of length $\mathcal{Q}_\ell$ in γ, i.e., the suffix of γ of length $\mathcal{Q}_\ell$ of the form $\gamma_{\sum_{l=1}^{\ell} \mathcal{R}_l + \sum_{l=1}^{\ell-1}(\lceil \log n \rceil - 1)\mathcal{Q}_l + (\lceil \log n \rceil - 1)\mathcal{Q}_\ell} \dots \gamma_{\sum_{l=1}^{\ell} \mathcal{R}_l + \sum_{l=1}^{\ell-1}(\lceil \log n \rceil - 1)\mathcal{Q}_l + \lceil \log n \rceil \mathcal{Q}_\ell}$, $\wp_{\lceil \log n \rceil - 1}^{(\mathcal{Q}_\ell)}$ must check whether the triplet $\gamma_{\sum_{l=1}^{\ell} \mathcal{R}_l + \sum_{l=1}^{\ell-1}(\lceil \log n \rceil - 1)\mathcal{Q}_l + \lceil \log n \rceil \mathcal{Q}_\ell} = \gamma_n$ ends up the computation. This is done as for process $\wp_n$, Theorem 1.

Each cutting point $P_\ell^u = \sum_{l=1}^{u} \mathcal{R}_l + \sum_{l=1}^{u-1} i_l \mathcal{Q}_l + (i_u + 1)\mathcal{Q}_u$ can be equivalently rewritten as $\sum_{l=1}^{u+1} \mathcal{R}_l + \sum_{l=1}^{u} i_l \mathcal{Q}_l + \lceil \log n \rceil \mathcal{Q}_{u+1}$, due to the equality $\mathcal{Q}_u = \lceil \log n \rceil \mathcal{Q}_{u+1} + \mathcal{R}_{u+1}$, for any $1 \le u \le \ell - 1$. Furthermore, $\sum_{l=1}^{u+1} \mathcal{R}_l + \sum_{l=1}^{u} i_l \mathcal{Q}_l + \lceil \log n \rceil \mathcal{Q}_{u+1}$ is equal with $\sum_{l=1}^{u+1} \mathcal{R}_l + \mathcal{R}_{u+2} + \sum_{l=1}^{u} i_l \mathcal{Q}_l + (\lceil \log n \rceil - 1)\mathcal{Q}_{u+1} + \lceil \log n \rceil \mathcal{Q}_{u+2}$, due to the equality $\mathcal{Q}_{u+1} = \lceil \log n \rceil \mathcal{Q}_{u+2} + \mathcal{R}_{u+2}$, for any $1 \le u \le \ell - 2$. By applying this transformation k times, where $k = \ell - u$, each P_ℓ^u can be equivalently rewritten as $\sum_{l=1}^{u+1} \mathcal{R}_l + \mathcal{R}_{u+2} + ... + \mathcal{R}_{u+k} + \sum_{l=1}^{u} i_l \mathcal{Q}_l + (\lceil \log n \rceil - 1)(\mathcal{Q}_{u+1} + ... + \mathcal{Q}_{u+k-1}) + \lceil \log n \rceil \mathcal{Q}_{u+k}$, where $u + k = \ell$.

In this way each P_ℓ^u, yielded at Level $4u$ by $\mathfrak{R}_{\mathcal{R}_{u+1}}^c$, $1 \le u \le \ell - 1$, is in fact the right edge of an interval of the form $[\sum_{l=1}^{\ell} \mathcal{R}_l + \sum_{l=1}^{\ell-1} i_l \mathcal{Q}_l + i_\ell \mathcal{Q}_\ell \dots \sum_{l=1}^{\ell} \mathcal{R}_l + \sum_{l=1}^{\ell-1} i_l \mathcal{Q}_l + (i_\ell+1)\mathcal{Q}_\ell] = [x_{i_\ell} \dots x_{i_\ell+1}]$, for which $0 \le i_l \le \lceil \log n \rceil - 1$, $1 \le l \le \ell - 1$, $i_\ell = \lceil \log n \rceil - 1$. Hence, the decision on the correctness of each ranging vector $S(\gamma_{\sum_{l=1}^{u} \mathcal{R}_l + \sum_{l=1}^{u-1} i_l \mathcal{Q}_l + (i_u+1)\mathcal{Q}_u}) = S(\gamma_{P_\ell^u})$ will be actually taken by a process of type $\wp_{\lceil \log n \rceil - 1}^{(\mathcal{Q}_\ell)}$. Since the validity of each cutting point is decided by a process of type $\wp_{\lceil \log n \rceil - 1}^{(\mathcal{Q}_\ell)}$, the logical value returned by this process is "propagated" up to the level of the computation tree that has spawned the corresponding cutting point, and thus each ⋄ symbol receives a logical value. The input is accepted, if going up in the computation tree, with all $\diamond$'s changed into logical values, the root of the tree is labeled by 1.

The tuples $\Re_{\mathcal{R}_h}$, $\Re_{\mathcal{R}_h}^c$, $\Re_{\mathcal{Q}_\ell}$, $\Re_{\mathcal{Q}_\ell}^c$, $1 \leq \hbar \leq \ell$, vectors $V(r_j)$, $1 \leq j \leq k$, and auxiliary net effects computed by $\mathcal{A}$ during the algorithm, are stored by using $\mathcal{O}(\log n)$ space, in a similar manner as in Theorems 1 and 2.

It is easy to observe that $\mathcal{A}$ has $\mathcal{O}(\log n)$ levels. Since at each level $\mathcal{A}$ spawns either $\mathcal{O}(n^{c_1})$ or $\mathcal{O}(c_2^{\log n})$ existential branches, where c_1 and c_2 are constants, (each level being thus convertible into a binary tree with $\mathcal{O}(\log n)$ levels), and at each Level $4\hbar$, $1 \leq \hbar \leq \ell$, $\mathcal{A}$ performs a division operation, which requires $\mathcal{O}(\log n)$ time and space [9], $\mathcal{A}$ will perform the whole computation in $\mathcal{O}(\log^2 n)$ parallel time and $\mathcal{O}(\log n)$ space. □

Corollary 5. $SZRCL_i^{ac}(CF) \subset \mathcal{NC}^2$, $i \in \{2,3\}$.

Corollary 6. $SZRCL_i^{ac}(CF) \subset DSPACE(\log^2 n)$.

4   Remarks on SZLs of RCGs with PS Rules

The derivation mechanism in regulated rewriting grammars is quite similar to the derivation mechanism in Chomsky grammars. For the case of RCGs constraints are provided by the *permitting* and *forbidding* contexts that enable or disable a rule to be applied. These restrictions do increase the generative power of RCGs [5] but they do not change the complexity of the corresponding SZLs. On the other hand Definition 4 of leftmost-i, $i \in \{1,2,3\}$, derivations in RCGs with CF rules, can be naturally generalized for phrase-structure (PS) rules as follows.

Let $G = (N, T, P, S)$ be a RCG with PS rules, where $P = \{r_1, r_2, ..., r_k\}$, each $r_j \in P$, $1 \leq j \leq k$, is of the form $r_j = (p_j, Q_j, R_j)$, and each p_j is a PS rule of the form $\alpha_{p_j} \to \beta_{p_j}$, $\alpha_{p_j} \in (N \cup T)^* N (N \cup T)^*$, and $\beta_{p_j} \in (N \cup T)^*$. Consider $P_\alpha = \{\alpha_{p_j} | 1 \leq j \leq k\}$ the set of the left-hand sides of all rules in P.

Definition 6. Let G be a RCG^{ac} with PS rules. A derivation in G is called
  - *leftmost-1* if each rule used in the derivation rewrites the leftmost substring α occurring in the current sentential form, such that if $\alpha_0 \alpha$ is a prefix of the current sentential form, then $\alpha_0 \in T^*$ and $\alpha \in P_\alpha$,
  - *leftmost-2* if at each step of derivation, the leftmost occurrence of $\alpha \in P_\alpha$ that can be rewritten is rewritten,
  - *leftmost-3* if each rule used in the derivation rewrites the leftmost occurrence of its left-hand side in the current sentential form.,

In [3] we proved that leftmost SZLs of PSGs, and particularly of context-sensitive (CS) grammars, can be recognized in logarithmic time and space by indexing ATMs. It is easy to observe that leftmost-1 derivations in RCGs are not more restrictive than leftmost derivations in Chomsky grammars.

Denote by $SZRCL_1^{ac}(X)$ the class of leftmost-1 SZLs of RCGs^{ac} with X rules, $X \in \{CS, PS\}$, respectively. We have

Theorem 4. $SZRCL_1^{ac}(X) \subseteq ALOGTIME$, $X \in \{CS, PS\}$.

Sketch of Proof. The claim can be proved using a similar method as in [3]. However, besides checking the leftmost-1 condition of each RC rule γ_i of the form $(p_{\gamma_i}, Q_{\gamma_i}, R_{\gamma_i})$, $1 \leq i \leq n$, occurring in an input word $\gamma = \gamma_1 \gamma_2 ... \gamma_n \in P^*$, $\mathcal{A}$ also checks whether the sentential form obtained at the ith step of derivation, denoted by SF_i, contains all nonterminals in Q_{γ_i} and no nonterminal in R_{γ_i} (by omitting to count common occurrences of a nonterminal on SF_i and on the left-hand side of rule p_{γ_i}). $\qquad\square$

Corollary 7. $SZRCL_1^{ac}(X) \subset \mathcal{NC}^1$ $(SZRCL_1^{ac}(X) \subset DSPACE(\log n))$, $X \in \{CS, PS\}$.

However, leftmost-i, $i \in \{2, 3\}$, derivations in RCGs with PS rules, are more complex than the leftmost-1 case. We leave open these cases for further research.

5 On the Complexity of SZLs of Other Regulated Rewriting Grammars

The methods presented in this paper can be applied to several other regulated rewriting mechanisms. In this section we focus on the complexity of SZLs of programmed grammars (PGs), and briefly discuss what is going on for other regulated rewriting grammars. Results on the generative capacity of PGs can be found in [5], [17], and [18]. From [5] we have the following definitions.

Definition 7. A *programmed grammar* is a quadruple $G = (N, T, S, P)$ where S is the axiom, N and T, $N \cap T = \emptyset$, are finite sets of *nonterminals* and *terminals*, respectively. P is a finite set of *triplets* (programmed grammar rules) of the form $r = (p_r, \sigma_r, \varphi_r)$, where p_r is an unrestricted Chomsky rule, σ_r and φ_r are subsets of P, called the *success field* and *failure field* of r, respectively. If $\varphi_r = \emptyset$, for any $r \in P$, then G is a programmed grammar without *appearance checking*, otherwise G is a programmed grammar with *appearance checking* (henceforth PG^{ac}).

Definition 8. Let $G = (N, T, S, P)$ be a PG^{ac} and $V = N \cup T$. The language $L(G)$ generated by G is defined as the set of all words $w \in T^*$ such that there is a derivation $D: S = w_0 \Rightarrow_{r_{i_1}} w_1 \Rightarrow_{r_{i_2}} w_2 \Rightarrow_{r_{i_3}} ... \Rightarrow_{r_{i_s}} w_s = w$, $s \geq 1$, and for $r_{i_j} = (p_{r_{i_j}}, \sigma_{r_{i_j}}, \varphi_{r_{i_j}})$, where $p_{r_{i_j}}$ is a Chomsky rule of the form $\alpha_{i_j} \to \beta_{i_j}$, $1 \leq j \leq s - 1$, we have either $w_{j-1} = w'_{j-1} \alpha_{i_j} w''_{j-1}$, $w_j = w'_{j-1} \beta_{i_j} w''_{j-1}$ for some w'_{j-1}, $w''_{j-1} \in V^*$ and $r_{i_{j+1}} \in \sigma_{r_{i_j}}$, or α_{i_j} does not occur in w_{j-1}, $w_{j-1} = w_j$ and $r_{i_{j+1}} \in \varphi_{r_{i_j}}$.

Unrestricted SZLs and leftmost-i, $i \in \{1, 2, 3\}$, SZLs of PGs^{ac} can be defined in the same way as in Definition 3, with the specification that G is a PG^{ac} and D is either an unrestricted or a leftmost-i derivation of w.

We denote by $SZP^{ac}(CF)$ and $SZPL_i^{ac}(CF)$ the classes of SZLs and leftmost-i, $i \in \{1, 2, 3\}$, SZLs of PGs^{ac} with CF rules, respectively.

In the sequel, for the sake of simplicity (as in the case of RCGs) we use the same notation both for a PG rule and the label associated with it.

Let $G = (N, T, P, A_1)$ be a PG^{ac}, where A_1 is the axiom, $N = \{A_1, ..., A_m\}$ and $P = \{r_1, ..., r_k\}$ are the finite sets of ordered nonterminals and labels associated in one-to-one productions in P, respectively. A rule p_r in $r = (p_r, \sigma_r, \varphi_r)$ is of the form $\alpha_{p_r} \rightarrow \beta_{p_r}$, $\alpha_{p_r} \in N$, and $\beta_{p_r} \in (N \cup T)^*$. As for RCGs, the *net effect* of a PG rule r, with respect to each nonterminal $A_l \in N$, $1 \le l \le m$, is defined by $df_{A_l}(p_r) = |\beta_{p_r}|_{A_l} - |\alpha_{p_r}|_{A_l}$. To each PG rule r we associate a vector $V(r) \in \mathbf{Z}^m$ defined by $V(r) = (df_{A_1}(p_r), df_{A_2}(p_r), ..., df_{A_m}(p_r))$.

Theorem 5. *Each language $L \in SZP^{ac}(CF)$ can be recognized by an indexing ATM in $\mathcal{O}(\log n)$ time and space ($SZP^{ac}(CF) \subseteq ALOGTIME$).*

Proof. Let $G = (N, T, P, A_1)$ be a PG^{ac} with CF rules. Consider an indexing ATM $\mathcal{A}$ with a similar configuration as in Theorem 1, and $\gamma = \gamma_1 \gamma_2 ... \gamma_n \in P^*$ an input word of length n. Each label γ_i corresponds to a triplet in P of the form $(p_{\gamma_i}, \sigma_{\gamma_i}, \varphi_{\gamma_i})$, where p_{γ_i} is a CF rule of the form $\alpha_{\gamma_i} \rightarrow \beta_{\gamma_i}$, $1 \le i \le n$.

At the beginning of the computation the first track of the working tape of $\mathcal{A}$ stores $k + 1$ vectors, V^0 corresponding to the axiom, i.e., $V_1^0 = 1$ and $V_l^0 = 0$, $2 \le l \le m$, and $V(r_j)$, $1 \le j \le k$. In order to guess the length of γ, $\mathcal{A}$ proceeds with the procedure described at Level 1 (*Existential*), Theorem 1.

Levels 2-3 (*Universal-Existential*). $\mathcal{A}$ spawns n universal processes $\wp_i$, $1 \le i \le n$ (Level 2). On $\wp_1$ $\mathcal{A}$ checks whether $\alpha_{\gamma_1} = A_1$, while on $\wp_2$ $\mathcal{A}$ checks whether $\gamma_2 \in \sigma_{\gamma_1}$. For each $\wp_i$, $3 \le i \le n$, $\mathcal{A}$ counts the number of occurrences of each $r_j \in P$, $1 \le j \le k$, in $\gamma^{(i-1)} = \gamma_1 \gamma_2 ... \gamma_{i-2}$. Suppose that r_j occurs $c_j^{(i-1)}$ times in $\gamma^{(i-1)}$, $0 \le c_j^{(i-1)} \le i - 2$. Since for some occurrences of $r_j = (p_j, \sigma_j, \varphi_j)$ in $\gamma^{(i-1)}$, p_j may be either effectively applied (because its left-hand side α_{γ_j} occurs in the sentential form) or it is a "dummy" rule (because p_j cannot be applied), for each $1 \le j \le k$, $\mathcal{A}$ guesses a pair of arbitrarily large integers $t_j^{(i-1)} = (c_{j,a}^{(i-1)}, c_{j,d}^{(i-1)})$ such that $c_{j,a}^{(i-1)} + c_{j,d}^{(i-1)} = c_j^{(i-1)}$, where $c_{j,a}^{(i-1)}$ is the number of times r_j is effectively applied up to the $(i-1)^{th}$ step of derivation, and $c_{j,d}^{(i-1)}$ is the number of times r_j is a dummy rule in $\gamma^{(i-1)}$. Since there exist $\mathcal{O}(n^2)$ guesses, $\mathcal{A}$ spawns $\mathcal{O}(n^2)$ existential branches (Level 3). On each existential branch holding a pair $t_j^{(i-1)}$, $\mathcal{A}$ computes the sums $s_{A_l}^{(i-1)} = V_l^0 + \sum_{j=1}^k c_{j,a}^{(i-1)} V_l(r_j)$, $1 \le l \le m$, i.e., the number of occurrences of each A_l in the sentential form obtained at the $(i-1)^{th}$ step of derivation. Then, $\mathcal{A}$ checks whether one of the following conditions holds:

1. $s_{\alpha_{\gamma_{i-1}}}^{(i-1)} \ge 1$ and $\gamma_i \in \sigma_{i-1}$, i.e., γ_{i-1} is effectively applied and the next rule must be chosen from its success field,

2. $s_{\alpha_{\gamma_{i-1}}}^{(i-1)} = 0$ and $\gamma_i \in \varphi_{i-1}$, i.e., γ_{i-1} is a dummy rule and the next rule must be chosen from its failure field.

Besides, for the last process $\wp_n$, $\mathcal{A}$ computes $s_{A_l}^{(n, out, a)} = s_{A_l}^{(n-1)} + df_{A_l}(p_{\gamma_{n-1}}) + df_{A_l}(p_{\gamma_n})$ and $s_{A_l}^{(n, out, d)} = s_{A_l}^{(n-1)} + df_{A_l}(p_{\gamma_n})$, $1 \le l \le m$, and it checks whether one of the following conditions holds:

1. $s_{\alpha_{\gamma_{n-1}}}^{(n-1)} \geq 1$, $\gamma_n \in \sigma_{n-1}$, $s_{\alpha_{\gamma_n}}^{(n)} \geq 1$, $s_{A_l}^{(n,out,a)} = 0$, $1 \leq l \leq m$,

2. $s_{\alpha_{\gamma_{n-1}}}^{(n-1)} = 0$, $\gamma_n \in \varphi_{n-1}$, $s_{\alpha_{\gamma_n}}^{(n)} \geq 1$, $s_{A_l}^{(n,out,d)} = 0$, $1 \leq l \leq m$.

Each process $\wp_i$, $1 \leq i \leq n$, returns 1, if one of the conditions $1 - 2$ holds. Otherwise it returns 0. As in Theorem 1, $\mathcal{A}$ performs the whole computation in $\mathcal{O}(\log n)$ time and space. □

Corollary 8. $SZP^{ac}(CF) \subset \mathcal{NC}^1$ $(SZP_1^{ac}(CF) \subset DSPACE(\log n))$.

The algorithm described in the proof of Theorem 2 cannot be applied for the case of leftmost-1 SZLs of PGs^{ac}. The explanation is that, in the proof of Theorem 2, even if process $\wp_v$ ($\wp_l$) returns the true value, which means that at its turn γ_v (γ_l) can be applied in a leftmost-1 derivation manner on $\gamma_1...\gamma_{v-1}$ ($\gamma_1...\gamma_{l-1}$), the process $\wp_i$ cannot "see" whether γ_v (γ_l) has been effectively applied in the derivation, or it is only a dummy rule, since all branches spawned at the same level of the computation tree of $\mathcal{A}$ are independent on each other.

Denote by $SZPL_1(X)$ the class of leftmost-1 SZLs of PGs without appearance checking, with X-rules, $X \in \{CF, CS, PS\}$, and by $SZPL_i^{ac}(CF)$, $i \in \{1,2,3\}$, the class of leftmost-i SZLs of PGs with appearance checking and CF rules. Using a similar method as in Theorems 2, 3, and 4 we have, respectively

Theorem 6. $SZPL_1(CF) \subseteq ALOGTIME$ $(SZPL_1(CF) \subset \mathcal{NC}^1)$.

Theorem 7. Each language $L \in SZPL_i^{ac}(CF)$, $i \in \{1,2,3\}$, can be recognized by an indexing ATM in $\mathcal{O}(\log n)$ space and $\mathcal{O}(\log^2 n)$ time $(SZPL_i^{ac}(CF) \subset \mathcal{NC}^2)$.

Theorem 8. $SZPL_1(X) \subseteq ALOGTIME$ $(SZPL_1(X) \subset \mathcal{NC}^1)$, $X \in \{CS, PS\}$.

Brief discussion on other regulated rewriting grammars. Matrix grammars (MGs) are regulated rewriting grammars in which rules are grouped into *matrices* composed of a finite number of rules obeying a *predefined order*. For the case of MGs with appearance checking (MGs^{ac}) some rules in a matrix sequence can be passed over if they belong to a set of *forbidding rules* and if by applying them the derivation is blocked or never ends. If $\gamma = \gamma_1\gamma_2...\gamma_n$ is an input word for an indexing ATM $\mathcal{A}$, where each γ_i is the label of a matrix used in the derivation in a MG^{ac}, when spelling γ, $\mathcal{A}$ cannot estimate which of the forbidding rules of a matrix, applied at a certain step of derivation, have been used or not. Hence, as in the case of PGs^{ac} for each γ_i, $\mathcal{A}$ has to guess a $t_j^{(i-1)}$ tuple composed of a finite number of arbitrarily large integers that prescribes the number of times a certain ordered combination of rules in a matrix sequence has been applied, up to the ith step of derivation. Consequently, Theorems 5, 6, and 8 hold for SZLs of MGs without appearance checking, while Theorems 7 holds for leftmost-i, $i \in \{1,2,3\}$, SZLs of MGs^{ac}. The same observation holds for *regularly controlled grammars*. The method used in Theorem 7 (or 3) can be applied to prove that the class of unrestricted SZLs of MGs^{ac} is contained in $\mathcal{NC}^2$. Theorems 1, 2, 3, and 4 hold also for *additive* and *multiplicative valence grammars*, and *conditional* RCGs, since the membership problem for regular languages is in $\mathcal{NC}^1$.

References

1. Balcázar, J.L., Díaz, J., Gabarró, J.: Structural Complexity, vol. II. Springer, Heidelberg (1990)
2. Chandra, A., Kozen, D., Stockmeyer, L.: Alternation. J. ACM 28(1), 114–133 (1981)
3. Cojocaru, L., Mäkinen, E., Ţiplea, F.L.: Classes of Szilard Languages in NC^1. In: 11th International Symposium on Symbolic and Numeric Algorithms for Scientific Computing, pp. 299–306. IEEE Computer Society Press, Los Alamitos (2009)
4. Cremers, A.B., Maurer, H.A., Mayer, O.: A Note On Leftmost Restricted Random Context Grammars. Inf. Process. Lett. 2(2), 31–33 (1973)
5. Dassow, J., Păun, G.: Regulated Rewriting in Formal Language Theory. Springer, Heidelberg (1989)
6. Duske, J., Parchmann, R., Specht, J.: Szilard Languages of IO-Grammars. Information and Control 40(3), 319–331 (1979)
7. Ewert, S., van der Walt, A.P.J.: A Pumping Lemma for Random Permitting Context Languages. Theor. Comput. Sci. 270(1-2), 959–967 (2002)
8. Fischer, P., Meyer, A., Rosenberg, A.: Counter Machines and Counter Languages. Theory of Computing Systems 2(3), 265–283 (1968)
9. Hesse, W.: Division Is in Uniform TC^0. In: Orejas, F., Spirakis, P.G., van Leeuwen, J. (eds.) ICALP 2001. LNCS, vol. 2076, pp. 104–114. Springer, Heidelberg (2001)
10. Hopcroft, J., Ullman, J.: Introduction to Automata Theory, Languages and Computation. Addison-Wesley, Reading, Massachusetts (1979)
11. Igarashi, Y.: The Tape Complexity of Some Classes of Szilard Languages. SIAM J. Comput. 6(3), 460–466 (1977)
12. Mäkinen, E.: On Certain Properties of Left Szilard Languages. EIK 19(10/11), 497–501 (1983)
13. Mäkinen, E.: On Context-Free and Szilard Languages. BIT Numerical Mathematics 24(2), 164–170 (1984)
14. Păun, G.: On Szilard's Languages Associated to a Matrix Grammar. Inf. Process. Lett. 8(2), 104–105 (1979)
15. Penttonen, M.: On Derivation Language Corresponding to Context-Free Grammars. Acta Inf. 3, 285–291 (1974)
16. Penttonen, M.: Szilard Languages Are log n Tape Recognizable. EIK 13(11), 595–602 (1977)
17. Rosenkrantz, D.J.: Programmed Grammars - a New Device for Generating Formal Languages. PhD Thesis, Columbia University, New York (1967)
18. Rosenkrantz, D.J.: Programmed Grammars and Classes of Formal Languages. J. ACM 16(1), 107–131 (1969)
19. Ruzzo, W.: On Uniform Circuit Complexity. J. Comput. Syst. Sci. 22(3), 365–383 (1981)
20. Salomaa, A.: Matrix Grammars with a Leftmost Restriction. Information and Control 20(2), 143–149 (1972)
21. Salomaa, A.: Formal Languages. Academic Press, London (1973)
22. Vollmer, H.: Introduction to Circuit Complexity A Uniform Approach. Springer, Heidelberg (1999)
23. van der Walt, A.P.J.: Random Context Languages. In: Information Processing. Proceedings of IFIP Congress, vol. 1, pp. 66–68. North-Holland, Amsterdam (1972)
24. van der Walt, A.P.J., Ewert, S.: A Shrinking Lemma for Random Forbidding Context Languages. Theor. Comput. Sci. 237(1-2), 149–158 (2000)

Energy Games in Multiweighted Automata*

Uli Fahrenberg[1], Line Juhl[2], Kim G. Larsen[2], and Jiří Srba[2,**]

[1] INRIA/IRISA, Rennes Cedex, France
ulrich.fahrenberg@irisa.fr
[2] Aalborg University, Department of Computer Science, Denmark
{linej,kgl,srba}@cs.aau.dk

Abstract. Energy games have recently attracted a lot of attention. These are games played on finite weighted automata and concern the existence of infinite runs subject to boundary constraints on the accumulated weight, allowing e.g. only for behaviours where a resource is always available (nonnegative accumulated weight), yet does not exceed a given maximum capacity. We extend energy games to a multiweighted and parameterized setting, allowing us to model systems with multiple quantitative aspects. We present reductions between Petri nets and multiweighted automata and among different types of multiweighted automata and identify new complexity and (un)decidability results for both one- and two-player games. We also investigate the tractability of an extension of multiweighted energy games in the setting of timed automata.

1 Introduction

Energy games are two-player games played on finite weighted graphs with the objective of finding an infinite run where the accumulated weight is constrained by a lower and possibly also an upper bound. Such games have attracted considerable attention [4,5,6,7,8,9,10,11,12,17] in recent years, as they find natural applications in design and analysis of resource-constrained reactive systems, e.g. embedded or hybrid systems.

We study *multiweighted* energy games, where the weight vectors can have an arbitrary dimension. Let us motivate the study by a small example of an automatic lawn mower with a rechargeable battery and a container for collecting grass. Both the battery and the container have a maximum capacity that cannot be exceeded. We assume that the battery can be recharged and the container can be emptied at nearby servicing stations. The charger is an old-fashioned one, and it charges only for a fixed amount of energy corresponding to going from discharged to fully charged. If the lawn mower starts charging while the battery is not fully discharged, the battery will break. The station for emptying the container removes a unit amount of grass at a time and consumes a unit of battery energy. The container will break if too much grass is stored in it.

* Supported by the VKR Center of Excellence MT-LAB.
** Partially supported by Ministry of Education of Czech Republic, MSM 0021622419.

A. Cerone and P. Pihlajasaari (Eds.): ICTAC 2011, LNCS 6916, pp. 95–115, 2011.
© Springer-Verlag Berlin Heidelberg 2011

96   U. Fahrenberg et al.

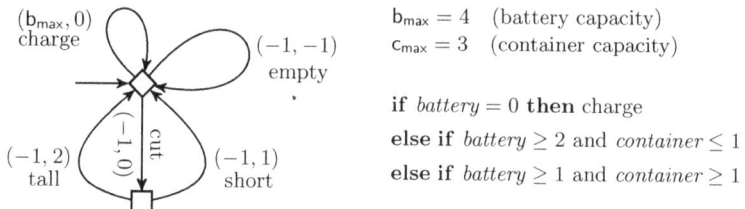

(a) A lawn mower 2-weighted game

$b_{max} = 4$ (battery capacity)
$c_{max} = 3$ (container capacity)

if $battery = 0$ then charge
else if $battery \geq 2$ and $container \leq 1$ then cut
else if $battery \geq 1$ and $container \geq 1$ then empty

(b) A winning strategy for Player 1

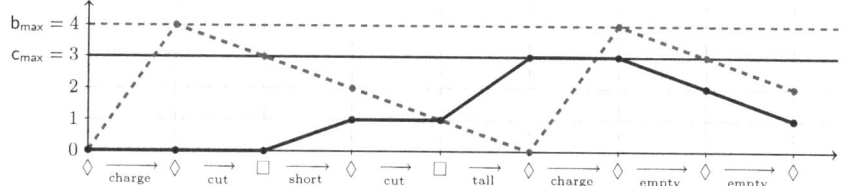

(c) A run of the game (dashed line shows battery level, solid line container content)

Fig. 1. A lawn mower example

A weighted game describing the lawn mower behaviour is given in Figure 1a. Each transition has a 2-dimensional vector representing the change to the accumulated battery level in the first coordinate and to the accumulated volume of grass in the container in the second coordinate. The numbers b_{max} and c_{max} represent the maximum capacity of the battery and the container, respectively. The initial state drawn as a diamond is controlled by Player 1 (the existential player), while the other state drawn as a square is controlled by Player 2 (the universal player). In the initial state, Player 1 has the choice of either charging the battery, emptying the container or cutting the grass. Moving to the lawn costs one unit of battery energy, and then Player 2 (the environment) controls whether the actual mowing, which costs again one energy unit, will fill the container with one or two units of grass, depending on whether the grass was short or tall. A *configuration* of the game consists of the state and the accumulated weight in all coordinates. A *run* is a sequence of transitions between configurations formed by the players of the game and starting from the initial state with zero accumulated weight.

The question we ask now (the problem called *energy games with lower and upper bounds*) is whether Player 1 has a strategy so that in the infinite run of actions the lawn mower performs, starting with empty battery and empty container, both the accumulated battery level as well as the container content stay invariantly above zero and do not exceed the given upper bounds $b_{max} = 4$ and $c_{max} = 3$. Such a strategy exists and it is depicted in Figure 1b. Figure 1c illustrates a finite run of the lawn mower game according to this strategy.

If we lower the volume of the container to $c_{max} = 2$, no such strategy exists. Player 1 must take the charge transition as the first step, after which cutting is the only opportunity. Player 2 can now choose to cut the short grass, leading to battery level 2 and grass volume 1. From here Player 1 can only empty the container, as cutting would allow Player 2 to break the container. After emptying the container, battery level is 1 and no transition (apart from cutting) is possible.

There are several variants of the above energy game problem. If we e.g. assume a modern battery charger which does not break the battery when it is not empty, then we have another variant of the problem called *energy games with weak upper bounds*. The weak upper bound game allows taking transitions that will exceed the upper bounds, but these will never accumulate more energy than the maximum capacity. We may also consider infinite runs that are constrained only by a given lower bound but with no upper bound. Finally, we ask questions regarding *parameterization*. We want to decide whether there *exists* some battery capacity b_{max} and some initial battery level such that Player 1 wins the energy game with lower and upper bound (or some of its variants). In our example one can by a simple reasoning argue that for a container capacity $c_{max} = 2$, there is no battery capacity b_{max} so that Player 1 can guarantee an infinite behaviour of the lawn mower.

Contributions. We define the variants of multiweighted energy games (Section 2) and present reductions involving these games, leading to new decidability and complexity results. Some reductions are to/from Petri nets (Section 3) while others are between different multiweighted energy games (Section 4). This is followed by a summary of decidability and complexity results we achieved. In Section 6 we consider a parameterized version of existential one-player games and show that some variants of the problem lead to undecidability while others are decidable in polynomial time. We conclude by presenting an undecidability result for a natural timed extension of the energy games (Section 7).

Related Work. The idea of checking whether a given resource stays above zero at all times was first presented by Chakrabarti et al. in [7], treating the subject in relation to interfaces. The lower and (weak) upper bound problems were first formulated in [5] for the case with a single weight. The paper presents several complexity results for the 1-weighted case, both timed and untimed, and has given rise to a number of recent papers on 1-weighted energy games [9,10,11].

The multiweighted extension has been studied in [6], but only for energy games with *unary* weights, i.e. updates by 1, 0 or −1. A continuation of this work presents a polynomial time algorithm for the 2-weighted case with unary inputs [8]. Contrary to this line of work, we consider *binary* input encoding, hence weight updates are now drawn from the full set of integers. Also in contrast to [6,8], where only complexity *upper* bounds are given, we give complexity *lower* bounds that in most cases match the upper bounds.

Multiweighted energy games with general integer updates have been considered in [9], where the authors show that the problem of deciding the existence of an initial weight vector such that Player 1 can win the lower bound energy game is solvable in polynomial time. In contrast to this, we show here that the non-parameterized variant of this problem—can Player 1 win with a *given* initial weight vector—is EXPSPACE-hard. We also treat the parameterized setting, where we show that the existential lower and (weak) upper bound problems with both bounds and initial weight vector parameterized are also decidable in polynomial time, unless the upper bound parameter is used in the transitions of the automaton, in which case the problem becomes undecidable.

2   Multiweighted Automata and Games

We denote by $\mathbb{Z}^k$ the set of integer vectors of dimension $k > 0$ and by $\bar{w}[i]$ the i'th coordinate of a vector $\bar{w} \in \mathbb{Z}^k$. A k-*weighted game* G is a four-tuple $(Q_1, Q_2, q_0, \longrightarrow)$ where Q_1 and Q_2 are finite, disjoint sets of *existential* and *universal* states, respectively, $q_0 \in Q_1 \cup Q_2$ is the initial state and $\longrightarrow \subseteq (Q_1 \cup Q_2) \times \mathbb{Z}^k \times (Q_1 \cup Q_2)$ is a finite weighted transition relation, written as $q \xrightarrow{\bar{w}} q'$ whenever $(q, \bar{w}, q') \in \longrightarrow$. We refer to Figure 1a in the introduction for an example of a k-weighted game with $k = 2$.

We are interested only in infinite runs in multiweighted games, hence for the rest of the paper, we assume that the game G is non-blocking, i.e. for every $q \in Q_1 \cup Q_2$ we have $q \xrightarrow{\bar{w}} q'$ for some $\bar{w} \in \mathbb{Z}^k$ and $q' \in Q_1 \cup Q_2$.

A *weighted run* in a k-weighted game $G = (Q_1, Q_2, q_0, \longrightarrow)$ restricted to a *weak upper bound* $\bar{b} \in (\mathbb{N}_0 \cup \infty)^k$ is an infinite sequence $(q_0, \bar{v}_0), (q_1, \bar{v}_1), (q_2, \bar{v}_2), \dots$ where $q_0, q_1, \dots \in Q_1 \cup Q_2$, $\bar{v}_0 = \bar{0} = (0, 0, \dots, 0)$ and $\bar{v}_1, \bar{v}_2, \dots \in \mathbb{Z}^k$ such that for all $j \geq 0$ we have $q_j \xrightarrow{\bar{w}_j} q_{j+1}$ and

$$\bar{v}_{j+1}[i] = \min \left\{ \bar{v}_j[i] + \bar{w}_j[i], \bar{b}[i] \right\}$$

for all coordinates i. An illustration of a run in a 2-weighted game is given in Figure 1c in the introduction. Intuitively, a weighted run is a sequence of states together with the accumulated weight gathered along the path. Moreover, the accumulated weight is truncated, should it exceed in some coordinate the given maximum weight $\bar{b}$. By $\mathsf{WR}_{\bar{b}}(G)$ we shall denote the set of all weighted runs in G restricted to the maximum accumulated weight $\bar{b}$.

A *strategy* for Player $i \in \{1, 2\}$ in a k-weighted game $G = (Q_1, Q_2, q_0, \longrightarrow)$ (restricted to a weak upper bound $\bar{b}$) is a mapping σ from each finite prefix of a weighted run in $\mathsf{WR}_{\bar{b}}(G)$ of the form $(q_0, \bar{v}_0), \dots, (q_n, \bar{v}_n)$ with $q_n \in Q_i$ to a configuration $(q_{n+1}, \bar{v}_{n+1})$ such that $(q_0, \bar{v}_0), \dots, (q_n, \bar{v}_n), (q_{n+1}, \bar{v}_{n+1})$ is a prefix of some weighted run in $\mathsf{WR}_{\bar{b}}(G)$. A weighted run $(q_0, \bar{v}_0), (q_1, \bar{v}_1), \dots$ *respects* a strategy σ of Player i if $\sigma((q_0, \bar{v}_0), \dots, (q_n, \bar{v}_n)) = (q_{n+1}, \bar{v}_{n+1})$ for all n such that $q_n \in Q_i$. Figure 1b in the introduction shows a strategy for the 2-weighted game from Figure 1a; note that the run of the game depicted in Figure 1c indeed respects this strategy.

We shall consider three decision problems related to energy games on a given k-weighted game $G = (Q_1, Q_2, q_0, \longrightarrow)$. Below we let $\overline{\infty} = (\infty, \infty, \dots, \infty)$, and we write $\bar{w} \leq \bar{v}$ if $\bar{w}[i] \leq \bar{v}[i]$ for all i, $1 \leq i \leq k$.

Energy Game with Lower bound (GL): Given a game G, is there a strategy σ for Player 1 such that any weighted run $(q_0, \bar{v}_0), (q_1, \bar{v}_1), \dots \in \mathsf{WR}_{\overline{\infty}}(G)$ respecting σ satisfies $\bar{0} \leq \bar{v}_i$ for all $i \geq 0$?

Hence we ask whether Player 1 has a winning strategy such that during any play the accumulated weight stays above zero in all coordinates.

Energy Game with Lower and Weak upper bound (GLW): Given a game G and a vector of upper bounds $\bar{b} \in \mathbb{N}_0^k$, is there a strategy σ for Player 1 such that any weighted run $(q_0, \bar{v}_0), (q_1, \bar{v}_1), \dots \in \mathsf{WR}_{\bar{b}}(G)$ respecting σ satisfies $\bar{0} \leq \bar{v}_i$ for all $i \geq 0$?

Hence we ask whether Player 1 has a winning strategy such that during any play the accumulated weight, which is truncated whenever it exceeds the given upper bound, stays in all coordinates above zero.

Energy Game with Lower and Upper bound (GLU): Given a game G and a vector of upper bounds $\bar{b} \in \mathbb{N}_0^k$, is there a strategy σ for Player 1 such that any weighted run $(q_0, \bar{v}_0), (q_1, \bar{v}_1), \dots \in \mathsf{WR}_{\overline{\infty}}(G)$ respecting σ satisfies $\bar{0} \leq \bar{v}_i \leq \bar{b}$ for all i?

Hence we ask whether Player 1 has a winning strategy such that during any play the accumulated weight stays in all coordinates above zero and below the given upper bound.

The problems GL, GLW and GLU can be specialized in two different ways. Either by giving Player 1 the full control over the game by setting $Q_2 = \emptyset$ or dually by giving the full control to Player 2 by assuming that $Q_1 = \emptyset$. The first problem is called the *existential variant* as we essentially ask whether there *exists* some weighted run with the accumulated weight within the given bounds. The second problem is called the *universal variant* as we now require that *all* weighted runs satisfy the constraints of the energy game. We will denote the respective existential problems by EL, ELW and ELU, and the universal problems by AL, ALW and ALU. These special cases are known as one-player games or simply as multiweighted automata, and we denote such games as only a triple $(Q, q_0, \longrightarrow)$.

In the general formulation of energy games there is no fixed bound on the dimension of the weight vectors, in other words, the dimension k is a part of the input. If we want to consider problems of a fixed dimension k, we use the notation $\mathrm{GL}(k)$, $\mathrm{GLW}(k)$, $\mathrm{GLU}(k)$, $\mathrm{EL}(k)$ etc.

As the inputs to our decision problems are numbers, it is important to agree on their encoding. We will use the *binary encoding*, unlike some other recent work [6,8] where unary notation is considered and thus enables to achieve better complexity bounds as the size of their input instance is exponentially larger.

We may also easily allow an initial weight vector $\bar{w}_0$ different from $\bar{0}$. This is evident by adding a new fresh start state with one transition labeled with $\bar{w}_0$ pointing to the original start state. In addition we may assume that in any given upper bound or weak upper bound vector $\bar{b}$ we have $\bar{b}[1] = \bar{b}[2] = \cdots = \bar{b}[k]$. This can be achieved by scaling every i'th coordinate of all weight vectors on transitions with $\frac{\bar{b}[1] \cdot \ldots \cdot \bar{b}[k]}{\bar{b}[i]}$ in order to obtain equality on the coordinates of $\bar{b}$. Such a scaling implies only polynomial increase in the size (in binary encoding) of the upper bound constants.

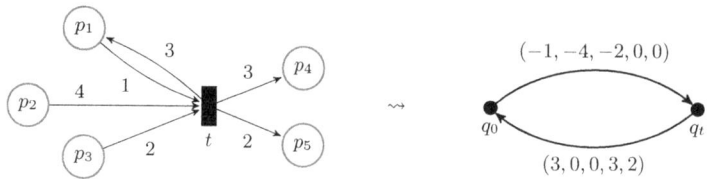

Fig. 2. Translation of a Petri net to a 5-weighted automaton

3 Relationship to Petri Nets

We show that the existential variants of the infinite run problems on multi-weighted automata can be reduced to the corresponding problems on Petri nets and vice versa. This will allow us to transfer some of the decidability and complexity results from the Petri net theory to our setting.

We shall first define the Petri net model with weighted arcs (that allow to consume more than one token from a given place). A *Petri net* is a triple $N = (P, T, W)$ where P is a finite set of places, T is a finite set of transitions, and $W : (P \times T) \cup (T \times P) \to \mathbb{N}_0$ is a function assigning a weight to each arc in the net. A *marking* on N is a function $M : P \to \mathbb{N}_0$ denoting the number of tokens present in the places. A *marked Petri net* is a pair (N, M_0) where N is a Petri net and M_0 is an initial marking on N.

A transition $t \in T$ is *enabled* in a marking M if $M(p) \geq W(p, t)$ for all $p \in P$. An enabled transition may *fire*. When a transition t fires, it produces a new marking M' obtained as $M'(p) = M(p) - W(p, t) + W(t, p)$ for all places $p \in P$. Then we write $M \xrightarrow{t} M'$. A marking M is *reachable* in N if $M_0 \longrightarrow^* M$ where $\longrightarrow = \bigcup_{t \in T} \xrightarrow{t}$. A marked Petri net is called *1-safe* if for any reachable marking M the number of tokens in any place is at most one, i.e. $M(p) \leq 1$ for all $p \in P$. We say that a marked net (N, M_0) has an infinite run if there is a sequence of markings $M_1, M_2, \dots$ and transitions $t_1, t_2, \dots$ such that $M_0 \xrightarrow{t_1} M_1 \xrightarrow{t_2} M_2 \xrightarrow{t_3} \dots$ The *infinite run problem* for Petri nets (see e.g. [13]) is to decide whether a given Petri net has an infinite run.

Lemma 1. *The infinite run Petri net problem is polynomial time reducible to EL. The infinite run Petri net problem for 1-safe nets is polynomial time reducible to ELU and ELW. The problem EL is polynomial time reducible to the infinite run problem of Petri nets.*

Proof. We first prove the first part of the lemma. Given a Petri net $N = (P, T, W)$ where $P = \{p_1, \dots, p_k\}$ we construct a k-weighted automaton $A = (Q, q_0, \longrightarrow)$ such that $Q = \{q_0\} \cup \{q_t \mid t \in T\}$. Now for every $t \in T$ we add to A two transitions $q_0 \xrightarrow{\bar{w}_t^-} q_t$ and $q_t \xrightarrow{\bar{w}_t^+} q_0$ where $\bar{w}_t^-[i] = -W(p_i, t)$ and $\bar{w}_t^+[i] = W(t, p_i)$ for all i, $1 \leq i \leq k$. Consult Figure 2 for an example. The initial weight vector then corresponds to the initial marking of the net in the expected way. It follows from the construction that each transition firing can

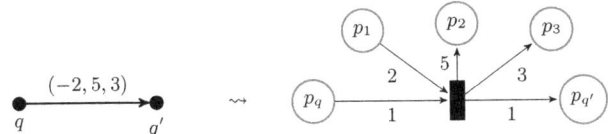

Fig. 3. Translation of a 3-weighted automaton to a Petri net

be simulated by two transitions in the constructed weighted automaton and vice versa. Observe that the reachable Petri net markings are represented as accumulated weight vectors in the automaton and hence are nonnegative in all coordinates. It is easy to verify that the net has an infinite run if and only if the EL problem has a solution. The reduction clearly runs in polynomial time.

For the second part, observe that if the net is 1-safe then by taking the upper bound $\bar{b} = (1, 1, \ldots, 1)$ we have a reduction from the infinite run problem for 1-safe nets to ELU and ELW.

The reduction from k-weighted automata to Petri nets works in a similar way. Given a k-weighted automaton $A = (Q, q_0, \longrightarrow)$ we construct a Petri net $N = (P, T, W)$ where $P = \{p_1, \ldots, p_k\} \cup \{p_q \mid q \in Q\}$ and $T = \{t_{(q,\bar{w},q')} \mid q \xrightarrow{\bar{w}} q'\}$. For each $t_{(q,\bar{w},q')}$ we set $W(p_q, t_{(q,\bar{w},q')}) = 1$, $W(t_{(q,\bar{w},q')}, p_{q'}) = 1$ and for all i, $1 \leq i \leq k$, $W(p_i, t_{(q,\bar{w},q')}) = -\bar{w}[i]$ if $\bar{w}[i] < 0$ and $W(t_{(q,\bar{w},q')}, p_i) = \bar{w}[i]$ if $\bar{w}[i] \geq 0$. See Figure 3 for an example of the reduction. The initial marking corresponds to the initial weight vector in the natural way, and there is one extra token in the place p_{q_0} representing the current state of the automaton. As before, it is easy to verify that the constructed Petri net has an infinite run if and only if the EL problem has a solution. The reduction clearly runs in polynomial time. □

Theorem 1. *The problem EL is EXPSPACE-complete. The problems ELU and ELW are PSPACE-complete.*

Proof. The complexity bounds for EL follow from Lemma 1 and from the fact that the existence of an infinite run in a Petri net is decidable in EXPSPACE [16,2] and EXPSPACE-hard (see e.g. [13]). The same problem for 1-safe Petri nets is PSPACE-complete (see again [13]) and by Lemma 1 we get PSPACE-hardness also for ELU and ELW. The containment of the ELU and ELW problems in PSPACE can be shown by noticing that these problems have an infinite run $(q_0, \bar{v}_0), (q_1, \bar{v}_1), \ldots$ if and only if there are two indices $i < j$ such that $(q_i, \bar{v}_i) = (q_j, \bar{v}_j)$. As the size of any configuration $(q, \bar{v})$ appearing on such a run is polynomially bounded by the size of the input (which includes the upper bound vector), we can use a nondeterministic algorithm to guess such a repeated configuration $(q_i, \bar{v}_i)$ and nondeterministically verify whether it forms a loop which is reachable from the initial pair $(q_0, \bar{v}_0)$. This completes the argument for the containment of ELU and ELW in PSPACE. □

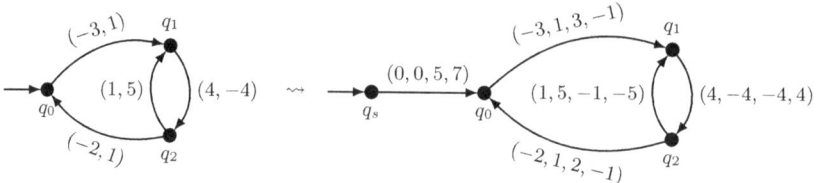

Fig. 4. Example of reduction from GLU with $\bar{b} = (5,7)$ to GL

4   Reductions among Energy Games

In this section we present reductions among the variants of one- and two-player energy games with a particular focus on the size of the weight vectors.

Theorem 2. *The problem $GLU(k)$ is polynomial time reducible to $GL(2k)$ and $GLW(2k)$ for all $k > 0$. The reduction preserves the existential and universal variants of the problems.*

Proof. Let $G_k = (Q_1, Q_2, q_0, \longrightarrow)$ be a k-weighted game and let $\bar{b}$ be a given upper bound vector for the GLU problem. We construct a $2k$-weighted game $G_{2k} = (Q_1 \uplus \{q_s\}, Q_2, q_s, \longrightarrow)$ where $q \xrightarrow{(\bar{w}[1], \bar{w}[2], ..., \bar{w}[k], -\bar{w}[1], -\bar{w}[2], ..., -\bar{w}[k])} q'$ in G_{2k} if and only if $q \xrightarrow{\bar{w}} q'$ in G_k. We moreover add the initial transition $q_s \xrightarrow{\bar{w}_0} q_0$ where $\bar{w}_0[i] = 0$ and $\bar{w}_0[k+i] = \bar{b}[i]$ for all i, $1 \leq i \leq k$. Figure 4 illustrates the construction on an example. Intuitively, every coordinate in the weight vector is duplicated and the duplicated coordinate gets initially the value from the vector $\bar{b}$, while the original coordinate is 0. It is now easy to verify that during any run in G_{2k} all its configurations $(q, \bar{v})$ satisfy the invariant $\bar{v}[i] + \bar{v}[k+i] = \bar{b}[i]$ for all i, $1 \leq i \leq k$.

The upper bound check is hence replaced with a lower bound on the duplicate coordinates and hence the GLU problem is reduced to GL and also to GLW (by using the weak upper bound vector $\bar{b}$), while the size of the weight vectors doubles. The reduction also clearly preserves the existential and universal variants of the problems.   □

Since we already know that ELU(1) is NP-hard [5], using Theorem 2 with $k = 1$ gives that EL(2) is NP-hard too, which is of course then also the case for EL. Similarly as GLU(1) is known to be EXPTIME-hard [5], we get EXPTIME-hardness also for GL(2) and hence also for GL.

Our next reductions show (perhaps surprisingly) that allowing multiple weights is not that crucial in terms of complexity. The first theorem shows that for upper bound games, it suffices to work with one weight only; Theorem 4 then shows that for the existential variant, two weights are enough.

Theorem 3. *The problem GLU is polynomial time reducible to $GLU(1)$.*

Proof. Let $G = (Q_1, Q_2, q_0, \longrightarrow)$ be a k-weighted game and $\bar{b}$ a given upper bound vector for the GLU problem. We assume that G is encoded in binary and let n denote the size of such encoding. This means that all constants that appear in the description of G are less than 2^n. We will construct a corresponding 1-weighted game $G' = (Q'_1, Q'_2, q_s, \longrightarrow)$ where $Q'_1 = Q_1 \cup \{q_2, q_3, \ldots, q_{k+5} \mid q \in Q_1\} \cup \{q_s\}$ and $Q'_2 = Q_2 \cup \{q_1 \mid q \in Q_2\}$ that simulates G.

Let $\bar{w}$ denote any weight vector present in G. Clearly, $0 \leq \bar{w}[1], \ldots, \bar{w}[k] < 2^n$ due to the encoding of the input. Without loss of generality we can assume that all coordinates of $\bar{b}$ are the same, i.e. that $\bar{b} = (b, \ldots, b)$ for some $0 \leq b < 2^n$.

We need to encode the weights from G using only one weight. We will do so by placing them into the single (large) weight w'. Since $b < 2^n$, at most n bits are needed to represent each weight $\bar{w}[i]$. The weight w' is constructed by appending the weights from G in higher and higher bit positions, with a suitable separation sequence to ensure that weights cannot get 'entangled' should their bounds overflow or underflow. Formally, we introduce the following notation for any integer $\ell \in \mathbb{Z}$ and any i, $1 \leq i \leq k$:

$$\langle \ell \rangle^i = \ell \cdot 2^{(i-1)(n+2)} \ .$$

For example, if $n = 4$ then $\langle 6 \rangle^2 = 6 \cdot 2^6 =$ (in binary) $= 110 \cdot 1000000 = 110000000$. A weight vector $\bar{w}$ of size k in G is now represented by the number

$$\langle \bar{w} \rangle \stackrel{\text{def}}{=} \langle \bar{w}[1] \rangle^1 + \langle 2^{n+1} \rangle^1 + \langle \bar{w}[2] \rangle^2 + \langle 2^{n+1} \rangle^2 + \ldots + \langle \bar{w}[k] \rangle^k + \langle 2^{n+1} \rangle^k$$

where the weights $\bar{w}[1], \ldots, \bar{w}[k]$ written in binary from the less significant bits to more significant ones are separated by the binary string '10'. For example if again $n = 4$ then the weight vector $\bar{w} = (110, 1, 1011)$ with the weights written in binary is represented by the binary number $\langle \bar{w} \rangle = 10\ 1011\ 10\ 0001\ 10\ 0110$.

The new upper bound B for G' is defined by $B = \langle b \rangle^{k+1} + \langle \bar{b} \rangle$ where apart from the standard encoding of all upper bounds for all coordinates we add one more time the constant b at the most significant bits (we will use these bits for counting in our construction).

Each transition $q \xrightarrow{\bar{w}} q'$ in G is transformed into a number of transitions in G' as depicted in Figure 5 where Player 1 (existential) states are drawn as diamonds and Player 2 (universal) states are drawn as squares. The states drawn as filled circles can be of either type, and their type is preserved in the translation. We also add the initial transition $q_s \xrightarrow{\langle \bar{0} \rangle} q_0$ which inserts the separation strings 10 at the correct positions.

The idea is that the update of the accumulated weight vector $\bar{v}$ in G via adding a vector $\bar{w}$ like in Figure 5 is simulated by adding the numbers $\langle \bar{w}[1] \rangle^1$, $\langle \bar{w}[2] \rangle^2$, $\ldots, \langle \bar{w}[k] \rangle^k$ to the accumulated weight in G'. The chosen encoding of k weights into a single weight is crucial to preserve the soundness of the construction as discussed in the following remark.

Remark 1. Given an accumulated weight vector $\bar{v}$ and a weight update vector $\bar{w}$ where $\bar{0} \leq \bar{v}, \bar{w} \leq \bar{b} < (2^n, \ldots, 2^n)$, then adding the numbers $\langle \bar{v} \rangle$ and $\langle \bar{w}[i] \rangle^i$ in $\langle \bar{v} \rangle$ changes at most the bits that are designated for representing the weight coordinate $\bar{w}[i]$ and the separating two bits 10 just before it. This can be easily seen by analyzing the two extreme cases of adding $11 \ldots 1$ to an accumulated

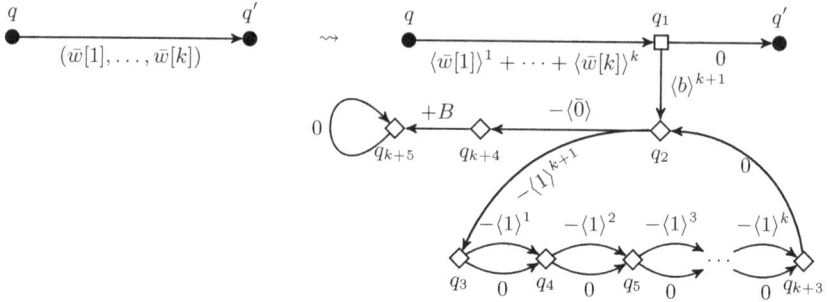

Fig. 5. Simulation of a transition in a k-weighted game by a 1-weighted game

weight coordinate with full capacity and subtracting $11\ldots1$ from an accumulated weight coordinate that represents zero as showed in the following two examples.

$$
\begin{array}{r}
\ldots 10\ 111\ldots111\ 10\ldots \\
+\ldots 00\ 111\ldots111\ 00\ldots \\
\hline
\ldots 11\ 111\ldots110\ 10\ldots
\end{array}
\qquad
\begin{array}{r}
\ldots 10\ 000\ldots000\ 10\ldots \\
-\ldots 00\ 111\ldots111\ 00\ldots \\
\hline
\ldots 01\ 000\ldots001\ 10\ldots
\end{array}
$$

Let us now argue about the correctness of this polynomial time construction. Assume that Player 1 has a winning strategy in the game G. As the accumulated weight stays within the bounds during any such play in G, it is clear that the same winning strategy can be performed also in G' using only a single weight. One complication is that each transition in G is split in G' and a new node for Player 2 (q_1 in Figure 5) is inserted. Hence Player 2 could possibly have an extra winning strategy by playing $q_1 \xrightarrow{\langle b\rangle^{k+1}} q_2$, instead of the expected move to q'. However, because the accumulated weight vector $\bar{v}$ satisfies $0 \le \bar{v}[i] \le b < 2^n$ for all i, we can see that Player 1 wins in this case, by taking the loop $q_2, q_3, \ldots q_{k+3}, q_2$ exactly b times while choosing the zero or $-\langle 1\rangle^i$ transitions (for all i) in such a way that the bits representing the weight $\bar{v}[i]$ are all set to 0. What remains in G' as the accumulated weight is then the value $\langle \bar{0}\rangle$ which consists only of the separation symbols. From here Player 1 takes the transition with weight $-\langle \bar{0}\rangle$, setting the accumulated weight to zero, and wins by performing the transition labeled with $+B$ (which is possible only if the accumulated weight is exactly zero) and repeatedly performing in q_{k+5} the self-loop with weight zero.

On the other hand, assume that a play in G causes the accumulated weight in some coordinate i, $1 \le i \le k$, to get out of the bounds; we shall argue that Player 2 has a winning strategy in G' in this case. Should this happen during a transition from q to q' in G, then in G', Player 2 will simply move from the intermediate state q_1 to q_2, while the counter value of size b is added to the most significant bits of the accumulated weight via adding the number $\langle b\rangle^{k+1}$. It is clear that it is possible to move from q_2 to q_{k+5} only if the accumulated weight is exactly $\langle \bar{0}\rangle$. In order to achieve this value, the accumulated weight needs to be decreased exactly b times via taking the loop $q_2, q_3, \ldots, q_{k+3}, q_2$. Because of Remark 1 we can see that only the bits relevant to each weight coordinate were

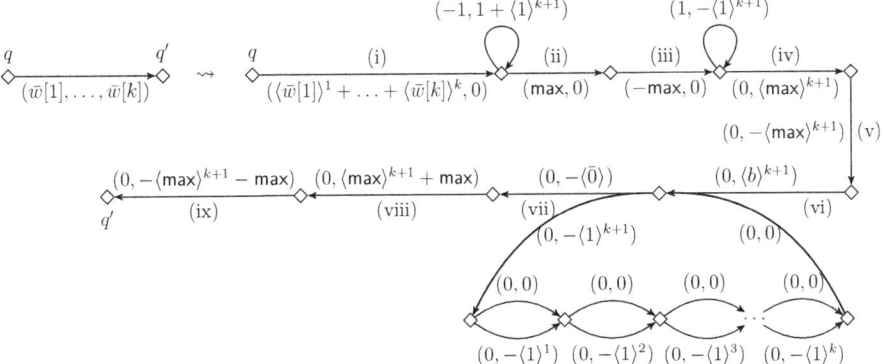

Fig. 6. Simulation of a k-weighted transition by a 2-weighted automaton

changed before entering the loop, so it is impossible to zero all bits corresponding to the coordinate i while preserving the separation bits 10.   □

Theorem 4. *The problem ELU is polynomial time reducible to ELU(2).*

Proof. The reduction idea is similar to the one in the proof of Theorem 3. The main complication is that Player 2 has no states in control, hence checking the underflow and overflow of weights has to be performed without resorting to an opponent. As the original weight values are destroyed during such a check, we need to employ a second weight for saving them.

Let $A = (Q, q_0, \longrightarrow)$ be a k-weighted automaton and $\bar{b}$ the upper bound vector for the ELU problem. We construct a corresponding 2-weighted automaton $A' = (Q', q_s, \longrightarrow)$. Let $\bar{w}$ denote the weight vectors in A and $\bar{v}[1], \bar{v}[2]$ the two weights in A'. As before for an input automaton of size n we may assume that all weights in A have the same upper bound $\bar{b} = (b, b, \ldots, b)$ where $b < 2^n$.

The upper bound $\bar{b}'$ for the ELU(2) problem in A' is given by $\bar{b}' = (\mathsf{max}, \langle\mathsf{max}\rangle^{k+1} + \mathsf{max})$ with $\mathsf{max} = \langle b\rangle^{k+1} + \langle\bar{b}\rangle$. The reason for reserving twice as many bits in the second weight is that we need to save there *two* copies of the first weight. Figure 6 shows how to simulate one transition in A by a number of transitions in A'. From the newly added initial state q_s we also add the transition $q_s \xrightarrow{(\langle\bar{0}\rangle,0)} q_0$ which inserts the separation strings '10' into the first weight.

We shall now argue that the automaton A' faithfully simulates A. We will examine the effect of the sequence of transitions between q and q' added to the automaton A' (here numbered with (i), (ii), ..., (ix) for convenience) and argue at the same time that the part of the run between q and q' in A' is uniquely determined. By construction, $\bar{v}[2]$ will be zero when entering q, and then the transition (i) adds the encoded weights of the original transition in A to $\bar{v}[1]$. Transition (ii) will add the upper bound to $\bar{v}[1]$, hence before this, we need to take the loop with weight $(-1, 1 + \langle 1\rangle^{k+1})$ until $\bar{v}[1]$ equals zero, thereby copying twice the value of $\bar{v}[1]$ to $\bar{v}[2]$ (first copy in the less significant bits, second copy in the more significant bits). After the transitions (ii) and (iii), $\bar{v}[1]$ is then

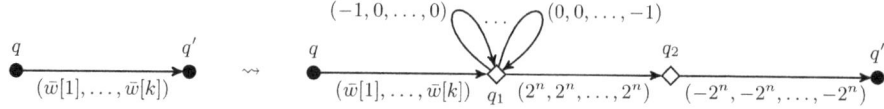

Fig. 7. Simulation of a transition in a LW game by a LU game

again at zero. Now transition (iv) wants to add the upper bound to the most significant bits of $\bar{v}[2]$, hence before this, we need to take the loop with weight $(1, -\langle 1\rangle^{k+1})$ until the value of the most significant bits in $\bar{v}[2]$ is copied to $\bar{v}[1]$, thereby restoring the original weight in $\bar{v}[1]$.

After the transitions (iv) and (v), we are in a situation where both coordinates in the accumulated weight store the same number, and we can afford to destroy the second copy during the verification phase for bound overflow/underflow performed by transitions (vi), the long loop, and transitions (vii), (viii) and (ix). This is identical to the construction in the previous proof (except for the extra coordinate $\bar{v}[1]$ which is not updated). Provided that no violation of bounds was detected, we will reach q' with $\bar{v}[1]$ encoding the weight vector of A at q' and $\bar{v}[2]$ equal to zero.

Hence a transition between two states in A can be performed if and only if the sequence of transitions between q and q' in A' can be performed. As the reduction is clearly in polynomial time, this concludes the proof. □

The next theorem finishes our considerations about reductions between different variants of energy games.

Theorem 5. *The problem GLW is polynomial time reducible to GLU, and ELW is polynomial time reducible to ELU.*

Proof. Let $G = (Q_1, Q_2, q_0, \longrightarrow)$ be a k-weighted game and let $\bar{b}$ be a given upper bound vector for the GLW problem. We will construct a corresponding k-weighted game $G' = (Q_1', Q_2', q_0, \longrightarrow)$ where $Q_1' = Q_1 \cup \{q_1, q_2 \mid q \in Q_1\}$ and $Q_2' = Q_2$ that simulates G.

As before we assume that the weak upper bound is $\bar{b} = (b, \dots, b)$ and that b is represented using at most n bits, hence $0 \le b < 2^n$. The new upper bound for G' is given as $\bar{b}' = (b', \dots, b')$ where $b' = 2^n + b$ (in binary the most significant bit 1 is appended to the binary encoding of b).

Each transition $q \xrightarrow{\bar{w}} q'$ in G is simulated by a number of transitions in G' as seen in Figure 7. Moving from q to q_1 adds $\bar{w}$ to the accumulated weights of G' in exactly the same way as in G. In q_1 Player 1 has the opportunity to decrement independently all weight coordinates with an arbitrary value. The two last transitions from q_1 to q' make sure that in all coordinates all weights are no more than b, otherwise the upper bound $\bar{b}'$ is exceeded.

It is now clear that if Player 1 has a winning strategy in G, then it has a winning strategy also in G' by lowering all weights above b to exactly b in the state q_1. On the other hand, if Player 1 does not have a winning strategy in G, then it cannot win in G' either. This can be observed by the fact that Player 1 is

Table 1. Complexity bounds; results obtained in this paper are in bold

Weights	Type	Existential	Game
One	L	$\in$ P [5]	$\in$ UP $\cap$ coUP [5]
	LW	$\in$ P [5]	$\in$ NP $\cap$ coNP [5]
	LU	NP-hard [5], $\in$ PSPACE [5]	EXPTIME-complete [5]
Fixed $(k>1)$	L	**NP-hard,** $\in k$-EXPTIME [6] (Rem. 2)	**EXPTIME-hard,** $\in k$-EXPTIME [6] (Rem. 3)
	LW	**NP-hard,** $\in$ **PSPACE** (Rem. 4) **PSPACE-complete** for $k \geq 4$	**EXPTIME-complete** (Rem. 5)
	LU	**PSPACE-complete** (Rem. 4)	**EXPTIME-complete** (Rem. 5)
Arbitrary	L	**EXPSPACE-complete** (Thm. 1)	**EXPSPACE-hard** (from EL) decidable [6]
	LW	**PSPACE-complete** (Thm. 1)	**EXPTIME-complete** (Rem. 5)
	LU	**PSPACE-complete** (Thm. 1)	**EXPTIME-complete** (Rem. 5)

forced to decrement all weights to at least b, and the player cannot benefit from decrementing them to any lower number as this makes the position of Player 1 in the weak upper bound game only worse.

Since the reduction is clearly in polynomial time and it adds only existential (Player 1) states, this concludes the proof. $\square$

Now, in combination with Theorems 3 and 4, we get the following corollary.

Corollary 1. *The problems GLW and ELW are polynomial time reducible to GLU(1) and ELU(2), respectively.*

5   Summary of Complexity Results

The collection of complexity results and reductions between different types of energy games and automata enables us to draw the conclusions presented in Table 1. Notice that the LU problems are computationally easier than the L problems for an arbitrary number of weights, even though they are harder than the L problems in the 1-weighted case. The configuration space for the LU (and LW) problems is bounded (see Theorem 1), whereas the same a priori does not apply to the L problem.

Observe also that any *universal* problem with k weights can be solved by checking the same problem for each coordinate independently. If the k-weighted problem violates the bounds at some coordinate, so will do the 1-weighted problem projected on this coordinate. On the other hand, if some coordinate in the 1-weighted problem violates the bounds then so will do the k-weighted game, as the same run leading to the violation in one coordinate leads to a violation in the k-weighted game (unless the violation occurs in some other coordinate before that). As AL(1), ALW(1) and ALU(1) are decidable in P [5], this implies polynomial upper bounds also for all the other k-weighted universal problems.

Remark 2. The problem ELU(1) is NP-hard, and Theorem 2 implies NP-hardness for EL(2). The upper bound follows from the game version of the problem (see also Remark 3).

Remark 3. The lower bound follows from EXPTIME-hardness of GLU(1) and Theorem 2. The upper bound is due to a result in [6] showing $(k-1)$-EXPTIME containment for GL(k) but for games where weight updates are only $+1$, 0, and -1. We can reduce updates with arbitrary weights into this setting by standard techniques (introducing intermediate transitions which repeatedly add or subtract 1) but this causes an exponential blowup in the size of the system. Hence the complexity upper bound increases by one exponent to k-EXPTIME.

Remark 4. The PSPACE upper bound follows from the results for an arbitrary number of weights (Theorem 1). The PSPACE lower bound for ELU(2) is due to the reduction in Theorem 4 and PSPACE-hardness of ELU. By using Theorem 2 we get PSPACE-hardness for ELW(4) because ELU(2) is PSPACE-hard, and we also get NP-hardness of ELW(2) as ELU(1) is NP-hard.

Remark 5. The upper bound for GLU follows from Theorem 3 and the EXPTIME upper bound for GLU(1); the upper bound for GLW follows additionally from Theorem 5. The lower bound for GLU is obvious and for GLW it is by Theorem 2 and the EXPTIME-hardness result for GLU(1).

6   Parameterized Existential Problems

In this section we shall focus in more detail on the existential one-player energy games. So far we have studied decision problems where both the initial weight vector and the upper bound were given as a part of the input. We will now consider parameterized versions of the problems where, given a weighted automaton, we ask whether there is some initial weight vector $\bar{v}_0$ (and some upper bound $\bar{b}$ in case of ELU and ELW) such that the automaton has a run where the accumulated weight satisfies the constraints imposed by the respective variant of the problem.

Recent work by Chatterjee et al. [9] proves that the parameterized version of the EL problem, asking if there is an initial weight vector such that the accumulated weight of some run in the automaton stays (component-wise) above zero, is decidable in polynomial time. Perhaps surprisingly, this result contrasts with our EXPSPACE-hardness result for the EL problem where the initial weight vector is fixed. An interesting fact, using Lemma 1, is that by the result of [9], it is also decidable in polynomial time whether there is an initial marking such that a given Petri net has an infinite run.

The situation can be, however, different when considering the problems ELU and ELW. Depending on whether the parameterized upper bound $\bar{b}$ is allowed to appear as a weight in transitions of the given weighted automaton (see Section 1 for an example where the upper bound appears as a weight), we shall show below that the problem is either decidable in polynomial time or undecidable.

We present first the positive result. Its proof is based on a polynomial time algorithm for zero-weight cycle detection in multiweighted automata by Kosaraju and Sullivan [14], and we acknowledge [9] where we found a pointer to this result, which is mentioned there in connection with the parameterized EL problem.

Theorem 6. *The parameterized ELU and ELW problems where the upper bound parameter does not appear as a weight in the underlying weighted automaton are decidable in polynomial time.*

Proof. We shall first focus on the ELU problem. Notice that a parameterized ELU problem has an infinite run $(q_0, \bar{v}_0), (q_1, \bar{v}_1), \ldots$ where $\bar{0} \leq \bar{v}_i \leq \bar{b}$ for all i and some $\bar{b}$ if and only if there are two indices $j < k$ such that $(q_j, \bar{v}_j) = (q_k, \bar{v}_k)$. In other words, there is a cycle such that the accumulated weight on that cycle is exactly $\bar{0}$. A result in [14] shows that the existence of such zero-weight cycle is decidable in polynomial time.

Assume without loss of generality that the given weighted automaton contains only states reachable (while disregarding the weights) from the initial state q_0. It is now clear that if the weighted automaton contains a zero-weight cycle then the parameterized ELU problem has a solution by choosing an appropriate initial weight vector $\bar{v}_0$ and a sufficiently large upper bound $\bar{b}$ which enables us to execute the whole cycle plus reach the cycle from the initial pair $(q_0, \bar{v}_0)$. On the other hand, if there is no zero-weight cycle then the parameterized ELU does not have a solution, as for any choice of $\bar{v}_0$ and $\bar{b}$, every run will eventually violate either the lower bound or the upper bound.

By similar arguments, it is easy to see that a parameterized ELW problem has a solution if and only if the weighted automaton contains a nonnegative-weight cycle. To check for the existence of such a cycle in polynomial time we can use the trick described in [9]. We simply add to each state in the automaton a number of self-loops with weights $(-1, 0, \ldots, 0), (0, -1, 0, \ldots, 0), \ldots (0, \ldots, 0, -1)$ and then ask for the existence of a zero-weight cycle. □

However, if the upper bound can appear as a weight, we get undecidability.

Recall that a *Minsky machine* with two nonnegative counters c_1 and c_2 is a sequence of labeled instructions $1 : \mathsf{inst}_1; \ 2 : \mathsf{inst}_2; \ \ldots, n : \mathsf{inst}_n$ where $\mathsf{inst}_n = \mathsf{HALT}$ and each inst_i, $1 \leq i < n$, is of one of the following forms:

(Inc) $i\colon c_j\ \mathsf{:=}\ c_j\ \mathsf{+}\ 1;\ \mathtt{goto}\ k$

(Test-Dec) $i\colon \mathtt{if}\ c_j\ \mathsf{=}\ 0\ \mathtt{then\ goto}\ k\ \mathtt{else}\ (c_j\ \mathsf{:=}\ c_j\ \mathsf{-}\ 1;\ \mathtt{goto}\ \ell)$

for $j \in \{1, 2\}$ and $1 \leq k, \ell \leq n$. Instructions of type (Inc) are called *increment* instructions and of type (Test-Dec) are called *test and decrement* instructions. A configuration is a triple (i, v_1, v_2) where i is the current instruction and v_1 and v_2 are the values of the counters c_1 and c_2 respectively. A computation step between configurations is defined in the natural way. If starting from the initial configuration $(1, 0, 0)$ the machine reaches the instruction HALT then we say it *halts*.

It is well known that the problem whether a given Minsky machine halts is undecidable [15].

Theorem 7. *The parameterized $ELU(2)$ and $ELW(4)$ problems where the upper bound parameter can appear as a weight in the underlying weighted automaton are undecidable.*

Proof. We provide a reduction from the undecidable halting problem of Minsky machines [15] to ELU(3). Let $1 : \mathsf{inst}_1$; $2 : \mathsf{inst}_2$; $\ldots, n : \mathsf{inst}_n$ be a Minsky machine over the nonnegative counters c_1 and c_2. We construct a 3-weighted automaton $(Q, q_0, \longrightarrow)$ where $Q = \{q_i, q_i' \mid 0 \le i \le n\}$ and where the initial weight vector $\bar{v}_0$ and the upper bound $\bar{b}$ are parameterized. The intuition is that the first and second coordinates will record the accumulated values of counters c_1 and c_2, respectively, and the third coordinate will be used for counting the number of steps the machine performs. The transitions are of four types:

1. $q_0 \xrightarrow{+\bar{b}} q_0' \xrightarrow{-\bar{b}} q_1$
2. For each instruction i: c_j := c_j + 1; goto k, we add the transitions
   - $q_i \xrightarrow{(+1,0,+1)} q_k$ if $j = 1$, and $q_i \xrightarrow{(0,+1,+1)} q_k$ if $j = 2$.
3. For each instruction i: if c_j = 0 then goto k else (c_j := c_j - 1; goto ℓ), we add the transitions
   - $q_i \xrightarrow{(+\bar{b}[1],0,0)} q_i' \xrightarrow{(-\bar{b}[1],0,+1)} q_k$ and $q_i \xrightarrow{(-1,0,+1)} q_\ell$ if $j = 1$, and
   - $q_i \xrightarrow{(0,+\bar{b}[2],0)} q_i' \xrightarrow{(0,-\bar{b}[2],+1)} q_k$ and $q_i \xrightarrow{(0,-1,+1)} q_\ell$ if $j = 2$.
4. Finally, we add the loop $q_n \xrightarrow{(0,0,0)} q_n$.

It is now easy to argue that the constructed 3-weighted automaton has an infinite run if and only if the Minsky machine halts.

From Theorem 4 we get that ELU(3) is reducible to ELU(2), hence the parameterized existential problem is undecidable for vectors of dimension two. By Theorem 2 we can reduce ELU(2) to ELW(4), which implies the undecidability of the problem also for weak upper bound and weight vectors of size at least four.   □

The parameterized problems ELU(1) and ELW(k) for $1 \le k \le 3$ where the upper bound parameter can appear in the automata are open.

7   Extension to Timed Automata

It is natural to ask for extensions of the results presented in this article to multi-weighted *timed* automata and games [1,3]. For the case with one weight and one clock only, such extensions have been discussed in [4,5]. In [5] it has been shown that the GLU(1) problem is already undecidable for one-clock multiweighted timed automata. By an adaptation of the technique introduced in [5], we can prove that the *existential* problem ELU with two weights and one clock is also undecidable. As the reductions from Theorem 2 apply also to timed automata, we altogether get the following undecidability results. The full version of the proof is in the appendix.

Theorem 8. *The problems $ELU(2)$, $EL(4)$ and $ELW(4)$, and $GLU(1)$, $GL(2)$ and $GLW(2)$ are undecidable for one-clock multiweighted timed automata.*

8   Conclusion and Future Work

We have presented an extension of different types of energy games to a setting with multiple weights and established a comprehensive account of the complexity of these problems. To derive our results, we have demonstrated a close connection of these problems with infinite run problems in Petri nets, together with a number of reductions between different variants of multiweighted energy games. We have also studied a parameterized version of these problems and shown that depending on the precise statement of the problem, it is either solvable in polynomial time or undecidable. Finally, we have demonstrated that for the timed automata extension of energy games, the lower and upper bound existential problem is undecidable already for one clock and two weights.

There are two main problems left open. The first one deals with settling the complexity of the one-weight lower and upper bound existential problem, which is only known to be between NP and PSPACE. This is closely related to the lower bound and weak upper bound problems with a fixed number of weights. The second problem deals with the complexity of energy games with lower bound only, as the present upper complexity bound depends on the number of weights and does not have a matching lower bound. Further extensions with e.g. different acceptance conditions and the optimization problems are also of future interest.

References

1. Alur, R., La Torre, S., Pappas, G.J.: Optimal paths in weighted timed automata. Theoretical Computer Science 318(3), 297–322 (2004)
2. Atig, M.F., Habermehl, P.: On Yen's Path Logic for Petri Nets. In: Bournez, O., Potapov, I. (eds.) RP 2009. LNCS, vol. 5797, pp. 51–63. Springer, Heidelberg (2009)
3. Behrmann, G., Fehnker, A., Hune, T., Larsen, K.G., Pettersson, P., Romijn, J.M.T., Vaandrager, F.W.: Minimum-Cost Reachability for Priced Timed Automata. In: Di Benedetto, M.D., Sangiovanni-Vincentelli, A.L. (eds.) HSCC 2001. LNCS, vol. 2034, pp. 147–161. Springer, Heidelberg (2001)
4. Bouyer, P., Fahrenberg, U., Larsen, K.G., Markey, N.: Timed automata with observers under energy constraints. In: Johansson, K.H., Yi, W. (eds.) HSCC, pp. 61–70. ACM, New York (2010)
5. Bouyer, P., Fahrenberg, U., Larsen, K.G., Markey, N., Srba, J.: Infinite Runs in Weighted Timed Automata with Energy Constraints. In: Cassez, F., Jard, C. (eds.) FORMATS 2008. LNCS, vol. 5215, pp. 33–47. Springer, Heidelberg (2008)
6. Brázdil, T., Jančar, P., Kučera, A.: Reachability games on extended vector addition systems with states. In: Abramsky, S., Gavoille, C., Kirchner, C., Meyer auf der Heide, F., Spirakis, P.G. (eds.) ICALP 2010. LNCS, vol. 6199, pp. 478–489. Springer, Heidelberg (2010)
7. Chakrabarti, A., de Alfaro, L., Henzinger, T.A., Stoelinga, M.: Resource Interfaces. In: Alur, R., Lee, I. (eds.) EMSOFT 2003. LNCS, vol. 2855, pp. 117–133. Springer, Heidelberg (2003)
8. Chaloupka, J.: Z-reachability problem for games on 2-dimensional vector addition systems with states is in P. In: Kučera, A., Potapov, I. (eds.) RP 2010. LNCS, vol. 6227, pp. 104–119. Springer, Heidelberg (2010)

9. Chatterjee, K., Doyen, L., Henzinger, T.A., Raskin, J.-F.: Generalized mean-payoff and energy games. In: Proceedings of FSTTCS 2010. LIPIcs, vol. 8, pp. 505–516. Schloss Dagstuhl - Leibniz-Zentrum fuer Informatik (2010)
10. Chatterjee, K., Doyen, L.: Energy Parity Games. In: Abramsky, S., Gavoille, C., Kirchner, C., Meyer auf der Heide, F., Spirakis, P.G. (eds.) ICALP 2010. LNCS, vol. 6199, pp. 599–610. Springer, Heidelberg (2010)
11. Degorre, A., Doyen, L., Gentilini, R., Raskin, J.-F., Toruńczyk, S.: Energy and Mean-Payoff Games with Imperfect Information. In: Dawar, A., Veith, H. (eds.) CSL 2010. LNCS, vol. 6247, pp. 260–274. Springer, Heidelberg (2010)
12. Ehrenfeucht, A., Mycielski, J.: Positional strategies for mean payoff games. International Journal of Game Theory 8(2), 109–113 (1979)
13. Esparza, J.: Decidability and complexity of Petri net problems — An introduction. In: Reisig, W., Rozenberg, G. (eds.) APN 1998. LNCS, vol. 1491, pp. 374–428. Springer, Heidelberg (1998)
14. Kosaraju, S.R., Sullivan, G.: Detecting cycles in dynamic graphs in polynomial time. In: Proceedings of the 20th Annual ACM Symposium on Theory of Computing (STOC 1988), pp. 398–406. ACM, New York (1988)
15. Minsky, M.L.: Computation: Finite and Infinite Machines. Prentice-Hall, Englewood Cliffs (1967)
16. Yen, H.C.: A unified approach for deciding the existence of certain Petri net paths. Information and Computation 96(1), 119–137 (1992)
17. Zwick, U., Paterson, M.: The complexity of mean payoff games on graphs. Theoretical Computer Science 158(1&2), 343–359 (1996)

Appendix

Definition of a k-weighted timed automaton. Let $\Phi(C)$ be the standard set of (diagonal-free) *clock constraints* over a finite set of *clocks* C given by conjunctions of constraints of the form $x \bowtie c$ with $x \in C$, $c \in \mathbb{Z}$, and $\bowtie$ any of the relations $\leq, <, =, >$, and $\geq$.

A k-weighted timed automaton is a tuple $T = (L, \ell_0, C, E, r, w)$, where L is a finite set of locations, $\ell_0 \in L$ is the initial location, C is a finite set of clocks, $E \subseteq L \times \Phi(C) \times 2^C \times L$ is a finite set of edges, and $r : L \to \mathbb{Z}^k$, $w : E \to \mathbb{Z}^k$ assign weight vectors to locations and edges.

Note that we allow weight updates on edges here; as shown in [4], this can have a significant influence on the complexity of the problems one wants to consider.

We also use the standard notation $v \models g$ for the fact that a *valuation* $v : C \to \mathbb{R}_{\geq 0}$ satisfies the clock constraint $g \in \Phi(C)$, $v + t$ for the valuation given by $(v + t)(x) = v(x) + t$, and $v[R]$ for the valuation with clocks in R reset to value 0.

The semantics of a k-weighted timed automaton is now given by a k-weighted automaton with states $Q = L \times \mathbb{R}_{\geq 0}^C$ and transitions

$$(\ell, v) \xrightarrow{t \cdot r(\ell)} (\ell, v + t) \text{ for all } t \in \mathbb{R}_{\geq 0} \text{ (delay)},$$

$$(\ell, v) \xrightarrow{w(e)} (\ell', v') \text{ for all } e = (\ell, g, R, \ell') \in E \text{ s.t. } v \models g \text{ and } v' = v[R] \text{ (switch)}.$$

We recall the fact that weights on delay transitions may be non-integer real numbers; formally we have to change the definition of a k-weighted game to allow an infinite weighted transition relation $\longrightarrow \subseteq Q \times \mathbb{R}^k \times Q$. A *run* in a multiweighted timed automaton is a sequence of alternating switch and delay transitions in the corresponding multiweighted automaton.

Proof (of Theorem 8). We start by proving the case of ELU(2). The proof is by reduction from Minsky machines to multiweighted timed automata, based on the technique of the proof of Theorem 17 in [5]. We construct a one-clock 2-multiweighted timed automaton T that simulates a Minsky machine such that the Minsky machine loops if and only if T is a positive instance of the ELU(2) problem.

The values c_1, c_2 of the counters will be encoded by the accumulated weight vector $\bar{w} = (5 - 2^{-c_1}, 5 - 2^{-c_2})$ and T will start with an initial weight vector of $\bar{v}_0 = (4, 4)$, and the upper bound vector is $\bar{b} = (5, 5)$.

In order to simulate the instructions of the Minsky machine we now describe two different modules of T.

Increment and decrement: Figure 8 shows the general module used for incrementing and decrementing counter c_1; by interchanging the two weights one obtains the module for c_2. Note that the second component $\bar{w}[2]$ of the weight vector is not changed in the module, and we assume that $\bar{w}[1] = 5 - e$ when entering the module and $0 \leq en \leq 30$. We now prove that when exiting the module, $\bar{w}[1] = 5 - \frac{en}{6}$.

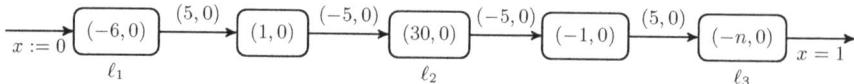

Fig. 8. The module for incrementing ($n = 3$) and decrementing ($n = 12$)

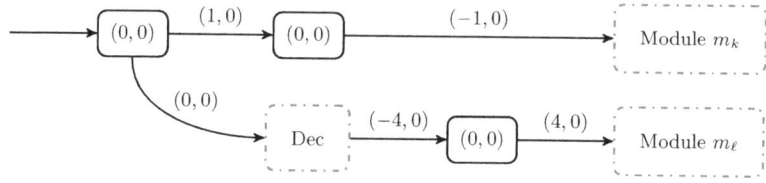

Fig. 9. The test-decrement module

Any legal run must decrease $\bar{w}[1]$ to value 0 while delaying in ℓ_1 (otherwise adding 5 to $\bar{w}[1]$ in the following transition exceeds the upper bound), hence the clock x has the value $\frac{5-e}{6}$ when leaving ℓ_1. We cannot delay in the next location, as this would exceed the upper bound, hence we arrive in ℓ_2 with $x = \frac{5-e}{6}$ and $\bar{w}[1] = 0$. We must delay in ℓ_2 until $\bar{w}[1]$ has the value 5, otherwise the following transition would exceed the lower bound, hence the delay in ℓ_2 is precisely $1/6$ time units. Location ℓ_3 is thus entered with $x = 1 - \frac{e}{6}$ and $\bar{w}[1] = 5$, and after delaying for $e/6$ time units, $\bar{w}[1] = 5 - \frac{en}{6}$.

Hence instantiating $n = 3$ converts an input of $\bar{w}[1] = 5 - e$ to $\bar{w}[1] = 5 - \frac{e}{2}$, thus incrementing counter c_1. Likewise, for $n = 12$ counter c_1 is decremented.

The test-decrement module: We have shown how to implement a module which increments a counter, so we miss to construct a module performing the instruction if $c_1 = 0$ then goto k else ($c_1 := c_1 - 1$; goto ℓ). This module is displayed in Figure 9; the construction for the corresponding c_2 module is symmetric.

We now argue that the module acts as claimed. If $c_1 = 0$ when entering, i.e. $\bar{w}[1] = 4$, then the upper path can be taken, leading to Module m_k with counter value $c_1 = 0$ (and c_2 unchanged). On the other hand, attempting to take the lower path exits the Dec module with a value $\bar{w}[1] = 3$, hence the following transition leads to a violation of the lower bound.

If $c_1 \geq 1$, i.e. $\bar{w}[1] \geq 4.5$, when entering the module, then the $(1,0)$ transition in the upper path will violate the upper bound. In the lower path, the Dec module is left with $\bar{w}[1] \geq 4$ and c_1 decreased by one, hence Module m_ℓ is entered with the correct c_1 value.

We have shown how to faithfully simulate a Minsky machine by a one-clock 2-multiweighted timed automaton such that the Minsky machine has an infinite computation if and only if the timed automaton has an infinite alternating run.

By undecidability of the halting problem for Minsky machines, this concludes the proof for the case of ELU(2).

For the case of $EL(4)$ and $ELW(4)$ we observe that the construction in the proof of Theorem 2 can be adapted also to multiweighted timed automata. Given a k-weighted timed automaton $T = (L, \ell_0, C, I, E, r, w)$ and an upper bound vector $\bar{b}$, we construct a $2k$-weighted timed automaton $T' = (L', \ell_0', C, I', E', r', w')$ with $L' = L \uplus \{\ell_0'\}$, $I'(\ell) = I(\ell)$ for $\ell \in L$, $I'(\ell_0') = (\bigwedge_{x \in C} x = 0)$, $E' = E \cup \{(\ell_0', (\bigwedge_{x \in C} x = 0), \emptyset, \ell_0)\}$, $r'(\ell_0') = \bar{0}$, and

$$r'(\ell) = (\bar{r}[1], \ldots, \bar{r}[k], -\bar{r}[1], \ldots, -\bar{r}[k]) \text{ for } \ell \in L \text{ and } \bar{r} = r(\ell),$$

$$w'(\ell, g, R, \ell') = (\bar{w}[1], \ldots, \bar{w}[k], -\bar{w}[1], \ldots, -\bar{w}[k])$$
$$\text{for } (\ell, g, R, \ell') \in E \text{ and } \bar{w} = w(\ell, g, R, \ell'),$$

$$w'(\ell_0', g, R, \ell_0) = (0, \ldots, 0, \bar{b}[1], \ldots, \bar{b}[k]).$$

Then T is a positive instance of the ELU problem with an upper bound vector $\bar{b}$ if and only if T' is a positive instance of the EL or ELW (with weak upper bound vector $\bar{b}$) problems. The claim then follows from Theorem 8.

The results for the game versions of the problems follow from undecidability of $GLU(1)$ [5] together with Theorem 2. ☐

Intersection Types
for the Resource Control Lambda Calculi

Silvia Ghilezan[1,*], Jelena Ivetić[1,*], Pierre Lescanne[2], and Silvia Likavec[3,*]

[1] University of Novi Sad, Faculty of Technical Sciences, Serbia
gsilvia@uns.ac.rs, jelenaivetic@uns.ac.rs
[2] University of Lyon, École Normal Supérieure de Lyon, France
pierre.lescanne@ens-lyon.fr
[3] Dipartimento di Informatica, Università di Torino, Italy
likavec@di.unito.it

Abstract. We propose intersection type assignment systems for two resource control term calculi: the lambda calculus and the sequent lambda calculus with explicit operators for weakening and contraction. These resource control calculi, $\lambda_{\circledR}$ and $\lambda_{\circledR}^{Gtz}$, respectively, capture the computational content of intuitionistic natural deduction and intuitionistic sequent logic with explicit structural rules. Our main contribution is the characterisation of strong normalisation of reductions in both calculi. We first prove that typability implies strong normalisation in $\lambda_{\circledR}$ by adapting the reducibility method. Then we prove that typability implies strong normalisation in $\lambda_{\circledR}^{Gtz}$ by using a combination of well-orders and a suitable embedding of $\lambda_{\circledR}^{Gtz}$-terms into $\lambda_{\circledR}$-terms which preserves types and enables the simulation of all its reductions by the operational semantics of the $\lambda_{\circledR}$-calculus. Finally, we prove that strong normalisation implies typability in both systems using head subject expansion.

Introduction

It is well known that simply typed λ-calculus captures the computational content of intuitionistic natural deduction through Curry-Howard correspondence [21]. This connection between logic and computation can be extended to other calculi and logical systems [19]: Parigot's $\lambda\mu$-calculus [28] corresponds to classical natural deduction, whereas in the realm of sequent calculus, Herbelin's $\overline{\lambda}$-calculus [20], Espírito Santo's λ^{Gtz}-calculus [14], Barbanera and Berardi's symmetric calculus [3] and Curien and Herbelin's $\overline{\lambda}\mu\tilde{\mu}$-calculus [11] correspond to its intuitionistic and classical versions. Extending λ-calculus (λ^{Gtz}-calculus) with explicit operators for weakening and contraction brings the same correspondence to intuitionistic natural deduction (intuitionistic sequent calculus) with explicit structural rules, as investigated in [22,23,18].

Among many extensions of the simple type discipline is the one with intersection types, originally introduced in [9,10,29,33] in order to characterise termination properties of term calculi [36,16,17]. The extension of Curry-Howard correspondence to

---

* Partially supported by the Ministry of Education and Science of Serbia, projects III44006 and ON174026.

A. Cerone and P. Pihlajasaari (Eds.): ICTAC 2011, LNCS 6916, pp. 116–134, 2011.

other formalisms brought the need for intersection types into many different settings [13,24,25,26].

Our work is inspired by Kesner and Lengrand's work on resource operators for λ-calculus [22]. Their linear λlxr calculus introduces operators for substitution, erasure and duplication, preserving at the same time strong normalisation, confluence and subject reduction property of its predecessor λx [8].

Explicit control of erasure and duplication leads to decomposing of reduction steps into more atomic steps, thus revealing the details of computation which are usually left implicit. Since erasing and duplicating of (sub)terms essentially changes the structure of a program, it is important to see how this mechanism really works and to be able to control this part of computation. We choose a direct approach to term calculi, namely lambda calculus and sequent lambda calculus, rather than taking a more common path through linear logic [1,7]. In practice, for instance in the description of compilers by rules with binders [31,32], the implementation of substitutions of linear variables by inlining is simple and efficient when substitution of duplicated variables requires the cumbersome and time consuming mechanism of pointers and it is therefore important to tightly control duplication. On the other hand, precise control of erasing does not require a garbage collector and prevents memory leaking.

We introduce the intersection types into $\lambda_{\circledR}$ and $\lambda_{\circledR}^{Gtz}$, λ-calculus and λ^{Gtz}-calculus with explicit rules for weakening and contraction. To the best of our knowledge, this is a first treatment of intersection types in the presence of resource control operators. Our intersection type assignment systems $\lambda_{\circledR} \cap$ and $\lambda_{\circledR}^{Gtz} \cap$ integrate intersection into logical rules, thus preserving syntax-directedness of the system. We assign restricted form of intersection types, namely strict types, therefore minimizing the need for pre-order on types. Using these intersection type assignment systems we prove that terms in both calculi enjoy the strong normalisation property if and only if they are typable.

We first prove that typability implies strong normalisation in $\lambda_{\circledR}$-calculus by adapting the reducibility method for explicit resource control operators. Then we prove strong normalisation for $\lambda_{\circledR}^{Gtz}$ by using a combination of well-orders and a suitable embedding of $\lambda_{\circledR}^{Gtz}$-terms into $\lambda_{\circledR}$-terms which preserves types and enables the simulation of all its reductions by the operational semantics of the $\lambda_{\circledR}$-calculus. Finally, we prove that strong normalisation implies typability in both systems using head subject expansion.

The paper is organised as follows. In Section 1 we extend the λ-calculus and λ^{Gtz}-calculus with explicit operators for weakening and contraction obtaining $\lambda_{\circledR}$-calculus and $\lambda_{\circledR}^{Gtz}$-calculus, respectively. Intersection type assignment systems with strict types are introduced to these calculi in Section 2. In Section 3 we first prove that typability implies strong normalization in $\lambda_{\circledR}$-calculus by adapting the reducibility method. Then we prove that typability implies strong normalization in $\lambda_{\circledR}^{Gtz}$-calculus by using a combination of well-orders and a suitable embedding of $\lambda_{\circledR}^{Gtz}$-terms into $\lambda_{\circledR}$-terms which preserves types and enables the simulation of all its reductions by the operational semantics of the $\lambda_{\circledR}$-calculus. Section 4 gives a proof of strong normalization of typable terms for both calculi using head subject expansion. We conclude in Section 5.

1 Untyped Resource Control Calculi

1.1 Resource Control Lambda Calculus $\lambda_{\circledR}$

The *resource control* lambda calculus, $\lambda_{\circledR}$, is an extension of the λ-calculus with explicit operators for weakening and contraction. It corresponds to the λcw-calculus of Kesner and Renaud, proposed in [23] as a vertex of "the prismoid of resources".

The *pre-terms* of $\lambda_{\circledR}$-calculus are given by the following abstract syntax:

$$\text{Pre-terms} \quad f ::= x \,|\, \lambda x.f \,|\, ff \,|\, x \odot f \,|\, x <_{x_2}^{x_1} f$$

where x ranges over a denumerable set of term variables. $\lambda x.f$ is an *abstraction*, ff is an *application*, $x \odot f$ is a *weakening* and $x <_{x_2}^{x_1} f$ is a *contraction*. The contraction operator is assumed to be insensitive to order of the arguments x_1 and x_2 i.e. $x <_{x_2}^{x_1} f = x <_{x_1}^{x_2} f$.

The set of free variables of a pre-term f, denoted by $Fv(f)$, is defined as follows:

$$Fv(x) = x; \quad Fv(\lambda x.f) = Fv(f) \setminus \{x\}; \quad Fv(fg) = Fv(f) \cup Fv(g);$$
$$Fv(x \odot f) = \{x\} \cup Fv(f); \quad Fv(x <_{x_2}^{x_1} f) = \{x\} \cup Fv(f) \setminus \{x_1, x_2\}.$$

In $x <_{x_2}^{x_1} f$, the contraction binds the variables x_1 and x_2 and a free variable x is introduced. The operator $x \odot f$ also introduces a free variable x. In order to avoid parentheses, we let the scope of all binders extend to the right as much as possible.

The set of $\lambda_{\circledR}$-*terms*, denoted by $\Lambda_{\circledR}$ and ranged over by $M, N, P, M_1, \dots$ is a subset of the set of pre-terms, defined in Figure 1.

$$\frac{}{x \in \Lambda_{\circledR}} \qquad \frac{f \in \Lambda_{\circledR} \quad x \in Fv(f)}{\lambda x.f \in \Lambda_{\circledR}}$$

$$\frac{f \in \Lambda_{\circledR} \quad g \in \Lambda_{\circledR} \quad Fv(f) \cap Fv(g) = \emptyset}{fg \in \Lambda_{\circledR}}$$

$$\frac{f \in \Lambda_{\circledR} \quad x \notin Fv(f)}{x \odot f \in \Lambda_{\circledR}} \qquad \frac{f \in \Lambda_{\circledR} \quad x_1, x_2 \in Fv(f) \quad x \notin Fv(f)}{x <_{x_2}^{x_1} f \in \Lambda_{\circledR}}$$

Fig. 1. $\Lambda_{\circledR}$: $\lambda_{\circledR}$-terms

Informally, we say that a term is a pre-term in which in every subterm every free variable occurs exactly once, and every binder binds (exactly one occurrence of) a free variable. This notion corresponds to the notion of linear terms in [22]. In that sense, only linear expressions are in the focus of our investigation. This assumption is not a restriction, since every non linear λ-term has its linear correspondent, as illustrated by the following example.

Example 1. Pre-terms $\lambda x.y$ and $\lambda x.xx$ are not $\lambda_{\circledR}$-terms, on the other hand pre-terms $\lambda x.(x \odot y)$ and $\lambda x.x <_{x_2}^{x_1} (x_1 x_2)$ are $\lambda_{\circledR}$-terms.

In the sequel, we use the notation $X \odot M$ for $x_1 \odot \dots x_n \odot M$ and $X <_Z^Y M$ for $x_1 <_{z_1}^{y_1} \dots x_n <_{z_n}^{y_n} M$, where X, Y and Z are lists of the size n, consisting of all distinct variables $x_1, \dots, x_n, y_1, \dots, y_n, z_1, \dots, z_n$.

$$
\begin{array}{ll}
(\beta) \quad (\lambda x.M)N \to M[N/x] & \\
(\gamma_1) \quad x <_{x_2}^{x_1} (\lambda y.M) \to \lambda y.x <_{x_2}^{x_1} M & (\omega_1) \quad \lambda x.(y \odot M) \to y \odot (\lambda x.M), \, x \neq y \\
(\gamma_2) \quad x <_{x_2}^{x_1} (MN) \to (x <_{x_2}^{x_1} M)N, \text{ if } x_1,x_2 \in Fv(M) & (\omega_2) \quad (x \odot M)N \to x \odot (MN) \\
(\gamma_3) \quad x <_{x_2}^{x_1} (MN) \to M(x <_{x_2}^{x_1} N), \text{ if } x_1,x_2 \in Fv(N) & (\omega_3) \quad M(x \odot N) \to x \odot (MN) \\
(\gamma\omega_1) \quad x <_{x_2}^{x_1} (y \odot M) \to y \odot (x <_{x_2}^{x_1} M), \, y \neq x_1,x_2 & (\gamma\omega_2) \quad x <_{x_2}^{x_1} (x_1 \odot M) \to M[x/x_2]
\end{array}
$$

Fig. 2. Reduction rules of $\lambda_{\circledR}$-calculus

The reduction rules of $\lambda_{\circledR}$-calculus are presented in Figure 2.

The inductive definition of the meta operator $[\,/\,]$, representing the substitution of free variables, is given in Figure 3. In this definition, the terms N_1 and N_2 are obtained from N by renaming of all the free variables in N by fresh variables.

$$
\begin{array}{ll}
x[N/x] \triangleq N & (y \odot M)[N/x] \triangleq y \odot M[N/x], \, x \neq y \\
(\lambda y.M)[N/x] \triangleq \lambda y.M[N/x], \, x \neq y & (x \odot M)[N/x] \triangleq Fv(N) \odot M \\
(MP)[N/x] \triangleq M[N/x]P, \, x \in Fv(M) & (y <_{y_2}^{y_1} M)[N/x] \triangleq y <_{y_2}^{y_1} M[N/x], \, x \neq y \\
(MP)[N/x] \triangleq MP[N/x], \, x \in Fv(P) & (x <_{x_2}^{x_1} M)[N/x] \triangleq Fv(N) <_{Fv(N_2)}^{Fv(N_1)} M[N_1/x_1][N_2/x_2]
\end{array}
$$

Fig. 3. Substitution in $\lambda_{\circledR}$-calculus

In the $\lambda_{\circledR}$, one works modulo equivalencies given in Figure 4.

$$
\begin{array}{ll}
x \odot (y \odot M) \equiv y \odot (x \odot M) & x <_{x_2}^{x_1} M \equiv x <_{x_1}^{x_2} M \\
x <_z^y (y <_v^u M) \equiv x <_u^y (y <_v^z M) & x <_{x_2}^{x_1} (y <_{y_2}^{y_1} M) \equiv y <_{y_2}^{y_1} (x <_{x_2}^{x_1} M), \, x \neq y_1,y_2, \, y \neq x_1,x_2 \\
M[(y \odot N)/x] \equiv y \odot M[N/x] & M[(y <_{y_2}^{y_1} N)/x] \equiv y <_{y_2}^{y_1} M[N/x], \, y_1,y_2 \in Fv(N)
\end{array}
$$

Fig. 4. Equivalences in $\lambda_{\circledR}$-calculus

1.2 Resource Control Sequent Lambda Calculus $\lambda_{\circledR}^{\mathsf{Gtz}}$

The *resource control lambda Gentzen* calculus $\lambda_{\circledR}^{\mathsf{Gtz}}$ is derived from the λ^{Gtz}-calculus (more precisely its confluent sub-calculus λ_V^{Gtz}) by adding the explicit operators for weakening and contraction. It is proposed in [18]. The abstract syntax of $\lambda_{\circledR}^{\mathsf{Gtz}}$ pre-expressions is the following:

$$
\begin{array}{ll}
\text{Pre-values} & F ::= x \mid \lambda x.f \mid x \odot f \mid x <_{x_2}^{x_1} f \\
\text{Pre-terms} & f ::= F \mid fc \\
\text{Pre-contexts} & c ::= \widehat{x}.f \mid f :: c \mid x \odot c \mid x <_{x_2}^{x_1} c
\end{array}
$$

where x ranges over a denumerable set of term variables.

A *pre-value* can be a variable, an abstraction, a weakening or a contraction; a *pre-term* is either a value or a cut (an application). A *pre-context* is one of the following: a selection, a context constructor (usually called cons), a weakening on pre-context or a contraction on a pre-context. Pre-terms and pre-contexts are together referred to as the *pre-expressions* and will be ranged over by E. Pre-contexts $x \odot c$ and $x <_{x_2}^{x_1} c$ behave exactly like corresponding pre-terms $x \odot f$ and $x <_{x_2}^{x_1} f$ in the untyped calculus, so they will not be treated separately. The set of free variables of a pre-expression is defined analogously to the free variables in $\lambda_{\circledR}$-calculus with the following additions:

$$Fv(fc) = Fv(f) \cup Fv(c); \quad Fv(\widehat{x}.f) = Fv(f) \setminus \{x\}; \quad Fv(f :: c) = Fv(f) \cup Fv(c).$$

Like in the case of $\lambda_{\circledR}$-calculus, the set of $\lambda_{\circledR}^{\mathsf{Gtz}}$-expressions (namely values, terms and contexts), denoted by $\Lambda_{\circledR}^{\mathsf{Gtz}} \cup \Lambda_{\circledR,C}^{\mathsf{Gtz}}$, is a subset of the set of pre-expressions, defined as in Figure 1 plus:

$$\frac{f \in \Lambda_{\circledR}^{\mathsf{Gtz}} \quad x \in Fv(f)}{\widehat{x}.f \in \Lambda_{\circledR,C}^{\mathsf{Gtz}}} \qquad \frac{f \in \Lambda_{\circledR}^{\mathsf{Gtz}} \quad c \in \Lambda_{\circledR,C}^{\mathsf{Gtz}} \quad Fv(f) \cap Fv(c) = \emptyset}{f :: c \in \Lambda_{\circledR,C}^{\mathsf{Gtz}}}$$

Values are denoted by T, terms by $t, u, v \ldots$, contexts by $k, k', \ldots$ and expressions by e, e'. The computation over the set of $\lambda_{\circledR}^{\mathsf{Gtz}}$-expressions reflects the cut-elimination process. Four groups of reductions in $\lambda_{\circledR}^{\mathsf{Gtz}}$-calculus are given in Figure 5.

(β)	$(\lambda x.t)(u :: k) \to u(\widehat{x}.tk)$		(σ)	$T(\widehat{x}.v) \to v[T/x]$
(π)	$(tk)k' \to t(k@k')$		(μ)	$\widehat{x}.xk \to k$
(γ_1)	$x <_{x_2}^{x_1} (\lambda y.t) \to \lambda y.x <_{x_2}^{x_1} t$		(ω_1)	$\lambda x.(y \odot t) \to y \odot (\lambda x.t), \ x \neq y$
(γ_2)	$x <_{x_2}^{x_1} (tk) \to (x <_{x_2}^{x_1} t)k, \ \text{if } x_1, x_2 \in Fv(t)$		(ω_2)	$(x \odot t)k \to x \odot (tk)$
(γ_3)	$x <_{x_2}^{x_1} (tk) \to t(x <_{x_2}^{x_1} k), \ \text{if } x_1, x_2 \in Fv(k)$		(ω_3)	$t(x \odot k) \to x \odot (tk)$
(γ_4)	$x <_{x_2}^{x_1} (\widehat{y}.t) \to \widehat{y}.(x <_{x_2}^{x_1} t)$		(ω_4)	$\widehat{x}.(y \odot t) \to y \odot (\widehat{x}.t), \ x \neq y$
(γ_5)	$x <_{x_2}^{x_1} (t :: k) \to (x <_{x_2}^{x_1} t) :: k, \ \text{if } x_1, x_2 \in Fv(t)$		(ω_5)	$(x \odot t) :: k \to x \odot (t :: k)$
(γ_6)	$x <_{x_2}^{x_1} (t :: k) \to t :: (x <_{x_2}^{x_1} k), \ \text{if } x_1, x_2 \in Fv(k)$		(ω_6)	$t :: (x \odot k) \to x \odot (t :: k)$
$(\gamma\omega_1)$	$x <_{x_2}^{x_1} (y \odot e) \to y \odot (x <_{x_2}^{x_1} e) \qquad x_1 \neq y \neq x_2$		$(\gamma\omega_2)$	$x <_{x_2}^{x_1} (x_1 \odot e) \to e[x/x_2]$

Fig. 5. Reduction rules of $\lambda_{\circledR}^{\mathsf{Gtz}}$-calculus

The first group consists of β, π, σ and μ reductions from λ^{Gtz}. New reductions are added to deal with explicit contraction (γ reductions) and weakening (ω reductions). The groups of γ and ω reductions consist of rules that perform propagation of contraction into the expression and extraction of weakening out of the expression. This discipline allows us to optimize the computation by delaying the duplication of terms on the one hand, and by performing the erasure of terms as soon as possible on the other.

The meta-substitution $v[T/x]$ is defined as in Figure 3 with the following additions:

$$(tk)[u/x] = t[u/x]k, \ x \in Fv(t) \qquad (tk)[u/x] = tk[u/x], \ x \in Fv(k)$$
$$(\widehat{y}.t)[u/x] = \widehat{y}.t[u/x]$$
$$(t :: k)[u/x] = t[u/x] :: k, \ x \in Fv(t) \qquad (t :: k)[u/x] = t :: k[u/x], \ x \in Fv(k)$$

In the π rule, the meta-operator @, called *append*, joins two contexts and is defined as:

$$(\widehat{x}.t)@k' = \widehat{x}.tk'$$
$$(x \odot k)@k' = x \odot (k@k') \qquad (u :: k)@k' = u :: (k@k')$$
$$\qquad\qquad\qquad\qquad\qquad\qquad (x <_z^y k)@k' = x <_z^y (k@k').$$

2 Intersection Type Assignment Systems for Resource Control

In this section we introduce intersection type assignment systems which assign *strict* types to $\lambda_{\circledR}$-terms and $\lambda_{\circledR}^{Gtz}$-expressions. Strict types were proposed in [36] and already used in [15] for characterisation of strong normalisation in λ^{Gtz}-calculus.
The syntax of types is defined as follows:

$$\text{Strict types } \sigma ::= p \mid \alpha \to \sigma$$
$$\text{Types} \quad \alpha ::= \sigma \mid \sigma \cap \alpha$$

where p ranges over a denumerable set of type atoms. We denote types with $\alpha, \beta, \gamma...$ and strict types with $\sigma, \tau, \upsilon....$ We assume that intersection operator is idempotent, commutative and associative. Due to this property, equivalent terms have the same type.

Definition 1

(i) A basic type assignment *is an expression of the form* $x : \alpha$, *where* x *is a term variable and* α *is a type.*

(ii) A basis Γ *is a set* $\{x_1 : \alpha_1, ..., x_n : \alpha_n\}$ *of basic type assignments, where all term variables are different.* $Dom(\Gamma) = \{x_1, ..., x_n\}$. *A basis extension* $\Gamma, x : \alpha$ *denotes the set* $\Gamma \cup \{x : \alpha\}$, *where* $x \notin Dom(\Gamma)$.

(iii) A bases intersection *is* $\cap \Gamma_i = \{x : \cap \alpha_i \mid x : \alpha_i \in \Gamma_i\}$, *where for all* i, j, $Dom(\Gamma_i) = Dom(\Gamma_j)$.

2.1 Intersection Types for $\lambda_{\circledR}$

The type assignment system $\lambda_{\circledR} \cap$ is given in Figure 6.

$$\frac{}{x : \cap \sigma_i \vdash x : \sigma_i} \ (Ax)$$

$$\frac{\Gamma, x : \alpha \vdash M : \sigma}{\Gamma \vdash \lambda x.M : \alpha \to \sigma} \ (\to_I) \qquad \frac{\Gamma \vdash M : \cap \alpha_i \to \sigma \quad \Delta_i \vdash N : \alpha_i}{\Gamma, \cap \Delta_i \vdash MN : \sigma} \ (\to_E)$$

$$\frac{\Gamma, x : \alpha, y : \beta \vdash M : \sigma}{\Gamma, z : \alpha \cap \beta \vdash z <^x_y M : \sigma} \ (Cont) \qquad \frac{\Gamma \vdash M : \sigma}{\Gamma, x : \alpha \vdash x \odot M : \sigma} \ (Weak)$$

Fig. 6. $\lambda_{\circledR} \cap$: $\lambda_{\circledR}$-calculus with intersection types

The Generation lemma induced by the proposed system is the following:

Proposition 2 (Generation lemma for $\lambda_{\circledR} \cap$)

(i) $\Gamma \vdash \lambda x.M : \beta$ *iff there exist* α *and* σ *such that* $\beta \equiv \alpha \to \sigma$ *and* $\Gamma, x : \alpha \vdash M : \sigma$.

(ii) $\Gamma \vdash MN : \sigma$ *iff* $\Gamma = \Gamma', \cap \Delta_i$ *and there exists a type* $\cap \alpha_i$ *such that* $\Gamma' \vdash M : \cap \alpha_i \to \sigma$ *and for all* i $\Delta_i \vdash N : \alpha_i$.

(iii) $\Gamma \vdash z <_y^x M : \sigma$ *iff there exist* Γ', α, β *such that* $\Gamma = \Gamma', z : \alpha \cap \beta$
      and $\Gamma', x : \alpha, y : \beta \vdash M : \sigma$.

(iv) $\Gamma \vdash x \odot M : \sigma$ *iff there exist* Γ', β *such that* $\Gamma = \Gamma', x : \beta$ *and* $\Gamma' \vdash M : \sigma$.

The proposed system satisfies the following properties.

Proposition 3. *If* $M \to M'$ *then* $Fv(M) = Fv(M')$.

Proposition 4.   *(i)*   *If* $\Gamma \vdash M :$, *then* $Dom(\Gamma) = Fv(M)$.
(ii)   *If* $\Gamma_1 \vdash M : \sigma$ *and* $\Gamma_2 \vdash M : \sigma$, *then* $\Gamma_1 \cap \Gamma_2 \vdash M : \sigma$.

Proposition 5 (Substitution lemma). *If* $\Gamma, x : \cap \alpha_i \vdash M : \sigma$ *and for all* i, $\Delta_i \vdash N : \alpha_i$,
then $\Gamma, \cap \Delta_i \vdash M[N/x] : \sigma$.

Proposition 6 (Subject reduction and equivalence). *For every* $\lambda_{\circledR}$*-term* M*: if*
$\Gamma \vdash M : \sigma$ *and* $M \to M'$ *or* $M \equiv M$, *then* $\Gamma \vdash M' : \sigma$.

2.2   Intersection Types for $\lambda_{\circledR}^{\mathsf{Gtz}}$

The type assignment system $\lambda_{\circledR}^{\mathsf{Gtz}} \cap$ is given in Figure 7.

$$\frac{}{x : \cap \sigma_i \vdash x : \sigma_i} \ (Ax)$$

$$\frac{\Gamma, x : \alpha \vdash t : \sigma}{\Gamma \vdash \lambda x.t : \alpha \to \sigma} \ (\to_R) \qquad \frac{\Gamma_i \vdash t : \alpha_i \quad \Delta ; \sigma \vdash k : \tau}{\cap \Gamma_i, \Delta ; \cap \alpha_i \to \sigma \vdash t :: k : \tau} \ (\to_L)$$

$$\frac{\Gamma_i \vdash t : \alpha_i \quad \Delta ; \cap \alpha_i \vdash k : \sigma}{\cap \Gamma_i, \Delta \vdash tk : \sigma} \ (Cut) \qquad \frac{\Gamma, x : \alpha \vdash t : \sigma}{\Gamma ; \alpha \vdash \widehat{x}.t : \sigma} \ (Sel)$$

$$\frac{\Gamma, x : \alpha, y : \beta \vdash t : \sigma}{\Gamma, z : \alpha \cap \beta \vdash z <_y^x t : \sigma} \ (Cont_t) \qquad \frac{\Gamma \vdash t : \sigma}{\Gamma, x : \alpha \vdash x \odot t : \sigma} \ (Weak_t)$$

$$\frac{\Gamma, x : \alpha, y : \beta ; \gamma \vdash k : \sigma}{\Gamma, z : \alpha \cap \beta ; \gamma \vdash z <_y^x k : \sigma} \ (Cont_k) \qquad \frac{\Gamma ; \gamma \vdash k : \sigma}{\Gamma, x : \alpha ; \gamma \vdash x \odot k : \sigma} \ (Weak_k)$$

Fig. 7. $\lambda_{\circledR}^{\mathsf{Gtz}} \cap$: $\lambda_{\circledR}^{\mathsf{Gtz}}$-calculus with intersection types

The Generation lemma induced by the proposed system is the following:

Proposition 7 (Generation lemma for $\lambda_{\circledR}^{\mathsf{Gtz}} \cap$)

(i) $\Gamma \vdash \lambda x.t : \beta$ *iff there exist* α *and* σ *such that* $\beta \equiv \alpha \to \sigma$ *and* $\Gamma, x : \alpha \vdash t : \sigma$.
(ii) $\Gamma ; \gamma \vdash t :: k : \tau$ *iff* $\Gamma = \cap \Gamma_i, \Delta$, $\gamma \equiv \cap \alpha_i \to \sigma$, *and* $\Gamma_i \vdash t : \alpha_i, \forall i$ *and* $\Delta ; \sigma \vdash k : \tau$.
(iii) $\Gamma \vdash tk : \sigma$ *iff* $\Gamma = \cap \Gamma_i, \Delta$ *and there exists a type* $\cap \alpha_i$ *such that* $\Gamma_i \vdash t : \alpha_i$, $\forall i$
      and $\Delta ; \cap \alpha_i \vdash k : \sigma$.
(iv) $\Gamma ; \alpha \vdash \widehat{x}.t : \sigma$ *iff* $\Gamma, x : \alpha \vdash t : \sigma$.

(v) $\Gamma \vdash z <^x_y t : \sigma$ *iff there exist* Γ', α, β *such that* $\Gamma = \Gamma', z : \alpha \cap \beta$ *and*
        $\Gamma', x : \alpha, y : \beta \vdash t : \sigma$.

(vi) $\Gamma \vdash x \odot t : \sigma$ *iff there exist* Γ', β *such that* $\Gamma = \Gamma', x : \beta$ *and* $\Gamma' \vdash t : \sigma$.

(vii) $\Gamma; \varepsilon \vdash z <^x_y k : \sigma$ *iff there exist* Γ', α, β *such that* $\Gamma = \Gamma', z : \alpha \cap \beta$ *and*
        $\Gamma', x : \alpha, y : \beta; \varepsilon \vdash k : \sigma$.

(viii) $\Gamma; \gamma \vdash x \odot k : \sigma$ *iff there exist* Γ, β *such that* $\Gamma = \Gamma', x : \beta$ *and* $\Gamma; \gamma \vdash k : \sigma$.

3 Typability $\Rightarrow$ SN in Both Systems

3.1 Typeability $\Rightarrow$ SN in $\lambda_{\circledR} \cap$

The main idea of the reducibility method, introduced in Tait [35] for proving the strong normalization property for the simply typed lambda calculus, is to interpret types by suitable sets of lambda terms which satisfy certain realizability properties.

In the remainder of the paper we consider $\Lambda_{\circledR}$ as the *applicative structure* whose domain are $\lambda_{\circledR}$-terms and where the application is just the application of $\lambda_{\circledR}$-terms. We recall some notions from [4]. The set of *strongly normalizing terms* is defined as

$$\mathcal{SN} = \{M \in \Lambda_{\circledR} \mid \neg(\exists M_1, M_2, \ldots \in \Lambda_{\circledR}) M \to M_1 \to M_2 \to \ldots\}.$$

Definition 8. *For* $\mathcal{M}, \mathcal{N} \subseteq \Lambda_{\circledR}$, *we define* $\mathcal{M} \longrightarrow \mathcal{N} \subseteq \Lambda_{\circledR}$ *as*

$$\mathcal{M} \longrightarrow \mathcal{N} = \{N \in \Lambda_{\circledR} \mid \forall M \in \mathcal{M}. \quad (fv(\mathcal{M}) \cap fv(\mathcal{N}) = \emptyset \quad \Rightarrow \quad NM \in \mathcal{N})\}.$$

Definition 9. *The type interpretation* $[\![-]\!] : Types \to 2^{\Lambda_{\circledR}}$ *is defined by:*

(I1) $[\![p]\!] = \mathcal{SN}$, *where* p *is a type atom;*

(I2) $[\![\sigma \cap \alpha]\!] = [\![\sigma]\!] \cap [\![\alpha]\!]$;

(I3) $[\![\alpha \to \sigma]\!] = ([\![\alpha]\!] \longrightarrow [\![\sigma]\!]) = \{M \in \Lambda_{\circledR} \mid \forall N \in [\![\alpha]\!] \quad MN \in [\![\sigma]\!]\}$.

Next, we introduce the notions of *saturation property*, obtained by extending the saturation property given in [5], and *weakening property*. To this aim we introduce the following notation: if R denotes the set of reductions given in Figure 2, $r \in R \setminus (\beta)$, then $redex_r$ ($contr_r$) denote the left (right) hand side of the reduction r (its redex and contractum, respectively).

Definition 10

- *A set* $X \subseteq \mathcal{SN}$ *satisfies the* saturation property, *notation* SAT(X), *if*
  - VAR(X): $(\forall n \geq 0) (\forall x \in var) (\forall M_1, \ldots, M_n \in \mathcal{SN})$
    $(x \cap fv(M_1) \cap \ldots \cap fv(M_n) = \emptyset \quad \Rightarrow \quad xM_1 \ldots M_n \in X.$
  - SAT$_\beta$(X):[1] $(\forall n \geq 0) (\forall M_1, \ldots, M_n \in \mathcal{SN})$
    $M[N/x]M_1 \ldots M_n \in X \quad \Rightarrow \quad (\lambda x.M)NM_1 \ldots M_n \in X.$
  - SAT$_r$(X): $(\forall n \geq 0) (\forall M_1, \ldots, M_n \in \mathcal{SN})$
    $contr_r M_1 \ldots M_n \in X \quad \Rightarrow \quad redex_r M_1 \ldots M_n \in X.$

---

[1] Notice that we do not need a condition that $N \in \mathcal{SN}$ in SAT$_\beta$(X) since we only work with linear terms, hence if the contractum $M[N/x] \in \mathcal{SN}$, then $N \in \mathcal{SN}$.

124   S. Ghilezan et al.

- A set $X \subseteq S\mathcal{N}$ satisfies the weakening property, notation WEAK(X),
  - WEAK(X): $(\forall x \in \text{var})\ M \in X,\ x \notin Fv(M)\ \Rightarrow\ x \odot M \in X$.

Definition 11 (®-Saturated set). *A set $X \subseteq \Lambda_®$ is called ®-saturated, if it satisfies the saturation and weakening properties.*

Proposition 12. *Let $\mathcal{M}, \mathcal{N} \subseteq \Lambda_®$.*

(i) $S\mathcal{N}$ is ®-saturated.
(ii) If $\mathcal{M}$ and $\mathcal{N}$ are ®-saturated, then $\mathcal{M} \longrightarrow \mathcal{N}$ is ®-saturated.
(iii) If $\mathcal{M}$ and $\mathcal{N}$ are ®-saturated, then $\mathcal{M} \cap \mathcal{N}$ is ®-saturated.
(iv) For all types $\varphi \in Types$, $[\![\varphi]\!]$ is ®-saturated.

We further define a *valuation of terms* $[\![-]\!]_\rho : \Lambda_® \to \Lambda_®$ and the *semantic satisfiability relation* $\models$ which connects the type interpretation with the term valuation.

Definition 13. *Let $\rho : \text{var} \to \Lambda_®$ be a valuation of term variables in $\Lambda_®$. For $M \in \Lambda_®$, with $Fv(M) = x_1, \ldots, x_n$ the term valuation $[\![-]\!]_\rho : \Lambda_® \to \Lambda_®$ is defined as:*

(i) $[\![x]\!]_\rho = \rho(x)$;

(ii) $[\![MN]\!]_\rho \equiv \begin{cases} [\![M]\!]_\rho [\![N]\!]_\rho, & \text{if } Fv([\![M]\!]_\rho) \cap Fv([\![N]\!]_\rho) = \emptyset \\ Y <_{Y''}^{Y'} ([\![M]\!]_{\rho(Y'/Y)} [\![N]\!]_{\rho(Y''/Y)}), & \text{if } Fv([\![M]\!]_\rho) \cap Fv([\![N]\!]_\rho) = \{y_1, \ldots, y_k\} \end{cases}$ *where*
$Y = \{y_1, \ldots, y_k\}, Y' = \{y_1', \ldots, y_k'\}$ *and* $Y'' = \{y_1'', \ldots, y_k''\}$ *and*
$\rho(Y'/Y)$ *denotes* $\rho(y_1'/y_1, \ldots, y_k'/y_k)$ *(similarly for* $\rho(Y''/Y)$ *).*
(iii) $[\![\lambda x.M]\!]_\rho \equiv \lambda x.[\![M]\!]_{\rho(x/x)}$.
(iv) $[\![x \odot M]\!]_\rho \equiv Fv(\rho(x)) \odot [\![M]\!]_\rho$.
(v) $[\![z <_y^x M]\!]_\rho \equiv Fv(\rho(z)) <_{Fv(N_2)}^{Fv(N_1)} [\![M]\!]_{\rho(N_1/x, N_2/y)}$
where N_1 and N_2 are obtained from $\rho(z)$ by renaming its free variables.

Lemma 14

(i) $[\![M]\!]_{\rho(N/x)} \equiv [\![M]\!]_{\rho(x/x)}[N/x]$.
(ii) $[\![z <_y^x M]\!]_{\rho(N/z)} \equiv (z <_y^x [\![M]\!]_{\rho(x/x,y/y)})[N/z]$.
(iii) $[\![M]\!]_{\rho(N/x,N/y)} \equiv Fv(N) <_{Fv(N'')}^{Fv(N')} [\![M]\!]_{\rho(N'/x,N''/y)}$, *where N' and N'' are obtained from N by renaming all free variables of N with fresh variables.*

Proof. By induction on the construction of M. For the cases (i)-(iv) we consider only the base cases when M is a variable, other cases being straightforward using IH.

(i) $[\![y]\!]_{\rho(N/x)} = y[N/x, \rho(y)/y] = \rho(y)$.
  $[\![y]\!]_{\rho(x/x)}[N/x] = y[x/x, \rho(y)/y][N/x] = \rho(y)$.
(ii) Using (i) and the definition of substitution.
  $[\![z <_y^x M]\!]_{\rho(N/z)} = [\![z <_y^x M]\!]_{\rho(z/z)}[N/z] = (z <_y^x [\![M]\!]_{\rho(x/x,y/y)})[N/z] =$
  $Fv(N) <_{Fv(N_2)}^{Fv(N_1)} [\![M]\!]_{\rho(x/x,y/y)}[N_1/x][N_2/y] = Fv(N) <_{Fv(N_2)}^{Fv(N_1)} [\![M]\!]_{\rho(N_1/x,N_2/y)} =$
  $Fv(N) <_{Fv(N_2)}^{Fv(N_1)} [\![M]\!]_{\rho(x/x,y/y)}[N_1/x][N_2/y] = (z <_y^x [\![M]\!]_{\rho(x/x,y/y)})[N/z]$.
(iii) By straightforward application od Definition 13.

Definition 15

(i) $\rho \models M : \alpha \iff [\![M]\!]_\rho \in [\![\alpha]\!];$
(ii) $\rho \models \Gamma \iff (\forall (x : \alpha) \in \Gamma) \; \rho(x) \in [\![\alpha]\!];$
(iii) $\Gamma \models M : \alpha \iff (\forall \rho, \rho \models \Gamma \Rightarrow \rho \models M : \alpha).$

Proposition 16 (Soundness of $\lambda_{\circledR} \cap$). *If $\Gamma \vdash M : \alpha$, then $\Gamma \models M : \alpha$.*

Proof. By induction on the derivation of $\Gamma \vdash M : \alpha$. The cases (Ax) and $(\to_I)$ are analogous to the corresponding rules in ordinary λ calculus. We prove the statement for the remaining inference rules.

– The last rule applied is $(\to_E)$, i.e., $\Gamma \vdash M : \cap \alpha_i \to \sigma, \Delta_i \vdash N : \alpha_i \Rightarrow \Gamma, \cap \Delta_i \vdash MN : \sigma$. By the IH $\Gamma \models M : \cap \alpha_i \to \sigma$ and $\Delta_i \models N : \alpha_i, \forall i$. Suppose that $\rho \models \Gamma, \cap \Delta_i$, then $\rho \models \Gamma$ and $\rho \models \cap \Delta_i$. From $\rho \models \Gamma$, using the IH we deduce that $[\![M]\!]_\rho \in [\![\cap \alpha_i \to \sigma]\!]$. From $\rho \models \cap \Delta_i$, we deduce that $\rho \models \Delta_i, \forall i$ (since every variable $x : \alpha \in \cap \Delta_i$ is of the form $x : \cap \alpha_i, x : \alpha_i \in \Delta_i$), hence using the IH we deduce that $[\![N]\!]_\rho \in [\![\alpha_i]\!], \forall i$. This means that $[\![N]\!]_\rho \in \cap [\![\alpha_i]\!]_\rho = [\![\cap \alpha_i]\!]_\rho$. Using Definition 13(ii) we obtain that $[\![M]\!]_\rho [\![N]\!]_\rho = [\![MN]\!]_\rho \in [\![\sigma]\!]$.

– The last rule applied is $(Weak)$, i.e., $\Gamma \vdash M : \alpha \Rightarrow \Gamma, x : \beta \vdash x \odot M : \alpha$. By the IH $\Gamma \models M : \alpha$. Suppose that $\rho \models \Gamma, x : \beta \iff \rho \models \Gamma$ and $\rho \models x : \beta$. From $\rho \models \Gamma$ we obtain $[\![M]\!]_\rho \in [\![\alpha]\!]$. Using the weakening property WEAK and Definition 13(iv) we obtain $Fv(\rho(x)) \odot [\![M]\!]_\rho = [\![x \odot M]\!]_\rho \in [\![\alpha]\!]$, since $Fv(\rho(x)) \cap Fv([\![M]\!]_\rho) = \emptyset$.

– The last rule applied is $(Cont)$, i.e., $\Gamma, x : \alpha, y : \beta \vdash M : \gamma \Rightarrow \Gamma, z : \alpha \cap \beta \vdash z <^x_y M : \gamma$. By the IH $\Gamma, x : \alpha, y : \beta \models M : \gamma$. Suppose that $\rho \models \Gamma, z : \alpha \cap \beta$, in order to prove $[\![z <^x_y M]\!]_\rho \in [\![\gamma]\!]$. This means that $\rho \models \Gamma$ and $\rho \models z : \alpha \cap \beta \iff \rho(z) \in [\![\alpha]\!]$ and $\rho(z) \in [\![\beta]\!]$. For the sake of simplicity let $\rho(z) \equiv N$. We define a new ρ' such that $\rho' = \rho(N/x, N/y)$. Then $\rho' \models \Gamma, x : \alpha, y : \beta$ since $x, y \notin Dom(\Gamma)$, $N \in [\![\alpha]\!]$ and $N \in [\![\beta]\!]$. By the IH $[\![M]\!]_{\rho'} \in [\![\gamma]\!]$. By the definition of term valuation (Definition 13), Lemma 14(i), (ii) and (iii) and the definition of substitution we obtain $[\![M]\!]_{\rho'} = [\![M]\!]_{\rho(N/x, N/y)} = Fv(N) <^{Fv(N')}_{Fv(N'')} [\![M]\!]_{\rho(N'/x, N''/y)} = Fv(N) <^{Fv(N')}_{Fv(N'')}$ $[\![M]\!]_{\rho(x/x, y/y)} [N'/x][N''/y] = (z <^x_y [\![M]\!]_{\rho(x/x, y/y)}) [N/z] = ([\![z <^x_y M]\!]_{\rho(z/z)}) [N/z] = [\![z <^x_y M]\!]_{\rho(N/z)} = [\![z <^x_y M]\!]_\rho$, since $\rho(z) = N$. Hence, $[\![z <^x_y M]\!]_\rho \in [\![\gamma]\!]$.   □

Theorem 17 ($\mathcal{SN}$ for $\lambda_{\circledR} \cap$). *If $\Gamma \vdash M : \alpha$, then M is strongly normalizing, i.e. $M \in \mathcal{SN}$.*

Proof. Suppose $\Gamma \vdash M : \alpha$. By Proposition 16 $\Gamma \models M : \alpha$. According to Definition 15(iii), this means that $(\forall \rho \models \Gamma) \; \rho \models M : \alpha$. We can choose a particular $\rho_0(x) = x$ for all $x \in \texttt{var}$. By Proposition 12(iv), $[\![\beta]\!]$ is saturated for each type β, hence $x = [\![x]\!]_\rho \in [\![\beta]\!]$ (variable condition for $n = 0$). Therefore, $\rho_0 \models \Gamma$ and we can conclude that $[\![M]\!]_{\rho_0} \in [\![\alpha]\!]$. On the other hand, $M = [\![M]\!]_{\rho_0}$ and $[\![\alpha]\!] \subseteq \mathcal{SN}$ (Proposition 12), hence $M \in \mathcal{SN}$.   □

3.2 Typeability $\Rightarrow$ SN in $\lambda^{\mathsf{Gtz}}_{\circledR} \cap$

In this section, we prove the strong normalisation property of the $\lambda^{\mathsf{Gtz}}_{\circledR}$-calculus with intersection types. The termination is proved by showing that the reduction on the set

$\Lambda_{\circledR}^{\mathsf{Gtz}} \cup \Lambda_{\circledR,C}^{\mathsf{Gtz}}$ of the typeable $\lambda_{\circledR}^{\mathsf{Gtz}}$-expressions is included in a particular well-founded relation, which we define as the lexicographic product of three well-founded component relations. The first one is based on the mapping of $\lambda_{\circledR}^{\mathsf{Gtz}}$-expressions into $\lambda_{\circledR}$-terms. We show that this mapping preserves types and that all $\lambda_{\circledR}^{\mathsf{Gtz}}$-reductions can be simulated by the reductions or identities of the $\lambda_{\circledR}$-calculus. The other two well-founded orders are based on the introduction of quantities designed to decrease a global measure associated with specific $\lambda_{\circledR}^{\mathsf{Gtz}}$-expressions during the computation.

Definition 18. *The mapping* $\lfloor \ \rfloor : \Lambda_{\circledR}^{\mathsf{Gtz}} \rightarrow \Lambda_{\circledR}$ *is defined together with the auxiliary mapping* $\lfloor \ \rfloor_k : \Lambda_{\circledR,C}^{\mathsf{Gtz}} \rightarrow (\Lambda_{\circledR} \rightarrow \Lambda_{\circledR})$ *in the following way:*

$$
\begin{aligned}
\lfloor x \rfloor &= x & \lfloor \widehat{x}.t \rfloor_k(M) &= (\lambda x.\lfloor t \rfloor)M \\
\lfloor \lambda x.t \rfloor &= \lambda x.\lfloor t \rfloor & \lfloor t :: k \rfloor_k(M) &= \lfloor k \rfloor_k(M\lfloor t \rfloor) \\
\lfloor x \odot t \rfloor &= x \odot \lfloor t \rfloor & \lfloor x \odot k \rfloor_k(M) &= x \odot \lfloor k \rfloor_k(M) \\
\lfloor x <_z^y t \rfloor &= x <_z^y \lfloor t \rfloor & \lfloor x <_z^y k \rfloor_k(M) &= x <_z^y \lfloor k \rfloor_k(M) \\
\lfloor tk \rfloor &= \lfloor k \rfloor_k(\lfloor t \rfloor)
\end{aligned}
$$

Lemma 19. *(i)* $Fv(t) = Fv(\lfloor t \rfloor)$, *for* $t \in \Lambda_{\circledR}^{\mathsf{Gtz}}$.
(ii) $\lfloor v[t/x] \rfloor = \lfloor v \rfloor [\lfloor t \rfloor/x]$, *for* $v,t \in \Lambda_{\circledR}^{\mathsf{Gtz}}$.

We prove that the mappings $\lfloor \ \rfloor$ and $\lfloor \ \rfloor_k$ preserve types. In the sequel, the notation $\Lambda_{\circledR}(\Gamma' \vdash_{\lambda_{\circledR}} \alpha)$ stands for $\{M \mid M \in \Lambda_{\circledR} \ \& \ \Gamma' \vdash_{\lambda_{\circledR}} M : \alpha\}$.

Proposition 20 (Type preservation with $\lfloor \ \rfloor$)

(i) If $\Gamma' \vdash t : \alpha$, *then* $\Gamma' \vdash_{\lambda_{\circledR}} \lfloor t \rfloor : \alpha$.
(ii) If $\Gamma'; \alpha \vdash k : \beta$, *then* $\lfloor k \rfloor_k : \Lambda_{\circledR}(\Gamma'' \vdash_{\lambda_{\circledR}} \alpha) \rightarrow \Lambda_{\circledR}(\Gamma',\Gamma'' \vdash_{\lambda_{\circledR}} \beta)$, *for some* Γ''.

Proof. The proposition is proved by simultaneous induction on derivations. We distinguish cases according to the last typing rule used.

- Cases (Ax), $(\rightarrow_R)$, $(Weak_t)$ and $(Cont_t)$ are easy, because the intersection type assignment system of $\lambda_{\circledR}$ has exactly the same rules.
- Case (Sel): the derivation ends with the rule

$$
\frac{\Gamma',x:\alpha \vdash t : \sigma}{\Gamma';\alpha \vdash \widehat{x}.t : \sigma} \ (Sel)
$$

By IH we have that $\Gamma',x:\alpha \vdash_{\lambda_{\circledR}} \lfloor t \rfloor : \sigma$. For any $M \in \Lambda^{\circledR}$ such that $\Gamma'' \vdash_{\lambda_{\circledR}} M : \alpha$, for some Γ'', we have

$$
\frac{\dfrac{\Gamma',x:\alpha \vdash_{\lambda_{\circledR}} \lfloor t \rfloor : \sigma}{\Gamma' \vdash_{\lambda_{\circledR}} \lambda x.\lfloor t \rfloor : \alpha \rightarrow \sigma} \ (\rightarrow_I) \qquad \Gamma'' \vdash_{\lambda_{\circledR}} M : \alpha}{\Gamma',\Gamma'' \vdash_{\lambda_{\circledR}} (\lambda x.\lfloor t \rfloor)M : \sigma} \ (\rightarrow_E)
$$

Since $(\lambda x.\lfloor t \rfloor)M = \lfloor \widehat{x}.t \rfloor_k(M)$, we conclude that $\lfloor \widehat{x}.t \rfloor_k : \Lambda_{\circledR}(\Gamma'' \vdash_{\lambda_{\circledR}} \alpha) \rightarrow \Lambda_{\circledR}(\Gamma',\Gamma'' \vdash_{\lambda_{\circledR}} \sigma)$.

- Case $(\to_L)$: the derivation ends with the rule

$$\frac{\Gamma'_i \vdash t : \alpha_i \quad \Delta; \sigma \vdash k : \beta}{\cap \Gamma'_i, \Delta; \cap \alpha_i \to \sigma \vdash t :: k : \beta} \ (\to_L)$$

By IH we have that $\Gamma'_i \vdash_{\lambda_\circledR} \lfloor t \rfloor : \alpha_i, \ \forall i$. For any $M \in \Lambda^\circledR$ such that $\Gamma''' \vdash_{\lambda_\circledR} M : \cap \alpha_i \to \sigma$, we have

$$\frac{\Gamma''' \vdash_{\lambda_\circledR} M : \cap \alpha_i \to \sigma \quad \Gamma'_i \vdash_{\lambda_\circledR} \lfloor t \rfloor : \alpha_i}{\cap \Gamma'_i, \Gamma''' \vdash_{\lambda_\circledR} M \lfloor t \rfloor : \sigma} \ (\to_E)$$

From the right-hand side premise in the $(\to_L)$ rule, by IH, we get that $\lfloor k \rfloor_k$ is the function with the scope $\lfloor k \rfloor_k : \Lambda_{\circledR(\Gamma'''' \vdash_{\lambda_\circledR} \sigma)} \to \Lambda_{\circledR(\Gamma''', \Gamma'' \vdash_{\lambda_\circledR} \beta)}$. For $\Gamma'''' \equiv \cap \Gamma'_i, \Gamma'''$ and by taking $M \lfloor t \rfloor$ as the argument of the function $\lfloor k \rfloor_k$, we get $\cap \Gamma'_i, \Delta, \Gamma''' \vdash_{\lambda_\circledR} \lfloor k \rfloor_k(M \lfloor t \rfloor) : \beta$. Since $\lfloor k \rfloor_k(M \lfloor t \rfloor) = \lfloor t :: k \rfloor_k(M)$, we have that $\cap \Gamma'_i, \Delta, \Gamma''' \vdash_{\lambda_\circledR} \lfloor t :: k \rfloor_k(M) : \beta$. This holds for any M of the appropriate type, yielding $\lfloor t :: k \rfloor_k : \Lambda_{\circledR(\Gamma''' \vdash_{\lambda_\circledR} \cap \alpha_i \to \sigma)} \to \Lambda_{\circledR(\cap \Gamma'_i, \Delta, \Gamma''' \vdash_{\lambda_\circledR} \beta)}$, which is exactly what we need.
- Case (Cut): the derivation ends with the rule

$$\frac{\Gamma'_i \vdash t : \alpha_i \quad \Delta; \cap \alpha_i \vdash k : \sigma}{\cap \Gamma'_i, \Delta \vdash tk : \sigma} \ (Cut)$$

By IH we have that $\Gamma'_i \vdash_{\lambda_\circledR} \lfloor t \rfloor : \alpha$ and $\lfloor k \rfloor_k : \Lambda_{\circledR(\Gamma'' \vdash_{\lambda_\circledR} \cap \alpha_i)} \to \Lambda_{\circledR(\Gamma'', \Delta \vdash_{\lambda_\circledR} \sigma)}$. Hence, for any $M \in \Lambda^{\lambda_\circledR}$ such that $\Gamma'' \vdash_{\lambda_\circledR} M : \cap \alpha_i$, it holds $\Gamma'', \Delta \vdash_{\lambda_\circledR} \lfloor k \rfloor_k(M) : \sigma$. By taking $M \equiv \lfloor t \rfloor$ and $\Gamma'' \equiv \cap \Gamma'_i$, we get $\cap \Gamma'_i, \Delta \vdash_{\lambda_\circledR} \lfloor k \rfloor_k(\lfloor t \rfloor) : \sigma$. But $\lfloor k \rfloor_k(\lfloor t \rfloor) = \lfloor tk \rfloor$, so the proof is done.
- Case $(Weak_k)$: the derivation ends with the rule

$$\frac{\Gamma'; \gamma \vdash k : \beta}{\Gamma', x : \alpha; \gamma \vdash x \odot k : \beta} \ (Weak_k)$$

By IH we have that $\lfloor k \rfloor_k$ is the function with the scope $\lfloor k \rfloor_k : \Lambda_{\circledR(\Gamma'' \vdash_{\lambda_\circledR} \gamma)} \to \Lambda_{\circledR(\Gamma', \Gamma'' \vdash_{\lambda_\circledR} \beta)}$, meaning that for each $M \in \Lambda^\circledR$ such that $\Gamma'' \vdash_{\lambda_\circledR} M : \gamma$ holds $\Gamma', \Gamma'' \vdash_{\lambda_\circledR} \lfloor k \rfloor_k(M) : \beta$. Now, we can apply $(Weak)$ rule:

$$\frac{\Gamma', \Gamma'' \vdash \lfloor k \rfloor_k(M) : \beta}{\Gamma', \Gamma'', x : \alpha \vdash x \odot \lfloor k \rfloor_k(M) : \beta} \ (Weak)$$

Since $x \odot \lfloor k \rfloor_k(M) = \lfloor x \odot k \rfloor_k(M)$, this means that $\lfloor x \odot k \rfloor_k : \Lambda_{\circledR(\Gamma'' \vdash_{\lambda_\circledR} \gamma)} \to \Lambda_{\circledR(\Gamma', \Gamma'', x : \alpha \vdash_{\lambda_\circledR} \beta)}$, which is exactly what we wanted to get.
- Case $(Cont_k)$: similar to the case $(Weak_k)$, relying on the rule $(Cont)$ in $\lambda_\circledR$.   □

For the given encoding $\lfloor \ \rfloor$, we show that each $\lambda_\circledR^{Gtz}$-reduction step can be simulated by $\lambda_\circledR$-reduction or identity. In order to do so, we prove the following lemmas. The proofs of Lemma 22 and Lemma 23 use Regnier's σ reductions, investigated in [30].

Lemma 21. *If $M \to_{\lambda_{\circledR}} M'$, then $\lfloor k \rfloor_k(M) \to_{\lambda_{\circledR}} \lfloor k \rfloor_k(M')$.*

Lemma 22. $\lfloor k \rfloor_k((\lambda x.P)N) \to_{\lambda_{\circledR}} (\lambda x.\lfloor k \rfloor_k(P))N$.

Lemma 23. *If $M \in \Lambda^{\circledR}$ and $k, k' \in \Lambda^{\mathsf{Gtz}}_{\circledR,C}$, then $\lfloor k' \rfloor_k \circ \lfloor k \rfloor_k(M) \to_{\lambda_{\circledR}} \lfloor k @ k' \rfloor_k(M)$.*

Lemma 24

(i) *If $x \notin Fv(k)$, then $(\lfloor k \rfloor_k(M))[N/x] = \lfloor k \rfloor_k(M[N/x])$.*
(ii) *If $x, y \notin Fv(k)$, then $z <^x_y (\lfloor k \rfloor_k(M)) \to_{\lambda_{\circledR}} \lfloor k \rfloor_k(z <^x_y M)$.*
(iii) $\lfloor k \rfloor_k(x \odot M) \to_{\lambda_{\circledR}} x \odot \lfloor k \rfloor_k(M)$.

Now we can prove that the reduction rules of $\lambda^{\mathsf{Gtz}}_{\circledR}$ can be simulated by the reduction rules or identities in $\lambda_{\circledR}$-calculus.

Theorem 25 (Simulation of $\lambda^{\mathsf{Gtz}}_{\circledR}$-reduction by $\lambda_{\circledR}$-reduction)

(i) *If term $M \to M'$, then $\lfloor M \rfloor \to_{\lambda_{\circledR}} \lfloor M' \rfloor$.*
(ii) *If context $k \to k'$ by γ_6 or ω_6 reduction, then $\lfloor k \rfloor_k(M) \equiv \lfloor k' \rfloor_k(M)$, for any $M \in \Lambda^{\circledR}$.*
(iii) *If context $k \to k'$ by some other reduction, then $\lfloor k \rfloor_k(M) \to_{\lambda_{\circledR}} \lfloor k' \rfloor_k(M)$, for any $M \in \Lambda^{\circledR}$.*

The previous proposition shows that each $\lambda^{\mathsf{Gtz}}_{\circledR}$-reduction step is interpreted either by a $\lambda_{\circledR}$-reduction or by an identity. If one wants to prove that there is no infinite sequence of $\lambda^{\mathsf{Gtz}}_{\circledR}$-reductions one has to prove that there cannot exist an infinite sequence of $\lambda^{\mathsf{Gtz}}_{\circledR}$-reductions which are all interpreted as identities. To prove this, one shows that if a term is reduced with such a $\lambda^{\mathsf{Gtz}}_{\circledR}$-reduction, it is reduced for another order that forbids infinite decreasing chains. This order is itself composed of several orders, free of infinite decreasing chains (Definition 29).

Definition 26. *The functions S, $\| \ \|_C$, $\| \ \|_W : (\Lambda^{\mathsf{Gtz}}_{\circledR} \cup \Lambda_{\circledR}) \to \mathbb{N}$ are defined in Figure 8.*

$S(x) = 1$	$\|x\|_C = 0$	$\|x\|_W = 1$
$S(\lambda x.t) = 1 + S(t)$	$\|\lambda x.t\|_C = \|t\|_C$	$\|\lambda x.t\|_W = 1 + \|t\|_W$
$S(x \odot e) = 1 + S(e)$	$\|x \odot e\|_C = \|e\|_C$	$\|x \odot e\|_W = 0$
$S(x <^y_z e) = 1 + S(e)$	$\|x <^y_z e\|_C = \|e\|_C + S(e)$	$\|x <^y_z e\|_W = 1 + \|e\|_W$
$S(tk) = S(t) + S(k)$	$\|tk\|_C = \|t\|_C + \|k\|_C$	$\|tk\|_W = 1 + \|t\|_W + \|k\|_W$
$S(\hat{x}.t) = 1 + S(t)$	$\|\hat{x}.t\|_C = \|t\|_C$	$\|\hat{x}.t\|_W = 1 + \|t\|_W$
$S(t :: k) = S(t) + S(k)$	$\|t :: k\|_C = \|t\|_C + \|k\|_C$	$\|t :: k\|_W = 1 + \|t\|_W + \|k\|_W$

Fig. 8. Definitions of $S(e), \|e\|_C, \|e\|_W$

Lemma 27. *For all $e, e' : \Lambda_{\circledR}$:*

(i) *If $e \to_{\gamma_6} e'$, then $\|e\|_C > \|e'\|_C$.*
(ii) *If $e \to_{\omega_6} e'$, then $\|e\|_C = \|e'\|_C$.*

Lemma 28. *For all $e, e' \in \Lambda_{\circledR}$: If $e \to_{\omega_6} e'$, then $\|e\|_W > \|e'\|_W$.*

Now we can define the following orders based on the previously introduced mapping and norms.

Definition 29. *We define the following strict orders and equivalences on* $\Lambda_{\circledR}^{\mathsf{Gtz}} \cap$:

(i) $t >_{\lambda_{\circledR}} t'$ *iff* $\lfloor t \rfloor \to_{\lambda_{\circledR}}^{+} \lfloor t' \rfloor$; $t =_{\lambda_{\circledR}} t'$ *iff* $\lfloor t \rfloor \equiv \lfloor t' \rfloor$;

   $k >_{\lambda_{\circledR}} k'$ *iff* $\lfloor k \rfloor_k (M) \to_{\lambda_{\circledR}}^{+} \lfloor k' \rfloor (M)$ *for every* $\lambda_{\circledR}$ *term M* ;

   $k =_{\lambda_{\circledR}} k'$ *iff* $\lfloor k \rfloor_k (M) \equiv \lfloor k' \rfloor_k (M)$ *for every* $\lambda_{\circledR}$ *term M;*

(ii) $e >_c e'$ *iff* $\|e\|_C > \|e'\|_C$; $e =_c e'$ *iff* $\|e\|_C = \|e'\|_C$;

(iii) $e >_w e'$ *iff* $\|e\|_W > \|e'\|_W$; $e =_w e'$ *iff* $\|e\|_W = \|e'\|_W$;

A lexicographic product of two orders $>_1$ and $>_2$ is usually defined as follows ([2]):
$$ a >_1 \times_{lex} >_2 b \iff a >_1 b \ or \ (a =_1 b \ and \ a >_2 b). $$

Definition 30. *We define the relation* $\gg$ *on* $\Lambda_{\circledR}^{\mathsf{Gtz}}$ *as the lexicographic product:*

$$ \gg \ = \ >_{\lambda_{\circledR}} \times_{lex} >_c \times_{lex} >_w . $$

The following propositions proves that the reduction relation on the set of typed $\lambda_{\circledR}^{\mathsf{Gtz}}$-expressions is included in the given lexicographic product $\gg$.

Proposition 31. *For each* $e \in \Lambda_{\circledR}^{\mathsf{Gtz}}$: *if* $e \to e'$, *then* $e \gg e'$.

Proof. The proof is by case analysis on the kind of reduction and the structure of $\gg$. If $e \to e'$ by β, σ, π, μ, γ_1, γ_2, γ_3, γ_4 γ_5, $\gamma\omega_1$, $\gamma\omega_2$, ω_1, ω_2, ω_3 ω_4 or ω_5 reduction, then $e >_{\lambda_{\circledR}} e'$ by Proposition 25.
If $e \to e'$ by γ_6, then $e =_{\lambda_{\circledR}} e'$ by Proposition 25, and $e >_c e'$ by Lemma 27.
Finally, if $e \to e'$ by ω_6, then $e =_{\lambda_{\circledR}} e'$ by Proposition 25, $e =_c e'$ by Lemma 27 and $e >_w e'$ by Lemma 28.   □

SN of $\to$ is another terminology for the well-foundness of the relation $\to$ and it is well-known that a relation included in a well-founded relation is well-founded and that the lexicographic product of well-founded relations is well-founded.

Theorem 32 (Strong normalization). *Each expression in* $\Lambda_{\circledR}^{\mathsf{Gtz}} \cap$ *is SN.*

Proof. The reduction $\to$ is well-founded on $\Lambda_{\circledR}^{\mathsf{Gtz}} \cap$ as it is included (Proposition 31) in the relation $\gg$ which is well-founded as the lexicographic product of the well-founded relations $>_{\lambda_{\circledR}}$, $>_c$ and $>_w$. Relation $>_{\lambda_{\circledR}}$ is based on the interpretation $\lfloor \ \rfloor : \Lambda_{\circledR}^{\mathsf{Gtz}} \to \Lambda_{\circledR}$. By Proposition 20 typeability is preserved by the interpretation $\lfloor \ \rfloor$ and $\to_{\lambda_{\circledR}}$ is SN (i.e., well-founded) on $\Lambda_{\circledR} \cap$ (Section 3.1), hence $>_{\lambda_{\circledR}}$ is well-founded on $\Lambda_{\circledR}^{\mathsf{Gtz}} \cap$. Similarly, $>_c$ and $>_w$ are well-founded, as they are based on interpretations into the well-founded relation $>$ on the set $\mathbb{N}$ of natural numbers.   □

4   SN $\Rightarrow$ Typability in Both Systems

4.1   SN $\Rightarrow$ Typability in $\lambda_{\circledR} \cap$

We want to prove that if a $\lambda_{\circledR}$-term is SN, then it is typable in the system $\lambda_{\circledR} \cap$. We proceed in two steps: 1) we show that all $\lambda_{\circledR}$-normal forms are typable and 2) we prove

The head subject expansion property. First, let us observe the structure of the $\lambda_\circledR$-normal forms, given by the following abstract syntax:

$$M_{nf} ::= x \mid \lambda x.M_{nf} \mid \lambda x.x \odot M_{nf} \mid xM_{nf}^1 \ldots M_{nf}^n \mid x <_{x_2}^{x_1} M_{nf}N_{nf}, \text{ if } x_1 \in Fv(M_{nf}), x_2 \in Fv(N_{nf})$$
$$W_{nf} ::= x \odot M_{nf} \mid x \odot W_{nf}$$

Proposition 33. $\lambda_\circledR$-normal forms are typable in the system $\lambda_\circledR \cap$.

Proposition 34 (Inverse substitution lemma). Let $\Gamma \vdash M[N/x] : \alpha$ and N typable. Then, there are Δ_i and β_i, $i \in I$ such that $\Delta_i \vdash N : \beta_i$, $\forall i$ and $\Gamma', x : \cap \beta_i \vdash M : \alpha$, where $\Gamma = \Gamma', \cap \Delta_i$.

Proof. By induction on the structure of M.   □

Proposition 35 (Head subject expansion). For every $\lambda_\circledR$-term M: if $M \to M'$, M is contracted redex and $\Gamma \vdash M' : \alpha$, then $\Gamma \vdash M : \alpha$, provided that if $M \equiv (\lambda x.N)P \to_\beta N[P/x] \equiv M'$, P is typable.

Proof. By the case study according to the applied reduction.   □

Theorem 36 (SN $\Rightarrow$ typability). All strongly normalising $\lambda_\circledR$-terms are typable in the $\lambda_\circledR \cap$ system.

Proof. The proof is by induction on the length of the longest reduction path out of a strongly normalising term M, with a subinduction on the size of M.

- If M is a normal form, then M is typable by Proposition 33.
- If M is itself a redex, let M' be the term obtained by contracting the redex M. M' is also strongly normalising, hence by IH it is typable. Then M is typable, by Proposition 35. Notice that, if $M \equiv (\lambda x.N)P \to_\beta N[P/x] \equiv M'$, then, by IH, P is typable, since the length of the longest reduction path out of P is smaller than that of M, and the size of P is smaller than the size of M.
- Next, suppose that M is not itself a redex nor a normal form. Then M is of one of the following forms: $\lambda x.N$, $\lambda x.x \odot N$, $xM_1 \ldots M_n$, $x \odot N$, or $x <_{x_2}^{x_1} NP$, $x_1 \in Fv(N)$, $x_2 \in Fv(P)$ (where $M_1, \ldots, M_n$, and NP are *not* normal forms). $M_1, \ldots, M_n$ and NP are typable by IH, as subterms of M. Then, it is easy to build the typing for M. For instance, let us consider the case $x <_{x_2}^{x_1} NP$ with $x_1 \in Fv(N)$, $x_2 \in Fv(P)$. By induction NP is typable, hence N is typable with say $\Gamma, x_1 : \beta \vdash N : \cap \alpha_i \to \sigma$ and P is typable with say $\Delta_i, x_2 : \gamma_i \vdash P : \alpha_i$. Then using the rule $(E \to)$ we obtain $\Gamma, \cap \Delta_i, x_1 : \beta, x_2 : \cap \gamma_i \vdash NP : \sigma$. Finally, the rule $(Cont)$ yields $\Gamma, \cap \Delta_i, x : \beta \cap (\cap \gamma_i) \vdash x <_{x_2}^{x_1} NP : \sigma$.   □

4.2   SN $\Rightarrow$ Typability in $\lambda_\circledR^{\text{Gtz}} \cap$

Finally, we want to prove that if a $\lambda_\circledR^{\text{Gtz}}$-term is SN, then it is typable in the system $\lambda_\circledR^{\text{Gtz}} \cap$. We follow the procedure used in Section 4.1. The proofs are similar to the ones in Section 4.1 and omitted due to the lack of space.

The abstract syntax of $\lambda_{\circledR}^{\text{Gtz}}$-normal forms is the following:

$$t_{nf} ::= x \mid \lambda x.t_{nf} \mid \lambda x.x \odot t_{nf} \mid x(t_{nf} :: k_{nf}) \mid x <_z^y y(t_{nf} :: k_{nf})$$
$$k_{nf} ::= \widehat{x}.t_{nf} \mid \widehat{x}.x \odot t_{nf} \mid t_{nf} :: k_{nf} \mid x <_z^y (t_{nf} :: k_{nf}), \; y \in F v(t_{nf}), z \in F v(k_{nf})$$
$$w_{nf} ::= x \odot e_{nf} \mid x \odot w_{nf}$$

We use e_{nf} for any $\lambda_{\circledR}^{\text{Gtz}}$-expression in the normal form.

Proposition 37. $\lambda_{\circledR}^{\text{Gtz}}$-normal forms are typable in the system $\lambda_{\circledR}^{\text{Gtz}}\cap$.

The following two lemmas explain the behavior of the meta operators $[\,/\,]$ and $@$ during expansion.

Lemma 38 (Inverse substitution lemma)

(i) Let $\Gamma \vdash t[u/x] : \alpha$ *and u typable. Then, there exist* $\cap\Delta_i$ *and* $\cap\beta_i$, $i \in I$ *such that* $\Delta_i \vdash u : \beta_i$, $\forall i$ *and* $\Gamma', x : \cap\beta_i \vdash t : \alpha$, *where* $\Gamma = \Gamma', \cap\Delta_i$.
(ii) Let $\Gamma; \gamma \vdash k[u/x] : \alpha$ *and u typable. Then, there exist* $\cap\Delta_i$ *and* $\cap\beta_i$, $i \in I$ *such that* $\Delta_i \vdash u : \beta_i$, $\forall i$ *and* $\Gamma', x : \cap\beta_i; \gamma \vdash k : \alpha$, *where* $\Gamma = \Gamma', \cap\Delta_i$.

Lemma 39 (Inverse append lemma). *If* $\Gamma; \alpha \vdash k@k' : \sigma$, *then* $\Gamma = \Gamma', \Gamma''$ *and there is a type* $\cap\beta_i$ *such that* $\Gamma'; \alpha \vdash k : \beta_i$, $\forall i$ *and* $\Gamma''; \cap\beta_i \vdash k' : \sigma$.

Now we prove that the type of a term is preserved during the expansion.

Proposition 40 (Head subject expansion). *For every* $\lambda_{\circledR}^{\text{Gtz}}$-term *t: if* $t \to t'$, *t is contracted redex and* $\Gamma \vdash t' : \alpha$, *then* $\Gamma \vdash t : \alpha$.

Theorem 41 (SN $\Rightarrow$ typability). *All strongly normalising* $\lambda_{\circledR}^{\text{Gtz}}$ *terms are typable in the* $\lambda_{\circledR}^{\text{Gtz}}\cap$ *system.*

5 Conclusions

In this paper, we have proposed intersection type assignment systems for $\lambda_{\circledR}$-calculus (λ_{CW} of [23]) and $\lambda_{\circledR}^{\text{Gtz}}$-calculus of [18]. The two intersection type systems proposed here, for resource control lambda and sequent lambda calculus, give a complete characterisation of strongly normalising terms for both calculi. The strong normalisation of typeable resource lambda terms is proved directly by appropriate modification of the reducibility method, whereas the same property for resource sequent lambda terms is proved by well-founded lexicographic order based on suitable embedding into the former calculus. Although the obtained results are not surprising, this paper expands the range of the intersection type techniques and combines different methods in the strict types environment. Unlike the approach of introducing non-idempotent intersection into the calculus with some kind of resource management [27], our intersection is idempotent. As a consequence, our type assignment system corresponds to full intuitionistic logic, while non-idempotent intersection type assignment systems correspond to intuitionistic linear logic.

Resource control lambda and sequent lambda calculi are good candidates to investigate the computational content of substructural logics ([34]) both in natural deduction and sequent calculus. The motivation for these logics comes from philosophy (Relevant Logics), linguistics (Lambek Calculus) to computing (Linear Logic). The basic idea of resource control is to explicitly handle structural rules, so the absence of (some) structural rules in substructural logics such as weakening, contraction, commutativity, associativity can possibly be handled by resource control operators, which is in the domain of further research. Another direction will involve the investigation of the use of intersection types, being a powerful means for building models of lambda calculus ([6,12]), in constructing models for sequent lambda calculi.

Acknowledgements. We would like to thank the anonymous referees for careful reading and many valuable comments, which helped us improve the final version of the paper. We would also like to thank Dragiša Žunić for participating in the earlier stages of the work.

References

1. Abramsky, S.: Computational interpretations of linear logic. Theor. Comput. Sci. 111(1&2), 3–57 (1993)
2. Baader, F., Nipkow, T.: Term Rewriting and All That. Cambridge University Press, UK (1998)
3. Barbanera, F., Berardi, S.: A symmetric lambda calculus for classical program extraction. Inform. Comput. 125(2), 103–117 (1996)
4. Barendregt, H.P.: The Lambda Calculus: its Syntax and Semantics. North-Holland, Amsterdam (1984), revised edition
5. Barendregt, H.P.: Lambda calculi with types. In: Abramsky, S., Gabbay, D.M., Maibaum, T.S.E. (eds.) Handbook of Logic in Computer Science, pp. 117–309. Oxford University Press, UK (1992)
6. Barendregt, H.P., Coppo, M., Dezani-Ciancaglini, M.: A filter lambda model and the completeness of type assignment. J. Symb. Logic 48(4), 931–940 (1984) (1983)
7. Benton, N., Bierman, G., de Paiva, V., Hyland, M.: A term calculus for intuitionistic linear logic. In: Bezem, M., Groote, J.F. (eds.) TLCA 1993. LNCS, vol. 664, pp. 75–90. Springer, Heidelberg (1993)
8. Bloo, R., Rose, K.H.: Preservation of strong normalisation in named lambda calculi with explicit substitution and garbage collection. In: Computer Science in the Netherlands, CSN 1995, pp. 62–72 (1995)
9. Coppo, M., Dezani-Ciancaglini, M.: A new type-assignment for lambda terms. Archiv für Mathematische Logik 19, 139–156 (1978)
10. Coppo, M., Dezani-Ciancaglini, M.: An extension of the basic functionality theory for the λ-calculus. Notre Dame J. Formal Logic 21(4), 685–693 (1980)
11. Curien, P.-L., Herbelin, H.: The duality of computation. In: 5th International Conference on Functional Programming, ICFP 2000, pp. 233–243. ACM Press, New York (2000)
12. Dezani-Ciancaglini, M., Ghilezan, S., Likavec, S.: Behavioural Inverse Limit Models. Theor. Comput Sci. 316(1-3), 49–74 (2004)
13. Dougherty, D.J., Ghilezan, S., Lescanne, P.: Characterizing strong normalization in the Curien-Herbelin symmetric lambda calculus: extending the Coppo-Dezani heritage. Theor. Comput Sci. 398, 114–128 (2008)

14. Espírito Santo, J.: Completing herbelin's programme. In: Della Rocca, S.R. (ed.) TLCA 2007. LNCS, vol. 4583, pp. 118–132. Springer, Heidelberg (2007)
15. Espírito Santo, J., Ivetić, J., Likavec, S.: Characterising strongly normalising intuitionistic terms. Fundamenta Informaticae (to appear 2011)
16. Gallier, J.: Typing untyped λ-terms, or reducibility strikes again! Ann. Pure Appl. Logic 91, 231–270 (1998)
17. Ghilezan, S.: Strong normalization and typability with intersection types. Notre Dame J. Formal Logic 37(1), 44–52 (1996)
18. Ghilezan, S., Ivetić, J., Lescanne, P., Žunić, D.: Intuitionistic sequent-style calculus with explicit structural rules. In: Bezhanishvili, N. (ed.) TbiLLC 2009. LNCS, vol. 6618, pp. 101–124. Springer, Heidelberg (2011)
19. Ghilezan, S., Likavec, S.: Computational interpretations of logics. In: Ognjanović, Z. (ed.) Collection of Papers, Special issue Logic in Computer Science, vol. 20(12), pp. 159–215. Mathematical Institute of Serbian Academy of Sciences and Arts (2009)
20. Herbelin, H.: A lambda calculus structure isomorphic to Gentzen-style sequent calculus structure. In: Pacholski, L., Tiuryn, J. (eds.) CSL 1994. LNCS, vol. 933, pp. 61–75. Springer, Heidelberg (1995)
21. Howard, W.A.: The formulas-as-types notion of construction. In: Seldin, J.P., Hindley, J.R. (eds.) To H. B. Curry: Essays on Combinatory Logic, Lambda Calculus and Formalism, pp. 479–490. Academic Press, London (1980)
22. Kesner, D., Lengrand, S.: Resource operators for lambda-calculus. Inform. Comput. 205(4), 419–473 (2007)
23. Kesner, D., Renaud, F.: The prismoid of resources. In: Královič, R., Niwiński, D. (eds.) MFCS 2009. LNCS, vol. 5734, pp. 464–476. Springer, Heidelberg (2009)
24. Kikuchi, K.: Simple proofs of characterizing strong normalization for explicit substitution calculi. In: Baader, F. (ed.) RTA 2007. LNCS, vol. 4533, pp. 257–272. Springer, Heidelberg (2007)
25. Matthes, R.: Characterizing strongly normalizing terms of a λ-calculus with generalized applications via intersection types. In: Hindley, J.R., et al. (eds.) ICALP Workshops 2000. Carleton Scientific (2000)
26. Neergaard, P.M.: Theoretical pearls: A bargain for intersection types: a simple strong normalization proof. J. Funct. Program. 15(5), 669–677 (2005)
27. Pagani, M., della Rocca, S.R.: Solvability in resource lambda-calculus. In: Ong, L. (ed.) FOSSACS 2010. LNCS, vol. 6014, pp. 358–373. Springer, Heidelberg (2010)
28. Parigot, M.: Lambda-mu-calculus: An algorithmic interpretation of classical natural deduction. In: Voronkov, A. (ed.) LPAR 1992. LNCS, vol. 624, pp. 190–201. Springer, Heidelberg (1992)
29. Pottinger, G.: A type assignment for the strongly normalizable λ-terms. In: Seldin, J.P., Hindley, J.R. (eds.) To H. B. Curry: Essays on Combinatory Logic, Lambda Calculus and Formalism, pp. 561–577. Academic Press, London (1980)
30. Regnier, L.: Une équivalence sur les lambda-termes. Theor. Comput Sci. 126(2), 281–292 (1994)
31. Rose, K.H.: CRSX - Combinatory Reduction Systems with Extensions. In: Schmidt-Schauß, M. (ed.) 22nd International Conference on Rewriting Techniques and Applications, RTA 2011. Leibniz International Proceedings in Informatics (LIPIcs), vol. 10, pp. 81–90. Schloss Dagstuhl–Leibniz-Zentrum fuer Informatik (2011)

32. Rose, K.H.: Implementation Tricks That Make CRSX Tick. Talk at IFIP 1.6 Workshop, RDP 2011 (May 2011)
33. Sallé, P.: Une extension de la théorie des types en lambda-calcul. In: Ausiello, G., Böhm, C. (eds.) ICALP 1978. LNCS, vol. 62, pp. 398–410. Springer, Heidelberg (1978)
34. Schroeder-Heister, P., Došen, K.: Substructural Logics. Oxford University Press, UK (1993)
35. Tait, W.W.: Intensional interpretations of functionals of finite type I. J. Symb. Logic 32, 198–212 (1967)
36. van Bakel, S.: Complete restrictions of the intersection type discipline. Theor. Comput Sci. 102(1), 135–163 (1992)

Modal Interface Theories for Communication-Safe Component Assemblies*

Rolf Hennicker[1] and Alexander Knapp[2]

[1] Ludwig-Maximilians-Universität München
`hennicke@pst.ifi.lmu.de`
[2] Universität Augsburg
`knapp@informatik.uni-augsburg.de`

Abstract. We propose an extension of the abstract rules for independent implementability of reactive components proposed in interface theories to take into account interface assemblies. As a concrete instantiation we extend existing interface theories for modal I/O-transition systems to support assemblies, (greybox) assembly refinement and assembly encapsulation. We introduce a new notion of communication-safety for N-ary assemblies which overcomes problems with previous definitions of interface compatibility. We show that communication-safety can be checked incrementally. We also show that communication-safety is preserved by assembly refinement, that blackbox refinement of component interfaces is compositional w.r.t. greybox refinement of assemblies and, conversely, that assembly encapsulation maps greybox to blackbox refinement. The methodology of our approach is illustrated by a small case study.

1 Introduction

Reactive software components are commonly understood as encapsulated units which communicate with their environment via well-defined interfaces. Interface specifications provide a means to describe the visible behaviour of interacting components. They serve, on the one hand, to express what is expected from the environment for a correct functioning of a component, and, on the other hand, to specify what is offered by a component. For the development of component systems on the basis of interfaces we can identify three key issues: the ability to build larger specifications from smaller ones (by composition), the (stepwise) refinement of interface specifications, and compatibility requirements ensuring safe communication of components. Of course, it is important that the different aspects fit properly together, i.e. that refinement is preserved by composition and that compatibility of interfaces is preserved by refinement, thus guaranteeing independent implementability of components.

1.1 Interface Languages

These crucial requirements, that any concrete interface theory should obey, are nicely formulated by the rules of an interface language stated in [7]. It assumes a domain $\mathcal{F}$

---

* This work has been partially sponsored by the Bavarian Ministry for Economics, Infrastructure, Traffic and Technology under the IuK-project RAJA, IUK-0805-0005 and by the European Union under the FP7-project ASCENS, 257414.

A. Cerone and P. Pihlajasaari (Eds.): ICTAC 2011, LNCS 6916, pp. 135–153, 2011.

of interfaces, a partial composition operator $\| : \mathcal{F} \times \mathcal{F} \rightarrow \mathcal{F}$, a binary compatibility relation $\sim \subseteq \mathcal{F} \times \mathcal{F}$, and a refinement relation $\leq \subseteq \mathcal{F} \times \mathcal{F}$ relating concrete and abstract specifications. On this basis the principle of independent implementability reads as follows:

Independent implementability: For all $F, F', G, G' \in \mathcal{F}$,
   if $F \sim G$ and $F' \leq F$, $G' \leq G$, then $F' \sim G'$ and $(F' \| G') \leq (F \| G)$.[1]

Particular instances of interface theories satisfying these requirements are formulated for interface automata in [7] and for modal I/O-transition systems (MIOs) in [10,2].

Following the ideas of an interface language, interfaces for complex components are constructed from smaller ones by interface composition, following, e.g., a synchronous communication scheme, like interface automata and MIOs, where shared actions of complementary types (input/output) are synchronised. The result of an interface composition yields again an interface describing the visible (blackbox) behaviour of a composite component. Hence, the architectural information behind interface composition is hidden and it is not possible to specify architectural requirements, which are important as well for the development of complex systems. In particular, the communication behaviour of interacting components is abstracted away during interface composition and can not be taken into account in further refinement, since interface refinement is inherently a blackbox refinement. For instance, assume that an interface for a credit card payment system is specified by composing an interface describing the customer's behaviour with another interface describing the clearing company's behaviour, which is responsible to verify the credit card. That the verification is really performed assumes a communication between the customer with the clearing company. But during interface composition this communication is made invisible and therefore the composite interface could be refined, for instance, by a primitive interface which has the same observable behaviour but which does not actually communicate with the clearing company.[2]

1.2   Interface Assemblies

As a consequence of this discussion, we claim that there is still a missing link in the notion of an interface language and in its concrete instantiations. What is still missing is the specification of architectural information and the explicit possibility to observe communications between components. Only in a next step, if the necessary communications are established, it should be legal to abstract them away and to construct a new interface specification by explicit encapsulation of the architectural one. To tackle this issue the most obvious approach is to consider interface networks as a distinguished concept. Interface networks are assemblies of connected interfaces thus providing architectural requirements for the planned system. Such assemblies can be refined only if the architectural requirements are respected. From the behavioural point of view this

---

[1] It is assumed that the composition of compatible interfaces is defined. Interface languages require also the property of incremental design which will be discussed later.

[2] A way out could be to require that refinements of composite interfaces not only can but must be performed piecewise; but this is not anchored in the formalism and anyway cannot be treated with alternating simulation refinement of interface-automata since, in contrast to modal I/O-transition systems, abstract outputs can always be omitted there in a refinement.

means that not only the visible actions to the outside but also specified communications between components within the assembly must be taken into account when assemblies are refined. Following the terminology of [12] such refinements are also called grey-box refinements. Hence, we can extend the abstract concept of an interface language by introducing, additionally to the domain $\mathcal{F}$ of interfaces, a domain $\mathcal{A}$ of assemblies. For the construction of assemblies we assume, for each natural number n, a partial (overloaded) operator $asm : \mathcal{F}^n \to \mathcal{A}$. Concerning compatibility of components, we extend the binary compatibility relation between interfaces to a communication-safety predicate $cs \subseteq \mathcal{A}$ on assemblies, which expresses that the interfaces belonging to an assembly can work together without communication errors. This could mean, e.g., that the assembly is deadlock-free, or, in the context of the I/O-transition systems considered below, that any output a component wants to issue to the remainder of the assembly is indeed accepted.[3] Concerning refinement, we distinguish between interface and assembly refinement, expressed by the binary relations $\preccurlyeq_{\mathrm{intf}} \subseteq \mathcal{F} \times \mathcal{F}$ and $\preccurlyeq_{\mathrm{asm}} \subseteq \mathcal{A} \times \mathcal{A}$ resp. Finally, we introduce an operation $pack : \mathcal{A} \to \mathcal{F}$ which allows to express encapsulation of an assembly into an interface (by hiding the architectural information of the assembly). The principle of independent implementability can now be rephrased as follows:

Independent implementability: For all $F_k, F'_k \in \mathcal{F}$ for $k = 1, \dots, n$,
  if $cs(asm(F_1, \dots, F_n))$ and $F'_k \preccurlyeq_{\mathrm{intf}} F_k$ for $k = 1, \dots, n$,
  then $cs(asm(F'_1, \dots, F'_n))$ and $asm(F'_1, \dots, F'_n) \preccurlyeq_{\mathrm{asm}} asm(F_1, \dots, F_n)$.

But obviously this does not suffice for extracting an interface from an assembly by encapsulation, i.e., by applying the *pack* operation. Then it must be ensured that packing two assemblies which are in refinement relation leads to interfaces which are in refinement relation again, which is expressed by the principle of refinement encapsulation:

Refinement encapsulation: For all $A, A' \in \mathcal{A}$,
  if $cs(A)$ and $A' \preccurlyeq_{\mathrm{asm}} A$, then $pack(A') \preccurlyeq_{\mathrm{intf}} pack(A)$.

1.3 Modal I/O-Automata for Interface and Assembly Specifications

As a concrete instantiation of our approach we will build upon modal I/O-transition systems (MIOs) introduced by Larsen et al. [10,11]. We have chosen MIOs as our basic formalism since they allow us to distinguish between transitions which are optional (may) or mandatory (must) for refinements. We extend the interface theory of MIOs presented in [2] by introducing interface assemblies together with a new notion of communication-safety and assembly refinement. In our approach, interface specifications are simply MIOs with input and output actions only, while assemblies are MIO networks formally presented by finitely indexed sets of (syntactically composable) MIOs. To any assembly a greybox behaviour is associated which is again a MIO having, additionally to input and output actions, distinguished communication actions. It is computed by the synchronous composition of the interface MIOs contained in the assembly, but synchronisations on complementary input and output actions are not

---

[3] We will show in the technical part of the paper that this requirement is different from deadlock-freedom.

hidden, as in the original MIO approach, but considered as visible communication actions. Our notion of communication-safety is inspired by the notion of weak modal compatibility proposed in [2]. However, it goes beyond that because, first, it allows to study the compatibility of arbitrarily many interfaces, and, secondly, it generalises significantly the behavioural requirements of weak modal compatibility. The idea is that whenever one component wants to send an output it finds the communication partner in a state where it must eventually take the corresponding input. Before taking the input the communication partner can still perform silent must-transitions *and/or* mandatory communications with other components of the assembly *and also* outputs which are a must and are directed outside of the assembly. The latter is a significant generalisation of weak modal compatibility needed in many practical applications. We show that communication-safe assemblies can be built up in an incremental way, i.e., given a communication-safe assembly A and an interface F which is compatible to A, the new assembly extending A by F will be communication-safe again. This result is related to the property of incremental design of an interface language [7].

Concerning refinement we distinguish, as explained above, between interface and assembly refinement. Interface refinement has to respect blackbox behaviours, it is formalised in terms of weak modal refinement of MIOs based on a simulation relation which abstracts from silent transitions (labelled with the invisible action τ). Assembly refinement has to respect the architectural requirements and the (greybox) behaviour of assemblies. Therefore it is defined as structure preserving pairwise refinement of the finitely indexed sets of interfaces which form the assemblies. The refinement of assembly behaviours abstracts away silent transitions (which stem from inner components), but transitions resulting from communications are considered as visible and therefore they are respected by the simulation relation. Interface refinement is also called blackbox refinement and assembly refinement corresponds to greybox refinement.

As central results of our approach we obtain that the property of independent implementability (second version from above) is satisfied. Indeed we even get stronger results, called compositionality of refinement and preservation of communication-safety, which read as follows and which obviously imply independent implementability:

Compositionality of refinement: For all $F_k, F_k' \in \mathcal{F}$ for $k = 1, \ldots, n$,
   if $F_k' \preceq_{\text{intf}} F_k$ for $k = 1, \ldots n$,
   then $asm(F_1', \ldots, F_n') \preceq_{\text{asm}} asm(F_1, \ldots, F_n)$.

Preservation of communication-safety: For all $A, A' \in \mathcal{A}$,
   if $cs(A)$ and $A' \preceq_{\text{asm}} A$, then $cs(A')$.

Last but not least we consider the encapsulation of MIO assemblies into interfaces, i.e. the *pack* operation, which moves the visible communications of assemblies into silent transitions of interfaces. We show that encapsulation is compatible with assembly and interface refinement, i.e., that the principle of refinement encapsulation stated above is satisfied as well. Also in this case we can prove a stronger version which does not need the communication-safety assumption of the abstract assembly. Our methodology and our results will be demonstrated on a small, but detailed case study.

The paper is structured as follows: In Sect. 2 we summarise the basic notions of modal I/O-transition systems and in Sect. 3 we introduce our running example. Then, in

Sect. 4, we consider formally interfaces, assemblies, their greybox behaviour and their communication-safety; we also define interface and assembly refinement and prove our central compatibility and compositionality results. Our methodology is illustrated by our small case study in Sect. 5. Finally, in Sect. 6, we finish with some concluding remarks.

2   Modal I/O-Transition Systems: Basic Definitions

Modal I/O-transition systems (MIOs) have been introduced by Larsen et al. [10,11] as a formalism to specify the behaviour of reactive components. They allow to distinguish between transitions which are optional (*may*) or mandatory (*must*) for refinements. We will use MIOs for describing interface behaviours as well as assembly behaviours. Technically this is achieved by distinguishing not only input, output, and internal labels, but also communication labels expressing synchronous communication. In contrast to [10] internal actions are not explicitly named here but represented by the internal, invisible action τ while communication labels are newly introduced here. In the following of this section we recall the technical definitions used hereafter. These definitions will be illustrated by our running example introduced in Sect. 3.

An *I/O-labelling* $L = (I_L, O_L, T_L)$ consists of pairwise disjoint sets of *input labels* I_L, *output labels* O_L, and *communication labels* T_L, such that $\tau \notin I_L \cup O_L \cup T_L$. We write $\bigcup L$ for $I_L \cup O_L \cup T_L$.

A *modal I/O-transition system (MIO)* $M = (L_M, S_M, s_{0,M}, \dashrightarrow_M, \rightarrow_M)$ consists of an I/O-labelling $L_M = (I_M, O_M, T_M)$, a set of *states* S_M, an *initial state* $s_{0,M} \in S_M$, a *may-transition relation* $\dashrightarrow_M \subseteq S_M \times (\bigcup L_M \cup \{\tau\}) \times S_M$, and a *must-transition relation* $\rightarrow_M \subseteq \dashrightarrow_M$. M is called an *implementation* if $\rightarrow_M = \dashrightarrow_M$. For $l \in \bigcup L_M$ we write $s \xrightarrow{\hat{l}}_M s'$ for $s \xrightarrow{\tau}^m_M \cdot \xrightarrow{l}_M \cdot \xrightarrow{\tau}^n_M s'$ with $m, n \geq 0$, and $s \xrightarrow{\hat{\tau}}_M s'$ for $s \xrightarrow{\tau}^n_M s'$ with $n \geq 0$ (and likewise for the must-transition relation). Furthermore, for $X \subseteq \bigcup L_M$, we write $s \xrightarrow{\hat{X}}_M s'$ for $s \xrightarrow{\hat{l_1}}_M \cdots \xrightarrow{\hat{l_n}}_M s'$ with $n \geq 0$ and $l_1, \ldots, l_n \in X$. The *reachable states* of M are denoted by $\mathscr{R}(M)$ with $s \in \mathscr{R}(M)$ if, and only if there is a finite sequence of may-transitions from $s_{0,M}$ to s in M.

The *hiding* of communication labels of a MIO M is given by $M\xi = (L_M\xi, S_M, s_{0,M}, \dashrightarrow_{M\xi}, \rightarrow_{M\xi})$ with $L_M\xi = (I_{L_M}, O_{L_M}, \emptyset)$, $\dashrightarrow_{M\xi} = \{(s, l, s') \mid s \xrightarrow{l}_M s', l \in I_M \cup O_M\} \cup \{(s, \tau, s') \mid s \xrightarrow{l}_M s', l \in T_M\}$ and likewise for $\rightarrow_{M\xi}$.

Two I/O-labellings K and L are *composable* if their labels overlap only on complementary types, i.e. $\bigcup K \cap \bigcup L \subseteq (I_K \cap O_L) \cup (I_L \cap O_K)$. The *synchronous composition* of two composable I/O-labellings K and L moves corresponding input/output labels to the set of communication labels, i.e., it yields the I/O-labelling $K \otimes^{sy} L = ((I_K \setminus O_L) \cup (I_L \setminus O_K), (O_K \setminus I_L) \cup (O_L \setminus I_K), T_K \cup T_L \cup (I_K \cap O_L) \cup (I_L \cap O_K))$.

Two MIOs M and N are *composable* if their I/O-labellings are composable. The *synchronous composition* of two composable MIOs M and N is denoted by $M \otimes^{sy} N$ and defined as the usual product of automata with synchronisation on shared labels, which are communication labels of the product; a synchronisation transition in $M \otimes^{sy} N$ is a must-transition if, and only if both synchronising transitions are must-transitions.

Composability and synchronous composition are straightforwardly extended to finitely indexed sets of I/O-labellings and MIOs: A finitely indexed set $(L_i)_{1\leq i\leq n}$ of I/O-labellings with $n \geq 1$ is *composable* if its I/O-labellings are pairwise composable. The *synchronous composition* of a composable finitely indexed set $(L_i)_{1\leq i\leq n}$ of I/O-labellings with $n \geq 1$ is inductively given by $\bigotimes^{\mathrm{sy}}_{1\leq i\leq n} L_i = L_1 \otimes^{\mathrm{sy}} \ldots \otimes^{\mathrm{sy}} L_n$. A finitely indexed set $(M_i)_{1\leq i\leq n}$ of MIOs with $n \geq 1$ is *composable* if the I/O-labellings of its MIOs are pairwise composable. The *synchronous composition* of a composable finitely indexed set $(M_i)_{1\leq i\leq n}$ of MIOs with $n \geq 1$ is inductively given by $\bigotimes^{\mathrm{sy}}_{1\leq i\leq n} M_i = M_1 \otimes^{\mathrm{sy}} \ldots \otimes^{\mathrm{sy}} M_n$. (Commutativity and associativity laws could be obtained up to strong bisimulation.)

3 Modelling Component Systems with MIOs: Example

We introduce a running example to explain our notions of interface and assembly, its greybox behaviour and encapsulation. We consider a simple cash desk application, inspired by [13]. Figure 1 shows the assembly CashDeskAssembly, which is a set of three interfaces, CashDeskGUI, CashDeskController and ClearingCompany. Each interface has input and output actions indicated by incoming and outgoing arrows on the frame of the interface which shows the interface's signature. Interfaces are connected by shared actions of complementary types. For instance, newSale, itemReady and finish are the shared actions of CashDeskGUI and CashDeskController where, e.g., newSale is an input for CashDeskGUI and an output of CashDeskController. The assembly itself has also a signature with communication actions given by the shared actions of the interfaces and

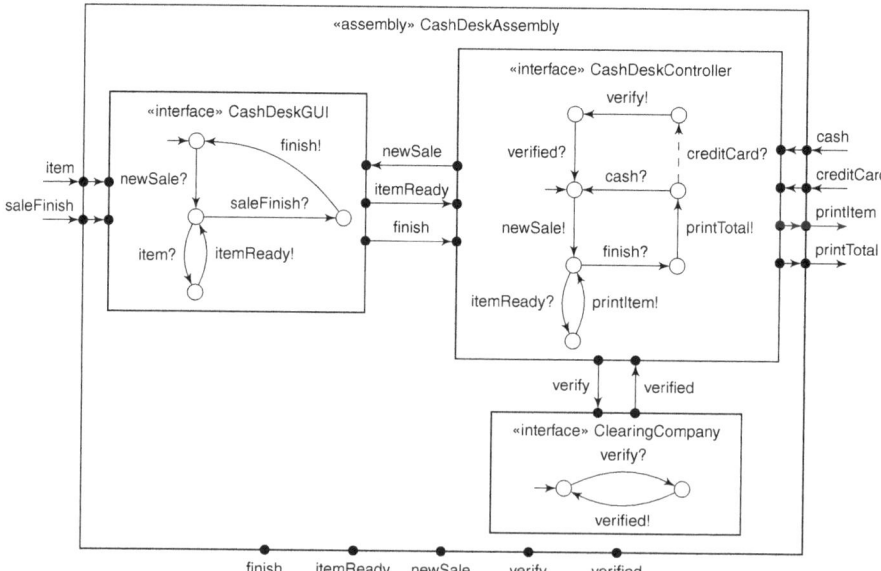

Fig. 1. Cash desk assembly with contained interfaces

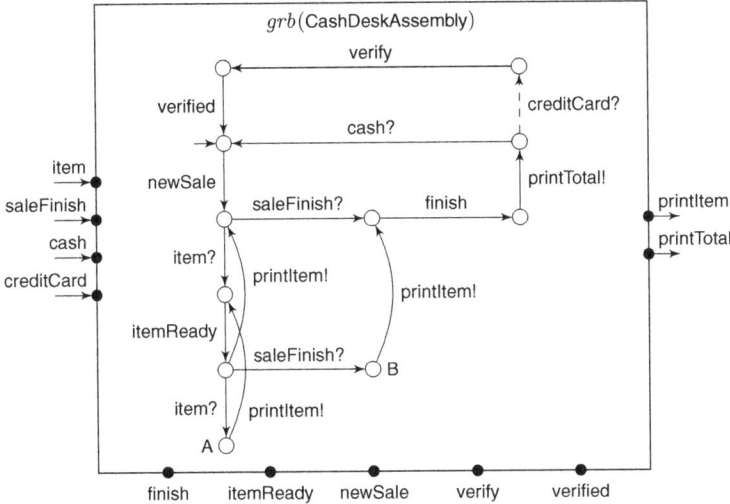

Fig. 2. Greybox behaviour of CashDeskAssembly in Fig. 1

with input/output actions given by the non-connected (open) actions of the interfaces. The communication actions are indicated by bullets on the frame of the assembly.

Each interface has a behaviour specification represented by a modal I/O-transition system with input/output labels but without communication labels. The I/O-labelling of the MIO determines the signature of the interface (shown on its frame). There may also be silent transitions labelled with τ, but those do not occur in the three example interfaces. In the drawings of the MIOs, labels suffixed with ? indicate inputs, those suffixed with ! outputs of the interface. The CashDeskGUI interface behaviour waits for a newSale? from the environment, then reacts to incoming item?s by issuing corresponding itemReady!s until a saleFinish? arrives, upon which it signals finish!. The CashDeskController interface behaviour starts each sale by issuing newSale! and then answers each itemReady? by printItem! until a finish? arrives, upon which a printTotal! is issued and either cash? or creditCard? is accepted. Only creditCard? is a may-transition, such that in a refinement of CashDeskController it may be absent or turned into a must-transition. The ClearingCompany waits for a verify? and then reacts with a verified!. For simplicity of presentation we have only specified the positive case where a credit card is validated.

To each assembly we associate a behaviour which is presented as a MIO with input, output, *and* communication labels. It is also called greybox behaviour since the communication labels are still visible, only τ actions possibly occurring in the contained interfaces of the assembly are hidden. Figure 2 shows the greybox behaviour of the CashDeskAssembly. It is constructed by the synchronous composition (see Sect. 2) of the three interface MIOs where communication happens if shared labels of complementary types match. The resulting communication labels are still visible but not usable for further input or output; i.e., we follow the binary communication scheme of interface automata and MIOs. Pictorially, the communication labels are drawn without a suffix on the transitions. Note that the signature of an assembly is determined by the I/O-labelling of its greybox view.

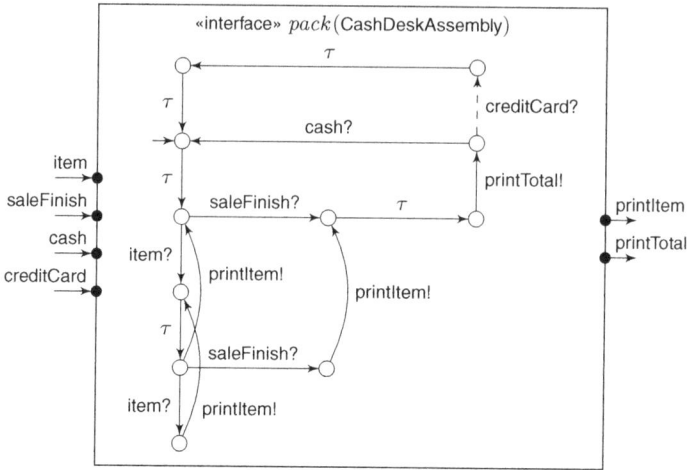

Fig. 3. Interface resulting from packing CashDeskAssembly in Fig. 1

An assembly can be encapsulated by "packing" its greybox view, i.e. by hiding all communication labels; see Sect. 2. Technically, this is achieved by replacing each transition with a communication label by a silent τ-transition. The result of assembly encapsulation yields an interface. Hence, assembly encapsulation is an important step for hierarchical system development. In our example, packing of the greybox behaviour of the CashDeskAssembly results in the interface shown in Fig. 3.

4 Interfaces and Assemblies

We now turn to a formal presentation of the notions of interface and assembly as motivated in the introduction and illustrated by the example. We discuss communication-safe assemblies and the refinement of interfaces and assemblies. In particular, we justify compositionality of refinement, preservation of communication-safety, and refinement encapsulation in our approach. We build on the definitions of MIOs, their composability and synchronous composition, as well as hiding of communication labels recalled in Sect. 2. All claims are reduced to corresponding lemmas for MIOs and their refinement; the proofs of these lemmas can be found in App. A.

The domain of *interfaces* $\mathcal{F}$ is constructed from all those MIOs whose I/O-labellings do not show communication labels. We write $F = intf(M)$ for an interface with underlying MIO M with I/O-labelling $L_M = (I_M, O_M, \emptyset)$. The *signature* of F is given by the I/O-labelling L_M and pictorially indicated in the examples on the frame of an interface. The labelling restriction reflects the blackbox characteristics of interfaces abstracting from communication. Two interfaces are *composable* if their underlying MIOs are composable, and a finitely indexed set $(F_i)_{1 \leq i \leq n}$ of interfaces is *composable* if the F_i are pairwise composable.

The domain of *assemblies* $\mathcal{A}$ is constructed from the composable finitely indexed sets of interfaces, and we write $A = asm((F_i)_{1 \leq i \leq n})$ for an assembly consisting of the interfaces $F_1, \ldots, F_n$. Each assembly A is assigned its *greybox behaviour* $grb(A)$ which is the synchronous composition of the MIOs underlying the constituting interfaces of the assembly, formally

$$grb(asm((intf(M_i))_{1 \leq i \leq n})) = \bigotimes_{1 \leq i \leq n}^{sy} M_i \, .$$

In particular, such a greybox behaviour leaves communications visible. The *signature* of an assembly A is given by the I/O-labelling $\bigotimes_{1 \leq i \leq n}^{sy} L_i$ of the MIO $\bigotimes_{1 \leq i \leq n}^{sy} M_i$.

We also construct an interface $pack(A)$ from an assembly A which abstracts from the communication labels in the greybox view. For this purpose we use the hiding operator ξ on MIOs defined in Sect. 2:

$$pack(A) = intf(grb(A)\xi) \, .$$

According to the hiding operator in the signature of $pack(A)$ all communication labels of A have become τ.

4.1 Communication-Safe Assemblies

Our notion of communication-safe assembly is inspired by the notion of weak modal compatibility in [2]. This compatibility notion, as well as the compatibility notions in [6,7] and [10], relies on the assumption that outputs are autonomous and must be accepted by a communication partner while inputs are subject to external choice and need not to be served. Hence the discrimination of inputs and outputs is essential here. For instance, the two interfaces shown in the assembly in Fig. 4(a) are (strongly) compatible, since the output x! issued by the interface on the left-hand side will be (immediately) accepted by the input x? of the MIO on the right-hand side. However, if we consider the assembly in Fig. 4(b), then the two interfaces are not compatible, since the interface on the right-hand side can autonomously decide to output y! which cannot be accepted by the interface on the left-hand side.

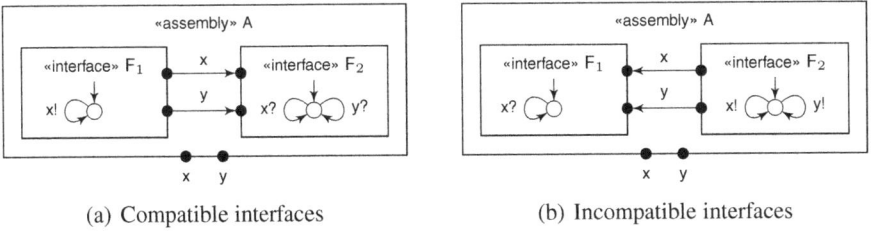

(a) Compatible interfaces   (b) Incompatible interfaces

Fig. 4. Autonomy of outputs

Strong modal compatibility is based on the idea that whenever one component wants to send an output it finds the communication partner in a state where it must take the corresponding input immediately. Weak modal compatibility is more liberal since it is sufficient if the communication partner must accept the message possibly after performing first some silent must-transitions. But simple examples show, see e.g. Ex. 1 below, that this compatibility requirement is still too strong. Therefore we generalise weak compatibility further and allow the communication partner to take the input only after performing silent must-transitions *and/or* mandatory communications with other components of the assembly *and also* outputs which are a must and are directed outside of the assembly. This works well because, assuming communication-safe developments, these (open) outputs are again guaranteed to be taken (possibly after a delay) when an assembly is further extended. We show that communication-safe assemblies can indeed be built up in an incremental way. Moreover, our notion of communication-safety goes beyond the compatibility notions because it allows to study the compatibility of arbitrarily many interfaces within an assembly.

We base our definition of communication-safety on the corresponding notion of output compatibility for MIO-families. Assume given a composable finitely indexed set $(M_i)_{1 \le i \le n}$ of MIOs and let M_j be an arbitrary MIO of the family. Then the rest of the family after omitting M_j, let us call it E_j, plays the role of the environment for M_j. We must ensure that in any reachable state of the product of the family, whenever M_j wants to send an output, then E_j must be able to take the corresponding input possibly after some autonomous must-transitions of E_j which do not concern communication with M_j. These autonomous transitions can be silent must-transitions or must-communication transitions or must-outputs of E_j which are not shared with the inputs of M_j.

Definition 1. *Let* $(M_i)_{1 \le i \le n}$ *be a composable finitely indexed set of MIOs. For each* j *with* $1 \le j \le n$, *let* $E_j = \bigotimes_{1 \le i \ne j \le n}^{sy} M_i$. *The MIO-family* $(M_i)_{1 \le i \le n}$ *is output compatible if for each* $1 \le j \le n$, *each* $(s_1, \ldots, s_n) \in \mathcal{R}(\bigotimes_{1 \le i \le n}^{sy} M_i)$, *and each* $l \in O_{M_j} \cap I_{E_j}$ *the following holds with* $X_j = T_{E_j} \cup (O_{E_j} \setminus I_{M_j})$.[4]

$$\exists s'_j \in S_{M_j} \cdot s_j \xrightarrow{l}_{M_j} s'_j \Rightarrow \exists (s'_1, \ldots, s'_{j-1}, s'_{j+1}, \ldots, s'_n) \in \mathcal{R}(E_j).$$

$$(s_1, \ldots, s_{j-1}, s_{j+1}, \ldots, s_n) \xrightarrow{\hat{X_j}}_{E_j} \cdot \xrightarrow{l}_{E_j} (s'_1, \ldots, s'_{j-1}, s'_{j+1}, \ldots, s'_n). \qquad \square$$

An assembly $A = asm((intf(M_i))_{1 \le i \le n})$ is *communication-safe*, denoted by $cs(A)$, if the family of MIOs $(M_i)_{1 \le i \le n}$ is output compatible .

Example 1. Consider the CashDeskAssembly in Fig. 1. To check communication-safety we have to consider the assembly's greybox behaviour shown in Fig. 2. Crucial states are the states A and B. For instance, in state A the CashDeskGUI has reached its lowest state in Fig. 1 where it wants to send out itemReady! and the CashDeskController has also reached its lowest state in Fig. 1 where it can perform the open output printItem! to the environment of the assembly. Only after this output it can input, as requested, itemReady?. This would not be allowed by weak compatibility since printItem! is not silent. On the other hand, sending printItem! before accepting itemReady? is not a problem, because we can expect that the whole assembly will only be put in a communication-safe context, where we can again assume that the output printItem! will eventually be

---

[4] Note that T_{E_j} is the set of communication labels of E_j and $(O_{E_j} \setminus I_{M_j})$ is the set of output labels of E_j which are not shared with the input labels of M_j, i.e. not used for communication between E_j and M_j. The silent must-transitions are anyway subsumed in the notation $\xrightarrow{\hat{X_j}}_{E_j}$; see Sect. 2.

accepted. A similar situation concerns state B of the assembly, where the CashDeskController accepts an output finish! of the CashDeskGUI only if it has performed an output of printItem! before.   □

Let us still point out that communication-safety does not coincide with deadlock-freedom. Indeed deadlock-freedom is neither necessary nor sufficient. For instance, the assembly in Fig. 4(b) is not communication-safe but deadlock-free. On the other hand, the assembly in Fig. 5 is communication-safe but does deadlock immediately since none of the inputs is served which is not required by our notion of communication-safety. (Of course one can also imagine other variants of communication correctness where inputs must be served.)

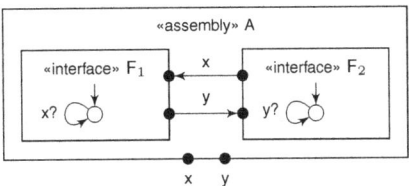

Fig. 5. Deadlocking interfaces

Communication-safety of an assembly can be shown incrementally, i.e. by enlarging the assembly by one interface at a time, each time checking that the assembly from the packed assembly up to now and the additional interface is communication-safe:

Proposition 1. *Let* $A = asm((F_i)_{1 \leq i \leq n+1})$ *be an assembly. If* $A' = asm((F_i)_{1 \leq i \leq n})$ *and* $asm(pack(A'), F_{n+1})$ *are communication-safe, then* A *is communication-safe.*

This claim follows immediately from a corresponding lemma for the underlying MIOs ensuring incremental checking of output compatibility:

Lemma 1. *Let* $(M_i)_{1 \leq i \leq n+1}$ *be a composable finitely indexed set of MIOs. If* $(M_i)_{1 \leq i \leq n}$ *and* $(\bigotimes_{1 \leq i \leq k}^{sy} M_i, M_{n+1})$ *are output compatible, then* $(M_i)_{1 \leq i \leq n+1}$ *is output compatible.*

However, for guaranteeing communication-safety of an assembly $asm((F_i)_{1 \leq i \leq n})$ it does not suffice to check pairwise communication-safety in the sense that each $asm(F_i, F_j)$ with $1 \leq i \neq j \leq n$ is communication-safe. Consider the assembly A in Fig. 6 consisting of three interfaces F_1, F_2, F_3. The three assemblies $asm(F_1, F_2)$, $asm(F_1, F_3)$, and $asm(F_2, F_3)$ are communication-safe; but $asm(F_1, F_2, F_3)$ is not communication-safe. For instance in the initial state of the whole assembly, F_1 wants to send x!, but the product of F_2 and F_3 does never take x? after autonomous actions which are not shared with F_1 (note that the output z! is shared).

4.2 Refinement of Interfaces and Assemblies

Refinement of interfaces and assemblies relies on the notion of weak modal refinement for MIOs [9]. The basic idea of *modal* refinement is that required (*must*) transitions

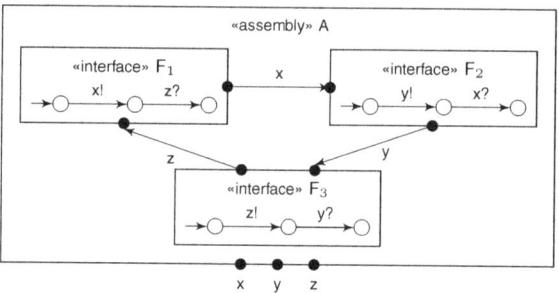

Fig. 6. Communication-safety does not follow from pairwise communication-safety

of an abstract specification must also occur in the concrete specification. Conversely, allowed (*may*) transitions of the concrete specification must be allowed by the abstract specification. The refinement relation is weak, because it supports observational abstraction, i.e., silent τ-transitions can be dropped and inserted as long as the modalities and the simulation relation are preserved. We first extend the notion of weak modal refinement given in [9] in a straightforward way to MIOs with communication labels. Like in [9], weak modal refinement abstracts from internal actions, but transitions with communication labels must be respected in the same way as input/output actions.

Definition 2. *Let M and N be MIOs with the same I/O-labelling. M weakly modally refines N, written $M \leq_m^* N$, if there exists a relation $R \subseteq S_M \times S_N$ containing $(s_{0,M}, s_{0,N})$ such that for all $(s_M, s_N) \in R$:*

1. $\forall l \in \bigcup L_N, s_N' \in S_N . s_N \xrightarrow{l}_N s_N' \Rightarrow \exists s_M' \in S_M . s_M \xrightarrow{\hat{l}}_M s_M' \wedge (s_M', s_N') \in R$
2. $\forall s_N' \in S_N . s_N \xrightarrow{\tau}_A s_N' \Rightarrow \exists s_M' \in S_M . s_M \xrightarrow{\hat{\tau}}_M s_M' \wedge (s_M', s_N') \in R$
3. $\forall l \in \bigcup L_M, s_M' \in S_M . s_M \dashrightarrow_M^l s_M' \Rightarrow \exists s_N' \in S_N . s_N \dashrightarrow_N^l s_N' \wedge (s_M', s_N') \in R$
4. $\forall s_M' \in S_M . s_M \dashrightarrow_M^\tau s_M' \Rightarrow \exists s_N' \in S_N . s_N \dashrightarrow_N^{\hat{\tau}} s_N' \wedge (s_M', s_N') \in R$

A MIO M co-simulates a MIO N, written $M =_m^* N$, if $M \leq_m^* N$ and $N \leq_m^* M$. □

Note that $\leq_m^*$ is reflexive and transitive. If all transitions of M are must-transitions co-simulation corresponds to weak bisimulation; if all transitions of M are may-transitions it is classical co-simulation.

Since interface refinement has to respect blackbox behaviours, and since interfaces do not show any communication labels, the notion of weak modal refinement is directly applicable to define interface refinement. An interface $F = intf(M)$ *refines* an interface $G = intf(N)$, written as $F \preccurlyeq_{\mathrm{intf}} G$, if $M \leq_m^* N$. The interfaces F and G are *equivalent*, written $F \approx_{\mathrm{intf}} G$, if $F \preccurlyeq_{\mathrm{intf}} G$ and $G \preccurlyeq_{\mathrm{intf}} F$, i.e., $M =_m^* N$.

Example 2. The interface $pack(\mathsf{CashDeskAssembly})$ in Fig. 3 was obtained by hiding the communication labels from the greybox behaviour of the $\mathsf{CashDeskAssembly}$. Figure 7 shows an equivalent but "smaller" interface behaviour. For this purpose one has to prove two refinement relations $pack(\mathsf{CashDeskAssembly}) \preccurlyeq_{\mathrm{intf}} min(pack(\mathsf{CashDeskAssembly}))$ and vice versa. Indeed both directions have been verified with the MIO-Workbench [2]. Note that for the first direction observational abstraction w.r.t. τ-transitions on the refinement side, i.e. on $pack(\mathsf{CashDeskAssembly})$,

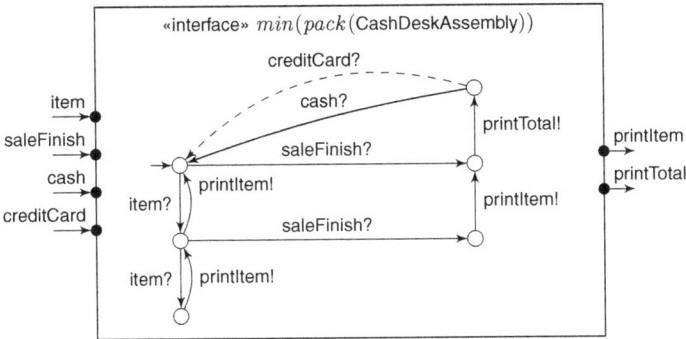

Fig. 7. Interface equivalent to the result from packing CashDeskAssembly in Fig. 3

is necessary which would not work for alternating simulation of interface automata. We believe that the interface $min(pack(\text{CashDeskAssembly}))$, as the name suggests, is minimal. However, whether minimal behaviours for equivalent interfaces exist and how they can be computed is an open issue for future research.   □

Assembly refinement has to respect the architectural requirements and the greybox behaviour of assemblies. The first requirement amounts to relate the interfaces of assemblies pairwise by interface refinement; the latter amounts to relate the greybox behaviours of assemblies by means of weak modal refinement, which abstracts away silent transitions (which stem from inner interfaces), but transitions resulting from communications are considered as visible and indeed they are respected by our generalised notion of weak modal refinement. In summary, an assembly $A = asm((F_i)_{1 \leq i \leq m})$ *refines* an assembly $B = asm((G_i)_{1 \leq i \leq n})$, written as $A \preccurlyeq_{\text{asm}} B$, if (1) $m = n$ and $F_i \preccurlyeq_{\text{intf}} G_i$ for all $1 \leq i \leq m$ and (2) $grb(A) \leq_{\text{m}}^* grb(B)$. In fact, the first condition implies already the second one which is a consequence of the following lemma:

Lemma 2. *Let* $(M_i)_{1 \leq i \leq n}$ *and* $(N_i)_{1 \leq i \leq n}$ *be composable finitely indexed sets of MIOs such that* $M_i \leq_{\text{m}}^* N_i$ *for all* $1 \leq i \leq n$. *Then* $\bigotimes_{1 \leq i \leq n}^{\text{sy}} M_i \leq_{\text{m}}^* \bigotimes_{1 \leq i \leq n}^{\text{sy}} N_i$.

Moreover, the lemma shows that our claim of *compositionality of refinement* in Sect. 1.3 — refinements of the interfaces constituting assemblies induce assembly refinements — is indeed valid in our approach:

Proposition 2. *Let* $(F_i)_{1 \leq i \leq n}$ *and* $(G_i)_{1 \leq i \leq n}$ *be finitely indexed sets of interfaces with* $F_i \preccurlyeq_{\text{intf}} G_i$ *for all* $1 \leq i \leq n$. *Then* $asm((F_i)_{1 \leq i \leq n}) \preccurlyeq_{\text{asm}} asm((G_i)_{1 \leq i \leq n})$.

The rule of *preservation of communication-safety* stated in Sect. 1.3 requires that each refinement of a communication-safe assembly is again communication-safe. Indeed, also this rule is valid here. The proof relies on the fact that must-transitions are preserved by refinements.

Proposition 3. *If* $cs(B)$ *and* $A \preccurlyeq_{\text{asm}} B$, *then* $cs(A)$.

The proof of this proposition is reduced to a corresponding lemma for the preservation of output compatibility w.r.t. weak modal refinements.

Lemma 3. *Let* $(M_i)_{1 \leq i \leq n}$ *and* $(N_i)_{1 \leq i \leq n}$ *be composable finitely indexed sets of MIOs such that* $M_i \leq^*_m N_i$ *for all* $1 \leq i \leq n$. *If* $(N_i)_{1 \leq i \leq n}$ *is output compatible, then also* $(M_i)_{1 \leq i \leq n}$ *is output compatible.*

Finally, we also obtain the (strong) version of *refinement encapsulation* discussed in Sect. 1.3 that assembly refinements induce interface refinements of their packings:

Proposition 4. *If* $A \preccurlyeq_{asm} B$, *then* $pack(A) \preccurlyeq_{intf} pack(B)$.

The proof of this proposition relies on Lem. 2 and the following simple observation that hiding preserves weak modal refinement:

Lemma 4. *If* $C \leq^*_m A$, *then* $C\xi \leq^*_m A\xi$.

5   Case Study

We will illustrate how our techniques work in terms of a (small) top-down development of the cash desk application. Figure 8 gives an overview of the different steps and their proof obligations. We start by an abstract requirements specification of the whole system which is given by the interface CashDesk in Fig. 9. The specification is rather loose having only a single must-transition requiring cash payment to be possible in any system implementation whenever a printTotal! has been performed before. The other transitions are may-transitions. At the start of a sale arbitrarily many items may be taken and printed; note that only as many printItem!s should be performed as item?s have been taken before, but this cannot be specified with finite state. Also a saleFinish? request may be accepted, possibly followed by printing items (that have not been printed yet) and then printing the total. Instead of cash payment, payment by credit card may be allowed by an implementation.

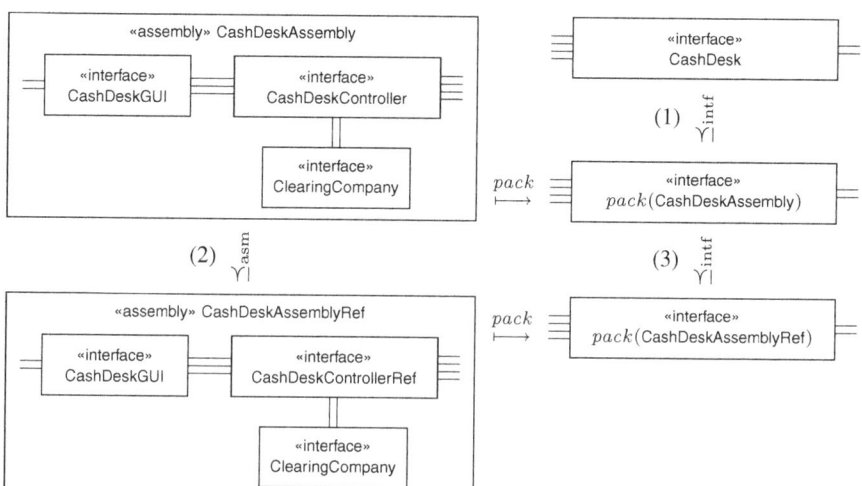

Fig. 8. Overview of top-down development of the cash desk application

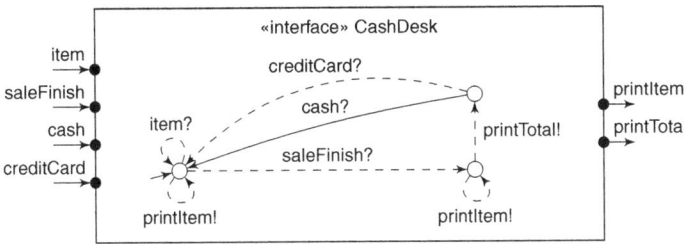

Fig. 9. Interface CashDesk

In the next step we specify an architecture for the intended system, which is given by the CashDeskAssembly known from Sect. 3, Fig. 1. As a first proof obligation, we have to show that the behaviour induced by the proposed assembly fits to the abstract requirements specification of the system. Formally this means that the interface of the encapsulated assembly is an interface refinement of CashDesk, i.e., that (1) in Fig. 8 is satisfied. For the proof it is obviously sufficient (cf. Sect. 4.2) to consider the minimised version of the interface shown in Fig. 7 and to prove $min(pack(\text{CashDeskAssembly})) \preccurlyeq_{intf}$ CashDesk. We have verified this statement with the MIO-Workbench.[5]

The CashDeskAssembly introduces architectural requirements *and* behavioural requirements in terms of the greybox behaviour of the assembly shown in Fig. 2. In our third step this assembly is refined by the assembly CashDeskAssemblyRef where the interface CashDeskController is replaced by the interface CashDeskControllerRef. The latter has the same behaviour specification as CashDeskController (see Fig. 1) but the previous may-transition for creditCard? is turned into a must-transition. Obviously, CashDeskControllerRef $\preccurlyeq_{intf}$ CashDeskController and therefore, by compositionality of refinement as stated in Sect. 4.2, we get the proof obligation (2) in Fig. 8. Since CashDeskAssembly is communication-safe, (2) implies that CashDeskControllerRef is communication-safe as well; cf. Sect. 4.2. Moreover, encapsulation of assemblies turns assembly (greybox) refinement into interface (blackbox) refinement (cf. Sect. 4.2), and therefore we obtain (3) in Fig. 8. Now we can utilise that interface refinement is transitive to be sure that the visible behaviour of the encapsulated assembly CashDeskAssemblyRef is conform to the system's interface specification.

Finally, we would like to emphasise the significance of proper assembly refinement, i.e. the importance of respecting communications during assembly refinement. Imagine that we would use instead of CashDeskAssemblyRef an assembly CashDeskAssemblyRef' where the interface CashDeskControllerRef is replaced by the interface CashDeskControllerRef' shown in Fig. 10. This interface accepts creditCard? without initiating a subsequent verification of the card with the clearing company. Obviously, CashDeskControllerRef' is not an interface refinement of CashDeskController and also CashDeskAssemblyRef' is not an assembly refinement of CashDeskAssembly since the required communications with the clearing company, see Fig. 2, do not

---

[5] It may be interesting to remark, that the refinement would not hold, if at least one of the remaining inputs of the CashDesk interface would be a must-transition; hence we could also not get an alternating simulation relation here.

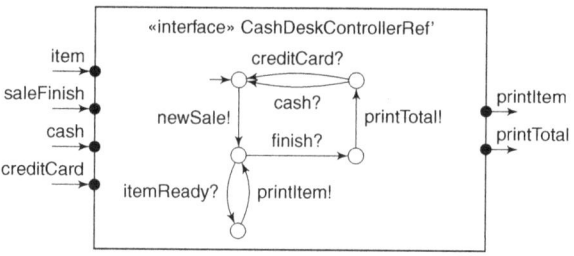

Fig. 10. Interface CashDeskControllerRef'

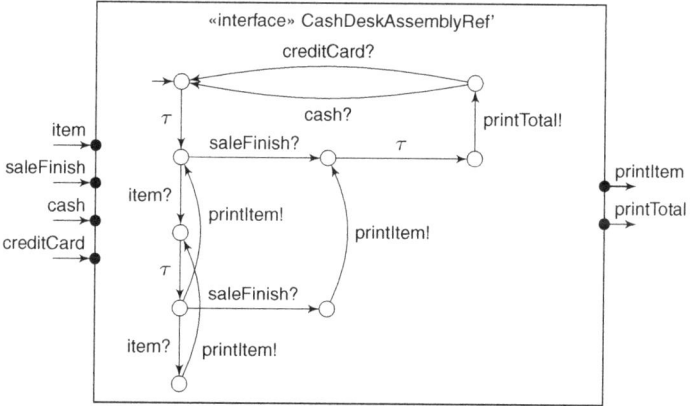

Fig. 11. Interface resulting from packing CashDeskAssemblyRef'

happen. However, if we would not check the assembly refinement but hide immediately all communications, which happens in approaches based on interface composition, then we obtain the interface *pack*(CashDeskAssemblyRef') shown in Fig. 11 which is obviously an interface refinement of *pack*(CashDeskAssembly); cf. Fig. 3. Thus the assembly CashDeskAssemblyRef' with no credit card verification could be used for the implementation of the system, which is certainly not intended.

6   Conclusion

Our study is motivated by an extension of the abstract rule of independent implementability of interface languages [7] to take into account architectural information given by interface assemblies. We have deliberately kept our approach to assemblies simple, not involving further constructs like connectors, but we believe that our fundamental research can be successfully applied to component models as well. As a concrete formalism we have chosen modal I/O-transition systems which we have adopted to take into account not only interface specifications and interface (black-box) refinement but also interface assemblies and assembly (grey-box) refinement. To our knowledge such an extension of the interface theory of MIOs did not exist yet. Also our notion of communication-safe assembly is an extension of previous work on compatibility of interfaces which we claim is strongly needed in practical examples. Of course many approaches in the literature support assemblies, i.e. networks of interface specifications and hierarchical constructions, in one or the other way. Among those based on labelled transition systems we want to mention interaction automata [5], pNets [1], symbolic transition systems (STS) [8], PADL [3], and communicating finite state machines (CF-SMs) [4]. CFSMs are based on asynchronous communication and introduce a notion of unspecified reception which is related to (a stronger version of) communication-safety not allowing "open" outputs. Otherwise usually deadlock checks are performed for assemblies which, however, are neither sufficient nor necessary for communication-safety, at least in our sense. Assembly refinement, however, is not a concern in these approaches. Most closely related to our result on compositional refinement is the interaction automata approach which studies substitutability of components w.r.t. a behavioural equivalence which can be tuned, e.g., to keep communications visible. In future work we want to investigate to what extent our notion of assembly refinement can be relaxed such that architectures can change in a controlled way. We are also interested to transfer our results to asynchronous communication, hybrid systems, and interfaces for components with data states.

Acknowledgements. We want to thank Sebastian Bauer for checking the examples with the MIO-Workbench, and Stephan Janisch for fruitful discussions on communication-safety.

References

1. Barros, T., Ameur-Boulifa, R., Cansado, A., Henrio, L., Madelaine, E.: Behavioural models for distributed Fractal components. Ann. Télécom. 64(1-2), 25–43 (2009)
2. Bauer, S.S., Mayer, P., Schroeder, A., Hennicker, R.: On weak modal compatibility, refinement, and the MIO workbench. In: Esparza, J., Majumdar, R. (eds.) TACAS 2010. LNCS, vol. 6015, pp. 175–189. Springer, Heidelberg (2010)
3. Bernardo, M., Ciancarini, P., Donatiello, L.: Architecting families of software systems with process algebras. ACM Trans. Softw. Eng. Methodol. 11(4), 386–426 (2002)
4. Brand, D., Zafiropulo, P.: On communicating finite-state machines. J. ACM 30(2), 323–342 (1983)
5. Cerná, I., Vareková, P., Zimmerova, B.: Component substitutability via equivalencies of component-interaction automata. Electr. Notes Theor. Comput. Sci. 182, 39–55 (2007)
6. de Alfaro, L., Henzinger, T.A.: Interface automata. In: Proc. 9th ACM SIGSOFT Ann. Symp. Foundations of Software Engineering (FSE 2001), pp. 109–120 (2001)
7. de Alfaro, L., Henzinger, T.A.: Interface-based design. In: Broy, M., Grünbauer, J., Harel, D., Hoare, C.A.R. (eds.) Engineering Theories of Software-intensive Systems. NATO Science Series: Mathematics, Physics, and Chemistry, vol. 195, pp. 83–104. Springer, Heidelberg (2005)
8. Fernandes, F., Royer, J.-C.: The STSLib project: Towards a formal component model based on STS. Electr. Notes Th. Comp. Sci. 215, 131–149 (2008)
9. Hüttel, H., Larsen, K.G.: The use of static constructs in a modal process logic. In: Meyer, A.R., Taitslin, M.A. (eds.) Logic at Botik. LNCS, vol. 363, pp. 163–180. Springer, Heidelberg (1989)

10. Larsen, K.G., Nyman, U., Wąsowski, A.: Modal I/O automata for interface and product line theories. In: De Nicola, R. (ed.) ESOP 2007. LNCS, vol. 4421, pp. 64–79. Springer, Heidelberg (2007)
11. Larsen, K.G., Thomsen, B.: A modal process logic. In: Proc. 3rd Ann. Symp. Logic in Computer Science (LICS 1988), pp. 203–210. IEEE Computer Society, Los Alamitos (1988)
12. Plášil, F., Višňovský, S.: Behavior protocols for software components. IEEE Trans. Software Eng. 28(11), 1056–1076 (2002)
13. Rausch, A., Reussner, R., Mirandola, R., Plášil, F. (eds.): The Common Component Modeling Example. LNCS, vol. 5153. Springer, Heidelberg (2008)

A   Proofs

Proof (of Lem. 1). For each $1 \leq j \leq n + 1$ let $E_j = \bigotimes_{1 \leq i \neq j \leq n+1}^{\mathrm{sy}} M_i$. For each $1 \leq j \leq n$ let $E_j' = \bigotimes_{1 \leq i \leq j \leq n}^{\mathrm{sy}}$. Let $(s_1, \ldots, s_{n+1}) \in \mathscr{R}(\bigotimes_{1 \leq i \leq n+1}^{\mathrm{sy}} M_i)$ and $s_j \overset{l}{\dashrightarrow}_{M_j} s_j'$ for $l \in O_{M_j} \cap I_{E_j}$.

Let $j = n + 1$. Then $E_j = \bigotimes_{1 \leq i \leq n}^{\mathrm{sy}} M_i$, and the claim follows since E_{n+1} and M_{n+1} are output compatible by assumption. Now let $1 \leq j \leq n$.

If $l \in O_{M_j} \cap I_{M_{n+1}}$, then $s_{n+1} \overset{\hat{X}}{\longrightarrow}_{M_{n+1}} \cdot \overset{l}{\longrightarrow}_{M_{n+1}} s_{n+1}'$ with $X = T_{M_{n+1}} \cup (O_{M_{n+1}} \setminus I_{E_{n+1}})$ since E_{n+1} and M_{n+1} are output compatible. Thus $(s_1, \ldots, s_{j-1}, s_{j+1}, \ldots, s_{n+1}) \overset{\hat{X}}{\longrightarrow}_{E_j} \cdot \overset{l}{\longrightarrow}_{E_j} (s_1, \ldots, s_{j-1}, s_{j+1}, \ldots, s_{n+1}')$ and $X \subseteq T_{E_j} \cup (O_{E_j} \setminus I_{M_j})$, since $T_{M_{n+1}} \subseteq T_{E_j}$, $O_{M_{n+1}} \setminus I_{E_{n+1}} \subseteq O_{E_j}$, and $(O_{M_{n+1}} \setminus I_{E_{n+1}}) \cap I_{M_k} = \emptyset$ for all $1 \leq k \leq n$.

If $l \in O_{M_j} \cap (\bigcup_{1 \leq i \neq j \leq n} I_i)$, then $(s_1, \ldots, s_{j-1}, s_{j+1}, \ldots, s_n) \overset{\hat{X}_j'}{\longrightarrow}_{E_j'} \cdot \overset{l}{\longrightarrow}_{E_j'} (s_1', \ldots, s_{j-1}', s_{j+1}', \ldots, s_n')$ with $X_j' = T_{E_j'} \cup (O_{E_j'} \setminus I_{M_j})$ by the output compatibility of $(M_i)_{1 \leq i \leq n}$. Let $(s_1'', \ldots, s_{j-1}'', s_{j+1}'', \ldots, s_n'') \overset{l'}{\longrightarrow}_{E_j'} (s_1''', \ldots, s_{j-1}''', s_{j+1}''', \ldots, s_n''')$ with $l' \in O_{M_k} \cap I_{M_{n+1}}$ for some $1 \leq k \leq n$ be the first transition to occur in this sequence. Then $s_{n+1} \overset{\hat{X}}{\longrightarrow}_{M_{n+1}} \cdot \overset{l'}{\longrightarrow}_{M_{n+1}} s_{n+1}'$ with $X = T_{M_{n+1}} \cup (O_{M_{n+1}} \setminus I_{E_{n+1}})$ since E_{n+1} and M_{n+1} are output compatible. As argued in the previous case $(s_1'', \ldots, s_{j-1}'', s_{j+1}'', \ldots, s_{n+1}) \overset{\hat{X}}{\longrightarrow}_{E_j} \cdot \overset{l'}{\longrightarrow}_{E_j} (s_1'', \ldots, s_{j-1}'', s_{j+1}'', \ldots, s_{n+1}')$ and thus inductively $(s_1, \ldots, s_{j-1}, s_{j+1}, \ldots, s_{n+1}) \overset{\hat{X}_j}{\longrightarrow}_{E_j} \cdot \overset{l}{\longrightarrow}_{E_j} (s_1', \ldots, s_{j-1}', s_{j+1}', \ldots, s_{n+1}')$ with $X_j = T_{E_j} \cup (O_{E_j} \setminus I_{M_j})$. □

Proof (of Lem. 2). We show that if M, N, and L are MIOs such that N and L are composable and $M \leq_{\mathrm{m}}^* N$, then $M \otimes^{\mathrm{sy}} L \leq_{\mathrm{m}}^* N \otimes^{\mathrm{sy}} L$. Then the claim follows by induction and symmetry.

Let such M, N, and L be given, let $ML = M \otimes^{\mathrm{sy}} L$, $NL = N \otimes^{\mathrm{sy}} L$, and let R_{MN} be a relation witnessing $M \leq_{\mathrm{m}}^* N$ with $(s_{0,M}, s_{0,N}) \in R_{MN}$. Let

$$R = \{((s_M, s_L), (s_N, s_L)) \mid (s_M, s_N) \in R_{MN}\} \, .$$

Then $((s_{0,M}, s_{0,L}), (s_{0,N}, s_{0,L})) \in R$. Let $((s_M, s_L), (s_N, s_L)) \in R$; we check the conditions of weak modal refinement for R:

(1) Let $l \in I_{NL} \cup O_{NL} \cup T_{NL}$ and $(s_N, s_L) \xrightarrow{l}_{NL} (s'_N, s'_L)$. If $l \in (I_N \setminus O_L) \cup (O_N \setminus I_L) \cup T_N$, then $s_N \xrightarrow{l}_N s'_N$ and $s_L = s'_L$. By (1) for R_{MN} there is an $s'_M \in S_M$ with $s_M \xrightarrow{\hat{l}}_M s'_M$ and, in particular, $(s_M, s_L) \xrightarrow{\hat{l}}_{ML} (s'_M, s_L)$; thus $((s'_M, s_L), (s'_N, s_L)) \in R$. — If $l \in (I_L \setminus O_N) \cup (O_L \setminus I_N) \cup T_L$, then $s_N = s'_N$ and $s_L \xrightarrow{l}_L s'_L$. Thus $(s_M, s_L) \xrightarrow{l}_{ML} (s_M, s'_L)$ and hence $((s_M, s'_L), (s_N, s'_L)) \in R$. — If $l \in (I_N \cap O_L) \cup (O_N \cap I_L)$, then $s_N \xrightarrow{l}_N s'_N$ and $s_L \xrightarrow{l}_L s'_L$ for some $s'_N \in S_N$ and $s'_L \in S_L$. By (1) for R_{MN} there is an $s'_M \in S_M$ with $s_M \xrightarrow{\hat{l}}_M s'_M$ and, in particular, $(s_M, s_L) \xrightarrow{\hat{l}}_{ML} (s'_M, s'_L)$; thus $((s'_M, s'_L), (s'_N, s'_L)) \in R$.

(2) Let $(s_N, s_L) \xrightarrow{\tau}_{NL} (s'_N, s'_L)$. If $s_N \xrightarrow{\tau}_N s'_N$ and $s_L = s'_L$, then $s_M \xrightarrow{\hat{\tau}}_M s'_M$ for some $s'_M \in S_M$ by (2) for R_{MN}; in particular, $(s_M, s_L) \xrightarrow{\hat{\tau}}_{ML} (s'_M, s_L)$ and hence $((s'_M, s_L), (s'_N, s_L)) \in R$. — If $s_N = s'_N$ and $s_L \xrightarrow{\tau}_L s'_L$ then $(s_M, s_L) \xrightarrow{\hat{\tau}}_{ML} (s_M, s'_L)$ and hence $((s_M, s'_L), (s_N, s'_L)) \in R$.

(3) Let $l \in I_{ML} \cup O_{ML} \cup T_{ML}$ and $(s_M, s_L) \dashrightarrow^{l}_{ML} (s'_M, s'_L)$. If $l \in (I_M \setminus O_L) \cup (O_M \setminus I_L) \cup T_M$, then $s_M \dashrightarrow^{l}_N s'_M$ and $s_L = s'_L$. By (3) for R_{MN} there is an $s'_N \in S_N$ with $s_N \dashrightarrow^{\hat{l}}_N s'_N$ and, in particular, $(s_N, s_L) \dashrightarrow^{\hat{l}}_{NL} (s'_N, s_L)$; thus $((s'_M, s_L), (s'_N, s_L)) \in R$. — If $l \in (I_L \setminus O_M) \cup (O_L \setminus I_M) \cup T_L$, then $s_M = s'_M$ and $s_L \dashrightarrow^{l}_L s'_L$. Thus $(s_N, s_L) \dashrightarrow^{l}_{NL} (s_M, s'_L)$ and hence $((s_M, s'_L), (s_N, s'_L)) \in R$. — If $l \in (I_M \cap O_L) \cup (O_M \cap I_L)$, then $s_M \dashrightarrow^{l}_M s'_M$ and $s_L \dashrightarrow^{l}_L s'_L$ for some $s'_M \in S_M$ and $s'_L \in S_L$. By (3) for R_{MN} there is an $s'_N \in S_N$ with $s_N \xrightarrow{\hat{l}}_N s'_N$ and, in particular, $(s_N, s_L) \dashrightarrow^{\hat{l}}_{NL} (s'_N, s'_L)$; thus $((s'_M, s'_L), (s'_N, s'_L)) \in R$.

(4) Let $(s_M, s_L) \xrightarrow{\tau}_{ML} (s'_M, s'_L)$. If $s_M \dashrightarrow^{\tau}_M s'_M$ and $s_L = s'_L$, then $s_N \dashrightarrow^{\hat{\tau}}_N s'_N$ for some $s'_N \in S_N$ by (4) for R_{MN}; in particular, $(s'_N, s_L) \dashrightarrow^{\hat{\tau}}_{NL} (s'_N, s_L)$ and hence $((s'_M, s_L), (s'_N, s_L)) \in R$. — If $s_M = s'_M$ and $s_L \dashrightarrow^{\tau}_L s'_L$ then $(s_N, s_L) \dashrightarrow^{\hat{\tau}}_{ML} (s_N, s'_L)$ and hence $((s_M, s'_L), (s_N, s'_L)) \in R$.   □

Proof (of Lem. 3). Let $R_1, \ldots, R_n$ be the weakly modal refinement relations witnessing $M_1 \leq^*_m N_1, \ldots, M_n \leq^*_m N_n$, respectively. Let $D_j = \bigotimes^{sy}_{1 \leq i \neq j \leq n} M_i$ and $E_j = \bigotimes^{sy}_{1 \leq i \neq j \leq n} N_i$ for all $1 \leq i \leq n$. Let $(s_1, \ldots, s_n) \in \mathscr{R}(\bigotimes^{sy}_{1 \leq i \leq n} M_i)$ and let $l \in O_{M_j} \cap I_{D_j}$ for some $1 \leq j \leq n$ such that $s_j \dashrightarrow^{l}_{M_j} s''_j$ for some $s''_j \in S_{M_j}$. Then there are $s'_1 \in S_{N_1}, \ldots, s'_n \in S_{N_n}$ with $(s_1, s'_1) \in R_1, \ldots, (s_n, s'_n) \in R_n$ and $(s'_1, \ldots, s'_n) \in \mathscr{R}(\bigotimes^{sy}_{1 \leq i \leq n} N_i)$ by conditions (3) and (4) of weakly modal refinement relations. Moreover, $s'_j \dashrightarrow^{l}_{N_j} s'''_j$ for some $s'''_j \in S_{N_j}$ by condition (3). Thus, $(s'_1, \ldots, s'_{j-1}, s'_{j+1}, \ldots, s'_n) \xrightarrow{\hat{Y}_j}_{E_j} \cdot \xrightarrow{l}_{E_j} (s'''_1, \ldots, s'''_{j-1}, s'''_{j+1}, \ldots, s'''_n)$ with $Y_j = T_{E_j} \cup (O_{E_j} \setminus I_{N_j})$ by output compatibility of $(N_i)_{1 \leq i \leq n}$. Now $Y_j = T_{D_j} \cup (O_{D_j} \setminus I_{M_j})$. From conditions (1) and (2) of weakly modal refinement relations it follows that $(s_1, \ldots, s_{j-1}, s_{j+1}, \ldots, s_n) \xrightarrow{\hat{Y}_j}_{D_j} \cdot \xrightarrow{l}_{D_j} (s''_1, \ldots, s''_{j-1}, s''_{j+1}, \ldots, s''_n)$.   □

Proof (of Lem. 4). Let R be a relation witnessing $C \leq^*_m A$. Then R is also a relation witnessing $C\xi \leq^*_m A\xi$.   □

WP Semantics and Behavioral Subtyping*

Yijing Liu, Zongyan Qiu, and Quan Long

LMAM and Department of Informatics, School of Mathematical Sciences, Peking University
{liuyijing,qzy}@math.pku.edu.cn,longquan78@gmail.com

Abstract. For the object oriented (OO) world, developing formal semantics for theoretical study and practical use is still an important topic despite of a decade's efforts. In this paper, for a sufficiently large subset of sequential Java with a pure reference semantics model, we define a Weakest Precondition (WP) semantics, and prove its soundness and completeness. Based on this WP semantics, we study specifications of methods and the refinement relationship between specifications, and we propose new definitions for object invariants and behavioral subtyping notation for general OO programs.

Keywords: Object Orientation, Weakest Precondition, Separation Logic, Specification, Refinement, Behavioral Subtyping.

1 Introduction

Object Orientation (OO) is and will be, for a long time, one of the mainstream techniques in software development. Recently, due to the even higher demands on the reliability and correctness of software systems (and in general, computer-based systems), developing powerful and useful frameworks for specifying and verifying OO programs becomes more urgent. For developing such frameworks, two mutually dependent issues must be considered: (1) a formal semantics for OO programs as the basis for verification, which should be powerful enough to capture the desired behaviors of various useful programs, and abstract enough so researchers do not suffer from the implementation details; (2) useful specification and verification techniques, which can support modular verification, thus offering scalability to program verification.

For the first issue, we believe that Weakest Precondition (WP) and Strongest Postcondition (SP) semantics are among the best choices. One reason is that such semantics may achieve completeness, thus can describe what a program does exactly. In addition, these semantics are relatively high-level because they define the semantics of programs as predicate transformers that is completely independent of any implementation. As the result, these semantics can be used not only directly to verify OO programs, but also as a solid foundation to define important OO concepts formally, and to validate verification frameworks and tools. In this paper, we will focus especially on the WP semantics for OO Programs.

According to our knowledge, people strive for a WP semantics for OO programs since 1999. [6] proposes a WP calculus for OO programs. Later Cavalcanti and Naumann gave a WP semantics [5] for an OO language, but it does not support object

---

* Supported by NNSF of China Grant No. 90718002.

A. Cerone and P. Pihlajasaari (Eds.): ICTAC 2011, LNCS 6916, pp. 154–172, 2011.
© Springer-Verlag Berlin Heidelberg 2011

reference and sharing. With more study on OO, various forms of WP semantics for OO programs are proposed. Noticeable works include ESC/JAVA [7], LOOP [4], JML [14] and Spec# [2]. All of these works use WP to generate verification conditions. However, although many works can be listed here, many central issues in OO languages and programs, especially those related to mutable object structures, have not been sufficiently addressed. After the emergence of Separation Logic [23], things begin to change. People use WP ideas in their work, explicitly or implicitly, to deal with problems related to OO programs. However, there is still not enough work directly on a WP semantics to establish a well-founded theoretical foundation which covers most of the important features of OO programs.

For the second issue, it is well known that *Behavioral Subtyping*, or *Liskov Substitutability Principle*, [16] plays a central role in verification of OO programs. Almost all recent works in this field adopt this principle as a part of their theoretical foundations. Liskov [17] gave the first formal treatment for behavioral subtyping by a group of constraint rules, and considered object invariants (or class invariants) in the rules. Some researchers offered various new definitions afterward, where the most influential one is [12], where Leavens and Naumann proposed a natural refinement order on specifications, and defined the behavioral subtyping based on the order. More importantly is that they proved that behavioral subtyping is equivalent to modular reasoning for OO programs. They also considered object invariants in subsequent work [13]. However, we will point out that their treatment for object invariant is not very adequate in practice.

In this paper we will discuss both of these two issues. We introduce a language μJava [27], which is a sufficiently large subset of sequential Java covering most important OO features, including reference types, subtypes, inheritance, dynamic binding, and sharing based parameters for methods, etc. We develop a WP semantics for μJava based on an OO Separation Logic (OOSL) [25]. The WP semantics is proved to be both sound and complete respect to μJava's operational semantics. Then we use the WP semantics as a theoretical tool to formalize and study specification, object invariant and behavioral subtyping, to show its power and effects.

Briefly, the main contributions of this work are as follows:

- Firstly, we answer a theoretical question: Can we have a sound and complete WP semantics for a typical class-based OO language that takes the pure reference semantic model for variables and fields? Here we can say that the answer is yes.
- We illustrate such a WP semantics is useful in OO field by use it to define specifications and their refinement relationship, prove some refinement judgments; and we offer a new definition for object invariant by this WP semantics.
- We give a new behavioral subtyping definition, which follows Liskov Substitutability Principle and Leavens's natural refinement order, but our formalism is more natural and closer to practice than these previous works.

The rest of the paper is organized as follows. We introduce briefly μJava in **Section 2**. The WP semantics is defined in **Section 3**, and some properties are provided, as well as the soundness and completeness. In **Section 4**, we study behavioral subtyping and other important issues in OO verification, including specification, refinement and object invariant. Due to the paper length limit, we left most of the proofs and other applications of the WP semantics in our report [26].

2 The Programming Language: μJava

The language used in this paper, μJava, is a sequential subset of Java. We consider mainly essential OO features relating to object sharing, updating, and creation. We choose the reference semantics for variables and fields, to reflect the reality in mainstream OO languages. μJava has a clear separation of store and heap operations. It is simple to facilitate theoretical study, and large enough for covering important OO features, e.g., dynamic binding, object sharing, aliasing, casting, etc.

The syntax of μJava is as follows:

$$
\begin{aligned}
v &::= \texttt{this} \mid x \qquad\qquad\qquad e ::= \texttt{true} \mid \texttt{false} \mid \texttt{null} \mid v \\
b &::= \texttt{true} \mid \texttt{false} \mid e = e \mid \neg b \mid b \wedge b \mid b \vee b \\
c &::= \texttt{skip} \mid x := e \mid x := v.a \mid x := (C)v \mid v.a := e \mid x := v.m(\overline{e}) \mid \\
&\qquad x := \texttt{new}\ C(\overline{e}) \mid \texttt{return}\ e \mid c; c \mid \texttt{if}\ b\ c\ \texttt{else}\ c \mid \texttt{while}\ b\ c \\
T &::= \texttt{Bool} \mid \texttt{Object} \mid C \qquad\quad M ::= T\ m(\overline{T\ z})\{\overline{T\ y};\ c\} \\
K &::= \texttt{class}\ C : C\{\overline{T\ a}; C(\overline{T\ z})\{\overline{T\ y};\ c\}; \overline{M}\} \\
G &::= K \mid K\ G
\end{aligned}
$$

here x is a variable, C a class name, a and m field and method names respectively. We use over-lined form to represent a sequence. Here are some explanations:

- We assume a built-in type Object, which has no field, as the supertype of all classes, and Null the subtype of any class. Null is the type of null, used only in definitions of the type system and semantics. The only primitive type Bool is not a supertype or subtype of any type. true and false are boolean values.
- We restrict expressions to those whose values depend only on the store, and restrict assignments to a number of special forms, including plain $x := e$, mutation $v.a := e$, and lookup $x := v.a$, where the right hand sides are only our expressions. We consider *cast* as a part of a special form of assignments. Command $x := \texttt{new}\ C(\overline{e})$ creates a new object, builds it with parameters $\overline{e}$ and assigns its reference to variable x. We take this also as a special form of assignment. More complex structures can be encoded with some auxiliary variables and/or assignments.
- We assume all references to fields of current object in methods are decorated with this, to make the field references uniformly of the form $v.a$. We can remove this restriction by adding repeated rules.
- The special $C(\overline{T\ z})\{\overline{T\ y};\ c\}$ in each class C is the constructor, which has the same name as the class. We assume return e only appears as the last statement in non-constructor methods. For recording the return value in semantic definitions, we assume an internal-variable res, which cannot be used in programs. We require that local variables and res initialized to special nil values (represented as nil) according to their types, i.e., rfalse for Bool and rnull for class types.
- We do not have access control here. A program is just a sequence of class declarations. We assume, as in Java, a main method in last class as the execution entry. If there is a main method in a μJava program, we say that it is a *closed program*, otherwise we say it is an *open program*.

In [5] a static environment is defined, then in the definition of the WP semantics, only well-typed expressions and commands need to be considered. We follow the idea, and define a static environment $\Gamma = (\Delta, \Theta)$ with Δ for typing, and Θ for method lookup. Both Δ and Θ can be established by scanning the program text. Now we introduce their skeletons with respect to the requirement of this paper.

The typing environment Δ_G for program G (abbr. Δ) records static structural information in G. Its construction is routine and omitted, and we only assume several notations here. We use $\mathsf{super}(C_1, C_2)$ to mean that C_2 is the immediate superclass of C_1, and use $T_1 <: T_2$ as the transitive closure of super, here we often omit the context Δ when it is clear. On the other hand, we record every method for each class in Θ. We will use notation $\Theta, C, m \rightarrowtail \lambda(\overline{z})\{\mathsf{var}\ \overline{y}; c\}$ to denote that $m(\overline{z})\{\mathsf{var}\ \overline{y}; c\}$ is a method in class C with parameters $\overline{z}$, local variables $\overline{y}$ and body code c.

The type judgment for expressions takes the form $\Gamma, C, m \vdash e : T$ to denote that e is of the type T in the scope of method m of C under Γ. On the other hand, $\Gamma, C, m \vdash c : \mathbf{com}$ means that c is a well-typed command in body of m of C. For a method m in class C, we use $\Gamma, C \vdash m : \mathbf{method}$ to assert that it is well-typed. We consider only the well-formed commands and methods in the rest of the paper.

In [27], we give rules for the construction of Δ and Θ, and rules for the typing, as well as an operational semantics. Due to space limitation, we omit the details here.

3   A WP Semantics for μJava

In this section, we define a Weakest Precondition (WP) semantics for μJava and investigate its properties.

3.1   The Assertion Language: OOSL

Separation Logic [23] is extension of Hoare logic, aims to reason programs in C like languages. It has been proved a powerful tool to handle mutable data structures. In our previous work [25], we proposed a revised Separation Logic, OO Separation Logic (OOSL), to describe OO programs' states. And we will use it as our assertion language in this work. Firstly we give a short introduction to OOSL. And readers can refer to the appendix or our report [25] to find more details.

We use a revised Stack-Heap storage model to represent the states of OO programs. A state $s = (\sigma, O) \in$ State consists of a store and a heap (object pool):

$$\mathsf{Store} \ \widehat{=} \ \mathsf{Name} \rightarrow_{\mathsf{fin}} \mathsf{Ref} \quad \mathsf{Heap} \ \widehat{=} \ \mathsf{Ref} \rightarrow_{\mathsf{fin}} \mathsf{Name} \rightarrow_{\mathsf{fin}} \mathsf{Ref}$$
$$\mathsf{State} \ \widehat{=} \ \mathsf{Store} \times \mathsf{Heap}$$

Here Name is an infinite name set. Special names $\mathtt{true}, \mathtt{false}, \mathtt{null} \in$ Name denote boolean constants and null. Type is an infinite set of types. $\mathtt{Object}, \mathtt{Null}, \mathtt{Bool} \in$ Type, where $\mathtt{Object}$ is the supertype of all classes, and $\mathtt{Null}$ is the subtype of all classes. Ref is an infinite set of references denoting object identities. It contains three constants: rtrue, rfalse refer $\mathtt{Bool}$ objects respectively, and rnull refers to nothing.

For any $\sigma \in$ Store, we assume $\sigma \mathtt{true} = \mathsf{rtrue}, \sigma \mathtt{false} = \mathsf{rfalse}$ and $\sigma \mathtt{null} = \mathsf{rnull}$. We will use $r, r_1, \ldots$ to denote references, and $a, a_1, \ldots$ for fields of objects.

The assertion language of OOSL is similar to that of Separation Logic, with some revisions to fit the needs of OO programs:

$$\rho ::= \text{true} \mid \text{false} \mid r_1 = r_2 \mid r : T \mid r <: T \mid v = r$$
$$\eta ::= \text{emp} \mid r_1.a \mapsto r_2 \mid \text{obj}(r, T)$$
$$\psi ::= \rho \mid \eta \mid \neg\psi \mid \psi \vee \psi \mid \psi \wedge \psi \mid \psi \Rightarrow \psi \mid \psi * \psi \mid \psi \mathbin{-\!\!*} \psi \mid \exists r \cdot \psi \mid \forall r \cdot \psi$$

where T is a type, v a variable or constant, r_1, r_2 references. We use Ψ to denote the set of assertions. Here are some explanations:

- ρ denotes assertions independent of heaps. References are atomic values here. For any two references r_1, r_2, $r_1 = r_2$ holds iff r_1 and r_2 are identical. $r : T$ indicates that r refers to an object with exact type T. $r <: T$ means that r refers to an object of T or subtype of T. And $v = r$ asserts that the value of variable or constant v is r.
- η denotes assertions involving heaps, where emp asserts the heap is empty. As a cell in heap is a field-value binding of an object (denoted by a reference), the singleton assertion takes the form $r_1.a \mapsto r_2$. In addition, $\text{obj}(r, T)$ indicates that the heap contains exact an entire object of type T, which r refers to. In Separation Logic, people use $l \mapsto -$ or $l \hookrightarrow -$ to denote that location l is allocated in current storage. But because the existence of empty objects in OO, we cannot use $r.a \mapsto -$ or $r.a \hookrightarrow -$ to express that object which r refers to is allocated in current heap. To solve this problem, we introduce assertion form $\text{obj}(r, T)$ in OOSL.
- Connectors $*$ and $-\!\!*$ are from Separation Logic. $\psi_1 * \psi_2$ means current heap can be split into two parts, where ψ_1 and ψ_2 hold on each part respectively; $\psi_1 -\!\!* \psi_2$ means that if we add a heap satisfying ψ_1 to current heap, the combined heap will satisfy ψ_2.

We use $\psi[v/x]$ (or $\psi[r/x]$, $\psi[r_1/r_2]$) to denote substitution of variable or constant v (or reference r_2). We treat $r = v$ the same as $v = r$, and define $v.a \mapsto r$ as $\exists r' \cdot (v = r' \wedge r'.a \mapsto r)$. And we have some abbreviations borrowed from Separation Logic:

$$r.a \mapsto - \; \hat{=} \; \exists r' \cdot r.a \mapsto r' \qquad r.a \hookrightarrow r' \; \hat{=} \; r.a \mapsto r' * \text{true}$$

We use notation $(\sigma, O) \models \psi$ to denote that assertion ψ holds on state (σ, O), its definition is given in appendix, and a complete treatment of OOSL's semantics can be found in [25].

3.2 The WP Semantics

As usual, the WP semantics of a command c will be defined as a predicate transformer, which maps any given predicate ψ to the weakest precondition of c with respect to ψ. We define the semantics only for well-typed commands, that is, for any command c in discussion, $\Gamma, C, m \vdash c : \textbf{com}$ is supposed true. The static necessities ensured by typing will not appear in semantic rules.

Remember Ψ denotes the set of assertions in OOSL, thus the set of predicate transformers is $\mathcal{T} = \Psi \to \Psi$. We use $\llbracket \Gamma, C, m \vdash c : \textbf{com} \rrbracket$ to denote the WP semantics

$$[\![\Gamma, C, m \vdash c_1; c_2]\!] = [\![c_1]\!] \circ [\![c_2]\!] \qquad \text{(SEQ)}$$

$$[\![\Gamma, C, m \vdash \text{if } b\ c_1 \text{ else } c_2]\!] = \lambda\psi \cdot (b \Rightarrow [\![c_1]\!]\psi) \wedge (\neg b \Rightarrow [\![c_2]\!]\psi) \qquad \text{(COND)}$$

$$[\![\Gamma, C, m \vdash \text{while } b\ c]\!] = \lambda\psi \cdot \mu\phi \cdot (\neg b \Rightarrow \psi) \wedge (b \Rightarrow [\![c]\!]\phi) \qquad \text{(ITER)}$$

$$[\![\Gamma, C, m \vdash \text{skip}]\!] = \lambda\psi \cdot \psi \qquad \text{(SKIP)}$$

$$[\![\Gamma, C, m \vdash x := e]\!] = \lambda\psi \cdot \psi[e/x] \qquad \text{(ASN)}$$

$$[\![\Gamma, C, m \vdash v.a := e]\!] = \lambda\psi \cdot \exists r_1, r_2 \cdot (v = r_1) \wedge (e = r_2) \wedge \qquad \text{(MUT)}$$
$$(r_1.a \mapsto - * (r_1.a \mapsto r_2 \twoheadrightarrow \psi))$$

$$[\![\Gamma, C, m \vdash x := v.a]\!] = \lambda\psi \cdot \exists r_1, r_2 \cdot (v = r_1) \wedge (r_1.a \hookrightarrow r_2) \wedge \psi[r_2/x] \qquad \text{(LKUP)}$$

$$[\![\Gamma, C, m \vdash x := (N)v]\!] = \lambda\psi \cdot \exists r \cdot (r <: N) \wedge (v = r) \wedge \psi[v/x] \qquad \text{(CAST)}$$

$$[\![\Gamma, C, m \vdash \text{return } e]\!] = \lambda\psi \cdot \psi[e/\text{res}] \qquad \text{(RET)}$$

$$\frac{\Theta, C, m \twoheadrightarrow \lambda(\overline{z})\{\text{var } \overline{y}; c\}, \quad [\![\Gamma, C, m \vdash c]\!] = f}{[\![\Gamma, C \vdash m : \text{method}]\!] = \lambda\, \text{this}, \overline{z} \cdot \lambda\psi \cdot f(\psi)[\overline{\text{nil}}/\overline{y}]} \qquad \text{(MTHD)}$$

$$\frac{\Gamma, C, m_0 \vdash v : T, \quad S_1, ..., S_k \text{ are all subtypes of } T,}{[\![\Gamma, S_i \vdash m : \text{method}]\!] = F_i(i = 1, ..., k)}{[\![\Gamma, C, m_0 \vdash x := v.m(\overline{e})]\!] = \lambda\psi \cdot \exists r \cdot (v = r) \wedge (\bigvee(r : S_i \wedge F_i(r, \overline{e})(\psi[\text{res}/x])))} \qquad \text{(INV)}$$

$$\frac{[\![\Gamma, N \vdash N : \text{method}]\!] = F}{[\![\Gamma, C, m \vdash x := \text{new } N(\overline{e})]\!] = \lambda\psi \cdot \forall r \cdot \text{raw}(r, N) \twoheadrightarrow F(r, \overline{e})(\psi[r/x])} \qquad \text{(NEW)}$$

Fig. 1. WP Semantics for μJava

of command c, and sometimes $[\![c]\!]$ if Γ, C and m are clear. In most cases, we use λ-notations. We use $f = g$ in the definition to mean that $\forall\psi \cdot f(\psi) \Leftrightarrow g(\psi)$.

The WP semantics rules for μJava are listed in **Fig. 1**. The semantics of sequential composition, choice, and iteration are routine, given as three rules (SEQ), (COND), and (ITER), where $\mu\phi \cdot f$ denotes the least fix-point of $\lambda\phi \cdot f$. Below we give some explanations to each group of the other rules.

Basic Commands: The semantics of skip is the identity transformer. The semantics of the plain assignment $x := e$ is ordinary, due to the restricted expression forms in μJava, and the clear separation of assertion forms for the stores and heaps in OOSL.

If any ψ holds after mutation $v.a := x$, it is necessary that variable v points to an object that has field a. The existence of field a is guaranteed by typing. After the assignment, $v.a$ holds the reference which is the value of x that is defined by rule (MUT). The last part of the rule takes the similar form as in the Separation Logic.

As shown in rule (LKUP), the lookup command $x := v.a$ is similar to the plain assignment. The only pre-requirement for executing this command is that v must point to an object containing field a.

Type cast is treated by rule (CAST). Here we ask for that the variable v must refer to an object with type N or N's subtype. Remember that for any type T, null $<: T$.

Before discussing the WP semantics of method invocations, as well as the new commands, we need to have some preparation.

Generally, a method can be thought as a parameterized command. Following this idea, we define the semantics of a method as a parameterized predicate transformer with type $\mathcal{PT}_{n+1} \,\widehat{=}\, \mathsf{Ref}^{n+1} \to \mathcal{T}$, where n is the number of the parameters of the method, and an extra one for current object of the invocation. For a $F : \mathcal{PT}_{n+1}$, we need to apply it to a set of references $r_0, r_1, \ldots, r_n$, which stand for the objects referred by this and all the arguments, to obtain a predicate transformer $F(r_0, r_1, \ldots, r_n)$. For convenience, we define an abbreviation form that for any expression e,

$$F(r_0, .., e, .., r_n) \,\widehat{=}\, \lambda \psi \cdot \exists r \cdot (e = r) \wedge F(r_0, .., r, .., r_n)(\psi).$$

We may also accept more than one expressions in this abbreviation. For example, we can see $F(r, \bar{e})$ in the last two rules in **Fig. 1**.

We use the notation $[\![\Gamma, C \vdash m : \mathbf{method}]\!]$, or short $[\![C.m]\!]$, to denote the WP semantics of a method m defined in class C. Here m could be C to denote the constructor of class C. Then we have the following rules.

Method: Rule (MTHD) gives the semantics of methods and constructors. Here all local variables are replaced with nil values. This means that, on one hand, all local variables are initialized with nil according to the requirements mentioned in **Section 2**; on the other hand, all local variables are inaccessible from outside of the method. So, if a given ψ contains names in $\bar{y}$, we should rename such local variables to avoid it.

If all methods are non-recursive, we can get their parameterized predicate transformers directly. Otherwise, by the rules, we can obtain a group of equations about parameterized predicate transformers. [8] tells us there exists a least fix-point solution for such a set of equations, and we define the solution as the WP semantics for these methods respectively. So the WP semantics for methods is well-defined.

Method Invocation: Based on the above definition, semantics for method invocation is given by rule (INV) which takes a similar form as the corresponding one in [5]. Here we collect all methods of the subclasses in the program (which are determined statically by the program text), and define the weakest precondition as the disjunction of the predicates produced by these subclasses. Note that $r : S_i$ ensures $r \neq$ rnull. When reasoning on a real invocation, this disjunction will be resolved by the type of current object and disappeared. In building the precondition, we replace x with res in ψ, because the invocation can be viewed as two "actions": the first one is the execution of the body of $v.m(\bar{e})$ which stores the return value in res at the end, and the second copies the value to x.

Clearly, this rule demands that the program been reasoned about is a closed program. In this case, our definition can describe the behavior of a method invocation precisely. The closeness of the program is one crucial condition, because only under this condition, the WP semantics can achieve completeness, which we will prove in **Section 3.4**.

Object Creation: Informally, object creation can be thought as two "actions" sequentially: the first one extends current heap by creating a new raw object (while all its fields take nil values) and obtains its reference; the second initiates the object's state. That is exactly the case for practical OO languages, and specified by rule (NEW). The rule states that if we append any new object of class N to current heap, after the execution of the constructor, ψ will hold. In this rule, the assertion raw(r, N) asserts that r refers to a raw object of N, with the definition as

$$\text{raw}(r, N) \ \widehat{=} \ \begin{cases} \text{obj}(r, N), & N \text{ has no field} \\ r : N \wedge (r.a_1 \mapsto \text{nil}) * .. * (r.a_k \mapsto \text{nil}), \\ \{a_1, .., a_k\} \text{ is the set of all attrs of } N \end{cases}$$

We will use $\text{raw}(r, -)$ if do not care the type. We can prove this assertion satisfies the following proposition, which says that separated objects must be different:

Proposition 1. $\text{raw}(r_1, -) * \text{raw}(r_2, -) \Rightarrow r_1 \neq r_2$. $\qquad\qquad\qquad\qquad\qquad\qquad$ □

3.3 Properties

Now we show some properties of the WP semantics for μJava defined above. We have the following theorems, with all their proofs in our report [26].

The first theorem says that the WP semantics is well-defined, i.e., it forms a well-defined function on all well-typed commands and methods.

Theorem 1. *Suppose we have built Γ for program G. For any c in G with $\Gamma, C, m \vdash c : \textbf{com}$, its semantics $\llbracket \Gamma, C, m \vdash c : \textbf{com} \rrbracket$ is a total function on all formulas. Additionally, if $\Gamma, C \vdash m : \textbf{method}$, the semantics $\llbracket \Gamma, C \vdash m : \textbf{method} \rrbracket$ is a well-defined parameterized predicate transformer.*

The WP semantics is monotonic, that is, the predicate transformer defined by any well-typed commands is a monotonic function. In fact, the monotonicity is essential to get a least fix-point solution for parameterized predicate transformers.

Theorem 2. *Suppose $f : \mathcal{T}$ is a predicate transformer produced by rules in* **Fig. 1,** *and ψ, ψ' are any well-formed predicates. If $\psi \Rightarrow \psi'$, then $f(\psi) \Rightarrow f(\psi')$.*

Theorem 3. *Given command c and assertions ψ_1, ψ_2, if $FV(\psi_2) \cap md(c) = \emptyset$, then*

$$(\llbracket c \rrbracket \psi_1) * \psi_2 \Rightarrow \llbracket c \rrbracket (\psi_1 * \psi_2)$$

where $FV(\psi_2)$ is the set of all program variables (including internal variable res*) in ψ_2, $md(c)$ is the variable set modified by c, defined as:*

$$md(c) = \begin{cases} \{x\}, & c \text{ is } x := \ldots \\ \{\text{res}\}, & c \text{ is } \texttt{return} \ldots \\ md(c_1) \cup md(c_2), & c \text{ is } c_1; c_2 \\ md(c_1) \cup md(c_2), & c \text{ is } \texttt{if } b \ c_1 \texttt{ else } c_2 \\ md(c), & c \text{ is } \texttt{while } b \ c \\ \emptyset, & \text{otherwise} \end{cases}$$

In fact, this theorem is the Frame Rule [23] in the WP style.

Example 1 (Empty Object Creation). Now we give a small example to show how to do verification with the WP semantics defined above. Suppose the body of the constructor of Object is skip, then by the WP semantics we have:

$$\llbracket \Gamma, \texttt{Object} \vdash \texttt{Object} : \textbf{method} \rrbracket = \lambda \psi \cdot \psi$$

Then we have the following calculation:

$$\llbracket x := \text{new Object}(); y := \text{new Object}(); \rrbracket (x \neq y)$$
$$= \llbracket x := \text{new Object}(); \rrbracket (\forall r \cdot \text{raw}(r, \text{Object}) \rightarrow\!\!\ast x \neq r)$$
$$= \forall r_1, r_2 \cdot \text{raw}(r_1, \text{Object}) \rightarrow\!\!\ast \text{raw}(r_2, \text{Object}) \rightarrow\!\!\ast r_1 \neq r_2$$
$$= \text{true}$$

This indicates that two newly created empty objects are different. In fact, this result also holds for non-empty objects, but the calculation is complicated.   □

More examples can be found in our report [26].

3.4   Soundness and Completeness

Now we give the soundness and completeness theorems of the WP semantics defined above. Due to the page limit, we leave their proofs in our report [26].

Informally, a WP semantics $\llbracket \bullet \rrbracket$ is *sound*, if for any command c and predicate ψ, if c executes from a state satisfying the weakest precondition $\psi' = \llbracket c \rrbracket \psi$, it terminates and the final state will satisfy ψ. A WP semantics is *complete*, if it really gives the weakest precondition, that is, if any command c executes from any state s and terminates on a state satisfying a condition ψ, then $\llbracket c \rrbracket \psi = \psi'$ holds on state s.

We take **COM** the space of legal commands, and use $\langle c, (\sigma, O) \rangle \rightsquigarrow^* (\sigma', O')$ to denote configuration transformation of μJava, that says when command c executes from current state (σ, O), after its execution of the state will be (σ', O'). More details about the transformation (operational semantics) can be found in our report [26].

Definition 1 (Soundness). *A WP predicate transformer generator* $\llbracket \bullet \rrbracket : \textbf{COM} \rightarrow \mathcal{T}$ *is* **sound**, *if and only if for any assertions* $\psi, \psi' \in \Psi$ *and command* $c \in \textbf{COM}$ *satisfying* $\llbracket \Gamma, C, m \vdash c : \textbf{com} \rrbracket \psi = \psi'$, *we have: For any pair of states* (σ, O) *and* (σ', O'), *if* $(\sigma, O) \models \psi'$ *and* $\langle c, (\sigma, O) \rangle \rightsquigarrow^* (\sigma', O')$, *then* $(\sigma', O') \models \psi$.

Definition 2 (Completeness). *A WP predicate transformer generator* $\llbracket \bullet \rrbracket : \textbf{COM} \rightarrow \mathcal{T}$ *is* **complete**, *if and only if for any* $\psi, \psi' \in \Psi$ *and command* $c \in \textbf{COM}$ *satisfying* $\llbracket \Gamma, C \vdash c : \textbf{com} \rrbracket \psi = \psi'$, *we have: For any pair of states* $((\sigma, O)$ *and* (σ', O'), *if* $(\sigma', O') \models \psi$ *and* $\langle c, (\sigma, O) \rangle \rightsquigarrow^* (\sigma', O')$, *then* $(\sigma, O) \models \psi'$.

In these definitions, we see the WP as a generator which produces for each command in **COM** a predicate transformer. In report [26], we give the detailed proofs for the soundness and completeness of our WP semantics, according to the operational semantics of the language. Thus we conclude that,

Theorem 4. *The WP semantics for* μJava *is both sound and complete.*

4   Behavioral Subtyping

Because the WP semantics defined above is both sound and complete, we can use it as a theoretical foundation to study various problems. In report [26], we prove a set of Hoare-style rules for reasoning about OO programs using the WP semantics, including the Frame Rule which is important in local reasoning. Here we study the behavioral subtyping concept, and this concept involves many important issues in OO program verification, including method specification, refinement and object invariants.

4.1 Method Specification and Refinement

The specification for a method (or a piece of code) is often given as a pair of pre and post conditions. In the following we will use $\{P\}$-$\{Q\}$ to denote a specification with precondition P and postcondition Q.

A method $C.m(\overline{z})$ satisfies the specification $\{P\}$-$\{Q\}$, if $C.m$ executes under a pre-state where P holds, then Q will hold on the post-state when $C.m$ terminates. This can be defined based on the WP semantics:

Definition 3 (Method Specification). *Given any method* $C.m(\overline{z})$, *we say that method* $C.m$ *satisfies specification* $\{P\}$-$\{Q\}$, *written as* $\{P\}\,C.m\,\{Q\}$, *iff:*

$$\forall r, \overline{r'} \cdot P[r, \overline{r'}/\text{this}, \overline{z}] \Rightarrow [\![C.m]\!](r, \overline{r'})(Q[r, \overline{r'}/\text{this}, \overline{z}]).$$

This definition is straightforward and intuitive. Based on this definition, we can define the refinement relationship between specifications.

Definition 4 (Refinement of Specifications). *We say a specification* $\{P_2\}$-$\{Q_2\}$ *refines another specification* $\{P_1\}$-$\{Q_1\}$, *written* $\{P_1\}$-$\{Q_1\} \sqsubseteq \{P_2\}$-$\{Q_2\}$, *iff for any command* c, $\{P_2\}\,c\,\{Q_2\}$ *implies* $\{P_1\}\,c\,\{Q_1\}$.

This definition implies that if $\{P_2\}$-$\{Q_2\}$ refines $\{P_1\}$-$\{Q_1\}$, then the former can substitute the latter anywhere. This idea follows the natural refinement order in [12].

Although this definition for refinement is simple and clear, it is not easy for us to use in practice, because we could hardly have ways to investigate all commands. Here we provide a sound condition for refinement judgement.

Theorem 5. *Given specification* $\{P_1\}$-$\{Q_1\}$ *and* $\{P_2\}$-$\{Q_2\}$, *we have* $\{P_1\}$-$\{Q_1\} \sqsubseteq \{P_2\}$-$\{Q_2\}$ *if there exists an assertion* R *such that: (1). R does not contains program variables, and (2).* $(P_1 \Rightarrow P_2 * R) \wedge (Q_2 * R \Rightarrow Q_1)$.

In fact, this theorem combines the consequence rule in Hoare Logic and Frame Rule in Separation Logic. It provides a useful way to check refinement relation in OO programs where the heap and heap extension are taken into account.

4.2 Object Invariant

Object invariant is an important concept in both practice and research, because it describes a kind of consistent object states we can rely on. A popular view about an object invariant is that it is a shorthand for the postcondition of constructor and default pre/post conditions for every public methods. This view leads to the following verification conditions for class C with object invariant I: (1) The postcondition of C's constructor implies I; and (2) for every method $C.m$ with specification $\{P\}$-$\{Q\}$, $\{P \wedge I\}\,C.m\,\{Q \wedge I\}$ holds. Point (2) shows that the "real" specification of a method is a combination of its declared specification and the object invariant. But we want to say that this treatment of object invariant is not adequate for practice.

We use the code in **Fig. 2** to illustrate our points, where are three classes: *Base* has a field a and methods f, g, h. Its object invariant demand that a always holds true. *Derive* inherits *Base* with a new field b, and strengthens the object invariant with that b should also hold true. *Client* may use *Base* and *Derive*. Here the rep modifier

```
class Base : Object {                          this.a = true; }
  rep Bool a;                              }
  invariant this.a ↪ true;
  Base() { this.a = true; }               class Derive : Base {
  void f()                                  rep Bool b;
    requires this.a ↪ -;                    invariant this.a ↪ true∗
    ensures this.a ↪ true;                            this.b ↪ true;
    { this.a = true ; }                     Derive()
  void g()                                    { this.a = true; this.b = true; }
    requires this.a ↪ -;                  }
    ensures true;
    { this.a = false; this.f(); }         class Client : Object {
  void h(C c)                               void m(Base b)
    requires this.a ↪ -;                      requires b.a ↪ -;
    ensures true;                             ensures true
    { this.a = false; c.fun(this);            { b.f(); }
                                          }
```

Fig. 2. Sample Code with Specifications and Object Invariants

denotes a *representation field* of a class, that is inaccessible to clients. This notation is from *ownership types* [19], and is adopted by many work about object invariants.

Firstly, a method may be invoked by methods of same class, including itself (recursive call). In these circumstances, the object invariant can be ignored, in fact, we may allow breaking the invariant for a while in a method. For example, before the invocation of $Base.f$ in $Base.g$, we do assignment this.a = false, this cause the invariant temporarily broken. Under a common treatment of invariants, invocation this.$f()$ is invalid, although $Base.g$ re-establishes the invariant before its termination, thus this temporary breakage is harmless. This tells us that a method invocation may appear in two kinds of scenarios, inside or outside the class it belongs to. The requirements for these two scenarios are different. As far as our knowledge, this problem is not well studied.

Secondly, the object invariant is often strengthened in subclasses. If we treated the precondition of a method as the conjunction of the object invariant and the declared precondition in method interface, then preconditions of subclass's methods would be stronger. In this example, if we took (this.a ↪ - ∧ this.a ↪ true) as the precondition for $Base.f$ and (this.a ↪ - ∧ this.a ↪ true ∧ this.b ↪ true) for $Derive.f$, we would find that $Derive.f$ is not a refinement of $Base.f$! Because for refinement, always we demand that precondition may only be weakened in a subclass. Existing solutions to this problem are abstracting away details of the objects [1,9,18]. For example, in [1], Barnett uses a model field st in specifications to indicate whether the object invariant holds. For this example, he suggest to write (this.a ↪ - ∧ this.st = $Valid$) as the precondition of $Base.f$, thus it can be validly inherited by $Derive$.

At last, the object invariant should be transparent for clients. In fact, clients often care only about the specification declared in a method's interface, but have no obligation to establish the object invariant before some invocation. Consider method $Client.m$ in above example, the invocation $b.f()$ is valid according $Base.f$'s specification. But if we required that "the real specification of $Base.f$ is this.a ↪ - ∧ this.a ↪ true", this invocation would become invalid. Barnett also considered this problem in [1], but because they also combine objects invariants with specifications, they cannot show the validity of $b.f()$ here with their methodology.

From the above analysis, we conclude that it is not adequate to treat an object invariants as a necessary part of method specifications. In fact, an object invariant has class scope, while a specification is only for particular method, they are independent with each other, and thus we have to verify them separately. **Definition 3** has provided a verification condition for a method specification. And we define what an object invariant is below:

Definition 5 (Object Invariant). *We say that assertion I is an object invariant of class C, written $C \models I$, iff:* (1),

$$\forall r, \overline{r'} \cdot (\llbracket C.C \rrbracket (r, \overline{r'}) \mathtt{true}) \Rightarrow (\llbracket C.C \rrbracket (r, \overline{r'})(I[r/\mathtt{this}])),$$

and (2), *for every client accessible method $C.m$*

$$\forall r, \overline{r'} \cdot ((\llbracket C.m \rrbracket (r, \overline{r'}) \mathtt{true}) \wedge I[r/\mathtt{this}]) \Rightarrow (\llbracket C.m \rrbracket (r, \overline{r'})I[r/\mathtt{this}]).$$

The first condition requires that constructor establish the object invariant, and the second condition ensures that every client accessible method preserves the invariant. Thus, the object invariant will always hold for clients. Please note that, this definition for the invariant does not involve method specifications, in addition, for a method, we need only verify that it satisfy *its specification*, and condition (2) if it is client accessible.

By this definition, we can see that the object invariant becomes a self-contained concept, and has nothing to do with particular method specification. Comparing to existing treatments for object invariants, such as [13, 1] and so on, our definition is a complete one. That is to say, our definition captures the nature of object invariants.

Back to our sample code, by definitions of method specification and object invariant, we can conclude the code meets its specifications except of method $Base.h$. We point that although $Base.h$ preserve the object invariant, but its implementation is not valid, because the object invariant does not hold before calling $c.fun(\mathtt{this})$. Barnett *et al* has studied this problem in [1]. They proposed a pair of new primitive statements **pack/unpack** to explicitly establish or break the object invariant. This invalid method call can be verified by Barnett's techniques. But we will not discuss this issue further, because it is out of this paper's scope.

4.3   Behavioral Subtyping

Now we give our definition for *Behavioral Subtyping* based on above discussion.

Definition 6 (Behavioral Subtype). *Given class C and B, we say C is a behavioral subtype of B, written $C \preceq B$, iff,* (1), *for every assertion I, $B \models I$ implies $C \models I$, and* (2), *for every client accessible method $B.m$ we have for any specification $\{P\}$-$\{Q\}$, $\{P\} B.m \{Q\}$ implies $\{P\} C.m \{Q\}$.*

The first condition requires that every object invariant of superclass is an object invariant of subclass; and the second requires that subclass obeys superclass's behavior. Clearly, this definition follows the thought of Liskov substitution principle.

Now we focus on the practical verification procedures. We will develop verification conditions for a program with behavioral subtyping requirement. At first, we introduce some notations. For a μJava program G, we suppose a specification environment Π_G containing specifications of all methods of classes in consideration, and an invariant environment Λ_G containing all object invariants. We will omit subscript G in what follows. More precisely, the specification environment Π is a map from a method/constructor to its specification. We will use $\{P\}\,C.m\,\{Q\} \in \Pi$ (or $\{P\}$ $\{C.C\} \in \Pi Q$ for constructor) to state that $\{P\}$-$\{Q\}$ is the specification for method $C.m$ (or constructor of C). And the invariant environment Λ mapping every class to its object invariant, which is just an assertion. We will use notation $\Lambda(C)$ to denote the object invariant of class C.

Definition 7 (Satisfaction of specification and invariant environment). *We say a program G satisfies specification environment Π and invariant environment Λ, written $G \models (\Pi, \Lambda)$, iff (1), for every $\{P\}\,C.m\,\{Q\} \in \Pi$, $\{P\}\,C.m\,\{Q\}$ holds, here m could be the constructor; and (2), for every class C in G, $C \models \Lambda(C)$ holds.*

This definition leads the following verification conditions for $G \models (\Pi, \Lambda)$:

Theorem 6. *Given a program G, a specification environment Π, and an invariant environment Λ, we have $G \models (\Pi, \Lambda)$, if following two conditions hold: (1), for every constructor specification $\{P\}\,C.C\,\{Q\} \in \Pi$, $\{P\}\,C.C\,\{Q \wedge \Lambda(C)\}$ holds, and (2), for every method specification $\{P\}\,C.m\,\{Q\} \in \Pi$, $\{P\}\,C.m\,\{Q\}$ holds; and if $C.m$ is client accessible, $\{P \wedge \Lambda(C)\}\,C.m\,\{\Lambda(C)\}$ holds.*

From this theorem, we can see that suppose $\Lambda(C) = I$, for the constructor of C with specification $\{P\}$-$\{Q\}$, we should verify that $\{P\}\,C.C\,\{Q \wedge I\}$; and for a method $C.m$ with specification $\{P\}$-$\{Q\}$, we have two proof obligations: $\{P\}\,C.m\,\{Q\}$ for its behavior, and $\{P \wedge I\}\,C.m\,\{I\}$ for the object invariant. This is very different from common treatment like [13, 1] in two aspects: First, method invocations now only rely on declared specifications $\{P\}$-$\{Q\}$, but not $\{P \wedge I\}$-$\{Q \wedge I\}$ with object invariant considered. Second, the object invariant is hidden inside a class and transparent to clients, but at any program point clients can assert the object invariant hold.

Although **Definition 6** gives a sound definition for behavioral subtype, it is not practical for real verification. As seen, we provide specifications and object invariants for classes with Π and Λ, and usually use them to do verification so that we need not explore the class details. In this sense, Π and Λ give the strongest specifications and object invariants. So we have the following behavioral subtype definition for practice:

Definition 8. *Given specification environment Π and invariant environment Λ for program G, and class C, B defined in G, we say C is a behavioral subtype of B under Π and Λ, written $(\Pi, \Lambda) \vdash C \preceq B$, iff, (1), $\Lambda(C) \Rightarrow \Lambda(B)$, and (2), for every client accessible method $B.m$ we have $\Pi(B.m) \sqsubseteq \Pi(C.m)$.*

In fact, this definition implies **Definition 6** with the meaning of that Π and Λ *give the strongest specifications and object invariants*. And clearly, this behavioral subtyping relationship is transitive.

Definition 9. *Given a program G with specification environment Π and invariant environment Λ, we say G satisfies the behavioral subtyping requirement under Π and Λ, iff for any class $C <: B$, we have $(\Pi, \Lambda) \vdash C \preceq B$.*

By **Definition 8** and its transitiveness, we can deduce that we only need check the behavioral subtype relationship for immediate super/sub classes. And, combining **Definition 9** and **Theorem 6**, we can obtain a kind of verification conditions for programs with behavioral subtyping requirements. These verification conditions have similar forms as Liskov's [17] and Leavens's [13], but the meanings are very different according to above discussions.

5 Related Work and Conclusion

In this paper, we investigate some important techniques in OO program verification: WP semantics, specification refinement, object invariant and behavioral subtyping. In this section, we discuss some related work and conclude.

WP semantics is one of the most powerful tools in theoretical study of procedural programming. Researchers apply it to define and validate semantics, generate verification conditions, validate refinement rules, and so on. But in OO world, after many years of efforts, WP has not yet fulfilled its potentials, since a satisfactory and well-studied WP semantics does not emerging yet. Efforts striving on a WP semantics for OO programs since 1999 [6] where a WP calculus was given for OO programs toward to support some object sharing. The semantics is restricted to the forms of syntactic substitution. To define the semantics syntactically, many restrictions to the programs and assertions are made, and many cases are treated specially. However, even many assertions cannot be checked statically, and the complicated special cases are hard to make accurately and completely. A. Cavalcanti and D. Naumann developed a WP semantics for OO language in [5]. Their language covers subtyping, dynamic binding, but not sharing. They introduce notations of OO refinement too. However, the semantics model in the work is not based on references, thus departs from the essentials of practical OO languages. This also makes the object sharing and updating hard to treat, if not impossible. With the rising and success of Separation Logic (SL), many problems related to programs with pointers or OO have been reexamined. Some papers mention or use WP semantics based on some form of SL. For example, the work presented in [20] use a WP semantics to prove the soundness of their framework on Separation Logic and Implicit Dynamic Frames [24]. However, the WP semantics is defined as state transformers, but not predicate transformers, that is not abstract enough, thus is not very useful practically. OO verification tools, such as ESC/JAVA [7], LOOP [4], JML [14, 10] and Spec# [2, 3] and so on, also utilize WP principle to generate verification conditions. But these work mainly focus on powerful, useful, yet succinct notations for proper specifications to support modular verification while ensuring information hiding, all these work put the important mutable object structures aside.

Behavioral subtyping is an important concept for OO program verification, and it always involves other crucial concepts like specification and object invariants. The essential formalisms on this topic is [16, 17], where Liskov proposed a group of constraint rules to ask that subtype methods preserve the supertype method's behavior, and subtype invariant implies supertype invariant. However, as pointed by Leavens and Naumann [12,13], the constraints given in [17] are too strong, so they offered a new behavioral subtyping definition by nature specification refinement, and provided a general notation for specification and refinement. But these works are based on state transition, thus is not high-level enough for practical verification framework. Besides, they treat object invariant as an always holding precondition of methods, this kind of requirement is not adequate as our discussion in Section 4.3. Specification refinement has been investigated by many other researchers. For example, rCOS [11] defines refinement relationship by graph transformation, Parkinson [21] defines refinement by a proof between specifications. In fact, all these definition follows the nature refinement order, and it seems that researchers have reached some consensus on specification refinement. The most famous work about object invariants are Hoare [9], Barnett [1], Leino [15] and Müller [18], and their techniques have applied to verification tools like ESC/JAVA [7], JML [14] and Spec# [2]. But they do not provide a complete formal definition for object invariant, and they treat object invariant as a part of method specification.

In this paper, based on an OO version of Separation Logic, we develop a WP semantics for a model OO language with typical OO features, and prove that the semantics is both sound and complete. In addition, some properties of the WP semantics are proposed and proved. As far as we know, this is the first work on the completeness of such a semantics for OO languages with pure reference semantic model. Based on the WP semantics, we investigate the behavioral subtyping notation which is central for OO verification. We introduction method specification and define refinement relationship on them, we propose new formal definitions for object invariants and behavioral subtying. And we provide verification conditions for a program with behavioral subtyping requirement. Conducting a comparison to existing works, e.g., [5,6,22,16,17,12,13], we might conclude that our WP semantics captures more essentials of object-orientation in an more adequate and useful way, and our treatment for object invariant and behavioral subtyping is more natural and closer to practice.

As for the future work, first, we will apply the WP semantics and our refinement and behavioral subtyping notation to OO program verification. We are working on a specification and verification framework for Java-like languages, with polymorphism, encapsulation and modular verification in mind. Second, we will extend our specification refinement to data refinement and program refinement, thus can study the refinement relationship between programs/specifications at different abstract levels, and provide the possibility of programming from specifications or/and code generation.

References

1. Barnett, M., DeLine, R., Fähndrich, M., Leino, K.R.M., Schulte, W., Rustan, K., Leino, M.: Verification of object-oriented programs with invariants. Journal of Object Technology 3, 2004 (2003)
2. Barnett, M., Leino, K.R.M., Schulte, W.: The spec# programming system: An overview. In: Barthe, G., Burdy, L., Huisman, M., Lanet, J.-L., Muntean, T. (eds.) CASSIS 2004. LNCS, vol. 3362, pp. 49–69. Springer, Heidelberg (2005)
3. Barnett, M., Leino, K.R.M.: Weakest-precondition of unstructured programs. In: Proceedings of the 6th ACM SIGPLAN-SIGSOFT Workshop on Program Analysis for Software Tools and Engineering, PASTE 2005, pp. 82–87. ACM, New York (2005)

4. Burdy, L., Requet, A., Lanet, J.-L.: Java applet correctness: A developer-oriented approach. In: Araki, K., Gnesi, S., Mandrioli, D. (eds.) FME 2003. LNCS, vol. 2805, pp. 422–439. Springer, Heidelberg (2003)

5. Cavalcanti, A.L.C., Naumann, D.: A weakest precondition semantics for refinement of object-oriented programs. IEEE Trans. on Software Engineering 26(8), 713–728 (2000)

6. de Boer, F.S.: A WP-calculus for OO. In: Thomas, W. (ed.) FOSSACS 1999. LNCS, vol. 1578, pp. 135–149. Springer, Heidelberg (1999), http://dx.doi.org/10.1007/3-540-49019-110

7. Flanagan, C., Leino, K.R.M., Lillibridge, M., Nelson, G., Saxe, J.B., Stata, R.: Extended static checking for java. SIGPLAN Not. 37, 234–245 (2002)

8. Hesselink, W.H.: Predicate-transformer semantics of general recursion. Acta Informatica 26, 309–332 (1989)

9. Hoare, C.A.R.: Proof of correctness of data representations. Acta Informatica 1, 271–281 (1972)

10. Jacobs, B.: Weakest precondition reasoning for java programs with jml annotations. Journal of Logic and Algebraic Programming 58, 2004 (2002)

11. Jifeng, H., Li, X., Liu, Z.: rcos: a refinement calculus of object systems. Theor. Comput. Sci. 365, 109–142 (2006)

12. Leavens, G.T., Naumann, D.A.: Behavioral subtyping is equivalent to modular reasoning for object-oriented programs. Technical Report 06-36, Department of Computer Science, Iowa State University, Ames, Iowa, 50011 (December 2006)

13. Leavens, G.T., Naumann, D.A.: Behavioral subtyping, specification inheritance, and modular reasoning. Technical Report 06-20b, Department of Computer Science, Iowa State University, Ames, Iowa, 50011 (September 2006)

14. Leavens, G.T., Baker, A.L., Ruby, C.: Preliminary design of JML: A behavioral interface specification language for Java. SIGSOFT Software Engineering Notes 31(3), 1–38 (2006)

15. Leino, K.R.M., Müller, P.: Object invariants in dynamic contexts. In: Odersky, M. (ed.) ECOOP 2004. LNCS, vol. 3086, pp. 491–515. Springer, Heidelberg (2004)

16. Liskov, B.: Keynote address - data abstraction and hierarchy. In: Addendum to the Proceedings on Object-Oriented Programming Systems, Languages and Applications (Addendum), OOPSLA 1987, pp. 17–34. ACM, New York (1987)

17. Liskov, B., Wing, J.M.: A behavioral notion of subtyping. ACM Trans. Program. Lang. Syst. 16(6), 1811–1841 (1994)

18. Müller, P.: Modular Specification and Verification of Object-Oriented Programs. LNCS, vol. 2262. Springer, Heidelberg (2002)

19. Noble, J., Vitek, J., Potter, J.: Flexible alias protection. In: Jul, E. (ed.) ECOOP 1998. LNCS, vol. 1445, pp. 158–185. Springer, Heidelberg (1998)

20. Parkinson, M., Summers, A.: The relationship between separation logic and implicit dynamic frames. In: Barthe, G. (ed.) ESOP 2011. LNCS, vol. 6602, pp. 439–458. Springer, Heidelberg (2011)

21. Parkinson, M.J., Bierman, G.M.: Separation logic, abstraction and inheritance. In: Proceedings of the 35th Annual ACM SIGPLAN-SIGACT Symposium on Principles of Programming Languages, POPL 2008, pp. 75–86. ACM, New York (2008)

22. Pierik, C., de Boer, F.S.: A proof outline logic for object-oriented programming. Theor. Comput. Sci. 343(3), 413–442 (2005)

23. Reynolds, J.C.: Separation logic: A logic for shared mutable data structures. In: Symposium on Logic in Computer Science, pp. 55–74. IEEE Computer Society, Los Alamitos (2002)

24. Smans, J., Jacobs, B., Piessens, F.: Implicit dynamic frames: Combining dynamic frames and separation logic. In: Drossopoulou, S. (ed.) ECOOP 2009. LNCS, vol. 5653, pp. 148–172. Springer, Heidelberg (2009)

25. Liu, Y., Qiu, Z.: A separation logic for OO programs. Technical Report 2010-42, School of Math., Peking University (2010) (preprints),
http://www.mathinst.pku.edu.cn/index.php?styleid=2
26. Liu, Y., Qiu, Z., Long, Q.: A weakest precondition semantics for Java. Technical Report 2010-46, School of Math., Peking University (2010) (preprints),
http://www.mathinst.pku.edu.cn/index.php?styleid=2
27. Qiu, Z., Wang, S., Long, Q.: Sequential μJava: Formal foundations. Technical Report 2007-35, School of Math., Peking University (2007) (preprints),
http://www.mathinst.pku.edu.cn/index.php?styleid=2

A   OOSL: Some Details and Semantics

Now we give some details about OOSL. A complete treatment can be found in [25], including a careful comparison with other similar works.

To represent the states of OO programs, we use an extension of classical Stack-Heap storage model based upon three basic sets Name, Type and Ref. Here we say something more for Ref. Because references are atomic, we assume two primitive functions:[1]

- eqref : Ref $\rightarrow$ Ref $\rightarrow$ bool, justifies whether two references are the same, i.e. for any $r_1, r_2 \in$ Ref, eqref(r_1, r_2) iff r_1 is same to r_2.
- type : Ref $\rightarrow$ Type decides the type of the object referred by some reference. We define type(rtrue) = type(rfalse) = Bool, and type(rnull) = Null.

A program state $s = (\sigma, O) \in$ State consists of a store and an object pool:

$$\text{Store} \,\widehat{=}\, \text{Name} \to_{\text{fin}} \text{Ref} \qquad \text{Heap} \,\widehat{=}\, \text{Ref} \to_{\text{fin}} \text{Name} \to_{\text{fin}} \text{Ref}$$
$$\text{State} \,\widehat{=}\, \text{Store} \times \text{Heap}$$

We use $r, \ldots$ to denote references, and $a, \ldots$ for fields. An element of O is a pair (r, f), where f is an abstraction of some object o pointed by r, a function from fields of o to values.[2] For domain of O, we refer to either a subset of Ref associated with objects, or a subset of Ref $\times$ Name associated with values. We use dom O to denote the domain of O, and define dom$_2$ $O \,\widehat{=}\, \{(r, a) \mid r \in \text{dom}\, O, a \in \text{dom}\, O(r)\}$ for the second case.

For the program states, we define the well-typedness as follows.

Definition 10 (Well-Typedness). *Store σ is well-typed iff*

$$\forall v \in \text{dom}\, \sigma \cdot \text{type}(\sigma(v)) <: \text{dtype}(v).$$

Heap O is well-typed iff

- $\forall (r, a) \in \text{dom}_2\, O \cdot a \in \text{fld}(r) \wedge \text{type}(O(r)(a)) <: \text{fields}(r)(a)$, *and*

---

[1] One possible implementation, for example, is to define a reference as a pair (t, id) where $t \in$ Type and $id \in \mathbf{N}$, and define eqref as the pair equality, and type$(r) = r.first$.

[2] Please pay attention that Ref $\to_{\text{fin}}$ Name $\to_{\text{fin}}$ Ref is very different from Ref $\times$ Name $\to_{\text{fin}}$ Ref. Informally speaking, the former is a map from references to objects, while the latter is a map from object fields to field values. So objects have no direct presentations in the latter, especially empty objects.

$$\mathcal{M}(\texttt{true}) \quad\quad = \text{State} \quad\quad\quad\quad\quad\quad\quad\quad\quad\quad\quad\quad\quad \text{(I-TRUE)}$$

$$\mathcal{M}(\texttt{false}) \quad\quad = \emptyset \quad\quad\quad\quad\quad\quad\quad\quad\quad\quad\quad\quad\quad\quad\quad\quad \text{(I-FALSE)}$$

$$\mathcal{M}(r_1 = r_2) \quad\quad = \text{State if eqref}(r_1, r_2), \quad \emptyset \quad \text{otherwise} \quad\quad \text{(I-REF)}$$

$$\mathcal{M}(r : T) \quad\quad = \text{State if type}(r) = T, \quad \emptyset \quad \text{otherwise} \quad\quad \text{(I-TYPE)}$$

$$\mathcal{M}(r <: T) \quad\quad = \text{State if type}(r) <: T, \quad \emptyset \quad \text{otherwise} \quad\quad \text{(I-SUBT)}$$

$$\mathcal{M}(v = r) \quad\quad = \{(\sigma, O) \mid \sigma(v) = r\} \quad\quad\quad\quad\quad\quad\quad \text{(I-VAL)}$$

$$\mathcal{M}(\textbf{emp}) \quad\quad = \{(\sigma, \emptyset)\} \quad\quad\quad\quad\quad\quad\quad\quad\quad\quad\quad \text{(I-EMP)}$$

$$\mathcal{M}(r_1.a \mapsto r_2) \quad\quad = \{(\sigma, \{(r_1, a, r_2)\})\} \quad\quad\quad\quad\quad\quad\quad \text{(I-SGL)}$$

$$\mathcal{M}(\textsf{obj}(r, T)) \quad\quad = \{(\sigma, O) \mid \text{type}(r) = T \wedge \text{dom } O = \{r\} \wedge \quad \text{(I-OBJ)}$$
$$\text{dom } (O(r)) = \text{dom } (\text{fields}(T))\}$$

$$\mathcal{M}(p(\bar{r})) \quad\quad = \mathcal{J}(p)(\bar{r}), \quad \mathcal{J} \text{ is the least fixpoint model of } \Lambda \quad\quad \text{(I-PRE)}$$

$$\mathcal{M}(\neg\psi) \quad\quad = \text{State} \setminus \mathcal{M}(\psi) \quad\quad\quad\quad\quad\quad\quad\quad\quad \text{(I-NEG)}$$

$$\mathcal{M}(\psi_1 \vee \psi_2) \quad\quad = \mathcal{M}(\psi_1) \cup \mathcal{M}(\psi_2) \quad\quad\quad\quad\quad\quad\quad \text{(I-OR)}$$

$$\mathcal{M}(\psi_1 \wedge \psi_2) \quad\quad = \mathcal{M}(\neg(\neg\psi_1 \vee \neg\psi_2)) \quad\quad\quad\quad\quad\quad \text{(I-AND)}$$

$$\mathcal{M}(\psi_1 \Rightarrow \psi_2) \quad\quad = \mathcal{M}(\neg\psi_1 \vee \psi_2) \quad\quad\quad\quad\quad\quad\quad \text{(I-IMP)}$$

$$\mathcal{M}(\psi_1 * \psi_2) \quad\quad = \{(\sigma, O) \mid \exists O_1, O_2 \cdot O_1 * O_2 = O \wedge (\sigma, O_1) \in \mathcal{M}(\psi_1) \quad \text{(I-SCON)}$$
$$\wedge (\sigma, O_2) \in \mathcal{M}(\psi_2)\}$$

$$\mathcal{M}(\psi_1 \mathbin{-\!\!*} \psi_2) \quad\quad = \{(\sigma, O) \mid \forall O_1 \cdot O_1 \perp O \wedge (\sigma, O_1) \in \mathcal{M}(\psi_1) \quad \text{(I-SIMP)}$$
$$\text{implies } (\sigma, O_1 * O) \in \mathcal{M}(\psi_2)\}$$

$$\mathcal{M}(\exists r \cdot \psi) \quad\quad = \{(\sigma, O) \mid \exists r \in \textsf{Ref} \cdot (\sigma, O) \in \mathcal{M}(\psi)\} \quad\quad \text{(I-EX)}$$

$$\mathcal{M}(\forall r \cdot \psi) \quad\quad = \mathcal{M}(\neg(\exists r \cdot \neg\psi)) \quad\quad\quad\quad\quad\quad\quad \text{(I-ALL)}$$

Fig. 3. Semantics of OOSL

– $\forall r \in \text{dom } O \cdot \textsf{fld}(r) = \emptyset \vee (\textsf{fld}(r) \cap \text{dom } O(r) \neq \emptyset)$.

$\textsf{fld}(r) = \text{dom fields}(r)$ *is the field set of the type of* r.
State $s = (\sigma, O)$ *is well-typed iff both* σ *and* O *are well-typed.* $\quad\quad \square$

A well-typed heap requires that: 1) all fields in O are valid according to their objects, and hold values of valid types; and 2) for a non-empty object (according to its type), only when at least one of its fields is in O, we can say the object is in O. Thus we can identify empty objects in any heap. We will only consider well-typed states.
We define a special overriding operator $\oplus$ on Heap:

$$(O_1 \oplus O_2)(r) \;\widehat{=}\; \begin{cases} O_1(r) \oplus O_2(r) & \text{if } r \in \text{dom } O_2 \\ O_1(r) & \text{otherwise} \end{cases}$$

The $\oplus$ operator on the right hand side is the standard function overriding. Thus, for heap O_1, $O_1 \oplus \{(r, a, r')\}$ gives a new heap, where only one field value (the value for a) of the object pointed by r is modified (denoted by r').

We use $O_1 \perp O_2$ to indicate that O_1 and O_2 are separated from each other:

$$O_1 \perp O_2 \ \hat{=} \ \forall r \in \text{dom } O_1 \cap \text{dom } O_2.$$
$$O_1(r) \neq \emptyset \wedge O_2(r) \neq \emptyset \ \wedge \text{dom } (O_1(r)) \cap \text{dom } (O_2(r)) = \emptyset.$$

If a reference to object o, is in both dom O_1 and dom O_2, then O_1 and O_2 must contain non-empty and disjoint subsets of o's fields (the well-typedness guarantees this). This means that we can separate fields of a non-empty object into different heaps, but not an empty object. We use $O_1 * O_2$ for the union of O_1 and O_2, when $O_1 \perp O_2$.

This storage model gives us both an object view and a field view. With it, we can correctly handle whole objects and their fields.

The assertion language of OOSL is in **Section 3.1**. Now we explain more about *user-defined assertions* and semantics of OOSL.

We allow user-defined predicates in OOSL. In fact, these predicates are indispensable to support specification and verification programs involving recursive data structures, e.g., lists, trees, etc. We record these definitions in a *Logic Environment* Λ:

$$\Lambda ::= \varepsilon \mid p(\bar{r}) \ \dot{=} \ \psi, \Lambda$$

Here ε denotes the empty environment, p is a symbol (a predicate name), $\bar{r}$ are (a list of) formal parameters of the predicate, and ψ is the body, which is an assertion correlated with $\bar{r}$. Recursive definitions are allowed.

As a well-formedness, the body ψ of any definition in Λ cannot use symbols not defined in Λ. Further, we require that Λ is *finite* and any body predicate ψ in it is *syntactically monotone*[3]. Under these conditions, we can define a *least fix-point model* for Λ by Tarski's theorem. Based on this model, we define semantics of assertions by a semantic function $\mathcal{M}_\Lambda : \Psi \rightarrow \mathbb{P}(\text{State})$ by rules listed in **Fig. 3**, where subscript Λ is omitted as default, and $\mathcal{J}$ is the least fix-point model of Λ. With this least fix-point model $\mathcal{J}$, we can define that some assertion holds on a given state:

Definition 11.

$$(\sigma, O) \models \psi \qquad \textit{iff} \qquad (\sigma, O) \in \mathcal{M}(\psi).$$

---

[3] For definition $p(\bar{r}) \ \dot{=} \ \psi$, every symbol occurred in ψ must lie under even number of negations.

Computing Preconditions and Postconditions of While Loops

Olfa Mraihi[1], Wided Ghardallou[2], Asma Louhichi[2], Lamia Labed Jilani[1], Khaled Bsaies[2], and Ali Mili[3]

[1] Institut Superieur de Gestion, Tunis, Tunisia
[2] Faculte des Sciences de Tunis, El Manar, Tunisia
[3] NJIT, Newark NJ, USA
louhichiasma@yahoo.fr, olfa.mraihi@yahoo.fr, wided.ghardallou@gmail.com,
lamia.labed@isg.rnu.tn, khaled.bsaies@fst.rnu.tn
mili@cis.njit.edu

Abstract. Weakest preconditions were introduced by Dijkstra as a tool to define the semantics of programming constructs, and thereby as a means to prove the correctness of programs; the dual concept of strongest postcondition was introduced subsequently as an alternative means for the same ends. In this paper, we present and discuss a method to compute weakest preconditions and strongest postconditions of while loops in a C-like programming language; to this effect, we use the concept of invariant relation. Whereas the task of computing weakest preconditions and strongest postconditions of while loops is usually approached by limiting the number of iterations and applying successive sequential compositions, invariant relations afford us a crisper, closed form solution.

Keywords: weakest precondition, strongest postcondition, while loop, invariant relation, programming language semantics, program correctness, relational calculus.

1 Introduction: Preconditions and Postconditions of Loops

Weakest preconditions were introduced by Dijkstra in [7], and further explored in [12,8] as a basis for a sound discipline of program derivation; specifically, they have been used to define the semantics of programming languages and design languages, and to prove the correctness of programs with respect to specifications represented by precondition/ postcondition pairs. Strongest postconditions, a dual concept, were introduced subsequently as means to essentially the same broad ends (defining semantics, proving correctness, capturing functional properties of programs and/ or designs). Like much of the research pertaining to programming language semantics and program correctness, weakest preconditions and strongest postconditions were the focus of much research interest in the seventies and eighties, and emerged again recently as important research topics [14,13,11,1,4,24,16,2,9]. Also, like most program correctness methods, weakest

A. Cerone and P. Pihlajasaari (Eds.): ICTAC 2011, LNCS 6916, pp. 173–193, 2011.

preconditions and strongest postconditions meet their toughest challenge when they deal with iterative constructs, most notably while loops.

In this paper, we use the concept of *invariant relation* of a while loop, introduced by us in earlier work [19], and explore how this concept can help us to compute or approximate weakest preconditions and strongest postconditions. Our approach is fairly orthogonal to existing methods for the derivation of preconditions and postconditions, and can be characterized by the following premises:

- It is applicable to loops written in actual programming languages, such as C, C++, Java, etc.
- It proceeds by a divide-and-conquer discipline, which allows us to handle large programs (loops) in near linear time (as a function of the size of the loop); hence it is fairly scalable.
- It is automatable, and proceeds by matching (some representation of) the source code against pre-catalogued code patterns.
- For strongest postconditions, it may proceed by successive approximations, generating (arbitrary) postconditions that culminate in the strongest postcondition or an approximation thereof (depending on whether our tool has the necessary programming knowledge and domain knowledge required to fully analyze the loop).
- It allows us to compute weakest preconditions once we have captured all the relevant functional details of the loop.

In section 3 we briefly introduce the concept of invariant relations, using the mathematical background discussed in section 2. In sections 4 and 5 we introduce weakest preconditions and strongest postconditions, and discuss how invariant relations help us compute these by means of invariant relations. Then, in section 6 we discuss how we generate invariant relations in practice. Finally, in section 7 we conclude by summarizing our results, assessing them by comparison with related work, and sketching venues for further research.

2   Mathematical Background

2.1   Elements of Relations

Definitions and Notations. We consider a set S defined by the values of some program variables, say x, y and z; we typically denote elements of S by s, and we note that s has the form $s = \langle x, y, z \rangle$. We use the notation $x(s)$, $y(s)$, $z(s)$ to denote the x-component, y-component and z-component of s. We may sometimes use x to refer to $x(s)$ and x' to refer to $x(s')$, when this raises no ambiguity. We refer to elements s of S as *program states* and to S as the *space* of the program. A relation on S is a subset of the cartesian product $S \times S$. Constant relations on some set S include the *universal* relation, denoted by L, the *identity* relation, denoted by I, and the *empty* relation, denoted by $\emptyset$.

Operations on Relations. Because relations are sets, we apply the usual set theoretic operations between relations: union ($\cup$), intersection ($\cap$), and complement ($\overline{R}$). Operations on relations also include

- The *converse*, denoted by $\widehat{R}$, and defined by $\widehat{R} = \{(s, s')|(s', s) \in R\}$.
- The *product* of relations R and R' is the relation denoted by $R \circ R'$ (or RR') and defined by $R \circ R' = \{(s, s')|\exists s'' : (s, s'') \in R \wedge (s'', s') \in R'\}$. We admit without proof that $\widehat{RR'} = \widehat{R'}\widehat{R}$ and that $\widehat{\widehat{R}} = R$.
- The *pre-restriction* (resp. *post-restriction*) of relation R to predicate t is the relation $\{(s, s')|t(s) \wedge (s, s') \in R\}$ (resp. $\{(s, s')|(s, s') \in R \wedge t(s')\}$). Given a predicate t, we denote by T the relation defined as $T = \{(s, s')|t(s)\}$. We admit without proof that the pre-restriction of a relation R to predicate t can be written as $T \cap R$, and the post-restriction of relation R to predicate t can be written as $R \cap \widehat{T}$.
- The *domain* of relation R is defined as $dom(R) = \{s|\exists s' : (s, s') \in R\}$. We admit without proof that for a relation R, $RL = \{(s, s')|s \in dom(R)\}$.
- The nth power of relation R, for natural number n, is denoted by R^n and defined as follows:

$$R^0 = I,$$
$$\text{For } n > 0, \ R^n = R^{n-1} \circ R.$$

- The *transitive closure* of relation R is the relation denoted by R^+ and defined by $R^+ = \{(s, s')|\exists n > 0 : (s, s') \in R^n\}$.
- The *reflexive transitive closure* of relation R is the relation denoted by R^* and defined by $R^* = R^+ \cup I$.

We apply the usual conventions with regards to operator precedence.

Properties of Relations. We say that R is *deterministic* (or that it is a *function*) if and only if $\widehat{R}R \subseteq I$, and we say that R is *total* if and only if $I \subseteq R\widehat{R}$, or equivalently, $RL = L$. A *vector* V is a relation that satisfies $VL = V$; in set theoretic terms, a vector on set S has the form $C \times S$, for some subset C of S. A relation R is said to be *reflexive* if and only if $I \subseteq R$, *transitive* if and only if $RR \subseteq R$ and *symmetric* if and only if $R = \widehat{R}$. We admit without proof that the transitive closure of a relation R is the smallest transitive superset of R; and that the reflexive transitive closure of relation R is the smallest reflexive transitive superset of R. A relation R is said to be *inductive* if and only if it can be written as $R = \overline{A} \cup \widehat{A}$ for some vector A; we leave it to the reader to check that if A is written as $\{(s, s')|\alpha(s)\}$, then $\overline{A} \cup \widehat{A}$ can be written as $\{(s, s')|\alpha(s) \Rightarrow \alpha(s')\}$.

2.2 Refinement Ordering

We define an ordering relation on relational specifications under the name *refinement ordering*:

Definition 1. *A relation R is said to* refine *a relation R' if and only if*

$$RL \cap R'L \cap (R \cup R') = R'.$$

In set theoretic terms, this equation means that the domain of R is a superset of (or equal to) the domain of R', and that for each element s in the domain of R', the set of images of s by R is a subset of (or equal to) the set of images of s by R'. This is similar to, but different from, refining a pre/postcondition specification by weakening its precondition and/or strengthening its postcondition [12,22]. We denote this relation by $R \sqsupseteq R'$ or $R' \sqsubseteq R$. We consider a program g on space S written in some C-like programming language. Because g is written in a deterministic programming language, its semantics is captured by a function, which we denote by G and define by

$$G = \{(s, s')|\ \text{if } g \text{ starts execution in state } s \text{ then it terminates in state } s'\}.$$

From this definition, it stems that $dom(G)$ can be interpreted as

$$dom(G) = \{s|\ \text{if } g \text{ starts execution in state } s \text{ then it terminates}\}.$$

We admit that, modulo traditional definitions of total correctness [8,12,20], the following propositions hold:

– A program g is correct with respect to a specification R if and only if $G \sqsupseteq R$.
– $R \sqsupseteq R'$ implies that any program correct with respect to R is correct with respect to R'.

In other words, R refines R' if and only if R represents a stronger requirement than R'.

2.3   Lattice Properties

We admit without proof that the refinement relation is a partial ordering. In [3] Boudriga et al. analyze the lattice properties of this ordering and find the following results:

– Any two relations R and R' have a greatest lower bound, which we refer to as the *meet*, denote by $\sqcap$, and define by:

$$R \sqcap R' = RL \cap R'L \cap (R \cup R').$$

– Two relations R and R' have a least upper bound if and only if they satisfy the following condition (which we refer to as the *consistency condition*): $RL \cap R'L = (R \cap R')L$. Under this condition, their least upper bound is referred to as the *join*, denoted by $\sqcup$, and defined by:

$$R \sqcup R' = (\overline{RL} \cap R') \cup (\overline{R'L} \cap R) \cup (R \cap R').$$

Intuitively, the join of R and R', when it exists, behaves like R outside the domain of R', behaves like R' outside the domain of R, and behaves like the intersection of R and R' on the intersection of their domain.
– Two relations R and R' have a least upper bound if and only if they have an upper bound.

- The lattice of refinement admits a *universal lower bound*, which is the empty relation.
- The lattice of refinement admits no *universal upper bound*.
- Maximal elements of this lattice are total deterministic relations.

Figure 1 (a) shows the overall structure of the lattice of specifications.

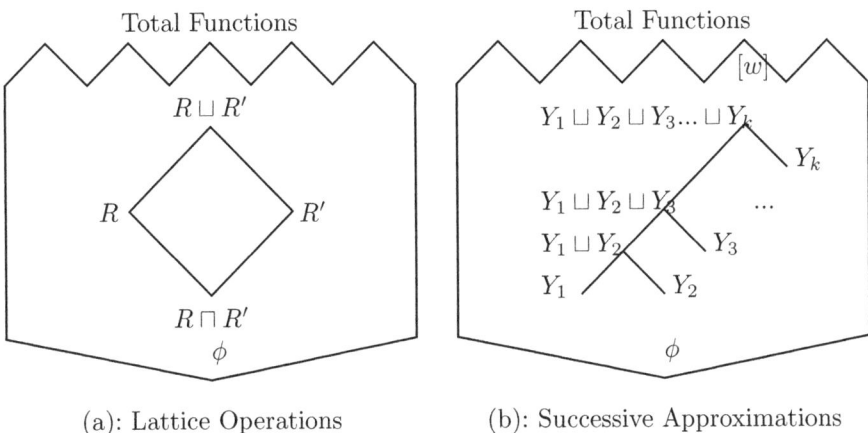

(a): Lattice Operations   (b): Successive Approximations

Fig. 1. Lattice Structure of Refinement

3   Invariant Relations

In this section, we discuss invariant relations; first, we introduce some background notations and results about loops, in subsection 3.1.

3.1   Loop Semantics

We consider while loops written in some C-like programming language, and we submit the following theorem, due to [21], which we use as the semantic definition of a while loop.

Theorem 1. *(Mili et. al. 2009 [21]) We consider a while statement of the form* $w = $ while t do b *that terminates for all the states in* S. *Then its function* W *is given by:*

$$W = (T \cap B)^* \cap \widehat{\overline{T}}.$$

For the sake of simplicity, we limit our investigation to while loops that terminate for all initial states, i.e. such that $WL = L$. In [21], we have discussed why this hypothesis does not, in theory, restrict the generality of our study; although we concede that in practice it makes for less interesting results.

To illustrate our subsequent discussions, we use a simple running example, which is the following while loop on natural variables n, f, k, such that $1 \le k \le n+1$:

```
w:   while k!=n+1 {f=f*k; k=k+1}.
```

3.2   Invariant Relations

Intuitively, an invariant relation is a relation that contains all the pairs of states (s, s') such that s' can be derived from s by application of an arbitrary number (including zero) of iterations of the loop body. We define it formally as follows.

Definition 2. *Given a while loop of the form* $w = $ while t do b *on some space* S, *we say that relation* R *is an* invariant relation *for* w *if and only if it is a reflexive and transitive superset of* $(T \cap B)$.

As a rationale for the concept of invariant relation, consider that a reflexive transitive closure of a relation is the *smallest* reflexive transitive superset of the relation. Had we been able to derive the reflexive transitive closure of $(T \cap B)$, we would apply Theorem 1 to compute the function of the loop, and we would dispose of/ dispense with all other means to analyze the loop. But computing the reflexive transitive closure of $(T \cap B)$, i.e. the *smallest* reflexive transitive superset of $(T \cap B)$, is usually difficult; as a substitute, invariant relations provide arbitrary (not necessarily smallest) reflexive transitive supersets of $(T \cap B)$. By taking the intersection of a sufficient number of invariant relations, we may attain the reflexive transitive closure of $(T \cap B)$.

To illustrate this concept, we consider the loop of the running example, and we submit the following relation:

$$R = \left\{ (s, s') \mid \frac{f}{(k-1)!} = \frac{f'}{(k'-1)!} \right\}.$$

This relation is clearly reflexive and transitive; to prove that it is a superset of $(T \cap B)$, we take an arbitrary pair (s, s') in $(T \cap B)$, and we proceed as follows:

$$(s, s') \in (T \cap B)$$
$\Rightarrow$ { substitution }
$$k \ne n+1 \wedge n' = n \wedge f' = f \times k \wedge k' = k+1$$
$\Rightarrow$ { substitution }
$$\frac{f'}{(k'-1)!} = \frac{f \times k}{(k+1-1)!}$$
$\Rightarrow$ { simplification }
$$\frac{f'}{(k'-1)!} = \frac{f}{(k-1)!}$$
$\Rightarrow$ { substitution }
$$(s, s') \in R.$$

4   Weakest Preconditions

4.1   A Relational Formula

We consider a while loop $w = $ while t do b on space S, we let W be the function computed by w, and we assume that w terminates for all s in S, i.e. that $WL = L$.

The weakest precondition p of the loop w with respect to postcondition q is the weakest predicate p such that the Hoare triplet [15]

$$\{p\}w\{q\}$$

is valid. We wish to rewrite this condition in relational terms, using vector $P = \{(s, s')|p(s)\}$ and vector $Q = \{(s, s')|q(s)\}$ to represent predicates p and q. We rewrite the Hoare triplet as follows:

$$\forall s : p(s) \Rightarrow \exists s' : (s, s') \in W \wedge q(s')$$
$$\Leftrightarrow \quad \{ \text{ tautology } \}$$
$$\forall s, s'' : p(s) \wedge s'' \in S \Rightarrow \exists s' : (s, s') \in W \wedge q(s') \wedge s'' \in S$$
$$\Leftrightarrow \quad \{ \text{ definition of } P \text{ and } Q \}$$
$$\forall s, s'' : (s, s'') \in P \Rightarrow \exists s' : (s, s') \in W \wedge (s', s'') \in Q$$
$$\Leftrightarrow \quad \{ \text{ definition of relational product } \}$$
$$\forall s, s'' : (s, s'') \in P \Rightarrow (s, s'') \in WQ$$
$$\Leftrightarrow \quad \{ \text{ set theory } \}$$
$$P \subseteq WQ.$$

Whence we submit the following definition.

Definition 3. *We consider a while loop w on space S whose function is W, and we let q be a predicate on S, represented by a vector Q on S, that we use as postcondition for w. A precondition of W with respect to q is any subset of WQ; the weakest precondition of W with respect to Q is WQ.*

Indeed, the largest subset (representing the weakest precondition) of WQ is WQ itself. In the remainder of the paper, we make no distinction between a predicate (p or q) and the vector that represents it (respectively, P or Q).

4.2 Invariant Relations and Weakest Preconditions

In [21], we have outlined a method to compute the function of the while loop (W) by successive approximations using invariant relations. The method is based on the following proposition.

Proposition 1. *Let w be a while statement while t do b on space S, let W be the function of w and let R be an invariant relation of w. Then $R \cap \widehat{T}$ is refined by W.*

Proof. If we let R' be defined as $R \cap \widehat{T}$, then we must prove that $W \sqsupseteq R'$, i.e. that $WL \cap R'L \cap (W \cup R') = R'$. Before we do that, we establish a lemma to the effect that W is a subset of R'. We proceed as follows:

$$R'$$
$$= \quad \{ \text{ substitution } \}$$
$$R \cap \widehat{T}$$
$$= \quad \{ \text{ because } R \text{ is reflexive and transitive } \}$$

$$R^* \cap \widehat{\widehat{T}}$$
$$\supseteq \qquad \{ \text{ because } R \text{ is a superset of } (T \cap B) \}$$
$$(T \cap B)^* \cap \widehat{\widehat{T}}$$
$$= \qquad \{ \text{ semantic definition of loops, Theorem 1 } \}$$
$$W.$$

Now we check the condition of refinement:

$$WL \cap R'L \cap (W \cup R')$$
$$= \qquad \{ \text{ because } R' \supseteq W \}$$
$$WL \cap R'L \cap (R')$$
$$= \qquad \{ \text{ because } R'L \supseteq WL \}$$
$$WL \cap (R')$$
$$= \qquad \{ \text{ because } W \text{ is total } \}$$
$$R'.$$

qed

In other words, $Y = R \cap \widehat{\widehat{T}}$ is a lower bound of W. Because W is total (by hypothesis: section 3.1) and deterministic (since we are considering actual C-like programming languages), it is maximal in the refinement ordering (see Figure 1); hence we can approximate it using nothing but lower bounds. To compute the function of the loop, we proceed as follows:

- We generate as many invariant relations as we can; this step is carried out by an automated tool, whose algorithm we will discuss in section 6. The performance of this tool is dependent on a knowledge base that contains programming knowledge and domain knowledge, and can handle loops that fall within the boundaries of the knowledge base.
- We transform the invariant relations of w into lower bounds of W (the function of w), using the formula given in Proposition 1.
- We compose the lower bounds by the join operation in the refinement lattice, to record all the functional information that we have collected on the loop (see Figure 1 (b)); all this information is represented as equations between initial states and final states, written in Mathematica (©Wolfram Research).
- We solve the Mathematica equations obtained above taking the final values of state variables as unknowns and the initial state variables as parameters; if the result is a total and deterministic relation (i.e. no condition on the input variables, and all output variables are uniquely specified) then we have obtained the function of the loop; else we have obtained the best approximation of the function of the loop we can get, given the current contents of our knowledge base.

As a brief illustration, we consider the sample program we had introduced in section 3.1, and we let the postcondition be: $Q = \{(s, s')|f = n!\}$. To compute the weakest precondition P of w with respect to Q, we must first compute W, then we derive P as WQ. We propose two invariant relations for this loop, namely:

$$R_0 = \{(s, s') | \frac{f}{(k-1)!} = \frac{f'}{(k'-1)!}\}$$
$$R_1 = \{(s, s') | n' = n\}.$$

We have already checked that R_0 is an invariant relation for w; checking that R_1 is also an invariant relation for w is trivial. From these invariant relations, we infer the following lower bounds of W:

$$Y_0 = \{(s, s') | \frac{f}{(k-1)!} = \frac{f'}{(k'-1)!} \wedge k' = n' + 1\}$$
$$Y_1 = \{(s, s') | n' = n \wedge k' = n' + 1\}.$$

Taking the join of these lower bounds, we find:

$$Y_0 \sqcup Y_1$$
$$= \quad \{ \text{ definition of join } \}$$
$$Y_0 \cap \overline{Y_1 L} \cup Y_1 \cap \overline{Y_0 L} \cup Y_0 \cap Y_1$$
$$= \quad \{ Y_0 \text{ and } Y_1 \text{ are both total } \}$$
$$Y_0 \cap \overline{L} \cup Y_1 \cap \overline{L} \cup Y_0 \cap Y_1$$
$$= \quad \{ \overline{L} = \phi \}$$
$$Y_0 \cap Y_1$$
$$= \quad \{ \text{ substitution } \}$$
$$\{(s, s') | k' = n + 1 \wedge n' = n \wedge f' = n! \times \frac{f}{(k-1)!}\}.$$

Because this relation is total and deterministic, the only relation that is more refined than it is itself. Hence

$$W = \{(s, s') | k' = n + 1 \wedge n' = n \wedge f' = n! \times \frac{f}{(k-1)!}\}.$$

whence the weakest precondition is:

$$WQ$$
$$= \quad \{ \text{ substitution } \}$$
$$\{(s, s') | k' = n + 1 \wedge n' = n \wedge f' = n! \times \frac{f}{(k-1)!}\} \circ \{(s, s') | f = n!\}$$
$$= \quad \{ \text{ product } \}$$
$$\{(s, s') | \exists s'' : k'' = n + 1 \wedge n'' = n \wedge f'' = n! \times \frac{f}{(k-1)!} \wedge f'' = n''!\}$$
$$= \quad \{ \text{ logic inference } \}$$
$$\{(s, s') | \frac{f}{(k-1)!} = 1 \wedge \exists s'' : k'' = n + 1 \wedge n'' = n \wedge f'' = n! \times \frac{f}{(k-1)!}\}$$
$$= \quad \{ \text{ logic simplification } \}$$
$$\{(s, s') | \frac{f}{(k-1)!} = 1\}$$
$$= \quad \{ \text{ numeric simplification } \}$$
$$\{(s, s') | f = (k - 1)!\}.$$

4.3   Illustration: A Larger Example

We consider the following program; this program is written in C++ syntax, except for two minor details, namely that constants are not assigned values (since, for our purposes, we may want to keep them as arbitrary parameters), and that #include statements are packed on one line (to save space).

```
#include <iostream> #include <list> using namespace std;//header
int main () {const int cn; int x, y, y, i, j, z, u, v;// scalars
list <int> l1, l2;   int aa[cn], bb[cn];//lists and arrays
while (! l2.empty()) {x=x+aa[i]; y=y+bb[j]; j=j+i; i=i+1; u=z;
 z=v+u; v=u; j=j-i; l1.push_back(l2.front()); l2.pop_front();}}
```

Our tool produces the following function for the loop (where $sl2$ is an abbreviation for $size(l2)$, F is the Fibonacci function, and the dot (.) represents list concatenation):

$$W = \{(s, s')|l2 = \langle\rangle \wedge s' = s\} \cup$$

$$\left\{ (s, s') \middle| \begin{array}{l} l2 \neq \langle\rangle \wedge i' = i + sl2 \wedge j' = j - sl2 \wedge l1' = l1.l2 \wedge \\ l2' = \langle\rangle \wedge x' = x + \sum_{h=i}^{sl2+i-1} aa[h] \wedge y' = y + \sum_{h=j+1-sl2}^{j} bb[h] \wedge \\ v' = vF(sl2 - 1) + zF(sl2) \wedge z' = vF(sl2) + zF(sl2 + 1) \\ \wedge aa' = aa \wedge bb' = bb \wedge u' = vF(sl2 - 1) + zF(sl2) \end{array} \right\}.$$

Using this function, we compute the weakest precondition of w for the following postconditions.

– Postcondition $Q_0 = \{(s, s')|x = \sum_{k=0}^{cN-1} aa[k]\}$. The weakest precondition of w for postcondition Q_0 is $P_0 = WQ_0$. We compute it in Mathematica by reducing the expression $\exists s' : (s, s') \in W \wedge q_0(s')$. We find:

$$P_0 = \overline{T} \cap Q_0 \cup$$

$$\{(s, s')|l2 \neq \langle\rangle \wedge \sum_{h=0}^{cN-1} aa[h] = x + \sum_{h=i}^{sl2+i-1} aa[h]\}.$$

Note that this precondition can be satisfied by the following initialization: i=1; x=0; // sl2=cN-1; the latter condition is achieved by making list $l2$ one shorter than cN.

– Postcondition $Q_1 = \{(s, s')|x = \sum_{k=0}^{cN-1} aa[k] \wedge y = \sum_{k=0}^{cN-1} bb[k]\}$. The weakest precondition of w for postcondition Q_1 is $P_1 = WQ_1$. We compute it in Mathematica by reducing the expression $\exists s' : (s, s') \in W \wedge q_1(s')$. We find:

$$P_1 = \overline{T} \cap Q_1 \cup$$

$$\{(s, s')|l2 \neq \langle\rangle \wedge \sum_{h=0}^{cN-1} aa[h] = x + \sum_{h=i}^{sl2+i-1} aa[h] \wedge \sum_{h=0}^{cN-1} bb[h] = y + \sum_{h=1+j-sl2}^{j} bb[h]\}.$$

Note that this precondition can be satisfied by the following initialization: i=1; j=cN-1; x=0; y=0;// sl2=cN-1;

– Postcondition $Q_2 = \{(s, s')|z = F(cN + 1)\}$. The weakest precondition of w for postcondition Q_2 is $P_2 = WQ_2$. We compute it in Mathematica by reducing the expression $\exists s' : (s, s') \in W \wedge q_2(s')$. We find:

$$P_2 = \overline{T} \cap Q_2 \cup \{(s, s')|l2 \neq \langle\rangle \wedge F(cN + 1) = vF(sl2) + zF(sl2 + 1)\}.$$

Note that this precondition can be satisfied by the following initialization:
`v=1; z=1; // sl2=cN-1;`

For this example, the generation of invariant relations took 953 ms of CPU time, and the resolution of the equations took 12.932 sec; as for the generation of weakest precondition, it took 156 ms for Q_0, 296 ms for Q_1, and 140 ms for Q_2.

5   Strongest Postconditions

5.1   Relational Definition

We consider a while loop $w = $ `while t do b` on space S, we let W be the function computed by w, and we assume that it terminates for all s in S, i.e. that $WL = L$. The strongest postcondition of w for precondition p is represented by the smallest vector Q such that (according to the relational interpretation we made earlier of the Hoare triplet $\{p\}$ w $\{q\}$):

$$P \subseteq WQ,$$

where P is the vector that represents predicate p. To better characterize the strongest postcondition, we use the following proposition.

Proposition 2. *Let P and Q be vectors on S and let W be a total function on S. Then $P \subseteq WQ$ is logically equivalent to $Q \supseteq \widehat{W}P$.*

Proof. Left to Right:

$$P \subseteq WQ$$
$$\Rightarrow \qquad \{ \text{ monotonicity } \}$$
$$\widehat{W}P \subseteq \widehat{W}WQ$$
$$\Rightarrow \qquad \{ \text{ determinacy of } W \}$$
$$\widehat{W}P \subseteq Q.$$

Right to Left:

$$Q \supseteq \widehat{W}P$$
$$\Rightarrow \qquad \{ \text{ monotonicity } \}$$
$$WQ \supseteq W\widehat{W}P$$
$$\Rightarrow \qquad \{ \text{ totality of } W \}$$
$$WQ \supseteq P$$

$\square$

Using the equation $Q \supseteq \widehat{W}P$, we can say that a postcondition of w with respect to P is any superset of $\widehat{W}P$; the strongest postcondition of w with respect to P corresponds to the smallest superset of $\widehat{W}P$, which is $\widehat{W}P$ itself. We formulate this in the following definition.

Definition 4. *Given a while loop w on space S whose function is W, and given a precondition p of w, which we represent by vector P on S; then any superset of $\widehat{W}P$ is said to be a* postcondition *of w with respect to p, and $\widehat{W}P$ is said to be the* strongest postcondition *of w with respect to p.*

5.2   Invariant Relations and Strongest Postconditions

In section 4.2, we found that in order to derive the weakest precondition, we had to generate a sufficient number of invariant relations to compute the function of the loop, which we then use to compute the weakest precondition WQ. The following proposition indicates that for postconditions, we can proceed in a more stepwise manner.

Proposition 3. *Let w be a while loop on space S and let R be an invariant relation for w; given a vector P, the vector $(\overline{T} \cap \widehat{R}P)$ is a postcondition of w with respect to P.*

Proof. From $T \cap B \subseteq R$ we infer $(T \cap B)^* \subseteq R^*$ which is equivalent to $(T \cap B)^* \subseteq R$ since R is reflexive and transitive. By monotonicity we infer $(T \cap B)^* \cap \widehat{\overline{T}} \subseteq R \cap \widehat{\overline{T}}$. By Proposition 1, we rewrite this as $W \subseteq R \cap \widehat{\overline{T}}$. Taking the inverse on both sides and multiplying on the right by P preserves the inequation: $\widehat{W}P \subseteq (\widehat{R \cap \overline{T}})P$. By a vector identity (which provides that $(v \cap R)Q = v \cap RQ$ for any vector v and any relations R and Q), this can be rewritten as: $\widehat{W}P \subseteq \widehat{R}P \cap \overline{T}$. □

The interest of this proposition is that any invariant relation gives rise to a post-condition (an approximation of the strongest postcondition); we can compute the strongest postcondition by finding enough invariant relations to compute W; but even if we do not find all the necessary invariant relations, we obtain an approximation of the strongest postcondition.

As a brief illustration, we consider the sample program we had introduced in section 3.1, and we let the precondition P be $\{(s, s')|f = (k-1)!\}$. Note that this precondition represents initial conditions such as: `f=1; k=1;` or `f=1; k=2;`, or `f=6; k=4;`, etc. We consider two invariant relations,

$$R_0 = \{(s, s')|\tfrac{f}{(k-1)!} = \tfrac{f'}{(k'-1)!}\}$$
$$R_1 = \{(s, s')|n' = n\}.$$

for which we generate the associated postconditions:

$$Q_0 = \{(s, s')|\tfrac{f}{(k-1)!} = \tfrac{f'}{(k'-1)!}\} \circ \{(s, s')|f = (k-1)!\} \cap \{(s, s')|k = n+1\}$$
$$Q_1 = \{(s, s')|n = n'\} \circ \{(s, s')|f = (k-1)!\} \cap \{(s, s')|k = n+1\}.$$

These can be simplified into:

$$Q_0 = \{(s, s')|k = n+1 \wedge f = n!\}$$
$$Q_1 = \{(s, s')|k = n+1\}$$

Taking their intersection, we find $Q = \{(s, s')|k = n+1 \wedge f = n!\}$. Note that in this case the postcondition generated from R_1 did not add any information.

5.3   Illustration: A Larger Example

As an illustration of how our tool for generating invariant relations can help us compute strongest postconditions of non-trivial loops, we consider the following program written in C++ (with slight syntactic modifications: `#include` statements are written on the same line, constants are left unspecified, and function declarations are left undefined):

```
#include <iostream>  #include <list>  #include<math.h>
using namespace std;  int fact (int z); int f(int x);
// fact is factorial, f is an arbitrary function
int main() {const int ca,cb,cd,ce,cN;  int i,j,k,h,y,m,q,w,x2,fx;
float ma,st,ut,x1,t,p,n,g,r,s,u,v,z,ta,ka,la,uv;
list <int> l1,l2; float aa[]; float ab[];
while (l2.size()!=0)
    {r=pow(i,5) + r; s=s+2*u; k=ca*h+k; la=pow(x1,j)/fact(j) + la;
    l1.push_back(l2.front()); h=h+j; m=m+1;  j=j+i; fx=f(fx);
    g=g-15*cd; q= 1+2*i + q; ma=ka-ma; i=i+1; st=st+aa[i]; j= j-i;
    w=4*w; ut=ut+ab[j]; ma=(cd+1)*ka - ma; ka=ka-1; ta=pow(ta,3);
    if(x2%4==0) {x2=x2/4; y= y+2; t= t*4;}
    else {if (x2%2==0) {x2= x2/2; y= y+1; t= t*2;}
        else {x2= x2-1; z=z+t;}}
    ka=3+3*ka; w= cd+ w/2; p= 2*pow(p,3); m=2*m -2; n=1 + n/2;
    s=(cb-2)*u + s; h=h-1+cb-j; g=3*cd + g/5; v=pow(v,4); u=ca+u;
    uv=pow(uv,5); l2.pop_front();}
}
```

We are interested to compute the strongest postcondition of this while loop for the precondition p defined by:

$$size(l2) = 5 \wedge x2 = 66 \wedge y = 0 \wedge t = 1 \wedge ut = 0 \wedge st = 0 \wedge la = 0 \wedge j = 5 \wedge i = 0.$$

To this effect, we compute the function of the loop, then we submit the following formula (as per Proposition 3) to Mathematica:

```
    simplify(!(l2.size()!=0 & (exists s': R(s',s)& P(s'))).
```

The result is (where Γ is Euler's Gamma function):

$$Q = \left\{ (s,s') \mid \begin{array}{l} i = 5 \wedge j = 0 \wedge 120(la + 1) = e^{x1} \Gamma(6, x1) \wedge st = \sum_{H=1}^{5} aa[H] \wedge \\ t = 2^{6 - \lfloor \frac{log(x2)}{log(2)} \rfloor} \wedge ut = \sum_{H=0}^{4} ab[H] \wedge y + \lfloor \frac{log(x2)}{log(2)} \rfloor = 6 \end{array} \right\}.$$

On this example, our tool needed 136.531 seconds of CPU time to generate invariant relations, and 53.243 seconds to compute the strongest postcondition for precondition P.

6 Computing Invariant Relations

While in the previous sections we discussed how to use invariant relations, in this section we discuss how to generate them. The detailed discussion of the algorithm is beyond the scope of this paper; we will content ourselves with presenting the main mathematical results behind its design, as well as some empirical observations of its operation.

6.1   Mathematical Foundations

As we recall, an invariant relation is a reflexive transitive superset of the function of the loop body; invariant relations are interesting because they help us to approximate the transitive closure of $(T \cap B)$, which is the *smallest* reflexive transitive superset of $(T \cap B)$. Clearly, smaller invariant relations are better; the following proposition provides means to obtain small invariant relations.

Proposition 4. *Let w be a while loop on space S and let R and R' be invariant relations for w; then $R \cap R'$ is an invariant relation for w.*

Proof. The intersection of two reflexive relations is reflexive; the intersection of two transitive relations is transitive; and the intersection of two supersets of $(T \cap B)$ is a superset of $(T \cap B)$.   □

Consequently, we can generate smaller invariant relations by taking the intersection of arbitrary invariant relations. As for how to generate elementary invariant relations, consider that in order to find supersets of $(T \cap B)$, it helps to write it as an intersection, such as:

$$(T \cap B) = B_1 \cap B_2 \cap B_3 \cap ... \cap B_n.$$

Then, any superset of B_1 is a superset of $(T \cap B)$; any superset of $B_1 \cap B_2$ is a superset of $(T \cap B)$; any superset of $B_1 \cap B_2 \cap B_3$ is a superset of $(T \cap B)$; etc. This is the basis of our divide-and-conquer strategy: we can invariant relations for an arbitrarily large loop, by writing the function of its loop body as an intersection, then by looking at one term at a time, or two at a time, or three at a time, etc. Specifically, our algorithm proceeds as follows:

- The source code is mapped into a notation that rewrites the function of the loop body as an intersection; when the loop body is merely a sequence of assignments, this can be done by eliminating sequential dependencies. When the loop body has more complex control structures, we invoke a more general procedure, which we discuss subsequently. We refer to this notation as CCA, for conditional concurrent assignments; there are as many CCA statements in the loop body as the program has variables, where each statement records the cumulative effect of the sequential statements on a variable.
- We deploy a pattern-matching algorithm that matches the terms of the intersection one a time, then two at a time, then three at a time against pre-stored patterns (called the *recognizers*) for which we store the corresponding invariant relation pattern. Whenever a match is successful, we instantiate the invariant relation pattern to obtain an actual invariant relation. We limit ourselves to no more than three terms for the time being, but we do not exclude to consider bigger recognizers.
- We take the intersection of all the invariant relations that are generated, to obtain a smaller invariant relation.

It is easy to write the function of the loop body as an intersection when the loop body is made up of a sequence of assignments. When the loop body contains more complex control structures, such as nested if-then-else statements, then the outermost structure of the function of loop body is a union. In that case, we apply the pattern matching algorithm discussed above to each term of the union, to obtain the following structure:

$$R = (R_{1,1} \cap R_{1,2} \cap ...R_{1,n1})$$
$$\cup(R_{2,1} \cap R_{2,2} \cap ...R_{2,n2}) \cup ...$$
$$\cup(R_{m,1} \cap R_{m,2} \cap ...R_{m,nm}).$$

This relation is a superset of the function of the loop body, and it is reflexive; but it is not transitive, as the union of transitive relations is not transitive; hence it is not an invariant relation. To derive an invariant relation from it, it suffices to compute a transitive superset of it. To explain how this is done, we consider two terms of the union, where each term is the intersection of two factors:

$$R = (R_{11} \cap R_{12}) \cup (R_{21} \cap R_{22}).$$

If we find, for example, that $(R_{21} \cap R_{22}) \subseteq R_{11}$ then we conclude that R_{11} is an invariant relation, since it is reflexive and transitive (by construction), and it is a superset of each term of the union. If, for example, we find also that $(R_{11} \cap R_{12}) \subseteq R_{22}$ then we can infer (for the same reasons as above) that R_{22} is an invariant relation. From which we conclude that $R_{11} \cap R_{22}$ is an invariant relation. As an illustration, consider the following simple loop:

```
while (y!=0) {if (y%2==0) {y=y/2;x=2*x;} else {z=z+x;y=y-1;}}
```

As a reflexive transitive superset of the first branch (which we call B_1), our tool finds $R_1 = R_{11} \cap R_{12}$, where $R_{11} = \{(s, s')|xy = x'y'\}$ and $R_{12} = \{(s, s')|z = z'\}$. As a reflexive transitive superset of the second branch (which we call B_2), our tool finds $R_2 = R_{21} \cap R_{22}$, where $R_{21} = \{(s, s')|x = x'\}$ and $R_{22} = \{(s, s')|z + xy = z' + x'y'\}$. The relation $R = R_1 \cup R_2$ is a superset of $(T \cap B)$ (by construction); and it is reflexive (as the union of reflexive relations); but it is not necessarily transitive (as the union of transitive relations). However, we note that R_{22} is a superset of R_1 (by inspection); on the other hand, it is also a superset of R_2. Hence R_{22} is a superset of $R_1 \cup R_2$; because by construction $R_1 \supseteq B_1$ and $R_2 \supseteq B_2$ we infer that R_{22} is a superset of $B_1 \cup B_2$, which is $(T \cap B)$. On the other hand, because it is generated by our tool, R_{22} is by construction reflexive and transitive. As a reflexive transitive superset of $(T \cap B)$, R_{22} is an invariant relation for the while loop.

6.2   Scaling Up

Two obvious issues arise when we are dealing with large programs:

– First, the combinatorial explosion that results from trying to match p statements of the loop body out of N CCA statements, against K recognizers, trying in turn all permutations of the statements. The number of operations required for this task is bound by $O(\frac{N!}{(N-p)!} \times K \times p!)$, where N is the number of CCA statements (which is the same as the number of program variables), p is the maximum recognizer size (currently 3), and K is the number of recognizers in the database. For small values of p, $p!$ is a small constant, and the expression above is linear in K; hence the factor that we must focus on is $\frac{N!}{(N-p)!}$. A simple observation enables us to scale that factor down from $O(N^p)$ to $O(N)$: We observe that invariant relations reflect the property that the statements they involve are executed an equal number of times. We let G be the graph whose nodes are the CCA statements of the loop body, and we let there be an arc between two nodes of this graph if and only if we have matched a recognizer against the statements representing these nodes. Because the relation "being executed the same number of times" is transitive, it is not necessary to build a complete graph on the nodes representing CCA statements; rather, it is sufficient to build a connected graph. For a set of N nodes, $N-1$ arcs are sufficient to make the graph connected. Hence, as we try to match combinations of CCA statements against recognizers, we maintain a graph G that represents direct connections between statements and a graph G^* that represents transitive links between statements. We conclude the matching process whenever we have tried all the recognizers, or when G^* becomes full.

- Second, when we exhaust all our available recognizers and still cannot fill graph G^*, we conclude that it is because we are missing recognizers for the loop at hand. In that case, our tool uses matrix G^* to offer suggestions for the statements that ought to be linked by recognizers. Whenever G^* has a zero in some entry, say $G^*(i,j)$, the system proposes the pair of statements (i,j) as a candidate for a 2-recognizer; also, whenever G^* has two zeros in the same row or the same column, say $G^*(i,j)$ and $G^*(i,k)$, then the system proposes the triplet (i,j,k) as a possible candidate for a 3-recognizer.

7   Conclusion: Summary, Comparison and Prospects

7.1   Summary

Weakest preconditions and strongest postconditions have been introduced by Dijkstra in the seventies, and have been widely adopted as means to define programming language semantics and to prove the correctness of designs and programs. Like many other program analysis artifacts, weakest preconditions and strongest postconditions show their limitations when they come up against iterative programs. In this paper, we use the concept of invariant relation, introduced in [19], to compute or approximate weakest preconditions and strongest postconditions of while loops. Among the results of this paper, we mention:

- Explicit relational formulas for weakest precondition and strongest postcondition.
- The ability to compute the weakest precondition of a while loop with respect to a given postcondition, by identifying enough invariant relations of the loop to compute its function.

- The ability to compute the strongest postcondition of a while loop with respect to a given precondition, by identifying enough invariant relations of the loop to compute its function.
- The ability to compute arbitrary (not necessarily strongest) postconditions of a while loop with respect to a given precondition, by identifying any invariant relation of the loop.

Hence there is a difference between how invariant relations are used to generate preconditions and post conditions: for preconditions, we must derive the function of the loop in full before we can compute any precondition; once we have the function in full, then we can use it to compute the weakest precondition for any given postcondition. By contrast, for postconditions, any invariant relation yields a postcondition; when we have enough invariant relations to compute the function of the loop, then we can compute the strongest postcondition.

7.2   Related Work

Dijsktra [8] introduced weakest preconditions in 1976, and used them to specify the semantics of a non-deterministic design language; his ideas were taken further by Gries [12], who put them in practice as the basis for his scientific discipline of programming. Weakest preconditions were further used subsequently to define the semantics of emerging programming paradigms and constructs, such as object oriented programming [5], exception handling [18], Java's method invocation [24,25], unstructured programming constructs [13,1], system security attributes [4], procedural abstraction [11], and proof carrying code [23], to cite some.

As for the generation of weakest preconditions and strongest postconditions, it is a challenge that remains largely unfulfilled as far as while loops are concerned. In [10], Flanagan and Saxe acknowledge the combinatorial complexity that stems from trying to generate weakest preconditions by analyzing large segments of code, and propose an algorithm that produces weakest preconditions whose size (in terms of number of clauses) is $O(M^2)$ as a function of the program size. Subsequent research by Jager and Brumley [16] and by Leino [18,17] focuses on minimizing or at least controlling predicate size and predicate generation time. Others focus on minimizing predicate size by performing simplifications after the generation phase [6]. All the efforts we have seen so far compute preconditions and postconditions of while loops by relying on loop invariants, which some attempt to generate and some assume to be available. Our approach relies on invariant relations, which are generated by a static analysis of the code, once it is mapped into a quasi-relational representation that highlights its structure as an intersection, or a union of intersections. Another difference that our approach has with most of the works cited above is that we have a way to test whether our invariant relation is sufficiently strong: it is sufficiently strong if the approximation it generate for the loop function (by the formula of Proposition 1) is total and deterministic. Then, we know, by virtue of Definitions 3 and 4, that we are indeed computing the *weakest* precondition and the *strongest* postcondition.

7.3 Prospects

As practical extensions of our work, we envision two directions:

- First, consolidating the pattern matching algorithm that is used to generate invariant relations. Currently, our pattern matching operates syntactically, by matching code patterns against pre-stored recognizers one token at a time; we intend to replace this syntactic matching algorithm by a semantic algorithm, that recognizes a match as soon as two expressions are equivalent; we anticipate that this will greatly enhance the recall, without affecting the precision of the algorithm.
- Second, expanding the capability of our approach beyond numeric computations; we have started this expansion, as the examples discussed in this paper show, but much remains to be done, in terms of capturing domain knowledge and using inference mechanisms that may be domain specific.

As for theoretical extensions, we are considering to lift the hypothesis that loops terminate for all states in the space; we anticipate that lifting this hypothesis will require a more sophisticated theoretical background, but also yield more interesting results.

References

1. Barnett, M., Rustan Leino, K.: Weakest precondition of unstructured programs. In: Proceedings, Sixth ACM SIGPLAN-SIGSOFT Workshop on Program Analysis for Software Tools and Engineering, Lisbon, Portugal (2005)
2. Berghammer, R.: Soundness of a purely syntactical formalization of weakest preconditions. Electronic Notes in Theoretical Computer Science. Elsevier Science Publisher, Amsterdam (2000)
3. Boudriga, N., Elloumi, F., Mili, A.: The lattice of specifications: Applications to a specification methodology. Formal Aspects of Computing 4, 544–571 (1992)
4. Brumley, D., Wang, H., Jha, S., Song, D.: Creating vulnerability signatures using weakest preconditions. In: Proceedings, 20th Computer Security Foundations Symposium, Venice, Italy, pp. 311–325 (2007)
5. Cavalcanti, A., Naumann, D.: A weakest precondition semantics for refinement of object oriented programs. IEEE Transactions on Software Engineering 26(8), 713–728 (2000)
6. Costa, M., Castro, M., Zhou, L., Zhang, L., Peinado, M.: Bouncer: Securing software by blocking bad input. In: Proceedings, ACM Symposium on Operating Systems Principles (October 2007)
7. Dijkstra, E.W.: Guarded commands, non dterminacy, and formal derivation of programs. Communications of the ACM 18(8), 453–457 (1975)
8. Dijkstra, E.W.: A Discipline of Programming. Prentice-Hall, Englewood Cliffs (1976)
9. Flanagan, C., Qadeer, S.: Predicate abstraction for software verification. In: Proceedings, POPL 2002: The 29th SIGPLAN-SIGACT Symposium on Principles of Programming Languages (2002)
10. Flanagan, C., Saxe, J.B.: Avoiding exponential explosion: Generating compact verification conditions. In: Proceedings, Symposium on Principles of Programming Languages (2001)

11. Gannod, G.C., Cheng, B.H.C.: Strongest postcondition semantics as the formal basis for reverse engineering. In: Proceedings, Second Working Conference on Reverse Engineering, Toronto, Ontario, Canada, pp. 188–197 (1995)
12. Gries, D.: The Science of programming. Springer, Heidelberg (1981)
13. Grigore, R., Charles, J., Fairmichael, F., Kiniry, J.: Strongest postcondition of unstructured programs. In: Proceedings of the 11th International Workshop on Formal Techniques for Java-like Programs (2009)
14. Gulwani, S., Srivastava, S., Venkatesan, R.: Program analysis as constraint solving. In: Proceedings, PLDI 2008: ACM SIGPLAN 2008 Conference on Programming Languages and their Implementation, Tuscon, AZ (2008)
15. Hoare, C.A.R.: An axiomatic basis for computer programming. Communications of the ACM 12(10), 576–583 (1969)
16. Jager, I., Brumley, D.: Efficient directionless weakest preconditions. Technical Report CMU-CyLab-10-002, Carnegie Mellon University (February 2010)
17. Leino, K.R.M.: Efficient weakest preconditions. Information Processing Letters 93(6), 281–288 (2005)
18. Leino, K.R.: Towards reliable modular programs. Technical report, California Institute of Technology, Pasadena, CA (1995)
19. Louhichi, A., Mraihi, O., Jilani, L.L., Mili, A.: Invariant assertions, invariant relations and invariant functions. In: Proceedings, 2nd International Workshop on Invariant Generation, York, UK (2009)
20. Manna, Z.: A Mathematical Theory of Computation. McGraw-Hill, New York (1974)
21. Mili, A., Aharon, S., Nadkarni, C.: Mathematics for reasoning about loop. Science of Computer Programming, 989–1020 (2009)
22. Morgan, C.C.: Programming from Specifications. International Series in Computer Sciences. Prentice Hall, London (1998)
23. Necula, G.C.: Proof carrying code. In: Proceedings, Symposium on Principles of Programming Languages (1997)
24. Rauch, N.: Precondition generation for a Java subset. In: Proceedings, FM-TOOLS 2002: The Fifth Workshop on Tools for System Design and Verification, Reisensberg, Germany (2002)
25. von Oheimb, D.: Analyzing java in isabelle/hol: Formalization, type safety, and hoare logic. Technical report, Technische Universitaet Muenchen (2001)

A   Illustration: A Fibonacci Example

We consider the following program on natural variables i, u, z, v, where cN is a constant that we assume to be greater than or equal to 1, and we further assume that $i \leq cN$.

```
const int cN; int i, z, u, v;
while (i!=cN) {i=i+1; u=z; z=v+u; v=u;}
```

A.1   Invariant Relations

The invariant relations that we generate for this program, written in Mathematica notation, are as follows:

```
i<=iP && zP==z*Fibonacci[iP+1-i]+v*Fibonacci[iP-i] &&
vP==z*Fibonacci[iP-i]+v*Fibonacci[iP-i-1] &&
((i==cN && iP==i && zP==z && uP==u && vP==v) ||
 (i!=cN && Exists [{iPP,uPP,vPP,zPP} iPP!=cn &&
    (uP==zPP && vP==zPP && zP==vPP+zPP && iP=iPP+1)]))
```

Using this information, we compute the function of the loop, and find the following relation (where F is the Fibonacci function):

$$W = \{(s,s')|i = cN \wedge s' = s\}\cup$$

$$\left\{(s,s')\middle| \begin{array}{c} i \neq cN \wedge u' = v \times F(cN - i - 1) + z \times F(cN - i) \\ \wedge i' = cN \wedge v' = v \times F(cN - i - 1) + z \times F(cN - i) \\ \wedge z' = v \times F(cN - i) + z \times F(cN - i + 1) \end{array}\right\}.$$

The derivation of the invariant relations took 78 ms and the derivation of the loop's function from the invariant relations took 47 ms of CPU time.

A.2   Weakest Precondition

Using the function of the loop, computed above, we can compute the weakest precondition of the loop with respect to any postcondition. We take postcondition P defined by

$$Q = \{(s,s')|z = F(cN + 2)\},$$

and we find

$$P = \{(s,s')|i = cN \wedge z = F(cN + 2)\}\cup$$

$$\{(s,s')|i < cN \wedge F(cN + 2) = v \times F(cN - i) + z \times F(cN - i + 1)\}.$$

Note that this precondition can be satisfied by setting i to zero and setting v and z to 1 before the loop. The calculation of the weakest precondition took 15 ms of CPU time.

A.3 Postconditions

We can generate arbitrary (not necessarily strongest) postconditions from any invariant relation (not necessarily the smallest invariant relation). We consider the precondition

$$P = \{(s, s') | i = 0 \wedge v = 1 \wedge z = 1\}.$$

With invariant relation

$$R_0 = \{(s, s') | i \leq i' \wedge z' = z \times F(i' + 1 - i) + v \times F(i' - i)\},$$

We find the post condition

$$Q_0 = \{(s, s') | i = cN \wedge z = F(i) + F(i + 1)\}.$$

Mathematica takes 16 ms of CPU time to generate this (straightforward) postcondition; we are not sure why it fails to reduce $F(i) + F(i + 1)$ to $F(i + 2)$.

With invariant relation

$$R_1 = \{(s, s') | i \leq i' \wedge v' = z \times F(i' - i) + v \times F(i' - i - 1)\},$$

We find the post condition

$$Q_1 = \{(s, s') | i = cN \wedge v = F(i - 1) + F(i)\}.$$

Mathematica takes 16 ms of CPU time to generate this (straightforward) postcondition; we are not sure why it fails to reduce $F(i - 1) + F(i)$ to $F(i + 1)$.

To compute the strongest postcondition for precondition P, we use all the invariant relations we have derived, and we find:

$$Q_2 = \{(s, s') | i = cN \wedge u = F(cN + 1) \wedge v = F(cN + 1) \wedge z = F(cN + 2)\}.$$

Mathematica takes 63 ms of CPU time to compute this (simple) strongest postcondition.

A Framework for Instantiating Pedagogic mLearning Objects Applications

Paul Birevu Muyinda[1,*], Jude T. Lubega[1], Kathy Lynch[2], and Theo van der Weide[3]

[1] Department of Open and Distance Learning
Makerere University
P.O. Box 7062
Kampala, Uganda
mpbirevu@iace.mak.ac.ug, jlubega@cit.mak.ac.ug
[2] University of the Sunshine Coast
Maroochydore
Queensland, Australia
KLynch1@usc.edu.au
[3] Information Retrieval and Information Systems
Digital Security
Institute for Computing and Information Sciences
Radboud University Nijmegen, Netherlands
Th.P.vanderWeide@cs.ru.nl

Abstract. An increasing desire to port learning objects on mobile phones exists. However, there is limited understanding on how to pedagogically obtain access to and use learning objects on mobile phones. The limited understanding is caused by a dearth in frameworks for underpinning the development of mobile learning objects applications. Following Design Research methodology, we developed a Mobile Learning Objects Deployment and Utilisation Framework (*MoLODUF*) to address this problem. *MoLODUF* is composed of twelve dimensions, including: MLearning Objects, MLearning Device, MLearning Interface, MLearning Connectivity, MLearning Process, MLearning Costs, MLearning Resources, MLearning Context, MLearning Pedagogy, MLearning Ethics, MLearning Policy and MLearning Evaluation. The *MoLODUF* makes significant extensions to existing electronic and mLearning frameworks. It provides a competency set of guidelines for developing and/or evaluating applications for deploying and utilising learning objects on mobile phones.

Keywords: mLearning, mLearning Objects, Framework, mLearning Objects Framework, mLearning Objects Deployment, mLearning Objects Utilization, *MoLODUF*, mLearning Objects Applications, Makerere University.

1 Introduction

Of recent, learner mobility has been enabled by use of mobile devices in their learning processes. This process has been termed 'mobile learning' or 'mLearning' for short.

---

* Corresponding author.

A. Cerone and P. Pihlajasaari (Eds.): ICTAC 2011, LNCS 6916, pp. 194–217, 2011.

Due to its embryonic nature, the practice of mLearning is still insignificant. As such, mLearning requires increasing research attention to let it mature. Research related to mLearning development, practice and evaluation is necessary. More so, little research attention has been accorded to the development of frameworks for instantiating pedagogic application for mLearning objects deployment and utilisation.

In [32], a pedagogic framework for mLearning is given. The framework categorizes educational applications of mobile technologies into four types, namely: 1) high transactional distance socialized mLearning, 2) high transactional distance individualized mLearning, 3) low transactional distance socialized mLearning, and 4) low transactional distance individualized mLearning (p.1). Other researchers [4, 5, 13] have also developed frameworks for theorizing about mLearning. All these frameworks are aloof to issues necessary for instantiating and/or evaluating pedagogic mLearning objects applications and environments. In [21, 34, 43], research that specifically targets development of frameworks for guiding the instantiation of applications for obtaining access to and utilising learning objects on mobile devices is called for.

In this paper, we have developed a Mobile Learning Objects Deployment and Utilization Framework (*MoLODUF*). *MOLODUF* provides process steps for instantiating pedagogic applications that can enable learners in developing countries obtain access to and use learning objects, delivered over the Internet, regardless of their proximity to higher education institutions, through the use of mobile phones. *MoLODUF* can also be used to evaluate mLearning environments in developing countries. Developing countries are faced with a hoard of infrastructural constraints which inhibit conventional eLearning [11] but on the other hand, they are embracing mobile telephony at unprecedented rates [18]. For instance, by the end of 2009, the Compound Annual Growth Rate (CAGR) for mobile telephony stood at 28.7 Percent for Uganda, 92.7 Percent for South Africa, 63.4 Percent for Ghana and 66.7 Percent for Egypt [18]. Such impressive mobile telephony permeation statistics are good recipe for mLearning [28, 41].

MLearning is a subset of eLearning [5]. Research into mLearning should thus be informed by earlier developments in eLearning. To develop a mLearning framework, one has to draw from existing eLearning frameworks. In [13], [20] and others, eLearning frameworks have been developed. A review of these frameworks posts the Global eLearning Framework in [20] as being the most comprehensive of all eLearning frameworks. For this reason, the development of the *MoLODUF* was guided by the Global eLearning Framework in [20]. The Global eLearning Framework [20] suggests implementation of eight dimensions for meaningful eLearning to occur. These are the *Pedagogical, Technological, Interface Design, Ethical, Institutional, Evaluation, Management* and *Resource Support* dimensions. Through *Design Research* [2], the Global eLearning Framework in [20] was extended to include dimensions that allow for learner mobility.

Design research is; "... a systematic but flexible methodology aimed [at improving] educational practices through iterative analysis, design, development, and implementation, based on collaboration among researchers and practitioners in real-world settings, and leading to contextually-sensitive design principles and theories". [48, p.6]. The framework developed in this study provides important guidelines for developing and evaluating mLearning objects applications and environments. It was developed from dimensions adduced from answers to the following six research questions;

    i.   What are the current learner contexts, practices and prospects for the development and growth of mLearning?
    ii.   What learning processes can be accomplished through mLearning?
    iii. What kinds of learning objects can be used to service the identified learning processes?
    iv. What are the issues and factors to obtain access to and use learning objects in mLearning?
    v.   What are the major dimensions and sub-dimensions of the *MoLODUF*?
    vi. How is the *MoLODUF* related with existing mLearning and eLearning frameworks?

The rest of this paper is organized in six sections. In *Section 2*, we review the concept of mLearning, mLearning objects, traditional learning theories and mLearning, mLearning objects frameworks and the Global eLearning Framework in [20]. In *Section 3*, we detail the methodology we used to get the dimensions for the *MoLODUF* and in *Section 4* we present and discuss results of the study with a view of developing the *MoLODUF*. The process steps for instantiating or evaluating mLearning objects applications and environments are given in *Section 5* before drawing the conclusion and future work from the study in *Section 6*.

2 Related Work

2.1 Mobile Learning (MLearning)

Wireless tiny handheld devices are making it possible for learners not to be tethered in orchestrated fixed classrooms for learning purposes. Such "anytime", "anywhere" computing platforms have ignited a paradigm shift from eLearning models to mLearning models [25, p.1]. Hence increasing research attention is unfolding in the area of mLearning from industrialists, researchers, educationist and policy makers [3, 5, 7, 22, 25, 43, 45]. As a consequence, mLearning has been variously defined. While considering a mobile device as an enabler of learner mobility, [43] defined mLearning as learning which takes place at anytime in anyplace using a mobile device. As such, mLearning is more than just the use of mobile devices for learning but the ability for one to electronically learn on-the-go (ibid). In [32, p.79], "mobile learning refers to the use of mobile or wireless devices for the purpose of learning while on the move". A view earlier espoused by [5] emphasized that mLearning is eLearning which uses mobile devices to deliver learning. It is evident from the various definitions that mLearning is a form of eLearning which takes place at anytime in any place using wireless tiny handheld technologies.

    MLearning enables learner mobility and as such exposes a learner to different learning environments/contexts [3, 43, 45]. Research has shown that a learner acquires a rich learning experience when exposed to an environment with other learners that have different learning experiences acquired from different contexts [7, 22, 45]. MLearning enables high transactional socialized learning [32] in different contexts. Context relates to information which describes the situation of a learner in a given location [45]. Learning from one's known context increases ones ability to relate what is being learnt to the surroundings, thus increasing learning experience and flexibility in learning.

In mLearning, the accumulation of different learning experiences is brought about by the advantages inherent in mobile devices since they facilitate just-in-time and just-in-place interaction and collaboration in specific contexts through exchange of mLearning objects [45]. In developing countries, contextualized learning is oftentimes lost because of the tethered technologies usually employed in conventional eLearning [5, 26]. A blend of mLearning and eLearning would suffice to bridge the gaps that exist in each of these models. By implementing mLearning, on-the-go, contextualized and flexible learning can be introduced in eLearning. However, the extent of development and use of mLearning in different contexts is still embryonic [41, 45]. Likewise, the development of content for mobile devices cum mLearning objects is also still embryonic [3].

2.2 MLearning Objects

The concept of mLearning objects started way back in 2002 [36]. Since then, little research attention was realized until recently when the Internet became increasingly accessible via mobile devices. It is now possible to deliver content to learners via their mobile phones [3]. However, because of the limitations of mobile devices [15], the content has to be "leaner than content prepared for eLearning systems" [24, p.9]. The content has to be granular, sequenceable, reusable and contextualiseable [3, 45]. These requirements are a perfect match for the characteristics of a learning object. In [49], a learning object is defined as a digital educational resource/content which is granulated into units that are reusable, adaptive, and can be re-purposed to different learning styles, knowledge levels and conditions. In [38, p.2], a learning object is defined as "one or more files or 'chunks' of materials, which might consist of graphics, text, audio, animation, calculator, or interactive notebook, designed to be used as a standalone learning experience". Elsewhere, a learning object is "any entity, digital or non-digital, which can be used, reused or referenced during technology supported learning" [17, p.1].

Whereas resources are abundantly available for desktop computer learning objects, learning objects for mobile devices have to be granulated so that they are viewable and sequenceable on tiny screens via limited bandwidth pipes. Learning objects that can be accessed by and delivered on mobile devices are called mLearning objects [3, 30, 36, 42, 44, 50]. Also a mLearning object can be "an interactive software component, personalized and reusable in different contexts, designed to support an educational objective through a mobile device in situated learning or collaborative learning activities" [3, p.153]. This implies that a mLearning object is not only restricted to content on the mobile device but also the interface to the content or activities related to the use of the content or all of these. An SMS to learners providing them with a URL to content in the WWW could be regarded as a mLearning object.

Research into the development, deployment and utilization of mLearning objects is ongoing [3, 13, 30, 36, 42, 44, 50, 51]. This research is however skewed in favor of developed countries' contexts and is mainly still in trial or prototype phases. Since uptake of mobile phones in developing countries has surpassed industry analyst's predictions, it is important to undertake research into development of frameworks for instantiating applications for deploying and utilizing mLearning objects and evaluating mLearning in those contexts.

MLearning objects could take the form of carefully designed materials that take cognizance of mobile device limitations. However, according to [3], considering mobile devices limitations alone in the design of mLearning objects is being short sighted. Designing for learner personalization, collaboration and interaction completes the picture of a mLearning object (ibid). It means even considering the capability of the mobile device owned by the target learner. It also means taking into consideration exogenous factors that could have an influence on mLearning objects deployment and utilization.

MLearning objects could be delivered in traditional classroom environments, could be used for online performance support to guide a learner working through a task, could be used for augmenting classroom instructions and other learning materials and could be used as instructions for operating a given device [36]. The size, presentation and scope of a mLearning object is dependant upon the capacity of the mobile device in question and how a given institution conceptualizes a learning object. In [3], a software component is regarded as a mLearning object. In developing countries where learners own mainly low end mobile phones, text based learning objects are more feasible than resource heavy learning objects such as software modules [5].

Software modules extending academic and administrative support to students can be run on Java enabled mobile phones. Multiple choice quizzes, exams and lecture calendars, reminders for important events and frequent errors committed by students in a given subject can be developed as Java midlets and delivered on java enabled mobile phones [42]. The success of mLearning lies in the need to recognize the limitation of mobile devices so as to deploy learning objects onto them which address pedagogic assistance. Consequently, mLearning objects should be characterized by appropriate pedagogic values. Just like any other learning delivery model, mLearning is intended to contribute to student learning. Therefore, the pedagogic values inherent in mLearning should as well be underpinned by the traditional learning theories.

2.3 Traditional Learning Theories and MLearning

While learning, learners collaborate, interact and communicate with each other to accomplish group or individual learning activities. Collaboration, interaction and communication are functions that can be accomplished using mobile communication technologies. These learning tenets are inherent in the Social Constructivist Learning Theory [46], Conversational Learning Theory [33], Behaviorist Learning Theory [39], Learning and Teaching Support Theory [29], and Informal and Lifelong Learning Theory [10].

The Social Constructivist Learning Theory is an extension of the Constructivist Learning Theory [46]. The Constructivist Learning Theory recognizes learning as an active process in which a learner constructs new ideas or concepts based on his/her current and past knowledge. The Constructivist Learning Theory takes an individualistic angle that negates the fact that learning occurs in social settings. Consequently, critiques of the Constructivist Learning Theory such as [35] have argued for the Social Constructivist Learning Theory [46]. The Social Constructivist Learning Theory proponents posit that knowledge creation is shared rather than an individual experience. Their position is inline with that of [14] who contends that knowledge is constructed through interaction of a number of minds and not just one. Hence knowledge is a social product [35]. Tools and raw materials for creating this social product can arise from technologies that encourage interaction and collaboration. The mobile phone is a good example of such technologies. Mobile teleconferencing and SMS can scaffold learning in communities of practice (CoP). Members of a given CoP and their facilitator (s) may use collaborative and interactive tools afforded by mobile technologies to interplay their minds on topical issue so as to generate new knowledge. In this case collaboration and interaction afforded by mobile technologies become key tenets for social learning.

Another traditional learning theory which can underpin mLearning is the Conversational Learning Theory [33]. According to this theory, learning takes place if there is a continuous two-way conversation and interaction between the teacher and learner and amongst the learners themselves. Indeed, learning will take place if two parties participating in a conversation can understand each other. As [29, p.15] observed, learning will take place if "Person A [makes] sense of B's explanations of what B knows, and person B can make sense of A's explanation of what A knows". The Conversational Learning Theory emphasizes the need for continuous conversation with peers and the teacher or a device which subsumes the role of a teacher. Mobile technologies such as mobile phones are well suited at providing this conversational space.

Learning occurs if there is a force in the learning process which reinforces a relationship between a stimulus and a response. This exposition derives from the Behaviorist Learning Theory [39]. This theory emphasizes activities that promote learning as a change in learner's observable actions. In the case of mLearning, an SMS message, for example, invokes a stimulus that may lead to an action as a response. When a message is received on a learner's mobile phone, for example, the learner will be triggered to respond or provide feedback. The message received on the learner's phone presents a problem (stimulus) that requires the learner to solve through a response. In this case, the mobile phone which presented the problem reinforces the relationship between the problem (stimulus) and the solution (response). Moreover, once learners are conditioned to an SMS as a conveyor of educational related messages, they will be conditioned to immediately read them as they are delivered. This abets just-in-time and just-in-place learning.

Provision of learning is not just about providing content and learning activities to learners. It also involves a great deal of coordination of learners and resources [29]. Besides, access, communication and support are the three canonical uses of ICTs in education [5]. The Learning and Teaching Support Theory [29] emphasizes the need for support systems in learning and teaching. The support systems assist in the "coordination of learners and resources for learning activities" [29, p.11]. By using SMS and voice calls, a lecturer can be able to coordinate class activities and organize resources for the class. The lecturer can be able to support learners through reminders of learning events and provide URLs to reading materials. Learners can also support each other using their mobile phones.

As per the Informal and Lifelong Learning Theory [10] learning can take place at any time, in any place and at any age. According to this theory, "learning happens all of the time and is influenced both by our environment and the particular situations we are faced with" [29, p.17]. Informal and lifelong learning can occur as a result of intentional or accidental learning episodes that are orchestrated by exchange of information and knowledge [31]. Intentional learning episodes occur when learning is planned while accidental learning episodes occur from scenes which have no direct learning intentions, such as experiencing an accident, watching television, engaging in casual conversations, reading a newspapers or even listening to radio talk shows (ibid). It means that accidental learning can occur at anytime in anyplace. Learners carry their mobile phones at all times in anyplace, implying that they can be a source of information for accidental learning.

The above learning theories have been at the forefront of research for formulating mLearning and eLearning frameworks and models. Some of these frameworks and models are reviewed in *Sections 2.4* and *2.5* respectively.

2.4   The Global eLearning Framework

In [20], an eLearning framework addressing global eLearning issues is presented. The framework has eight (8) major dimensions that are instrumental to meaningful implementation of eLearning. These dimensions are presented in the framework shown in *Figure 1* below.

The eight (8) major dimensions in the Global eLearning Framework [20] presented in *Figure 1* below are: *Institutional, Pedagogical, Interface Design, Evaluation, Management, Resource Support, Ethical* and *Technological* dimensions. Each of the major dimensions consists of several sub-dimensions as is detailed below.

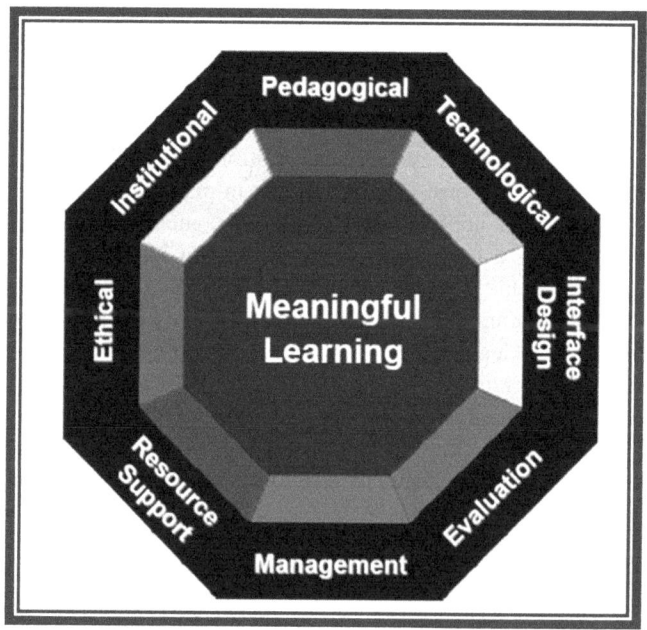

Fig. 1. Showing the Global eLearning Framework [20, p.1]

The *Institutional* dimension implores institutions wishing to adopt eLearning to examine their administrative, academic and student support affairs. In the *Administrative* sub-dimension, an institution should determine whether it is ready to offer eLearning or not. In the *Academic* sub-dimension, the institution should determine whether the quality of programs to be offered via eLearning meet quality standards similar to those offered through traditional programs. In the *Student Support* sub-dimension, the institution should determine that the instructors/administrators are available and ready to support the students during online learning.

The *Pedagogical* dimension consists of the *Content, Audience, Goal and Objectives, Medium, Design, Organization* and *Methods* sub-dimensions. The *Content* sub-dimension requires institutions to determine the type of content that can be delivered over different learning technologies. The *Audience* sub-dimension requires institutions to profile their learners. The *Goal and Objectives* sub-dimension requires institutions to provide clear expectations of what the learners are expected to achieve. The *Medium* sub-dimension requires institutions to determine whether they should utilize multiple media content (text, audio, video, graphics or a combination of these) in their delivery. The *Design* sub-dimension determines the role of the instructor. Is it more facilitative than didactic, more didactic than facilitative or a combination of both? The *Organization* sub-dimension is concerned with whether eLearning provides a sense of continuity in the learning process. It answers questions related to whether in eLearning, one unit of a lesson builds on the previous unit. The *Methods* sub-dimension asks whether the eLearning environment being proposed provides means and mechanisms for collaboration among learners and learners and their tutors and administrators.

In the *Interface Design* dimension are sub-dimensions such as *Page and Site Design, Content Design, Navigation, Accessibility* and *Usability Testing*. The *Page and Site Design* sub-dimension is concerned with the appearance of the web-pages to the learners. Pages must appear good and appealing to learners. The *Content Design* sub-dimension implores content developers to follow a 'one idea per paragraph' rule while designing content. The *Navigation* sub-dimension requires an eLearning program to provide structural aid or site map to guide learner's navigation. The *Accessibility* sub-dimension requires that an eLearning program should be designed in such a way as to be accessed by a wider user population. The *Usability Testing* sub-dimension requires that an eLearning program provides instant feedback to frequently asked questions in the program itself.

The *Evaluation* dimension considers the assessment of learners and evaluation of instruction and learning environment. The *Assessment of Learners* sub-dimension requires the eLearning program to have a mechanism for truly measuring the learner's learning achievements without having loopholes for cheating. The *Evaluation of Instruction* and *Learning Environment* sub-dimension requires that eLearning program should have mechanism to enable learners to evaluate the content, instructor, learning environment, learning resources, course design and technical support.

The *Management* dimension has two sub-dimensions, namely: *Content Development* and *Maintenance*. In *Content Development* sub-dimension, a requirement for a project support site for eLearning production team is placed. In the *Maintenance* sub-dimension, a requirement for constant and timely updates within the eLearning program is placed. The updates to the learners could be made through e-mail, announcement page, alert boxes, running footer added to a page or phone call. The *Resource Support* dimension has the *Online Support* and *Resources Support* sub-dimensions. The online support sub-dimension requires that eLearning should have troubleshooting expertise or helpdesk support. The *Resources* and *Support* sub-dimension requires the eLearning program to facilitate learning by providing examples of prior work of the student in digitized formats.

The *Ethical* dimension includes the *Social/Political Influence, Cultural Diversity, Bias, Geographical Diversity, Learner Diversity, Digital Divide, Etiquette* and *Legal Issues* sub-dimensions. In the *Social/Political Influence* sub-dimension, an institution should determine whether there are social/political forces that might curtail the implementation of eLearning. In the *Cultural Diversity* sub-dimension, counsel is provided to reduce or avoid the use of idioms, jargons, ambiguous words or cute humor and acronyms. The *Bias* sub-dimension requires that more than one view point be presented to a controversial issue. The *Geographical* sub-dimension requires that eLearning should be provided to learners located in different geographical areas and must therefore take care of different time zones so as to appropriately schedule synchronous communication. The *Learner Diversity* sub-dimension recognizes that there are slow, medium and fast learners. Therefore an eLearning system must take care of all these learners. The *Digital Divide* sub-dimension is important in that it considers access to technology. The system should not disadvantage learners who lack the necessary learning technologies. The digital divide issue should be considered while designing the eLearning content. The *Etiquette* sub-dimension provides guidance to learners on how to behave during eLearning. It provides the dos and don'ts in eLearning. The *Legal Issues* sub-dimension requires the eLearning program to seek permission to post on the Web, students' photographs and projects.

The *Technological* dimension has *Infrastructure Planning* and *Hardware and Software* sub-dimensions. *Infrastructure Planning* sub-dimension requires the institution to ascertain whether it has the necessary personnel who can assist learners to get onto eLearning. The *Hardware and Software* sub-dimension is important for profiling the necessary hardware and software requirements for the eLearning program (ibid).

The dimensions espoused in the Global eLearning Framework [20] do not cater for mLearning objects deployment and utilization on mobile phones. In the Global eLearning Framework [20] , no dimension(s) is/are included for enabling learning on-the-go. Using *Design Research* [2] approach, this paper has developed a global framework, underpinned by the Global eLearning Framework [20], for instantiating mLearning objects applications.

2.5   MLearning Objects Frameworks

Table 1 below provides a review of some mLearning objects frameworks and models. From *Table 1*, it is worth noting that the models and frameworks therein are not global in nature in as far as mLearning objects deployment and utilization is concerned. They address endogenous factors needed for mLearning objects adaptation and aggregation while putting less emphasis on exogenous factors that have potential influence on the deployment and utilization of learning objects on mobile phones.

Table 1. Some mLearning Objects Frameworks

Model/Framework	Characteristics/Features	Research Gap
Framework for flexible learning using mLearning objects [36]	- Uses the concept of learning objects to personalize learning. - It contextualizes learning	Does not model the limitations of mobile devices Does not consider cost dimension of mLearning Does not consider cognitive overload
Multi-dimensional framework for content adaptation [13]	- Adapts content to different device types and user profiles using five dimensions which include content, user, capability, connectivity and coordination dimensions	Lacks a dimension for learning objects usability and does not take into account mLearning objects acquisition issues. Limits pedagogy to content only yet mLearning pedagogy should be an overarching issue in all aspects of mLearning. Leaves out mLearning policy and strategy.
MLearning content hoarding model [44]	- Picks content from the WWW which it transforms into mobile formats and prepares it for online and offline sessions - Uses PDAs as the mobile devices - Caters for intermittency in network connections - Hoards content in the PDA's memory for use during offline sessions	Whereas the model addresses intermittency in network condition, something common in developing countries, memory limitations on low and mid range mobile phones makes this model inapplicable in developing countries Has no costs dimension
J2ME midlets/learning objects access model [42]	- A model for offering support services to students in a blended learning environment. - Support services are offered using Java midlets because they offer offline access as opposed to WAP pages - Midlets are accessible either via mobile devices or PCs	No device and learner profiling is evident in the model. Though they offer pedagogic support the midlets are not interactive, collaborative and contextualized.
Adaptive framework for aggregating mLearning objects [50]	- Provides an approach for gathering feasible eLearning content and adapting it for mobile devices - The framework profiles and contextualizes the learner and the mobile device	The model assumes one source of learning content – WWW. It is also concerned more with content transformation than deployment and utilization
Push and pull framework for mLearning objects delivery [27]	- Integrates mobile connectivity with eLearning - Is based on the push and pull model for content delivery - Supports pedagogic approaches for content personalization and collaboration	Does not profile device and network conditions
Adaptive mLearning environment [30]	- Provides an adaptive self-learning environment - It is motivated by the need to use learning objects in mobile and PC based environments - Supports learner adaptation and offline learning using mobile phones - Takes SCORM 2004 to the mobile arena	Limits the source of learning objects only to SCORM based LMS. The mobile web, WWW, enterprise databases, repositories are other sources for learning objects. No pedagogic agents are evident in the model. Also there is no profiling of network condition in the model
Computational models for mLearning objects [3]	- A mLearning object is not simply that which has been adapted for display on a tiny screen of the mobile phone. Rather, it is one with the following characteristics: • Ability to be displayed on the tiny screens • Ability to be personalized • Ability to inculcate collaboration and interaction - Offers computational models based on learning objects personalization, collaboration and interaction	The models lack a component for profiling network conditions, an aspect which is of importance in mLearning in developing countries

3 Methodology

MoLODUF aims at widening the dissemination of knowledge through the mobile phone. Knowledge is a social product [35]. Research into the design, development and evaluation of artifacts for disseminating knowledge is socially responsible [37]. The social responsibility emanates from the belief that such research addresses the needs and aspiration of the masses pursuing an education. It implies that research approaches to be employed in such socially responsible studies must ensure the participation of the masses involved in the knowledge dissemination artifacts design, development, evaluation and use. Since *MoLODUF* was aimed at widening knowledge dissemination; it implies that its development was socially responsible.

Design Research has been fronted as the most suitable approach/methodology for accomplishing socially responsible studies [2, 8, 16, 37, 48]. *Design Research* combines research, design and practice [48] and its outputs include: constructs, models, methods/frameworks, instantiations and better theories [2]. "Constructs are vocabularies or symbols used to define a problem or solution while models are abstractions and representations of the problem or solution and methods/frameworks are algorithms and practices for implementing the artifact. Instantiations are implementations and prototype systems" [16, p.2]. Constructs provide building blocks for models and frameworks. A framework is a supporting structure around which something can be built [ibid]. *MoLODUF* was built following the *Design Research* methodology.

Design Research methodology is an iterative process for developing or evaluating artifacts. It is accomplished through five process steps shown in *Figure 2* below.

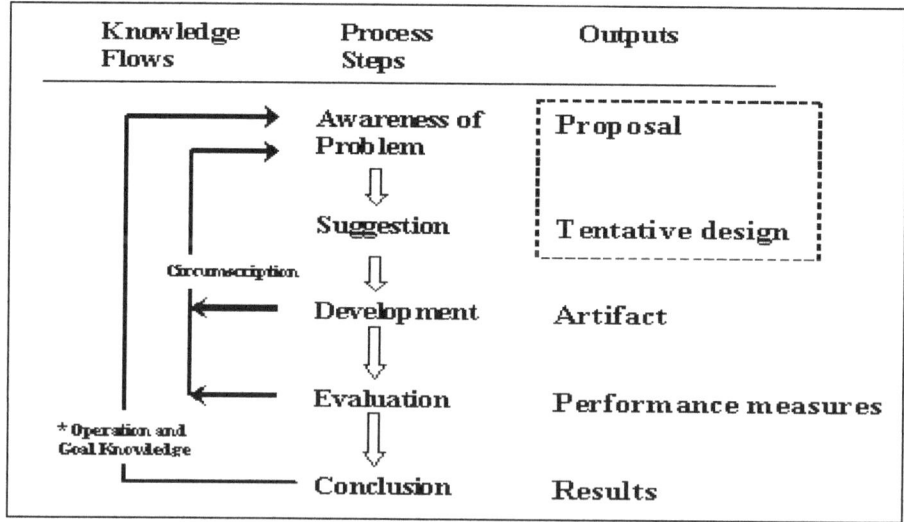

Fig. 2. Showing the *Design Research* Methodology [2, p.13]

The five process steps of *Design Research* as depicted in *Figure 2* above were followed in the development of the *MoLODUF*. The process steps are: the *Awareness of the Problem, Suggestion, Development, Evaluation* and *Conclusion*. At the *Awareness of the Problem* process step, a survey of 446 learners at Makerere University in Uganda was undertaken. The learners were selected using multi-stage sampling method involving cluster sampling at stage one and stratified random sampling at stage two. The learners were distributed as 48.9 Percent (n=218) distance learners and 51.1 Percent (n=228) campus-based learners. Males constituted 62.3 Percent while 37.7 Percent were female. Their minimum age was 18 while the maximum age was 46 with a mean age of 24.7 and mode of 21. The minimum age of 18 was recorded from amongst campus-based learners while the maximum age of 46 was recorded from distance learners. Forty three Percent of the learners surveyed were pursuing science related disciplines while 57.0 Percent were pursuing humanities related disciplines. Learners were drawn from all years of study, including: first year (15.9 Percent), second year (32.3 Percent), third year (35.2 Percent) and fourth year (16.6 Percent). Most of the learners were unemployed (67.5 Percent) and not married (79.8 Percent). They joined university after attaining 'A' Level (70.2 Percent), diploma (26.9 Percent), grade III teacher certificate (1.1 Percent), degree (1.1 Percent) or other qualifications (0.7 Percent).

A semi-structured, self-administered questionnaire was used to capture data. The survey consisted of open and close ended questions. The questionnaire collected data on mLearning context, mLearning activities, mLearning devices and technologies, mLearning resources, mLearning objects, mLearning institutional issues and mLearning environmental issues.

The survey results were triangulated with results from literature review and interviews held with key eLearning and mLearning stakeholders drawn from across Africa.

The *Awareness of the Problem* process step was useful for gathering requirements for suggesting and developing the *MoLODUF* during the *Suggestion* and *Development* process steps respectively. Using deductive reasoning, dimensions and sub-dimensions for constructing the *MoLODUF* were generated from the requirements. In the *Evaluation* process step the *MoLODUF* was compared with existing mLearning and eLearning frameworks with a view of establishing the novelty in our research. In the *Conclusion* process step, we drew conclusions from the novelty revealed in the *Evaluation* process step. The process of suggesting, developing and evaluating the *MoLODUF* and drawing conclusions from it resulted in new knowledge which was used in refining requirements for further development of the *MoLODUF*.

4 Results and Discussions

The results are presented and discussed following the six research questions formulated in this study and within the Design Research [2] framework.

4.1 Raising Awareness of the Problem and Making Suggestions for *MoLODUF* Dimensions

This *Section* is underpinned by the *Awareness of the Problem* and *Suggestion* process steps of Design Research methodology. These process steps were used to gather requirements for deducing dimensions and sub-dimensions for constructing the *MoLODUF*. The *Section* provides answers to four of the six research questions in this study, namely:

i.   What are the current learner contexts, practices and prospects for the development and growth of mLearning?
ii. What learning processes can be accomplished through mLearning?
iii. What kinds of learning objects can be used to service the identified learning processes?
iv. What are the issues and factors to obtain access to and use learning objects in mLearning?

Current Learner Contexts, Practices and Prospects for the Development and Growth of MLearning. Distance and campus-based learners faced similar contextual challenges and opportunities in as far as ICTs for learning was concerned. Mobile connectivity was available to all distance and campus-based learners ($p=0.062$). Urban areas were not a preserve for campus-based learners alone but they hosted distance learners as well ($p=0.532$). All the learners faced similar availability or intermittence in power supply ($p=0.199$) and Internet connectivity ($p=0.329$). This confirms the conclusion in [11] that developing countries of Africa are faced with a multitude of contextual constraints that undermine the development and growth of eLearning. Studies have indicated that mLearning has the potential to defy the odds that inhibit conventional eLearning [28]. For instance, there was no significant association between power supply and mobile network connectivity ($p=0.301$), yet Internet connectivity, which powers eLearning, was highly significantly associated ($p=0.000$) with availability of power supply. The implication in these findings is that there is need for equal planning for educational technologies aimed at enhancing learning amongst all learners in all learning contexts, which calls for a *mLearning Context* dimension in a framework for mLearning.

MLearning was practiced in a few instances, albeit inadvertently. In the majority of instances, it was established that learners could not be able to tell whether placing a call or text message for the purposes of learning or education constituted mLearning. These findings are not surprising because in [43], the infancy of mLearning is reiterated. MLearning just like any other infant field of study is likely to face limited epistemology. Consequently, the limited epistemology of mLearning has resulted into its limited practice.

Where mLearning existed, it was mainly practiced through text and audio learning objects in trial and pilot projects for collaborative and interactive learning. MLearning mainly occurred in a push nature with limited bi-directional synchronous and asynchronous collaboration and interaction through text messaging. The one way use of text messages was mainly due to the limitations imposed by low end mobile phones. Also, the use of text messaging in a push fashion was brought about by the high cost of using other media such as video and the prevalence of low end mobile phones which were owned by the majority (68.0 Percent) of learners. Low end mobile phones limitations curtail push and pull synchronous text messaging [15].

Through voice calls, the study showed that pull and push synchronous and asynchronous audio communication was practiced and preferred on low end mobile phones because voice calls imposed no character length limitations inherent in text messages. In [6] and [12], the use of audio mLearning objects on low end mobile phones is reported. In the mLearning project in [6], learners learn how to pronounce and spell English words by listening in to a word from the Hadeda system before being required to type it out. If a learner correctly types the word, the system congratulates him/her, otherwise it gives him/her the correct spelling. In the mLearning project in [12], a mobile audio-wikipedia system is reported. In this system, learners use their mobile phones to dial into it and listen to a definition of a given word. If the definition does not exist, the learner is given a chance to dictate a definition to the system.

Whereas audio learning objects for low end mobile phones were in use, earlier studies [4, 5, 26] on the practice of mLearning in Africa showed that text messaging was the most prevalent way of deploying and utilising learning objects in mLearning. In a report for the Commonwealth of Learning on the use of mobile phones for open schooling, [41] enumerated a number of innovative mLearning projects in which text messaging was the key technology for learning objects deployment and utilisation. One of such projects is the mobile research supervision initiative in Uganda in which lecturers and distance learning students interact with each other for the purpose of accomplishing field research activities. Another project is Dr. Math on Mxit, for collaborative learning in mathematics using instant text messaging [41].

All the projects discussed above considered the capabilities of learners' mobile device and the kind of learning objects that could be deployed and utilised on them. There must therefore be dimensions in the *MoLODUF* for *mLearning Devices* and *mLearning Objects*.

Through text and audio based mLearning objects, 77.7 Percent of the learners were able to collaboratively and interactively work on assignments and receive administrative and academic support. Learner support is one of the three imperatives of ICTs in education [5]. The other two being access to content and communication (ibid). When learners are adequately supported, a lot of their time is freed to participate in other learning activities. They also feel cared for and are motivated to learn. For distance learners who are separated by time and space [1, 7, 43, 47], collaborative and interactive learning can be an avenue for reducing the loneliness usually associated with distance learning. In so doing the 'distance' amongst the distance learners themselves and between the distance learners and their university can be bridged. In the learner support process, mLearning objects were used by learners, lecturers and university administrators which imply the need for *mLearning Pedagogy* dimension for profiling the *mLearning Object Users*.

The study revealed a number of prospects for the development and growth of mLearning. The prospects lay in the existence of possible learning activities that could be ported onto mLearning. MLearning was found to be suitable for out-of-classroom direct learning activities or activities meant to plan and support direct learning activities. While outside the classroom, learners participated in collaborative and interactive learning (41.0 Percent), co-curricular/extra-curricula activities (20.0 Percent), independent research (16.0 Percent), completed theoretical, practical and field courseworks and assignments (8.0 Percent), watched/listened to educative and entertaining music, news and movies (6.0 Percent), engaged in work related activities

(4 Percent), consulted their lecturers (7.0 Percent), acquainted themselves with the university environment (1.0 Percent) and took computer lessons (1.0 Percent). All these learning activities can be variously supported through mLearning to accomplish various learning processes. This calls for a *mLearning Processes* dimension in the *MoLODUF*.

Even if out-of-classroom learning activities can be ported on mobile phones, the tiny mobile phone screen and keyboard can be uncomforting to the mLearning object user. When asked to provide a view on using mobile phones to learn, one of the respondents said, "if it were not for the tiny screen and keyboard of my mobile phone, I would use it to learn". This calls for strategies to mitigate mobile phone limitations. One way could be blending mLearning devices with other eLearning devices and regularly evaluating the learning comfort afforded by the blend with the view of mitigating any discomfort. This suggests the need for a *mLearning Evaluation* dimension in the *MoLODUF*.

MLearning Processes. While considering learning activities that learners participated in while outside the classroom environment, the need to consider learning processes in mLearning was unearthed. Learning processes are value addition learning activities [9]. Since mLearning is of great value to out-of-classroom learning activities, it presents significant benefits to distance learning processes or learners on-the-go with limited access to web-based computers. From traditional learning theories reviewed in this study [10, 29, 33, 39, 46], learning processes related to *Co-Creation of New Knowledge, Knowledge Sharing, Collaborative and Interactive Learning, Reflective Learning, Problem-Based Learning, Academic and Administrative Support* and *Communication/Information Exchange* can be supported through mLearning.

Learning Objects for MLearning Processes. The study revealed that different mLearning objects could be used to service different mLearning processes identified above. MLearning objects could take the form of text messages, voice calls, MMSs, audio and video podcasts, Wapsites, software modules/components or games [3, 5, 19, 42]. The ability to deploy and utilize any of the aforementioned mLearning objects depends on financial, human and technological resources available, costs associated, constraints placed on mobile technologies, the learning processes in question, management/institutional policies and ethical considerations. Within the context of developing countries, text and audio based learning objects were found to be more feasible than any other learning objects. This discussion presents a need for profiling mLearning objects, hence the need for a *mLearning Objects* dimension in the *MoLODUF*. Other dimensions that can be adduced from these results include: *mLearning Processes, mLearning Ethics, mLearning Cost, mLearning Resources, mLearning Device* and *mLearning Policy*.

Issues and Factors for Obtaining Access to and Utilizing MLearning Objects. There are three design issues that can enable easy access to learning objects [40]. These include: designing for device independence, designing for multiple media content and allowing learners to control moving content [ibid]. In addition to these three issues, this research has established that mobile network connectivity/networking technology and intellectual property rights issues are also important factors to consider while obtaining access to learning objects in mLearning.

The interface of the mLearning device is yet another important factor to consider. The cultural appropriateness of using a learning object, the pedagogy chosen by the institution, the relationship between mLearning devices with other delivery devices and the cost of mLearning among others are important issues and factors for deploying and utilizing learning objects on mobile devices. These factors calls for *mLearning Objects, mLearning Connectivity, mLearning Ethics, mLearning Resources, mLearning Cost* and *mLearning Interface* dimensions in the *MoLODUF*.

4.2 Developing the *MoLODUF*

This *Section* is underpinned by the *Development* process step of Design Research methodology. It answers the research question - What are the major dimensions and sub-dimensions of the *MoLODUF*? In the *Development* process step, artifacts are developed from constructs adduced from the *Suggestion* process step [2]. From the awareness raised and suggestions made in *Section 4.1* above, twelve (12) major dimensions are apparent. These are: *mLearning Cost, mLearning Processes, mLearning Objects, mLearning Devices, mLearning Resources, mLearning Connectivity, mLearning Pedagogy, mLearning Interface, mLearning Evaluation, mLearning Ethics, mLearning Policy* and *mLearning Context* dimensions. These major dimensions are explained below and shown with their respective sub-dimensions in *Table 2* below.

MLearning Cost **Dimension.** The study has revealed that mLearning was practiced mainly in a push nature with limited bi-directional synchronous and asynchronous interaction because of its high cost. Mitigation of mLearning costs is therefore vital for successful mLearning. The *mLearning Costs* dimension is the 'midrib' or 'backbone' in the *MoLODUF*. For effective deployment and utilisation of learning objects in mLearning, there must be mechanisms to mitigate the usually high cost of mLearning. Thus there is need to determine the unit cost of mLearning and put in place a mLearning cost sustainability model.

MLearning Processes **Dimension.** *MLearning Processes* provide all the learning and teaching models commensurate with the limitations of mobile devices [43]. This research has adduced seven (7) learning processes that can be supported using mLearning. These are: *Co-Creation of New Knowledge, Knowledge Sharing, Collaboration and Interaction, Reflective Learning, Problem-Based Learning, Academic* and *Administrative Support* and *Communication/Information Exchange.* Consequently institutions wishing to effectively deploy and utilize learning objects in mLearning should first profile existing learning processes with the aim of determining those which are appropriate for mLearning. Learning processes can be abducted from the different learning activities partaken of by the learners especially when they are on-the-move or outside the classroom learning environment.

MLearning Objects **Dimension.** This dimension is responsible for modeling the learning objects for deploying and utilizing on mobile devices. It should have sub-dimensions for *mLearning Objects Organization, mLearning Objects Granulation, mLearning Objects Media Types, mLearning Objects Accessibility, mLearning Objects Utilization, mLearning Objects Pedagogy, mLearning Objects Repository* and *mLearning Objects Brokering.* The first three sub-dimensions are also available in the multi-dimensional framework for content adaptation [13].

MLearning Devices Dimension. This dimension profiles the mobile devices being used in mLearning objects deployment and utilization. By profiling the mobile devices in use, their *Generation Order, Properties, Capabilities* and *Limitations* can be determined and mitigated. Mobile devices limitations can constrain mLearning [15], hence they should be mitigated by adopting a device blend.

MLearning Resources Dimension. The *mLearning Resources* dimension has three sub-dimensions which are necessary for the successful implementation of mLearning, namely: *Infrastructural, Human* and *Financial Resources* sub-dimensions. The infrastructural resources needed for mLearning are: servers, fiber optic backbones, computers, fast Internet connectivity, e-mail, high end mobile phones, mobile network connectivity, learning management systems, local area networks (wired and wireless) and mobile applications development software. The human resources needed for mLearning are: flexible managers, administrators, lecturers and students willing to experiment with innovations in core educational practices. Other vital mLearning human resources are: mLearning researchers and systems analysts, mobile applications programmers, technicians, instructional and graphic designers, and content developers. The availability of financial resources is central for the acquisition, installation and maintenance of all the other mLearning resources. Financial resources are also necessary for sustaining mLearning costs. Therefore a budget vote for mLearning is a must for institutions wishing to deploy and utilize learning objects on mobile phones.

Table 2. MLearning Objects Deployment and Utilization Framework (*MoLODUF*)

1. *MLearning Costs*	5. *MLearning Resources*	9. *MLearning Evaluation*
• MLearning Unit Cost • MLearning Cost Sustainability Plan	• Infrastructural Resources • Human Resources • Financial Resources	• MCQ Quizzes • Learning Comfort • Learning Equity • MLearning Object Deployment Feedback
2. *MLearning Processes*	6. *MLearning Connectivity*	10. *MLearning Ethics*
• Co-creation of New Knowledge • Knowledge Sharing • Collaboration and Interaction • Reflective Learning • Problem-Based Learning • Academic & Administrative Support • Communication/Information Exchange	• Mobile Connectivity State • Mobile Networking Technology • Mobile Network Service Providers • Bandwidth	• Cognitive Overload • Cultural Appropriateness • Privacy and Security
3. *MLearning Objects*	7. *MLearning Pedagogy*	11. *MLearning Policy*
• MLearning Objects Organization • MLearning Objects Granulation • MLearning Objects Media Types • MLearning Objects Accessibility • MLearning Objects Usability • MLearning Objects Pedagogy • MLearning Objects Repository • MLearning Objects Brokering	• MLearning Objects User Role • MLearning Objects User Profile • MLearning Objects User Education	• Institutional Policies • Government Policies
4. *MLearning Devices*	8. *MLearning Interface*	12. *MLearning Context*
• Generation Order • Mobile Device Property • Capability • Limitations	• Mobile Device Interface • PC Interface	• MLearning Propellers • MLearning Inhibitors • Learning Environment

MLearning Connectivity **Dimension.** Internet and mobile network connectivity are not always available to all the learners. Also, the ability to deploy and utilize a given media type of a learning object depends not only on the capability of the mobile phone but also on the mobile networking technology at hand. Before embarking on any mLearning instance, it is important to profile the *Mobile Connectivity* State, *Mobile Networking Technology, Mobile Service Providers* and *Bandwidth* available to learners.

MLearning Pedagogy **Dimension.** The *mLearning Pedagogy* dimension profiles the users of mLearning objects. To be able to do so, it profiles the *mLearning Objects User Role, Profile* and *Education*. The actors in mLearning can be learners, lecturers or administrators. Their respective roles must be known before hand so as to deploy the right learning object to the right user. A user profile in terms of learning history, preferences, style and motivation for learning is vital for brokering the right learning objects. For users to be able to effectively utilize the learning objects, mobile phone user education is important.

MLearning Interface **Dimension.** In order to increase learning comfort in mLearning, mLearning devices should be blended with conventional eLearning devices. This implies that interfaces for mLearning are not strictly tied to *Mobile Devices Interfaces* alone. A blended approach means that mLearning objects could as well be deployed and utilised on *PC Interfaces*. This has learning objects design implication in the sense that a learning object should be designed with interoperability capability between mobile devices (*Mobile Device Interface* sub-dimension) and PCs (*PC Interface* sub-dimension).

MLearning Evaluation **Dimension.** "Evaluation is a reflective learning process" [23, p.43]. There must be mechanisms in a mLearning system for self evaluation. The *MoLODUF* has an *mLearning Evaluation* dimension whose functions are to establish: whether a mLearning objects user has understood the content in the object (using *MCQ Quizzes* sub-dimension), whether there is learning comfort in mLearning (using *Learning Comfort* sub-dimension), whether there is learning equity in mLearning (using *Learning Equity* sub-dimension) and whether a deployed learning object actually reached its intended recipients (using *mLearning Object Deployment Feedback* sub-dimension).

MLearning Ethics **Dimension.** This dimension is responsible for spelling out the mLearning etiquettes in a particular organization. It is responsible for protecting mLearning providers from unethical behaviors that may arise from the use of mLearning. It should be responsible for saving mLearning object users from cognitive overloads arising from multiple mLearning objects use and requests. It therefore spells out mechanisms for handling *Cognitive Overload, Culturally Inappropriate* communications and *Privacy* and *Security* of information being communicated.

MLearning Policy **Dimension.** This dimension consists of two sub-dimensions, namely: *Institutional Policies* and *Government Policies*. Institutional policies can curtail or propel the development and growth of mLearning. A favorable mLearning policy is therefore necessary. Likewise, if a government has an eLearning policy which takes cognizance of all learning platforms including mLearning, then mLearning will get support. The policies should be able to give guidelines and strategies for using mLearning in universities and other institutions of learning. The *mLearning Policy* dimension ensures that favorable mLearning policies, strategies, regulations and guidelines are put in place. Policies will inform the mLearning processes and therefore guide all mLearning activities in an institution. They will even provide regulations on the mobile devices to be used for mLearning and set aside resources for sustaining mLearning.

MLearning Context **Dimension.** In this study, it was established that learners lived and operated in different contexts. According to [45], learning context is an important factor in mLearning. Therefore the *MoLODUF* should have a *mLearning Context* dimension aimed at profiling mLearners' learning contexts. In so doing, *mLearning Propellers* can be established and exploited. Also, *mLearning Inhibitors* can be known and mitigated. The *Learning Environment* where the learner is based must also be profiled to determine the noise levels of the learner's usual learning environment, mobile connectivity in the area, availability of resources such as desktop computers and power connectivity and so on. The environment should be favorable for mLearning or if not, attempts must be made to make it favorable.

4.3   Evaluating the *MoLODUF*

This *Section* is underpinned by the *Evaluation* process step of *Design Research* methodology. It answers the research question - How is the *MoLODUF* related with existing key eLearning frameworks? Therefore the *MoLODUF* was evaluated by

Table 3. Summary Comparison of *MoLODUF* with mLearning and eLearning Frameworks

Frameworks	mLearning Cost	mLearning Resources	mLearning Processes	mLearning Evaluation	mLearning Connectivity	mLearning Devices	mLearning Interface	mLearning Pedagogy	mLearning Policy	mLearning Objects	mLearning Context	mLearning Ethics	Coordination
MoLODUF													
Global eLearning Framework [20]													
Multi-dimensional Framework for Content Adaptation [13]													
Framework for Flexible Learning Using mLearning Objects [36]													
Framework for Personalized mLearning Content [51]													
mLearning Content Hoarding Framework [44]													
Adaptive Framework for Aggregating mLearning Objects [50]													
Push and Pull Framework for mLearning Objects [27]													
Adaptive mLearning Environments [30]													
Computational Models for mLearning Objects [3]													

comparing it with existing mLearning and eLearning Frameworks in [3, 13, 20, 27, 30, 36, 44, 50, 51]. The differences and similarities of these frameworks with respect to the *MoLODUF* dimensions are presented in *Table 3* below.

A shaded box in the dimensions column indicates the existence of the corresponding dimension in the respective framework on the right. In the *Table*, it can be seen that existing mLearning frameworks do not have dimensions for *mLearning Costs, mLearning Processes, mLearning Evaluation, mLearning Policy* and *mLearning Ethics*. All the aforementioned dimensions are present in the *MoLODUF*. When the *MoLODUF* is compared with the Global eLearning Framework in [20], it can be deduced that the *mLearning Cost, mLearning Processes, mLearning Objects* and *mLearning Context* dimensions are *MoLODUF's* extension to that framework. The *Coordination* and *mLearning Pedagogy* dimensions are present in all frameworks. The *MoLODUF* has extended exiting mLearning frameworks with the *mLearning Costs, mLearning Processes, mLearning Evaluation, mLearning Policy* and *mLearning Ethics* dimensions. In the conventional eLearning arena, *MoLODUF* has contributed towards integrating mLearning with eLearning by suggesting the addition of *mLearning Cost, mLearning Processes, mLearning Objects* and *mLearning Context* dimensions into the Global eLearning Framework in [20].

5   Instantiating MLearning Objects Deployment and Utilization Applications

Whereas the *MoLODUF* process steps are not necessarily sequential in nature, we suggest that implementation of the *MoLODUF* guidelines/dimensions be based on the loose sequence provided in the process steps in *Figure 3* below.

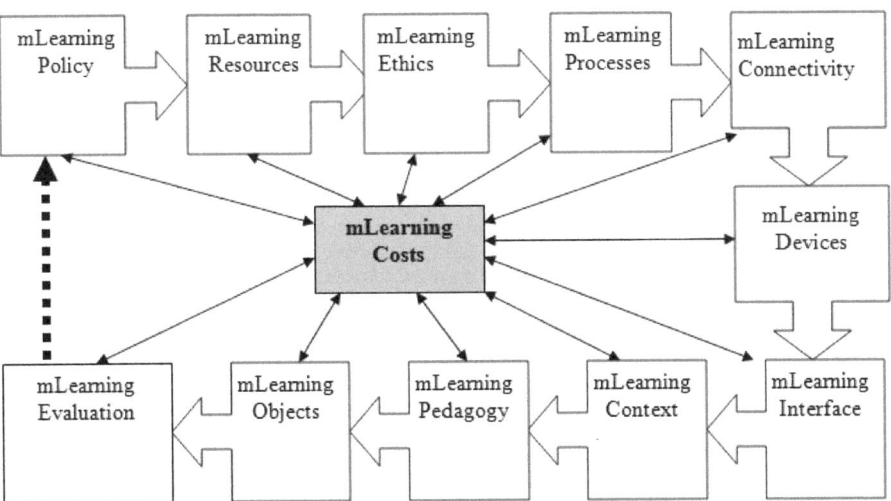

Fig. 3. Showing the Process Steps for Instantiating mLearning Applications using the *MoLODUF*

Loosely speaking, organizations wishing to create applications for deploying and utilizing learning objects on mobile phones should implement the guidelines/dimensions given in the *MoLODUF* dimensions following the sequence provided in *Figure 3* above. However, as can be seen in the *Figure*, mLearning costs present a central challenge that must be dealt with at all process steps. Further, sustainable deployment and utilization of mLearning objects will only be achieved if there is an appropriate mLearning policy. This is the reason why an mLearning policy must be put in place first before implementing any other dimension. Though formative mLearning evaluation is important to evaluate the mLearning applications development process, *Figure 3* above suggests the need for summative evaluation to measure the learning outcomes, learning comfort and learning equity emanating from the learning objects deployed and utilized by any mLearning application. *Figure 3* further shows that as a result of an mLearning summative evaluation, recommendation can be made to revise the mLearning policy and so on.

6 Conclusion and Future Work

This Section was underpinned by the *Conclusion* process step of Research Design methodology. The *MoLODUF* provides a competence set of dimensions and sub-dimensions for instantiating and/or evaluating mLearning objects applications and/or environments. By introducing four mobility dimensions, namely: *mLearning Cost, mLearning Processes, mLearning Objects* and *mLearning Context* into the Global eLearning Framework in [20], the *MoLODUF* provides a method for integrating mLearning with conventional eLearning. It also enhances research into adoption and implementation of mLearning. Further, *MoLODUF* offers guidelines for the pedagogic use of mobile phones. Future work emanating from this study include: a practical implementation of the *MoLODUF*, developing mLearning cost sustainability model and mobile phones limitation mitigation plan.

Acknowledgement. This work was part of the corresponding authors PhD research. Many thanks go to Makerere University, SIDA/SAREC and NUFFIC for funding this PhD Project.

References

1. Aderinoye, A.R., Ojokheta, O.K., Olojede, A.A.: Integrating Mobile Learning into Nomadic Education Programmes in Nigeria: Issues and perspectives. The International Review of Research in Open and Distance Learning 8(2), 1–17 (2007)
2. Association of Information Systems: Design Research in Information Systems (2007), http://www.isworld.org/Researchdesign/drisISworld.htm
3. Ayala, G., Castillo, S.: Towards Computational Models for Mobile Learning Objects. In: The Fifth IEEE International Conference on Wireless, Mobile, and Ubiquitous Technology in Education (WMTE 2005), Tokushima, Japan, March 23-26 (2008)
4. Barker, A., Krull, G., Mallinson, B.: A proposed Theoretical Model for M-Learning Adoption in Developing Countries. In: The 4th World conference on m-learning (MLearn 2005), Cape Town, SA, October 25-28 (2005)

5. Brown, H.T.: Towards a Model for m-Learning in Africa. International Journal on E-learning 4(3), 299–315 (2005)
6. Butgereit, L., Botha, A.: Hadeda: The Noisy Way to Practice Spelling Vocabulary using a Cell Phone. In: The IST-Africa 2009 Conference, Kampala, Uganda, May 6-8 (2009)
7. Caudill, G.J.: The Growth of m-Learning and the Growth of Mobile Computing: Parallel developments. The International Review of Research in Open and Distance Learning 8(2), 1–13 (2007)
8. Design-based research collective: Design-Based Research: An Emerging Paradigm for Educational Inquiry. Educational Researcher 32(1), 5–8 (2003)
9. Doos, M., Wilhelmson, L., Backlund, T., Dixon, N.: Functioning at the edge of knowledge. A study of learning processes in new product development. Journal of Workplace Learning 17(8), 481–492 (2005)
10. Eraut, M.: Non-formal learning, implicit learning and tacit knowledge in professional work. In: The Necessity of Informal Learning. The Policy Press, Bristol (2000)
11. Farrell, G., Isaacs, S.: Survey of ICT and Education in Africa. A Summary Report Based on 53 Country Surveys (2007),
    http://akgul.bcc.bilkent.edu.tr/egitim/ict-africa-survey.pdf
12. Ford, M., Botha, A.: MobiLED – Mobile-Led and Leading via Mobile. In: The IST-Africa 2009 Conference, Kampala, Uganda, May 6-8 (2009)
13. Goh, T., Kinshuk, D.: Getting Ready for Mobile Learning - Adaptation Perspectives. Journal of Educational Multimedia and Hypermedia 15(2), 175–198 (2006)
14. Goodman, N.: Mathematics as an objective science. In: Tymoezko, T. (ed.) New Directions in the Philosophy of Mathematics, pp. 79–94. Barkhauser, Boston (1986)
15. Grant, J., Lynch, K., Fisher, J.: Looks Can Cost; Especially On A Small Screen. In: The 7th IFIP International Conference on e-Business, e-Services, and e-Society (I3E 2007), Wuhan, China, October 10-12 (2007)
16. Hevner, R.A., March, T.S., Park, J., Ram, S.: Design Science in Information Systems research. MIS Quarterly 28(1), 75–105 (2004)
17. IEEE: WG12: Learning Object Metadata, http://ltsc.ieee.org/wg12/ (2010)
18. International Telecommunications Union: Mobile cellular subscribers (2009),
    http://www.itu.int/ITU-D/icteye/Reporting/
    ShowReportFrame.aspx?ReportName=/WTI/CellularSubscribersPubl
    ic&ReportFormat=HTML4.0&RP_intYear=2009&RP_intLanguageID=1&R
    P_bitLiveData=False
19. Ketterl, M., Heinrich, T., Mertens, R., Morisse, K.: Enhanced Content Utilization: Combined Re-Use of Multi-Type e-Learning Content on Mobile Devices. IEEE Multidisciplinary Engineering Education Magazine 2, 61–64 (2007)
20. Khan, B.: Elements of e-learning (2001), http://BadrulKhan.com
21. Kurubacak, G.: Identify Research Priorities and Needs for Mobile Learning Technologies in Open and Distance Education: A Delphi Study. College of Open Education, Anadolu University, Anadolu (2007)
22. Laurillard, D.: Pedagogical forms for mobile learning. In: Pachler, N. (ed.) Mobile Learning: Towards a Research Agenda. WLE Centre, London (2007)
23. Lin, X., Hmelo, C., Kinzer, K.C., Secules, J.T.: Designing Technology to Support Reflection. Educational Technology Research and Development 47(3), 43–62 (1999)
24. Low, L.: M-learning standards report. Background, discussion and recommendations for usable and accessible m-learning (2007),
    http://e-standards.flexiblelearning.net.au/docs/
    m-standards-report-v1-0.pdf

25. Luis de Marcos, H.R.J., Gutiérrez, A.J., Pagés, C., Martínez, J.J.: Implementing Learning Objects Repositories for Mobile Devices (2006), http://ftp.informatik.rwth-aachen.de/Publications/CEUR-WS/Vol-208/paper04.pdf
26. Masters, K.: Low-key m-learning: a realistic introduction of m-learning to developing countries, http://www.fil.hu/mobil/2005/Masters_final.pdf (nd)
27. Motiwalla, F.L.: Mobile learning: A framework and evaluation. Computers & Education 49(3), 581–596 (2007)
28. Muyinda, B.P., Lubega, J., Lynch, K.: Unleashing mobile phones for research supervision support at Makerere University, Uganda: the lessons learned. International Journal of Innovation and Learning 7(1), 14–34 (2010)
29. Naismith, L., Lonsdale, P., Vavoula, G., Sharples, M.: Literature Review in Mobile Technologies and Learning (No. 11). University of Birmingham, Birmingham (2006)
30. Nakabayashi, K., Hoshide, T., Hosokawa, M., Kawakami, T., Sato, K.: Design and Implementation of a Mobile Learning Environment as an Extension of SCORM 2004 Specifications. In: The Seventh IEEE International Conference on Advanced Learning Technologies (ICALT 2007), Niigata, Japan, July 18-20 (2007)
31. Nie, M.: The Pedagogical Perspectives of Mobile Learning (2007), https://lra.le.ac.uk/bitstream/2381/407/1/The%20Pedagogical%20Perspectives%20of%20Mobile%20Learning%20-%20A%20Literature%20Review.pdf
32. Park, Y.: A Pedagogical Framework for Mobile Learning: Categorizing Educational Applications of Mobile Technologies into Four Types. The International Review of Research in Open and Distance Learning 12(2), 78–102 (2011)
33. Pask, G.: Minds and media in education and entertainment: some theoretical comments illustrated by the design and operation of a system for exteriorizing and manipulating individual theses. In: Trappl, R., Pask, G. (eds.) Progress in Cybernetics and Systems Research, Hemisphere, London, pp. 38–50 (1975)
34. Pettit, J., Kukulska-Hulme, A.: Going with the grain: Mobile devices in practice. Australasian Journal of Educational Technology 23(1), 17–33 (2007)
35. Prawat, S.R., Floden, E.R.: Philosophical perspectives on constructivist views on learning. Educational Psychology 29(1), 37–48 (1994)
36. Quinn, N.C.: Flexible Learning: Mobile Learning Objects. Knowledge Anywhere (2002)
37. Reeves, C.T., Herrington, J., Oliver, R.: Design Research: A Socially Responsible Approach to Instructional Technology Research in Higher Education. Journal of Computing in Higher Education 16(2), 97–116 (2005)
38. Schibeci, R., Lake, D., Phillips, R., Lowe, K., Cummings, R., Miller, E.: Evaluating the use of learning objects in Australian and New Zealand schools. Computers & Education 50(1), 271–283 (2008)
39. Skinner, B.F.: The Technology of Teaching. Appleton-Century-Crofts (reprinted by the BF Skinner Foundation in 2003), New York (1968)
40. Smith, S.R.: Guidelines for Authors of Learning Objects (2004), http://archive.nmc.org/guidelines/NMC%20LO%20Guidelines.pdf
41. South African Institute for Distance Education: Using Mobile Technology for Learner Support in Open Schooling. Project report for: Commonwealth of Learning (2008), http://www.col.org/SiteCollectionDocuments/Mobile%20Technology_Final%20Report.pdf
42. Toledano, M.C.M.: Learning objects for mobile devices: A case study in the Actuarial Sciences degree. Current Developments in Technology-Assisted Education 2006, 2095–2099 (2006)

43. Traxler, J.: Defining, Discussing, and Evaluating Mobile Learning: The moving finger writes and having writ.... International Review of Research in Open and Distance Learning 8(2), 1–12 (2007)
44. Trifonova, A., Ronchetti, M.: Hoarding content for mobile learning. International Journal of Mobile Communications 4(4), 459–476 (2006)
45. Uden, L.: Activity theory for designing mobile learning. International Journal of Mobile Learning and Organization 1(1), 81–102 (2007)
46. Vygotsky, L.S.: Mind in Society: The Development of Higher Psychological Processes. Harvard University Press, Cambridge (1978)
47. Wang, C., Liu, Z.: Distance education: basic resource guide. Collection Building 22(3), 120–130 (2003)
48. Wang, F., Hannafin, J.M.: Design-Based Research and Technology Enhanced Learning Environments. ETR&D 53(4), 5–23 (2005)
49. Wiley, D.A.: The Instructional use of Learning Objects. Association for Educational Communication and Technology, Bloomington (2001)
50. Yang, M.: An Adaptive Framework for Aggregating Mobile Learning Materials. In: The Seventh IEEE International Conference on Advanced Learning Technologies (ICALT 2007) Los Alamitos, California, July 18-20 (2007)
51. Zhang, D.: Delivery of personalized and adaptive content to mobile devices: a framework and enabling technology. Communication of the Association for Information Systems 12, 183–202 (2003)

Emulating Primality with Multiset Representations of Natural Numbers

Paul Tarau

Department of Computer Science and Engineering
University of North Texas
Denton, Texas
tarau@cs.unt.edu

Abstract. Factorization results in multisets of primes and this mapping can be turned into a bijection between multisets of natural numbers and natural numbers. At the same time, simpler and more efficient bijections exist that share some interesting properties with the bijection derived from factorization.

This paper describes mechanisms to emulate properties of *prime numbers* through isomorphisms connecting them to computationally simpler representations involving bijections from natural numbers to *multisets* of natural numbers.

As a result, interesting automorphisms of $\mathbb{N}$ and emulations of the rad, Möbius and Mertens functions emerge in the world of our much simpler multiset representations.

The paper is organized as a self-contained *literate Haskell program*. The code extracted from the paper is available as a standalone program at http://logic.cse.unt.edu/tarau/research/2011/mprimes.hs.

Keywords: bijective datatype transformations, multiset encodings and prime numbers, Möbius and Mertens functions, experimental mathematics and functional programming, automorphisms of $\mathbb{N}$.

1   Introduction

Paul Erdös's statement, shortly before he died, that *"It will be another million years at least, before we understand the primes"* is indicative of the difficulty of the field as perceived by number theorists. The growing number of conjectures [1] and the large number of still unsolved problems involving prime numbers [2] shows that the field is still open to surprises, after thousands of years of effort by some of the brightest human minds.

Interestingly, some significant progress on prime numbers correlates with unexpected paradigm shifts, the prototypical example being Riemann's paper [3] connecting primality and complex analysis, all evolving around the still unsolved *Riemann Hypothesis* [4,5,6,7]. The genuine difficulty of the problems and the seemingly deeper and deeper connections with fields ranging from cryptography to quantum physics suggest that unusual venues might be worth trying out.

A. Cerone and P. Pihlajasaari (Eds.): ICTAC 2011, LNCS 6916, pp. 218–238, 2011.
© Springer-Verlag Berlin Heidelberg 2011

A number of breakthroughs in various sciences involve small scale emulation of complex phenomena. Common sense analogies thrive on our ability to extrapolate from simpler (or, at least, more frequently occurring and better understood) mechanisms to infer surprising properties in a more distant ontology.

Prime numbers exhibit a number of fundamental properties of natural phenomena and human artifacts in an unusually pure form. For instance, *reversibility* is present as the ability to recover the operands of a product of distinct primes. This relates to the information theoretical view of multiplication [8] and it suggests investigating connections between combinatorial properties of multisets and operations on multisets and multiplicative number theory.

With such methodological hints in mind, this paper will explore mappings between multiset encodings and prime numbers. It is based on our *data type transformation framework* connecting most of the fundamental data types used in computer science with a *groupoid of isomorphisms* [9,10,11].

The paper is organized as follows. Section 2 revisits the well-known connection between multisets and primes using a variant of Gödel's encoding [12]. Section 3 describes our computationally efficient multiset encoding. Based on these encodings, section 4 explores the analogy between multiset decompositions and factoring and describes a multiplicative monoid structure on multisets that "emulates" properties of the monoid induced by ordinary multiplication as well as generic definitions in terms of multiset encodings of the rad, Möbius and Mertens functions. Section 5 describes automorphisms of $\mathbb{N}$ derived from alternative multiset encodings. Section 6 overviews some related work and section 7 concludes the paper.

We organize our literate programming code as a Haskell module, relying only on the List library module:

```
module MPrimes where
import Data.List
```

2   Encoding Finite Multisets with Primes

2.1   Ranking/Unranking of Sets and Finite Sequences

First, we define an isomorphism between sets and finite sequences (the Hub of the groupoid of isomorphisms) as described in [9] (also in the Appendix), resulting in the Encoder set:

```
set2list xs = shift_tail pred (mset2list xs) where
  shift_tail _ [] = []
  shift_tail f (x:xs) = x:(map f xs)

list2set = (map pred) . list2mset . (map succ)

set :: Encoder [N]
set = Iso set2list list2set
```

We can *rank/unrank* a set represented as a list of distinct natural numbers by observing that it can be seen as the list of exponents of 2 in the number's base 2 representation.

```
nat_set = Iso nat2set set2nat

nat2set n | n>0 = nat2exps n 0 where
  nat2exps 0 _ = []
  nat2exps n x = if (even n) then xs else (x:xs) where
    xs=nat2exps (n 'div' 2) (succ x)

set2nat ns = sum (map (2^) ns)
```

The resulting Encoder is:

```
nat :: Encoder N
nat = compose nat_set set
```

2.2 Encoding Multisets

Multisets [13] are unordered collections with repeated elements. Non-decreasing sequences provide a canonical representation for multisets of natural numbers.

The mapping between finite multisets and primes described in this section goes back to Gödel's arithmetic encoding of formulae [12,14]. A factorization of a natural number is uniquely described as a multiset of primes. We can use the fact that each prime number is uniquely associated to its position in the infinite stream of primes to obtain a bijection from multisets of natural numbers to natural numbers. This mapping is the same as the *prime counting function* traditionally denoted $\pi(n)$, which associates to n the number of primes smaller or equal to n, restricted to primes. It is provided by the function to_prime_positions defined in Appendix. The function nat2pmset maps a natural number to the multiset of prime positions in its factoring[1].

```
nat2pmset 1 = []
nat2pmset n = to_prime_positions n
```

Clearly the following holds:

Proposition 1. *p is prime if and only if its decomposition in a multiset given by* nat2pmset *is a singleton.*

The function pmset2nat (relying on from_in and primes defined in Appendix) maps back a multiset of positions of primes to the result of the product of the corresponding primes.

```
pmset2nat [] = 1
pmset2nat ns = product (map (from_pos_in primes . pred) ns)
```

The operations nat2pmset and pmset2nat form an isomorphism that, using the combinator language defined in [9] (and summarized in the Appendix to ensure

---

[1] In contrast to [9], we will assume that our mappings are defined on $\mathbb{N}^+ = \mathbb{N} - \{0\}$ rather than $\mathbb{N}$.

that this paper is fully self-contained) provides *any-to-any encodings* between various data types. This gives the Encoder `pmset` for prime encoded multisets as follows:

```
pmset :: Encoder [N]
pmset = compose (Iso pmset2nat nat2pmset) nat
```

working as follows:

```
*MPrimes> as pmset nat 2010
[1,2,3,19]
*MPrimes> as nat pmset [1,2,3,19]
2010
```

For instance, as the factoring of 2010 is $2 * 3 * 5 * 67$, the list $[1,2,3,19]$ contains the positions of the factors, starting from 1, in the sequence of primes.

3 A Bijection between Finite Multisets and Natural Numbers

We will now define *ranking/unranking* functions for multisets i.e. bijective mappings to/from natural numbers. While finite multisets and sequences representing finite functions share a common representation $[N]$, multisets are subject to the implicit constraint that their ordering is immaterial. This suggest that a multiset like $[4, 4, 1, 3, 3, 3]$ could be represented canonically as sequence by first ordering it as $[1, 3, 3, 3, 4, 4]$ and then computing the differences between consecutive elements i.e. $[x_0, x_1 \ldots x_i, x_{i+1} \ldots] \rightarrow [x_0, x_1 - x_0, \ldots x_{i+1} - x_i \ldots]$. This gives $[1, 2, 0, 0, 1, 0]$, with the first element 1 followed by the increments $[2, 0, 0, 1, 0]$, as implemented by `mset2list`:

```
mset2list xs = zipWith (-) (xs) (0:xs)
```

It is now clear that incremental sums of the numbers in such a sequence return the original set as implemented by `list2mset`:

```
list2mset ns = tail (scanl (+) 0 ns)
```

Note that canonical representation (i.e. being sorted) is assumed for set and multisets.

The isomorphism between finite multisets and finite functions (seen as finite sequences in $\mathbb{N}$) is specified with two bijections `mset2list` and `list2mset`.

```
mset0 :: Encoder [N]
mset0 = Iso mset2list list2mset
```

The resulting isomorphism `mset0` can be applied by using its two components `mset2list` and `list2mset` directly.

```
*MPrimes> mset2list [1,3,3,3,4,4]
[1,2,0,0,1,0]
*MPrimes> list2mset [1,2,0,0,1,0]
[1,3,3,3,4,4]
```

Equivalently, following [9] (see also summary in Appendix), it can be expressed generically by using the "as" combinator:

```
*MPrimes> as list mset0 [1,3,3,3,4,4]
[1,2,0,0,1,0]
*MPrimes> as mset0 list [1,2,0,0,1,0]
[1,3,3,3,4,4]
```

The combinator "as" derives automatically *any-to-any* encodings, by routing through the appropriate one-to-one transformations (see [9] and the Appendix). As a result, we obtain "for free" a bijection from $\mathbb{N}$ to finite multisets of elements of $\mathbb{N}$:

```
*MPrimes> as mset0 nat 2011
[0,0,1,1,2,2,2,2,2]
*MPrimes> as nat mset0 it
2011
```

We will need one small change to convert this into a mapping on $\mathbb{N}^+$.

```
nat2mset1 n=map succ (as mset0 nat (pred n))
mset2nat1 ns=succ (as nat mset0 (map pred ns))

mset :: Encoder [N]
mset = compose (Iso mset2nat1 nat2mset1) nat
```

The resulting mapping, like pmset, now works on $\mathbb{N}^+$.

```
*MPrimes> as mset nat 2012
[1,1,2,2,3,3,3,3,3]
*MPrimes> as nat mset it
2012
*MPrimes> map (as mset nat) [1..7]
[[],[1],[2],[1,1],[3],[1,2],[2,2]]
```

Note that these mappings work in linear time and space in the bitsize of the numbers [15]. On the other hand, as prime number enumeration and factoring are involved in the mapping from numbers to multisets, the encoding described in section 2 is intractable for all but small values.

4   Exploring the Analogy between Multiset Decompositions and Factoring

As natural numbers can be uniquely represented as multisets of prime factors and, independently, they can also be represented as a multiset with the Encoder mset (described in section 3), the following question arises naturally:

Can the computationally efficient encoding mset *help emulate some properties of the the difficult to reverse factoring operation?*

4.1   A Multiset Analog to Multiplication

The first step is to define an analog of the multiplication operation in terms of the computationally easy multiset encoding `mset`. Clearly, it makes sense to take inspiration from the fact that factoring of an ordinary product of two numbers can be computed by *concatenating* the multisets of prime factors of its operands. We use the combinator `borrow_from` and the sorted concatenation `sortedConcat` operations (see Appendix) to express this:

```
mprod = borrow_from mset sortedConcat nat
```

Proposition 2. $\langle N^+, mprod, 1 \rangle$ *is a commutative monoid i.e.* `mprod` *is defined for all pairs of natural numbers and it is associative, commutative and has 1 as an identity element.*

Proof. After rewriting the definition of `mprod` as the equivalent:

```
mprod_alt n m = as nat mset
  (sortedConcat (as mset nat n) (as mset nat m))
```

the proposition follows immediately from the associativity of the concatenation operation and the order independence of the multiset encoding provided by `mset`.   □

Here are a few examples showing that `mprod` has properties similar to ordinary multiplication:

```
*MPrimes> mprod 41 (mprod 33 38) == mprod (mprod 41 33) 38
True
*MPrimes> mprod 33 46 == mprod 46 33
True
*MPrimes> mprod 1 712 == 712
True
```

Given the associativity of `mprod`, it makes sense to define the product of a list of numbers as

```
mproduct ns = foldl mprod 1 ns
```

Note also that any multiset encoding of natural numbers can be used to define a similar commutative monoid structure. In the case of `pmset` we obtain:

```
pmprod n m = as nat pmset
  (sortedConcat (as pmset nat n) (as pmset nat m))
```

This brings us back to observe that:

Proposition 3. $\langle N, pmprod, 1 \rangle$ *is a commutative monoid i.e.* `pmprod` *is defined for all pairs of natural numbers and it is associative, commutative and has 1 as an identity element.*

Unsurprisingly, this is the case indeed as one can deduce immediately from the definition of pmprod that, on $\mathbb{N}^+$:

$$pmprod \equiv * \tag{1}$$

As obvious as this equivalence is, note that computing $*$ is easy, while computing pmprod involves factoring which is intractable for large values.

Experimentally (including very large random integers), mprod x y $\leq$ pmprod x y, leading us to:

Conjecture 1. *mprod x $y = x * y$ if and only if $\exists n \geq 0$ such that $x = 2^n$ or $y = 2^n$. Otherwise, mprod x $y < x * y$.*

Fig. 1 shows the self-similar landscape generated by the function (mprod x y) / (x*y) for values of x,y in [1..128].

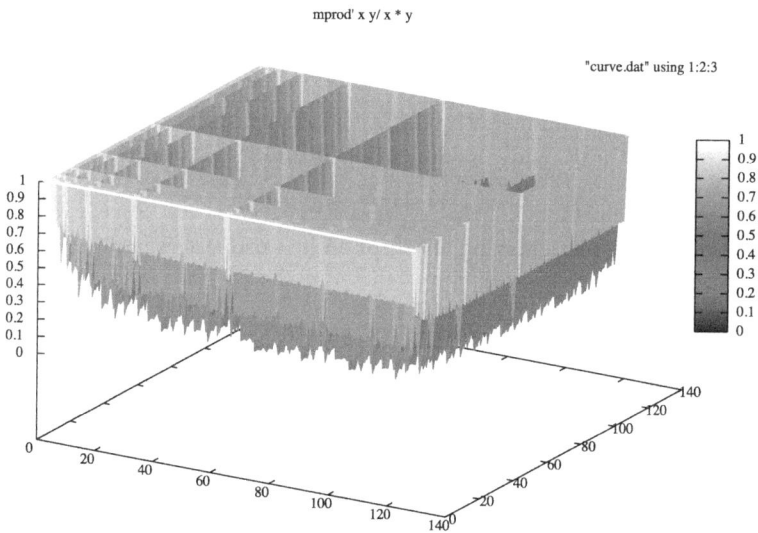

Fig. 1. Ratio between mprod and product

We can derive an exponentiation operation as a repeated application of mprod:

```
mexp n 1 = n
mexp n k = mprod n (mexp n (k-1))
```

Let us first observe that the ordinary exponent and our emulated variant correlate as follows:

```
*MPrimes> map (λx→mexp 2 x) [1..8]
[2,4,8,16,32,64,128,256]
*MPrimes> map (λx→2^x) [1..8]
[2,4,8,16,32,64,128,256]
```

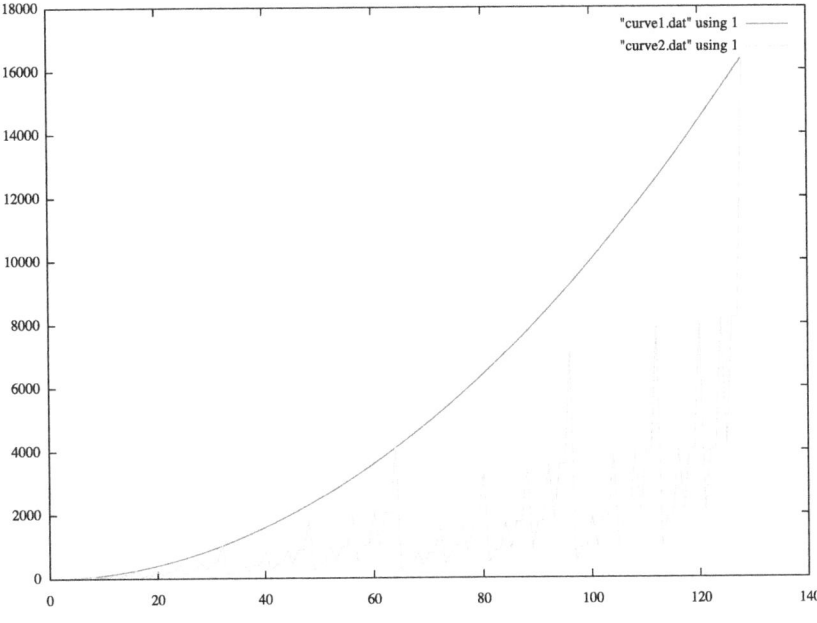

Fig. 2. Square vs. mexp n 2

```
*MPrimes> map (λx→mexp x 2) [1..16]
[1,4,7,16,13,28,31,64,25,52,55,112,61,124,127,256]
*MPrimes> map (λx→x^2) [1..16]
[1,4,9,16,25,36,49,64,81,100,121,144,169,196,225,256]
```

Fig. 2 shows that values for mexp x 2 follow from below those of the x^2 function and that equality only holds when x is a power of 2.

4.2   Multiset Analogues for div, gcd and lcd

Besides the connection with products, natural mappings worth investigating are the analogies between *multiset intersection* and gcd of the corresponding numbers or between *multiset union* and the lcm of the corresponding numbers. Assuming the definitions of multiset operations provided in the **Appendix**, one can define:

```
mgcd :: N → N → N
mgcd = borrow_from mset msetInter nat

mlcm :: N → N → N
mlcm = borrow_from mset msetUnion nat

mdivisible :: N→N→Bool
mdivisible n m = mgcd n m==m
```

```
mdiv :: N → N → N
mdiv = borrow_from mset msetDif nat

mexactdiv :: N → N → N
mexactdiv n m | mdivisible n m = mdiv n m
```

and note that properties similar to usual arithmetic operations hold:

$$mprod(mgcd\ x\ y)(mlcm\ x\ y) \equiv mprod\ x\ y \tag{2}$$

$$mexactdiv(mprod\ x\ y)\ y \equiv x \tag{3}$$

$$mexactdiv(mprod\ x\ y)\ x \equiv y \tag{4}$$

4.3 Multiset Primes

A remarkable algebraic property of $\mathbb{N}$ is that the lattice structure defined by the divisibility relation has an infinite *antichain*: the set of prime numbers. We will now provide a simple "emulation" of primality that shares this property.

Definition 1. *We say that $p > 1$ is a multiset-prime (or* mprime *shortly), if its decomposition as a multiset is a singleton.*

The following holds

Proposition 4. *$p > 1$ is a multiset prime if and only if it is not mdivisible by any number in $[2..p-1]$.*

Proof. This follows immediately by observing that singleton multisets are the first to contain a given number as the multiset [a,b] corresponds to a number strictly larger than the numbers corresponding to multisets [a] and [b].   □

We are now ready to "emulate" primality in our multiset monoid by defining is_mprime (or alternatively alt_is_mprime) as a recognizer for *multiset primes* and mprimes as a generator of their infinite stream:

```
is_mprime p | p >1 = 1==length (as mset nat p)

alt_is_mprime p | p>1 =
   []==[n|n←[2..p-1],p 'mdivisible' n]

mprimes = filter is_mprime [2..]
```

Trying out mprimes gives:

```
*MPrimes> take 10 mprimes
[2,3,5,9,17,33,65,129,257,513]
```

suggesting the following proposition:

Proposition 5. *There's an infinite number of* multiset *primes and they are exactly the numbers of the form $2^n + 1$.*

Proof. The proof follows immediately by observing that the first value of as mset nat n that contains k, is $n = 2^k + 1$ and that numbers of that form are exactly the numbers resulting in singleton multisets.   □

The following example illustrates this property.

```
*MPrimes> map (as mset nat) [1..9]
[[],[1],[2],[1,1],[3],[1,2],[2,2],[1,1,1],[4]]
      ~~~           ~~~                 ~~~

      2+1           4+1                 8+1
```

We can now implement faster versions of mprimes and is_mprime:

```
mprimes' = map (λx→2^x+1) [0..]


is_mprime' p | p>1 = p==
  last (takeWhile (λx→x≤p) mprimes')
```

4.4   An Analog to the "rad" Function

Definition 2. *n is square-free if each prime on its list of factors occurs exactly once.*

The rad(n) function (A007947 in [16]) is defined as follows:

Definition 3. *rad(n) is the largest square-free number that divides n*

Clearly, rad can be computed by factoring, then trimming multiple occurrences with the nub library function and finally by multiplying the resulting primes with product.

```
rad n = product (nub (to_primes n))
```

Note that rad can also be computed by trimming multiplicities in a multiset representation of n i.e. after defining respectively

```
pfactors n = nub (as pmset nat n)
mfactors n = nub (as mset nat n)
```

we can define prad ≡ rad and its multiset equivalent mrad:

```
prad n =  as nat pmset (pfactors n)

mrad n =  as nat mset (mfactors n)
```

```
*MPrimes> map rad [2..16]
[2,3,2,5,6,7,2,3,10,11,6,13,14,15,2]
*MPrimes> map prad [2..16]
[2,3,2,5,6,7,2,3,10,11,6,13,14,15,2]
*MPrimes> map mrad [2..16]
[2,3,2,5,6,3,2,9,10,11,6,5,6,3,2]
```

A comparison of the plots of the two functions (Fig. 3) shows that rad's chaotic behavior corresponds to a more regular, self-similar behavior in the case of mrad.

One can further explore if this "emulation" of the rad function can bring some light on the well known connections between the rad function and the famous *abc conjecture* [17].

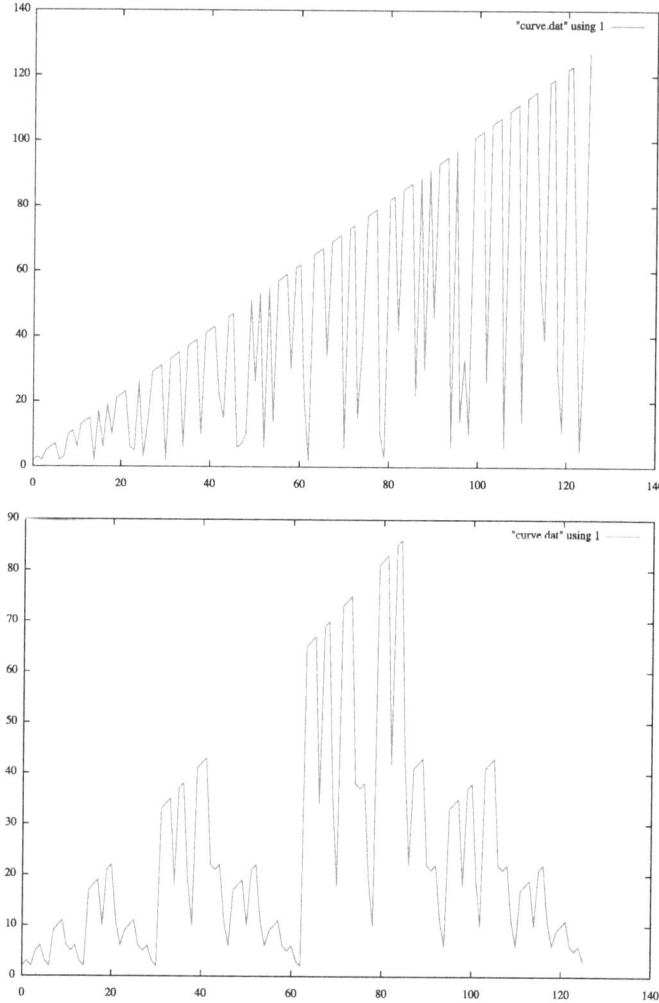

Fig. 3. rad(n) and mrad(n) on $[2..2^7 - 1]$

4.5   Emulating the Möbius and Mertens Functions

The Möbius function separates square free primes with even and odd number of factors from numbers that are not square free.

$$\mu(n) = \begin{cases} 1 & \text{if } n = 1 \\ 0 & \text{if } p^2 \text{ } divides \text{ } n \text{ for some prime } p \\ (-1)^r & \text{if } n \text{ has } r \text{ distinct prime factors} \end{cases}$$

A generalization that parameterizes it by the type t of a multiset encoding of natural numbers is given as follows.

```
mobius t n = if nub ns == ns then f ns else 0 where
  ns = as t nat n
  f ns = if even (genericLength ns) then 1 else -1
```

For t=pmset one obtains the instance corresponding to *primes* (sequence A008683 in [16]) while t=mset provides an instance corresponding to *mprimes*.

```
*MPrimes> map (mobius pmset) [1..16]
[1,-1,-1,0,-1,1,-1,0,0,1,-1,0,-1,1,1,0]

*MPrimes> map (mobius mset) [1..16]
[1,-1,-1,0,-1,1,0,0,-1,1,1,0,0,0,0,0]
```

Surprisingly this corresponds to the apparently identical sequences A132971 and A085357 in [16], related to enumeration of ternary trees and infinite Fibonacci words. We postpone exploring this connections for now, and define, in a similar way a generalization of the Mertens function (A002321 in [16])

$$M(x) = \sum_{n \leq x} \mu(n)$$

that accumulates values of the Möbius function up to n:

```
mertens t n = sum (map (mobius t) [1..n])
```

working as follows

```
*MPrimes> map (mertens pmset) [1..16]
[1,0,-1,-1,-2,-1,-2,-2,-2,-1,-2,-2,-3,-2,-1,-1]

*MPrimes> map (mertens mset) [1..16]
[1,0,-1,-1,-2,-1,-1,-1,-2,-1,0,0,0,0,0,0]
```

The Mertens conjecture (disproved by Odlyzko and te Riele, [18]) states that

$$|M(n)| < \sqrt{n},\ for\ n > 1$$

After defining

```
mertens2 t n = m^2 where m = mertens t n
```

```
counterex_mertens t m = [n|n←[2..m],mertens2 t n ≥ n^2]
```

we can show that it holds for small values for both t=mset and t=pmset

```
*MPrimes> counterex_mertens pmset 1000
[]
*MPrimes> counterex_mertens mset 1000
[]
```

Fig. 4 shows the more regular, fractal-like behavior of the Mertens function derived from mset in contrast with the more chaotic and strongly oscillating behavior of the original Mertens function derived from pmset.

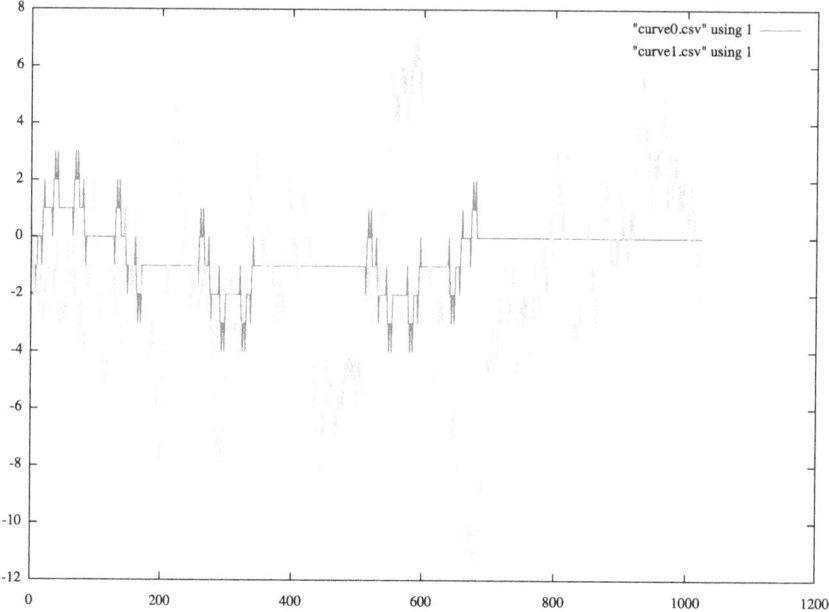

Fig. 4. Mertens functions for mset and pmset

A connection between the Riemann Hypothesis, originating from a representation of the inverse of the Riemann ζ function as

$$\frac{1}{\zeta(s)} = \sum_{n=1}^{\infty} \frac{\mu(n)}{n^s}$$

has lead to an equivalent elementary formulation (attributed to Littlewood) of the Riemann Hypothesis [6,19] as

$$M(x) = O(x^{1/2+\varepsilon}) \ \forall \varepsilon > 0 \tag{5}$$

By instantiating this statement to a Mertens function parameterized by a simple multiset representation like mset one obtains an analogue of the Riemann Hypothesis in much simpler and possibly more tractable context.

Conjecture 2. *The inequality 5 holds for the the instance of $M(x)$ derived from* mset *i.e. computed by the function* mertens mset.

This leads to speculating that, for instance, connecting values of ε between the emulation (derived from mset) and the original Martens function (derived from pmset) could provide interesting insight on the Riemann Hypothesis as such.

After defining:

```
mlt k m = [n|n←[k..m],mertens2 mset n< mertens2 pmset n]
meq k m = [n|n←[k..m],mertens2 mset n==mertens2 pmset n]
mgt k m = [n|n←[k..m],mertens2 mset n>mertens2 pmset n]
```

experiments indicate that bounds of the mset function might be dominated by bounds of the pmset function for large values of $k < m$.

```
*MPrimes> length (mlt 1000 1100)
95
*MPrimes> length (meq 1000 1100)
6

*MPrimes> length (mgt 1000 1100)
0
*MPrimes> length (mgt 2000 2100)
2
*MPrimes> length (mgt 3000 3100)
2
```

5   Deriving Automorphisms of $\mathbb{N}$

Definition 4. *An* automorphism *is an isomorphism for which the source and target are the same.*

A nice property of automorphisms is that, given the isomorphisms provided by the data transformation framework [9], they propagate from one data type to another. In our case, the multiset representations provided by pmset and mset induce two automorphisms on $\langle \mathbb{N}, *, 1 \rangle$

```
auto_m2p 0 = 0
auto_m2p n = as nat pmset (as mset nat n)

auto_p2m 0 = 0
auto_p2m n = as nat mset (as pmset nat n)
```

working as follows:

```
*MPrimes> map auto_m2p [0..31]
[0,1,2,3,4,5,6,9,8,7,10,15,12,25,18,27,16,11,14,
 21,20,35,30,45,24,49,50,75,36,125,54,81]

*MPrimes> map auto_p2m [0..31]
[0,1,2,3,4,5,6,9,8,7,10,17,12,33,18,11,16,65,14,
 129,20,19,34,257,24,13,66,15,36,513,22,1025]
```

After extending mprod to mimic pmprod (i.e. *) w.r.t. its behavior on 0

```
mprod' 0 _ = 0
mprod' _ 0 = 0
mprod' x y | x>0 && y>0= mprod x y
```

note that, as expected, one can define functors that transport mprod' into (*) and transport (*) into mprod' as follows:

```
emulated_mprod' x y =
  auto_p2m ((auto_m2p x) * (auto_m2p y))
```

```
emulated_prod x y =
  auto_m2p (mprod (auto_p2m x) (auto_p2m y))
```

Note that emulated_mprod' x y works as if defined by mprod' x y and emulated_prod x y works as if defined by x*y.

```
*MPrimes> mprod' 20 30
376
*MPrimes> emulated_mprod' 20 30
376
*MPrimes> 20*30
600
*MPrimes> emulated_prod 20 30
600
```

Fig. 5 shows the quickly amplifying reshuffling of the sequence [0..] generated by the functions auto_m2pfor values in $[0..2^6 - 1]$.

An experimental comparison is between the values for which auto_m2p is strictly larger or smaller than auto_p2m:

```
lt_mp n = length [x|x←[0..n],auto_m2p x < auto_p2m x]
eq_mp n = length [x|x←[0..n],auto_m2p x == auto_p2m x]
gt_mp n = length [x|x←[0..n],auto_m2p x > auto_p2m x]
```

indicates a shift from eq_mp for small numbers to lt_mp for larger ones.

```
*MPrimes> map eq_mp [0..15]
[1,2,3,4,5,6,7,8,9,10,11,11,12,12,13,13]
*MPrimes> map gt_mp [0..15]
[0,0,0,0,0,0,0,0,0,0,0,0,0,0,0,1]
*MPrimes> map lt_mp [0..15]
[0,0,0,0,0,0,0,0,0,0,0,1,1,2,2,2]

*MPrimes> map eq_mp [1000..1015]
[43,43,43,43,43,43,43,43,43,43,43,43,43,43,43,43]
*MPrimes> map gt_mp [1000..1015]
[321,322,322,323,323,323,323,324,325,325,325,325,326,326,327,328]
*MPrimes> map lt_mp [1000..1015]
[637,637,638,638,639,640,641,641,641,642,643,644,644,645,645,645]

*MPrimes> map eq_mp [2000..2015]
[48,48,48,48,48,48,48,48,48,48,48,48,48,48,48,48]
*MPrimes> map gt_mp [2000..2015]
[590,591,592,592,592,592,593,593,593,594,594,594,594,595,596,597]
*MPrimes> map lt_mp [2000..2015]
[1363,... 1364,1365,1366,1366,1367,1368,1368,1369,1370,1371,...,1371]
```

An interesting open problem related to these automorphisms is to prove or disprove that the permutations of $\mathbb{N}$ induced by auto_m2p and auto_p2m cannot contain infinite cycles.

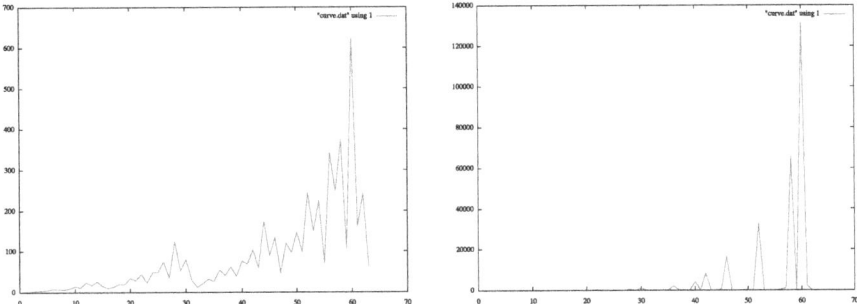

Fig. 5. The automorphisms auto_m2p and auto_p2m

6 Related Work

There's a huge amount of work on prime numbers and related aspects of multiplicative and additive number theory. Studies of prime number distribution and various probabilistic and information theoretic aspects also abound.

While we have not made use of any significantly advanced facts about prime numbers, the following references circumscribe the main topics to which our experiments can be connected [19,8,2,6,5].

Natural Number encodings of various set-theoretic constructs have triggered the interest of researchers in fields ranging from Axiomatic Set Theory and Foundations of Logic to Complexity Theory and Combinatorics [20,21,22]. In combinatorics they show up as *Ranking* functions [23] that can be traced back to Gödel numberings [12,14] associated to formulae. Together with their inverse *unranking* functions they are also used in combinatorial generation algorithms for various data types [24].

This paper relies on the compositional and extensible data transformation framework (summarized in the Appendix) that connects most of the fundamental data types used in computer science with a *groupoid of isomorphisms*. A large (100+ pages) unpublished draft [25], provides encodings between more than 60 different data types. The basic idea of the framework is described in [10] and some of its applications to computational mathematics in [9]. A compact Prolog implementation of the framework with focus on mapping between complex data structures is described in [11].

7 Conclusion and Future Work

We have explored some computational analogies between multisets, natural number encodings and prime numbers in a framework for experimental mathematics implemented as a literate Haskell program.

This has resulted in a methodology for emulating more difficult number theoretic phenomena through simpler isomorphic representations. In a way this parallels *abstract interpretation* [26] by using a simpler domain to approximate interesting properties in a more complex one. We are in the process of lifting our Haskell implementation to a generic type class based model, along the lines of [15], which allows experimenting with instances parameterized by arbitrary bijections between $\mathbb{N}$ and [$\mathbb{N}$]. Of special interest in this direction are multiset decompositions of a natural number in $O(log(log(n)))$ factors, similar to the $\omega(x)$ and $\Omega(x)$ functions counting the distinct and non-distinct prime factors of x, to mimic more closely the distribution of primes. Future work will also focus on finding a matching additive operation for the multiset induced commutative monoid.

Acknowledgment. We thank NSF (research grant 1018172) for support.

References

1. Cégielski, P., Richard, D., Vsemirnov, M.: On the additive theory of prime numbers. Fundam. Inform. 81(1-3), 83–96 (2007)
2. Crandall, R., Pomerance, C.: Prime Numbers–a Computational Approach, 2nd edn. Springer, New York (2005)
3. Riemann, B.: Ueber die anzahl der primzahlen unter einer gegebenen grösse. Monatsberichte der Berliner Akademie (November 1859)
4. Miller, G.L.: Riemann's hypothesis and tests for primality. In: STOC, pp. 234–239. ACM, New York (1975)
5. Lagarias, J.C.: An Elementary Problem Equivalent to the Riemann Hypothesis. The American Mathematical Monthly 109(6), 534–543 (2002)
6. Conrey, B.: The Riemann Hypothesis. Not. Amer. Math. Soc. 60, 341–353 (2003)
7. Chaitin, G.: Thoughts on the riemann hypothesis. Math. Intelligencer 26(1), 4–7 (2004)
8. Pippenger, N.: The average amount of information lost in multiplication. IEEE Transactions on Information Theory 51(2), 684–687 (2005)
9. Tarau, P.: A Groupoid of Isomorphic Data Transformations. In: Carette, J., Dixon, L., Coen, C.S., Watt, S.M. (eds.) MKM 2009, Held as Part of CICM 2009. LNCS, vol. 5625, pp. 170–185. Springer, Heidelberg (2009)
10. Tarau, P.: Isomorphisms, Hylomorphisms and Hereditarily Finite Data Types in Haskell. In: Proceedings of ACM SAC 2009, pp. 1898–1903. ACM, New York (2009)
11. Tarau, P.: An Embedded Declarative Data Transformation Language. In: Proceedings of 11th International ACM SIGPLAN Symposium PPDP 2009, Coimbra, Portugal, pp. 171–182. ACM, New York (2009)
12. Gödel, K.: Über formal unentscheidbare Sätze der Principia Mathematica und verwandter Systeme I. Monatshefte für Mathematik und Physik 38, 173–198 (1931)
13. Singh, D., Ibrahim, A.M., Yohanna, T., Singh, J.N.: An overview of the applications of multisets. Novi Sad J. Math 52(2), 73–92 (2007)
14. Hartmanis, J., Baker, T.P.: On Simple Goedel Numberings and Translations. In: Loeckx, J. (ed.) ICALP 1974. LNCS, vol. 14, pp. 301–316. Springer, Heidelberg (1974)
15. Tarau, P.: Declarative modeling of finite mathematics. In: PPDP 2010: Proceedings of the 12th International ACM SIGPLAN Symposium on Principles and Practice of Declarative Programming, pp. 131–142. ACM, New York (2010)

16. Sloane, N.J.A.: The On-Line Encyclopedia of Integer Sequences (2010), published electronically at http://www.research.att.com/~njas/sequences
17. Granville, A.: ABC allows us to count squarefrees. International Mathematics Research Notices (19), 991 (1998)
18. Odlyzko, A.M., Te Riele, A.M., Disproof, H.J.J.: of the Mertens conjecture. J. Reine Angew. Math. 357, 138–160 (1985)
19. Derbyshire, J.: Prime Obsession: Bernhard Riemann and the Greatest Unsolved Problem in Mathematics. Penguin, New York (2004)
20. Kaye, R., Wong, T.L.: On Interpretations of Arithmetic and Set Theory. Notre Dame J. Formal Logic 48(4), 497–510 (2007)
21. Avigad, J.: The Combinatorics of Propositional Provability. In: ASL Winter Meeting, San Diego (January 1997)
22. Kirby, L.: Addition and multiplication of sets. Math. Log. Q. 53(1), 52–65 (2007)
23. Martínez, C., Molinero, X.: Generic algorithms for the generation of combinatorial objects. In: Rovan, B., Vojtáš, P. (eds.) MFCS 2003. LNCS, vol. 2747, pp. 572–581. Springer, Heidelberg (2003)
24. Ruskey, F., Proskurowski, A.: Generating binary trees by transpositions. J. Algorithms 11, 68–84 (1990)
25. Tarau, P.: Declarative Combinatorics: Isomorphisms, Hylomorphisms and Hereditarily Finite Data Types in Haskell, p. 150 (January 2009), Unpublished draft, http://arXiv.org/abs/0808.2953, updated version at http://logic.cse.unt.edu/tarau/research/2010/ISO.pdf
26. Cousot, P., Cousot, R.: Abstract interpretation: A unified lattice model for static analysis of programs by construction or approximation of fixpoints. In: 4th ACM Symp. Principles of Programming Languages, pp. 238–278 (1977)

Appendix

An Embedded Data Transformation Language

We will describe briefly the embedded data transformation language used in this paper as a set of operations on a groupoid of isomorphisms. We refer to ([9,25]) for details.

The Groupoid of Isomorphisms. We implement an isomorphism between two objects X and Y as a Haskell data type encapsulating a bijection f and its inverse g.

$$X \xrightleftharpoons[{g = f^{-1}}]{f = g^{-1}} Y$$

We will call the *from* function the first component (a *section* in category theory parlance) and the *to* function the second component (a *retraction*) defining the isomorphism. The isomorphisms are naturally organized as a *groupoid*.

```
data Iso a b = Iso (a→b) (b→a)

from (Iso f _) = f

to (Iso _ g) = g

compose :: Iso a b → Iso b c → Iso a c
compose (Iso f g) (Iso f' g') = Iso (f' . f) (g . g')

itself = Iso id id

invert (Iso f g) = Iso g f
```

Assuming that for any pair of type Iso a b, $f \circ g = id_b$ and $g \circ f = id_a$, we can now formulate *laws* about these isomorphisms.

The data type Iso *has a groupoid structure, i.e. the* compose *operation, when defined, is associative,* itself *acts as an identity element and* invert *computes the inverse of an isomorphism.*

The Hub: Finite Sequences of Natural Numbers. To avoid defining $\frac{n(n-1)}{2}$ isomorphisms between n objects, we choose a *Hub* object to/from which we will actually implement isomorphisms.

Choosing a *Hub* object is somewhat arbitrary, but it makes sense to pick a representation that is relatively easy convertible to various others and scalable to accommodate large objects up to the runtime system's actual memory limits.

We will choose as our *Hub* object *finite sequences of natural numbers.* They can be seen as finite functions from an initial segment of $\mathbb{N}$, say $[0..n]$, to $\mathbb{N}$. We will represent them as lists i.e. their Haskell type is [N].

```
type N = Integer
type Hub = [N]
```

We can now define an *Encoder* as an isomorphism connecting an object to *Hub*

```
type Encoder a = Iso a Hub
```

together with the combinators *as* providing an *embedded transformation language* for routing isomorphisms through two *Encoders*.

```
as :: Encoder a → Encoder b → b → a
as that this x = g x where
    Iso _ g = compose that (invert this)
```

The combinator "**as**" adds a convenient syntax such that converters between A and B can be designed as:

```
a2b x = as B A x
b2a x = as A B x
```

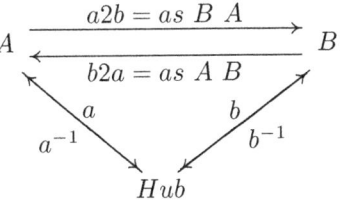

A particularly useful combinator that transports binary operations from an Encoder to another, `borrow_from`, can be defined as follows:

```
borrow_from :: Encoder a → (a → a → a) →
               Encoder b → (b → b → b)
borrow_from lender op borrower x y = as borrower lender
    (op (as lender borrower x) (as lender borrower y))
```

Given that [N] has been chosen as the root, we will define our finite function data type *list* simply as the identity isomorphism on sequences in [N].

```
list :: Encoder [N]
list = itself
```

Primes

The following code implements factoring function `to_primes` a primality test (`is_prime`) and a generator for the infinite stream of `primes`.

```
primes = 2 : filter is_prime [3,5..]

is_prime p = [p]==to_primes p

to_primes n|n>1 = to_factors n p ps where (p:ps) = primes
```

```
to_factors n p ps | p*p > n = [n]
to_factors n p ps | 0==n 'mod' p =
  p : to_factors (n 'div' p)  p ps
to_factors n p ps@(hd:tl) = to_factors n hd tl

to_prime_positions n =
  map (succ . (to_pos_in (h:ps))) qs where
    (h:ps)=genericTake n primes
    qs=to_factors n h ps

to_pos_in xs x = fromIntegral i where
  Just i=elemIndex x xs

from_pos_in xs n = xs !! (fromIntegral n)
```

Multiset Operations

The following functions provide multiset analogues of the usual set operations, under the assumption that multisets are represented as non-decreasing sequences.

```
msetInter, msetDif, msetSymDif, msetUnion ::
  (Ord a) => [a] -> [a] -> [a]

msetInter [] _ = []
msetInter _ [] = []
msetInter (x:xs) (y:ys) | x==y = x:msetInter xs ys
msetInter (x:xs) (y:ys) | x<y = msetInter xs (y:ys)
msetInter (x:xs) (y:ys) | x>y = msetInter (x:xs) ys

msetDif [] _ = []
msetDif xs [] = xs
msetDif (x:xs) (y:ys) | x==y = msetDif xs ys
msetDif (x:xs) (y:ys) | x<y = x:msetDif xs (y:ys)
msetDif (x:xs) (y:ys) | x>y = msetDif (x:xs) ys

msetSymDif xs ys =
  sortedConcat (msetDif xs ys) (msetDif ys xs)

msetUnion xs ys =
  sortedConcat (msetSymDif xs ys) (msetInter xs ys)

sortedConcat xs ys = sort (xs ++ ys)
```

Formal Verification of a Lock-Free Stack with Hazard Pointers

Bogdan Tofan, Gerhard Schellhorn, and Wolfgang Reif

Institute for Software and Systems Engineering
University of Augsburg
{tofan,schellhorn,reif}@informatik.uni-augsburg.de

Abstract. A significant problem of lock-free concurrent data structures in an environment without garbage collection is to ensure safe memory reclamation of objects that are removed from the data structure. An elegant solution to this problem is Michael's hazard pointers method. The formal verification of concurrent algorithms with hazard pointers is yet challenging. This work presents a mechanized proof of the major correctness and progress aspects of a lock-free stack with hazard pointers.

1 Introduction

Non-blocking implementations of concurrent data structures avoid major problems associated with blocking, such as convoying, deadlocks or priority inversion. In particular, lock-free [1] algorithms guarantee termination of some operation in a finite number of steps, even when individual operations are arbitrarily delayed or fail. Their main correctness property linearizability [2], ensures that each operation appears to take effect instantly at one step (the linearization point) between its invocation and response. Thus, from an external point of view, a linearizable operation executes atomically and can be used in a modular way. In addition, performance results show that lock-free implementations can outperform their lock-based counterparts significantly in the presence of contention or multiprogramming. These properties are even more important as multi-core architectures have become mainstream.

The advantages of lock-free implementations come at the price of an increased complexity to develop and verify them. These data structures are often used in programming environments without support for garbage collection (GC). There, the problem of safe memory reclamation of objects that have been removed from the data structure imposes significant additional challenges on design and verification. Memory occupied by a removed object can not be simply deallocated (e.g., using a *free* library call in C / C++) as other processes typically still access this object in their operations. The possible concurrent reuse of locations introduces a further fundamental problem of lock-free algorithms, the ABA-problem [3]. It becomes manifest in subtle errors such as wrong return values or data structure corruption, as we explain in Section 3.1 for a lock-free stack.

Several memory reclamation schemes that compensate the absence of GC exist. Hazard pointers [4] enable safe memory reclamation by extending concurrent

A. Cerone and P. Pihlajasaari (Eds.): ICTAC 2011, LNCS 6916, pp. 239–255, 2011.

algorithms with their own local, non-blocking garbage collection. The reclamation technique is applicable to a class of important concurrent algorithms. This work analyzes the central properties of the hazard pointers method and then applies the results to verify a well-known lock-free stack that uses hazard pointers. Proving safe memory reclamation and ABA-avoidance for such a stack has been declared a challenge for program verification [5].

Our main contribution is an intuitive verification that exploits the central properties of Michael's reclamation scheme. The proof is mechanized in the interactive theorem prover KIV [6] and addresses all major aspects: memory-safety, ABA-prevention as well as preservation of linearizability and lock-freedom of the stack with hazard pointers. We apply temporal logic and local rely-guarantee reasoning, but use neither complex history variables nor reasoning about the temporal past, as in other approaches (cf. Section 7). The proofs reveal that the correctness of the reclamation scheme can be expressed in terms of two contending processes. A further novel insight is that its relation to GC can be exploited to reuse central correctness arguments under GC.

To keep the presentation readable, we do not detail every formal aspect. In particular, the verification and an in-depth description of the applied decomposition theory is omitted. Further details can be found in [7]; a complete presentation that includes all KIV-proofs is available online [8].

The remainder of this paper is organized as follows: Section 2 gives an introduction to hazard pointers. Section 3 specifies the main case study of this paper, the extended stack algorithm. Section 4 briefly introduces the verification framework that forms the logical base for the applied decomposition theory, which is described in Section 5. Section 6 shows four central properties of the hazard pointers method and their specialization to formal verification conditions in the case study. Section 7 presents related work and a comparison. Finally, Section 8 concludes with a summary and discussion of the main results.

2   The Hazard Pointers Method

Figure 1 illustrates hazard pointers: (1) processes $p, q, \ldots$ can concurrently allocate and insert new objects NEW to a lock-free data structure LDS. Every process p collects the memory of objects r that it removes from LDS in a local pool of retired locations RL_p. These locations are candidates for deallocation. However, the contending use of these retired locations must be considered first.

(2) shows that each process is associated with a fixed (small) number of multi-reader single-writer shared pointers, so called hazard pointers. All hazard pointers of all processes are contained in a hazard pointer record HPR. By setting one of its hazard pointers to a location r, process p signals other contending processes not to deallocate this location. Crucially, to ensure that this signal is indeed considered, p subsequently checks whether r is still part of LDS. Only if this check – called hazard pointer validation – succeeds, p enters a hazardous code region where it accesses r.

To deallocate memory, a process p executes a scan operation in two phases (3) and (4). In (3), it consecutively collects all hazard pointers of all processes in

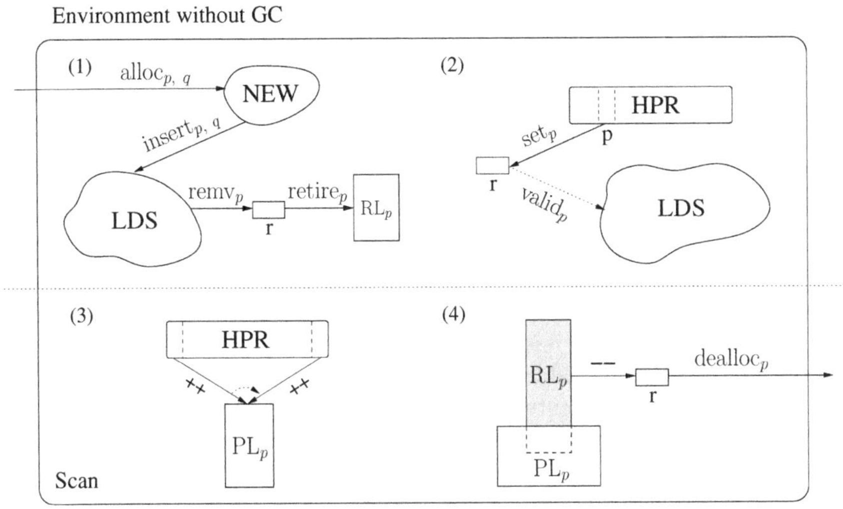

Environment without GC

Fig. 1. Michael's hazard pointers method

a local pointer list PL_p by traversing HPR. In (4), all retired memory locations r that were not found during this traversal ($r \in RL_p - PL_p$), are freed to the environment's memory management system for arbitrary reuse.

A properly extended lock-free algorithm with hazard pointers has the following central correctness property:

$$\boxed{\text{A validated hazard pointer is not concurrently freed.}} \tag{1}$$

This is because at the time of its successful validation, a hazard pointer is in LDS and hence in no retired list. Consequently, no currently running scan will deallocate it. After its successful validation, a hazard pointer might be concurrently retired, while still being used. Yet it is not freed, since the retiring process collects the pointer during its traversal of HPR. (We intuitively formalize this central argument in Section 6.)

3   A Lock-Free Stack with Hazard Pointers

3.1   The Lock-Free Stack

Instead of using locks, lock-free algorithms typically utilize atomic synchronization primitives such as the widely supported single-word CAS (Compare-And-Swap) instruction. A CAS compares a shared value SV with an older local copy of it Old, called snapshot. If these values are equal, then SV is updated to a new value New and true is returned; otherwise false is returned.

CAS($Old, New; SV, Succ$) {
  if* $SV = Old$ **then** {$SV := New, Succ := true$} **else** $Succ := false$}

Throughout this work, we use formal KIV-specifications to describe programs and thereby explain the introduced syntax. In the specification of CAS, the semicolon separates input from in-output parameters; the comma indicates parallel assignments and in **if*** evaluating the if-condition requires no extra step.

Figure 2 illustrates the lock-free stack which provides concurrent push and pop operations. The shaded code in pop, the scan and reset operations can be ignored for now. The algorithm is a prime example of a lock-free data structure, taken from Michael [4] and attributed to Treiber [3]. The shared stack is a singly linked list of cells – pairs of values and locations with .val and .nxt selector functions – in the application's memory heap H. The heap is a partial function from locations $r : ref$ (with $null \in ref$) to cells with standard operations, e.g., $H[r, ?]$ is allocation with arbitrary content "?", $r \in H$ tests if r is allocated, $H[r]$ is lookup and $H - r$ deallocation. A shared variable Top points to the top cell of the stack.

Whenever a process executes a push, it first allocates a new cell $UNew$ (lines U3 / U4 execute in one step) and initializes it with input value In. Then it repeatedly tries to CAS the shared top to point to this new cell (lines U6 – 9). A pop reads the shared top (if this snapshot is null, the special value $empty$ is returned) and locally stores the snapshot's next reference which becomes the target of the subsequent CAS. If it succeeds, the top cell is removed from the stack and its value is returned. Variables $UNew$, $USucc$, $OTop$ and $OSucc$ are local variables of "pUsh" resp. "pOp". They are defined as in-output parameters instead of using **let**, to allow us to reason about them.

Simply deallocating a removed cell at the end of pop can cause contending pop-processes to dereference an illegal snapshot pointer. If the reference is concurrently reused, an ABA-problem can occur: suppose that a pop-process p takes a snapshot of the top pointer when the stack consists of exactly one cell at location A. Process p is delayed after setting $ONxt$ to null in line O12 for another process q, which executes a successful pop, freeing A. Subsequently, q executes two successful push operations, thereby allocating reference B and then again A. Then p is rescheduled and its CAS operation in line O13 erroneously succeeds, violating the semantics of pop.

3.2   The Extended Stack

Applying the hazard pointers technique requires no modification of the push operation. The pop operation requires one hazard pointer to cover the hazardous usage of the snapshot pointer $OTop$ in lines O12 and O13. This hazard pointer is atomically set in line O9, using the shared hazard pointer record $HPR : \mathbb{N} \to ref$ and the identifier $Id : \mathbb{N}$ of the current process. In line O10, before any hazardous usage, the hazard pointer is validated. Crucially, only after this test succeeds, it can be guaranteed that the snapshot cell is not concurrently freed and possibly reused. An additional boolean flag $Hazard_{pc}$ marks the hazardous code region in which the validated hazard pointer equals (covers) the snapshot $OTop$. This simple auxiliary variable is required in the verification only, since our logic does not use program counters. In line O16, a location that has been removed from the stack is added to a local list of retired locations RL.

```
U1   Push(In;  UNew, USucc, Top, H) {
U2     let UTop = ? in {
U3       choose r with (r ≠ null ∧ r ∉ H) in {
U4         UNew := r, H := H[r, ?], USucc := false;
U5         H[UNew].val := In;
U6         while ¬ USucc do {
U7           UTop := Top;
U8           H[UNew].nxt := UTop;
U9           CAS(UTop, UNew; Top, USucc)}}}}


O1   Pop(; Id, Hazard_pc, OTop, OSucc, RL, Top, H, HPR, Out) {
O2     let ONxt = ?, Lo = empty in {
O3       OSucc := false;
O4       while ¬ OSucc do {
O5         OTop := Top, Hazard_pc := false;
O6         if OTop = null then {
O7           OSucc := true
O8         } else {
O9           HPR(Id) := OTop;
O10          if* OTop = Top then {
O11            Hazard_pc := true;
O12            ONxt := H[OTop].nxt;
O13            CAS(OTop, ONxt; Top, OSucc)}}}
O14      if OTop ≠ null then {
O15        Lo := H[OTop].val';
O16        RL := OTop + RL, Hazard_pc := false}
O17      Out := Lo}}


S1   Scan(; Scan, BefInc_pc, Lid, Lhp, PL, RL, H, HPR) {
S2     PL := [], Scan := true;
S3     while Lid ≤ MAXID do {
S4       Lhp := HPR(Lid), BefInc_pc := true;
S5       if Lhp ≠ null then {
S6         PL := Lhp + PL}
S7       Lid := Lid + 1, BefInc_pc := false};
S8     while Scan do {
S9       choose r with (r ∈ RL − PL) in {
S10        RL := RL − r, H := H − r}
S11      ifnone Scan := false, Lid := 0}}


R1   Reset(; Id, HPR) {HPR(Id) := null}
```

Fig. 2. A lock-free data-stack with hazard pointers

Operation *Scan*, characterized by boolean flag *Scan*, frees retired locations that are not concurrently used. In its first loop, a scan sequentially traverses the hazard pointer record, reading each hazard pointer and collecting it in a further local pointer list *PL*, where constant MAXID denotes the greatest occuring process identifier. This includes atomically taking a snapshot *Lhp* of the *HPR* entry at process index Lid ($BefInc_{pc}$ is a further simple program counter substitute used in the proofs). In the second loop, retired memory locations that are not in PL are consecutively deallocated.

To simplify verification while maintaining the core ideas of Michael's algorithm, our version of the extended stack uses several algebraic data structures. In particular, we use a function to model the hazard pointer record, while Michael proposes a singly linked heap list. In the second loop of the scan operation, the **choose** summarizes some merely local steps that are required to determine the deallocable references $RL - PL$. This avoids some standard sequential reasoning. Furthermore, we slightly generalize Michael's version, by allowing a scan to be performed arbitrarily between stack operations, while Michael calls a scan at the end of pop, depending on the current number of retired locations. As a further minor extension, we consider the possible reset of a hazard pointer $Reset$ between executions of push, pop or scan, while the original code does not explicitly reset.

4   The Verification Framework

4.1   Interval Temporal Logic

Interval temporal logic (ITL) [9] in KIV is based on algebras and intervals. Algebras define a semantic for the signature and intervals (executions) are finite or infinite sequences of states which evolve from program execution. A state maps variables to values in the algebra. In contrast to standard ITL, the logic explicitly includes the behavior of the program's environment in each step. Similar to "reactive sequences" [10], in an interval $I = [I(0), I'(0), I(1), I'(1), \ldots]$ the first transition from state $I(0)$ to the primed state $I'(0)$ is a program transition, whereas the next transition from state $I'(0)$ to $I(1)$ is a transition of a program's environment. In this manner program and environment transitions alternate. A variable V is evaluated over $I(0)$, whereas its primed resp. double primed version V' resp. V'' is evaluated over $I'(0)$ and $I(1)$ respectively. E.g., formula $V \neq V'$ denotes that variable V is changed in the first program transition, whereas $V' = V''$ states that V is not changed in the first environment transition. The last state of an interval is characterized by the atomic formula **last**.

The logic uses standard temporal operators to express future properties of an interval ($\Box, \Diamond, \bullet$, **until**). In rely-guarantee proofs, formulas $R(V', V'') \xrightarrow{+} G(V, V')$ are of particular interest, where G resp. R are guarantee resp. rely conditions and the "sustains" operator $\xrightarrow{+}$ ensures that the guarantee is sustained by a program, as long as its environment has not previously violated the rely (cf. Section 5).

$$R(V', V'') \xrightarrow{+} G(V, V') :\leftrightarrow \neg (R(V', V'') \textbf{ until } \neg G(V, V'))$$

The programming language provides the common sequential constructs, a construct for weak-fair and one for non-fair interleaving. Note that arbitrary programs α and formulas can be mixed, since they both evaluate to true or false over an algebra and an interval I. In particular, α evaluates to true in I iff I is an execution of α interleaved with arbitrary environment steps.

4.2 Symbolic Execution and Induction

The verification framework is based on the sequent calculus. A sequent is an assertion of the form $\Gamma \vdash \Delta$, where Γ, Δ are lists of formulas. It states that the conjunction of all formulas in antecedent Γ implies the disjunction of all formulas in succedent Δ. Sequents are implicitly universally closed. A typical sequent (proof obligation) about concurrent programs has the form $\alpha, E, F \vdash \varphi$ where a program α executes the program steps in an environment constrained by temporal formula E. Predicate logic formula F describes the current state of an α-execution and φ denotes the temporal property of interest. A sequent of the aforementioned form is:

$$(M := M + 1;\ \beta),\ M = 1 \ \vdash\ M' = M'' \xrightarrow{+} M' > M \tag{2}$$

The executed program is the sequential composition $M := M + 1;\ \beta$, environment behavior is unrestricted ($E = true$ omitted), the current state maps M to 1 and the succedent claims that the program increments M as long as its environment leaves M unchanged ($M' = M'' \xrightarrow{+} M' > M$).

Symbolic Execution. Proving sequents that contain temporal assertions is done by symbolically stepping forward to the next states of an interval, calculating strongest post conditions for each program step, possibly weakened according to environment assumptions. Thus the calculus is rather similar to classic symbolic execution of sequential programs [11], once environment behavior is suitably restricted.

A step computes by applying unwinding rules to both programs and formulas. A program is unwound by calculating the effect of its first statement and discarding it; the sustains operator is unwound using the rule $R \xrightarrow{+} G \equiv G \wedge (R \rightarrow \bullet (R \xrightarrow{+} G))$. Applying it on the succedent of (2) yields $M' > M \wedge (M' = M'' \rightarrow \bullet (M' = M'' \xrightarrow{+} M' > M))$. That is, we must prove that the counter is incremented by the (first) program transition as a first subgoal ($M' > M$). If the following environment transition leaves M unchanged ($M' = M''$), then the sustains formula must further hold in the rest of the interval ($\bullet$). Thus, we get a second subgoal when proving (2):

$$\beta,\ M = 2 \ \vdash\ M' = M'' \xrightarrow{+} M' > M$$

Induction. Well-founded induction is used to deal with loops. For infinite intervals a term for well-founded induction can often be derived from a known liveness property $\diamond \varphi$ as the number of steps N until φ holds.

$$\diamond \varphi \ \leftrightarrow\ \exists\, N.\ (N = N'' + 1)\ \textbf{until}\ \varphi.$$

This equivalence states that φ is eventually true iff there is a natural number N which can be decremented until φ becomes true. Note that N is a fresh variable and $N = N'' + 1$ is equivalent to $N'' = N - 1 \wedge N > 0$.

An induction term can be also extracted from a sustains formula.

$$R \xrightarrow{+} G \ \leftrightarrow\ \forall\, B.\ (\diamond B) \rightarrow ((R \wedge \neg B) \xrightarrow{+} G)$$

Thus, the proof of a sustains formula on an infinite interval I can be carried out by induction over the length of an arbitrary finite I-prefix, which ends when the fresh boolean variable B is true for the first time. Further details on the underlying calculus can be found, e.g., in [12,13].

5   The System Model and the Decomposition Theory

This section briefly describes the decomposition theory which we have applied to verify the case study. It contains several improvements over the theory used in [14,15], which are independent from verifying the stack. Their description is not in the scope of this paper (cf. [7] for more details).

The Concurrent System Model. The system model SPAWN($n; \ldots$) recursively spawns $n + 1$ processes ($n : \mathbb{N}$) to execute in parallel. Each process executes finitely or infinitely often operations COP($In; LS, S, Out$) on shared data structures. Variables In resp. Out are thereby used to insert resp. return values. Parameter $LS : lstate$ is the exclusive local state of the invoking process (with process identifier $LS.$id), whereas $S : sstate$ is the shared state.

In the stack case study, COP is instantiated with the non-deterministic choice between one of the operations that each legal process, having an identifier $\leq$ MAXID, can concurrently execute. Illegal processes just skip.

COP($In; LS, S, Out$) {
  if $LS.$id $\leq$ MAXID **then** {
    $Push(In; LS, S) \lor Pop(; LS, S, Out) \lor Scan(; LS, S) \lor Reset(; LS, S)$}}

The shared state S consists of the shared variables Top, H, HPR, whereas the local state LS is the tuple of all local variables $UNew$, $USucc$, $OTop$, $OSucc$, Id, $Hazard_{pc}$, $Scan$, $BefInc_{pc}$, Lid, Lhp, PL, and RL.

Local Rely-Guarantee Reasoning. To avoid reasoning about interleaved executions of SPAWN, we use a local version of rely-guarantee reasoning [16] that is embedded in the temporal logic framework. Different from the original approach [16], it does not enforce reasoning over the whole system state with $n + 1$ local states. Specifications instead consider two processes p resp. q with local states LS resp. LSQ. Such a reduction to a few representative processes is often useful for the verification of concurrent data types.

The rely-guarantee embedding abstracts from interference from other processes using rely conditions R_{ext}. In return, each process guarantees a certain behavior towards its environment according to guarantee conditions G_{ext}. Both G_{ext} and R_{ext} are structured into three categories: step invariant guarantee and rely conditions G and R, state invariant conditions Inv and $Disj$ (to symmetrically encode disjointness between the two local states), plus, local idle state conditions $Idle$ which hold between COP-executions only. (The use of these structural predicates in the case study is shown in Section 6.) Thus, the central proof obligation for rely-guarantee reasoning is:

$$\text{COP}(In; LS, S, Out), Idle(LS), Inv(LS, S),$$
$$LS.\text{id} \neq LSQ.\text{id}, Inv(LSQ, S), Disj(LS, LSQ) \vdash R_{ext} \xrightarrow{+} G_{ext} \tag{3}$$

According to G_{ext}, COP-steps maintain the guarantee conditions and the state invariants, plus, establish the idle state conditions.

$$G_{ext}(LS, LSQ, S, LS', LSQ', S') :\leftrightarrow$$
$$G(LS, LSQ, S, LS', S')$$
$$\wedge\ (\quad Inv(LS, S) \wedge Inv(LSQ, S) \wedge Disj(LS, LSQ)$$
$$\rightarrow Inv(LS', S') \wedge Inv(LSQ', S') \wedge Disj(LS', LSQ')) \wedge (\text{last} \rightarrow Idle(LS))$$

According to R_{ext}, transitions of COP's environment do not modify LS and they maintain R and the state invariants.

$$R_{ext}(LS', LSQ', S', LS'', LSQ'', S'') :\leftrightarrow$$
$$LS' = LS'' \wedge R(LS', S', S'')$$
$$\wedge\ (\quad Inv(LS', S') \wedge Inv(LSQ', S') \wedge Disj(LS', LSQ')$$
$$\rightarrow Inv(LS'', S'') \wedge Inv(LSQ'', S'') \wedge Disj(LS'', LSQ''))$$

Theorem 1 (Local Rely-Guarantee Reasoning). *If (3) can be proved for some transitive rely predicate R, reflexive predicate G with $G(LS, LSQ, S, LS', S')$ $\rightarrow R(LSQ, S, S')$, symmetric predicate Disj and predicates Idle and Inv, then each system step of $\text{SPAWN}(n; \dots)$ is a guarantee step G which does not modify the local state of other processes, the invariant conditions Inv and Disj hold for all processes at all times, and each process is Idle, just before it invokes COP.*

The Decomposition of Linearizability and Lock-Freedom. Linearizability [2] and lock-freedom [1] are major, global correctness resp. progress properties of concurrent systems. We define local proof obligations for COP which imply linearizability and lock-freedom of SPAWN. They are based on a local invariant property *ISR* that each process may always assume during its execution of COP($In; LS, S, Out$), according to Theorem 1.

$$ISR :\leftrightarrow Inv(LS, S) \wedge Inv(LS', S') \wedge LS' = LS'' \wedge R(LS', S', S'')$$

Linearizability. We prove linearizability by locating the linearization point (i.e., the step where a call appears to take effect) of each operation during its execution. Conceptually, the linearization point of an execution of COP is determined in a refinement proof using an abstraction function $Abs \subseteq sstate \times astate$ (a partial function defined on shared states that satisfy *Inv*, which returns a corresponding abstract state). In the stack example, Abs maps a linked list representation of the stack to a finite algebraic list St of its data values.

$$Abs(Top, H, [\,]) :\leftrightarrow Top = null$$
$$Abs(Top, H, v + St) :\leftrightarrow \quad Top \neq null \wedge Top \in H \wedge H[Top].\text{val} = v$$
$$\wedge\ Abs(H[Top].\text{nxt}, H, St)$$

To prove linearizability, one has to show that each concrete operation from COP, non-atomically refines a corresponding abstract operation, which is defined in a further generic procedure AOP on an abstract state AS. In the case study, AOP is the non-deterministic choice between an abstract push or pop on St, or a sequence of mere skip steps for the scan and reset operations, which leave the stack unchanged. Hence, a sufficient process-local proof obligation for linearizability is:

$$\text{COP}(In; LS, S, Out), \Box (ISR \wedge Abs(S, AS) \wedge Abs(S', AS')), Idle(LS)$$
$$\vdash \text{AOP}(In; AS, Out) \tag{4}$$

Theorem 2 (Decomposition of Linearizability). *In a setting in which the preconditions of Theorem 1 and proof obligation (4) hold for a suitable abstraction function Abs, the concurrent system* SPAWN *is linearizable.*

Lock-Freedom. Lock-free data structures ensure that even when single processes crash, neither deadlocks nor livelocks occur. In the stack example, single push and pop operations can be forced to always retry their loop if another process modifies the shared top pointer. If such an interference occurs, it is the interfering process which terminates its current execution and without interference, the current process terminates.

We capture this intuitive argument using an additional reflexive and transitive relation $U \subseteq sstate \times sstate$ to describe interference freedom ("unchanged"). To prove lock-freedom, one has to do two process-local termination proofs for each data structure operation. First, termination without U-interference and second, termination after violating U in a step. Thus, a sufficient process-local proof obligation for lock-freedom is (cf. [8,15] for more details):

$$\text{COP}(In; LS, S, Out), \Box ISR, Idle(LS)$$
$$\vdash \Box ((\Box U(S', S'')) \vee \neg U(S, S') \rightarrow \Diamond \mathbf{last}) \tag{5}$$

Theorem 3 (Decomposition of Lock-Freedom). *In a setting in which the preconditions of Theorem 1 and proof obligation (5) hold for a reflexive and transitive relation U, the concurrent system* SPAWN *is lock-free.*

6   Verifying the Stack with Hazard Pointers

This section shows central properties of hazard pointers and their specialization to formal verification conditions for the stack from Figure 2. To keep the presentation readable, we only give some major conditions explicitly (all formal conditions are described in [7]). All conditions are expressed in terms of at most two processes. This is possible, since a retired location r can only be freed by the process, which has removed r from the stack and then retired it. Thus, when a process is in its hazardous code region, there is at most one other process which could free its critical pointer.

6.1   Central Properties of Hazard Pointers

The following central invariant property of hazard pointers ensures that heap access errors do not occur in hazardous code regions.

$$\boxed{HPR_{valid} \subseteq H} \tag{6}$$

According to (6), each validated hazard pointer is in the application's heap at all times, i.e., it is never freed (cf. (1)). This property correlates with GC where one may assume that a heap location r is not concurrently freed if it is just referenced in some operation. With hazard pointers, one can make the same assumption if r is covered by a *validated* hazard pointer.

Before a process p validates a location r, however, it can be concurrently freed by another process q and arbitrarily reused even if p has already set its hazard pointer to r. This happens when $HPR_p := r$ is executed after the location has been retired by q, and q has passed p's hazard pointer entry in its current traversal of HPR. Therefore, we omit any assertions about hazard pointers which are not validated yet. This differs from Parkinson et al. [5], who include such locations in their main correctness argument (cf. Section 7).

A difference between hazard pointers and GC is that while locations that are reachable from a root location can be concurrently freed if they are no longer covered by a validated hazard pointer, they would typically not be freed under GC, as long as their root is used.

The next central property of hazard pointers ensures that retired locations are in the application's heap, but not in the lock-free data structure.

$$RL \subseteq (H - LDS) \tag{7}$$

This has two major consequences. First, deallocation steps are safe, as they do not affect locations which are not in the application's heap. Second, succeeding validations (a location is in LDS at that time) imply that the validated location is currently not retired, hence not a deallocation candidate of any current scan.

Two further central properties of hazard pointers ensure that no ABA-problem occurs.

$$\textbf{if } r \in HPR_{valid} \textbf{ then } r \notin NEW \tag{8}$$

$$\textbf{if } \text{under GC: } H'(r) = H''(r) \textbf{ then if } r \in HPR_{valid} : \ H'(r) = H''(r) \tag{9}$$

(8) states that if a location r is covered by a validated hazard pointer, then it is not reused, i.e., it is not reinserted in the data structure which averts the ABA-problem. This property is also related to GC, where a heap location is not reused as long as it is referenced in some operation. Hence, the environment assumption (9) holds: if the content of a heap location r is not concurrently changed in an environment with GC, then it is also unchanged when r is covered by a validated hazard pointer.

6.2   Verification Conditions for the Stack

Properties (6) - (9) are specialized to formal verification conditions which ensure memory-safety and ABA-avoidance for the stack. Properties in bold script are the corresponding verification conditions under GC, which we have simply reused.

Absence of Access Errors. The stack-specific counterpart of generic property (6) ensures that the snapshot pointer is allocated and covered by a validated hazard pointer in the hazardous code region of pop.

$$Hazard_{pc} \wedge \boldsymbol{OTop} \neq \boldsymbol{null} \rightarrow \boldsymbol{OTop} \in \boldsymbol{H} \wedge HPR(Id) = OTop \tag{10}$$

The stack-specific version of (7) implies that retired locations are allocated and disjoint from the stack, where a standard reachability predicate checks whether a location r is in the stack.

$$\forall \ r \in RL. \ r \neq null \wedge r \in H \wedge \neg \ reach(Top, r, H) \tag{11}$$

(10) and (11) ensure that heap access errors do not occur in pop and scan.

To sustain (10) at all times in every possible execution, the validated hazard pointer $OTop = HPR(Id)$ used in a pop operation of process p ($Hazard_{pc}$ holds, Id is the process identifier of p) must not be freed by any process q. The worst case is that q has retired $OTop$, just traverses HPR, but has not yet collected it ($OTop \in RLq - PLq$). Then q must not have passed the entry of p yet ($Lidq \leq Id$) and if it has reached p's entry, it must store $OTop$ in the local variable $Lhpq$ to ensure that it is collected. Invariant *ishazard* encodes this criterion precisely:

$ishazard(LS, LSQ) :\leftrightarrow$
$Hazard_{pc} \wedge OTop \in (RLq - PLq) \wedge Scanq \ \rightarrow$
if $BefIncq_{pc}$ **then** $Lidq < Id \vee (Lidq = Id \wedge Lhpq = OTop)$ **else** $Lidq \leq Id$

Note that *ishazard* is independent from the underlying data structure, except for mentioning the concrete hazardous reference $OTop$. It can be easily adapted to ensure memory-safety for other lock-free data structures as well.

To sustain invariant (11) at all times, we must establish that retired lists are always duplicate free and pairwise disjoint. Otherwise, a retired list might contain a freed location after a deallocation step. Furthermore, three basic heap-disjointness properties are necessary: removed locations, which are subsequently retired, must be disjoint from the stack and they must not be concurrently retired, plus, concurrently removed locations must be disjoint.

To ensure that heap access faults do not occur in push either, we claim that new cells that have not been inserted yet, are always allocated and never concurrently retired, hence never freed.

ABA-prevention. The stack-specific version of (8) ensures that the validated snapshot in pop is not reused, thus it is disjoint from other new cells.

$$Hazard_{pc} \wedge \neg \ \boldsymbol{USuccq} \rightarrow \boldsymbol{OTop} \neq \boldsymbol{UNewq} \tag{12}$$

The specialization of (9) yields the following rely condition which ensures that the snapshot's content is immutable in the hazardous code region of pop, to avoid an ABA-problem between the execution of lines O12 and O13.

$$Hazard_{pc}{}' \wedge \boldsymbol{OTop}' \neq \boldsymbol{null} \rightarrow H'[\boldsymbol{OTop}'] = H''[\boldsymbol{OTop}'] \tag{13}$$

An ABA-problem does not happen in push as well, since the content of a new cell remains unchanged.

$$\neg \ \boldsymbol{USucc}' \rightarrow H'[\boldsymbol{UNew}'] = H''[\boldsymbol{UNew}'] \tag{14}$$

To maintain rely (14) for the other process, when the current push process updates the new cell's next reference in line U8, new cells must be disjoint.

$$\neg\ USucc \wedge \neg\ USuccq \rightarrow UNew \neq UNewq \tag{15}$$

Verification conditions (10) and (11) are a main part of the structural predicate *Inv* from Section 5. Conditions *ishazard*, (12) and (15) are part of the symmetric predicate *Disj*, which is defined as:

$$Disj(LS, LSQ) :\leftrightarrow ishazard(LS, LSQ) \wedge ishazard(LSQ, LS) \wedge (12) \wedge \dots$$

Rely conditions (13) and (14) are the major part of R; guarantee G is defined to maintain R for the other process and a simple step-invariant which ensures that COP-steps do not create memory leaks. Finally, the *Idle* predicate encodes the following local restrictions:

$$USucc \wedge OSucc \wedge \neg\ Hazard_{pc} \wedge \neg\ Scan \wedge \neg\ BefInc_{pc} \wedge Lid = 0$$

6.3   The Main Proofs

Sustainment of the Verification Conditions. The main effort of the case study is to prove the rely-guarantee proof obligation (3) – sustainment of the verification conditions during steps of each operation. We proceed by case analysis over OP $\in$ {*Scan, Pop, Push, Reset*}. The proof resembles a Hoare-style proof of a sequential program. We use $\xrightarrow{+}$ induction for loops and consecutively, symbolically execute each program statement in OP according to Section 4. Only some major arguments are outlined.

OP $\equiv$ *Scan*: It is rather subtle to establish *ishazard*(LSQ, LS) when the current process switches to the next hazard pointer entry in line S7. This step must not miss a validated hazard pointer $OTopq$ of the other process q if the current process p has retired, but not yet collected it ($OTopq \in RL - PL$). If the snapshot Lhp of the current HPR entry is not null, we know from previous symbolic execution that it is in PL. If the current iteration examines q, *ishazard* before this step implies $Lhp = OTopq$, i.e., the validated hazard pointer has just been collected in the current iteration ($OTopq \in PL$), implying *ishazard*(LSQ, LS).

In the deallocation step (line S10), *ishazard* ensures that the validated snapshot location of the other process is not freed (10). The proof is by contradiction: if the other process is in its hazardous code region and its snapshot pointer is in $RL - PL$, then *ishazard* before this step implies that the current process must not have finished its traversal. However, the current process is in its second scan loop already (technically, the contradiction is MAXID + 1 = $Lid \leq Idq \leq$ MAXID).

OP $\equiv$ *Pop*: In the succeeding hazard pointer validation step (lines O10 / O11), *ishazard* and (10) can be established, since the hazard pointer is in the data structure, hence allocated and not concurrently retired. Immediately after removal of the snapshot $OTop$ from the stack in line O13, we know from (11) that it can not be in the current process' retired list RL. Hence, we can establish (11) again in the retiring step (line O16), since both $OTop$ and RL are local.

Op $\equiv$ *Push*: The allocation step (lines U3 / U4) resets the content of a new cell. However, it does not affect allocated locations and thus neither rely condition (13) nor (14) of the other process are violated. We additionally establish $UNew \notin RL$ in this step which allows to prove disjointness of retired locations from the data structure (11), when the new cell is added to the stack in line U9.

Op $\equiv$ *Reset*: The reset of a hazard pointer entry is safe, since it happens outside of the hazardous code region in pop.

Preservation of Linearizability. The proof of linearizability (4) distinguishes between the four possible concrete operations. In case of the hazard pointer operations scan and reset, each concrete step refines an abstract skip step. In particular, the deallocation step (lines S9 / S10) does not affect the stack, as retired locations are disjoint from the stack, according to (11).

The extended pop operation still has one linearization point in line O5 if the stack is empty, or else in line O13 if the CAS succeeds. Rely (13) ensures that the next reference of the snapshot cell and its value are immutable. Thus, the successful CAS corresponds to an abstract pop and returns the correct value. In case of a push operation, the linearization point is the successful CAS. Rely (14) ensures that the initial value of the new cell and its next reference are immutable. Hence, the successful CAS corresponds to an abstract push of the invoked value.

Preservation of Lock-Freedom. According to (5), the proof of lock-freedom requires termination proofs for each data structure operation if environment behavior is restricted according to U and if a step violates U. We determine the unchanged relation as identity of the top-of-stack pointer. It is then relatively simple to show that push and pop terminate. Since the scan operation is wait-free, we can prove its termination without U. Termination of the first scan loop uses well-founded induction over the term MAXID $-$ *Lid* which decreases in every iteration. Similarly, termination of the second loop follows by induction over the number of retired locations.

7   Related Work and Comparison

Current automatic techniques do not prove linearizability or lock-freedom without implicitly assuming GC, which significantly simplifies the proofs. Thus they are not directly related to this work. We do not know of any other mechanized verification of a lock-free algorithm with hazard pointers. [17] describes a mechanized proof of a lock-free queue with modification counters [3], which focuses on linearizability. Neither an ABA-problem nor lock-freedom are discussed.

Manual Proofs. Michael [4] gives a semantic verification condition which ensures safe memory reclamation for a lock-free algorithm with hazard pointers. This global condition requires the existence of a time in the past from which a hazardous location is safely covered by a hazard pointer. Michael verifies neither linearizability nor lock-freedom of the extended stack, but informally ensures safety by construction. Our verification of the stack formally resembles Michael's arguments, while avoiding both global reasoning and reasoning about the past. A key idea was to map Michael's temporal interval in which memory-safety and ABA-prevention are guaranteed, to a corresponding code interval ($Hazard_{pc}$).

There are two formal pen and paper proofs of a Treiber-like stack with hazard pointers. Parkinson et al. [5] apply concurrent separation logic (CSL) to verify a variant of the original stack, focusing on heap-modular reasoning and fractional permissions, which are used for simple properties such as (12) or (15). Their central correctness argument states that after a hazard pointer covers a location t, it can not be removed from the stack and then reinserted, which avoids the ABA-problem. Restricting this property to the case that t is covered by a *validated* hazard pointer better captures the essence of the reclamation scheme. While we use mainly simple formulas to ensure ABA-avoidance for validated hazard pointers, their proof requires rather complex auxiliary data structures.

Fu et al. [18] verify the stack in a program logic for history (HLRG). It provides temporal operators of the past only and evaluates state assertions in the last state of an execution. Their proof is based on rather complex global arguments about the temporal past of finite executions, while our verification conditions are just state/step invariants. Their implementation is not lock-free, since their *HPR*-traversal does not complete when a location is covered by a hazard pointer and the associated process fails. Michael's traversal, however, completes independent from environment behavior.

CSL and HLRG are based on separation logic and use abstract code annotations in their verification, while we use refinement, separating concrete from abstract code. They benefit from the implicit treatment of different heap locations by the separating conjunction operator, while we have to encode some disjointness properties explicitly. Their verification considers memory-safety and structural invariance of the stack only, but proves neither linearizability nor lock-freedom. They use process-global conditions and do not exploit symmetry.

8   Summary and Discussion

This work describes the first mechanized verification of a challenging lock-free stack. The proof intuitively applies central properties of the hazard pointers method and takes advantage of the relation between Michael's method and GC. It addresses the main safety and liveness aspects, avoiding process-global reasoning, complex history variables and reasoning about the past. Hence, it contributes an improved formal verification of the stack with hazard pointers.

Furthermore, we have applied our verification technique to the Michael-Scott queue with hazard pointers [4], where each process requires two hazard pointers. The central verification condition *ishazard* has been used analogously to ensure that the hazardous snapshot locations of the queue are not concurrently freed. The verification conditions from our previous proof under GC have been simply reused (cf. [8]). This indicates that the results of this work can be carried over to verify other lock-free algorithms in a similar way. A mechanized, schematic proof of correctness for an arbitrary underlying data structure, however, is left for future work.

As a further extension of our work, Maged Michael proposed that reading and writing hazard pointers non-atomically should be safe too, even though the scan algorithm may then read corrupted values. We confirmed this conjecture by replacing the atomic assignments with generic read and write procedures. These were specified to work correctly only if the environment does not concurrently modify the shared value. Just a few minor modifications of the proofs were necessary (cf. [8]).

Our current approach to verify linearizability suffices for algorithms that have an internal linearization point within the code of the executing process, even when its location depends on subsequent system behavior. This is possible, since future states of an interval can be easily analyzed in ITL (refer to [14] for more details). A generalization of the technique, using the results of [19], is part of current work.

Acknowledgments. We thank Jörg Pfähler for verifying the Michael-Scott queue with hazard pointers, resp. Alexander Knapp and Maged Michael for fruitful discussions.

References

1. Massalin, H., Pu, C.: A lock-free multiprocessor os kernel. Technical Report CUCS-005-91, Columbia University (1991)
2. Herlihy, M., Wing, J.: Linearizability: A correctness condition for concurrent objects. ACM Trans. on Prog. Languages and Systems 12(3), 463–492 (1990)
3. Treiber, R.K.: System programming: Coping with parallelism. Technical Report RJ 5118, IBM Almaden Research Center (1986)
4. Michael, M.M.: Hazard pointers: Safe memory reclamation for lock-free objects. IEEE Trans. Parallel Distrib. Syst. 15(6), 491–504 (2004)
5. Parkinson, M., Bornat, R., O'Hearn, P.: Modular verification of a non-blocking stack. SIGPLAN Not. 42(1), 297–302 (2007)
6. Reif, W., Schellhorn, G., Stenzel, K., Balser, M.: Structured specifications and interactive proofs with KIV. In: Bibel, W., Schmitt, P. (eds.) Automated Deduction—A Basis for Applications. Systems and Implementation Techniques, vol. II, pp. 13–39. Kluwer Academic Publishers, Dordrecht (1998)
7. Tofan, B., Schellhorn, G., Reif, W.: Verifying a stack with hazard pointers in temporal logic. Technical Report 2011-08, Universität Augsburg (2011), http://opus.bibliothek.uni-augsburg.de/volltexte/2011/1717/
8. KIV. Presentation of proofs for concurrent algorithms (2011), http://www.informatik.uni-augsburg.de/swt/projects/lock-free.html
9. Moszkowski, B.: Executing Temporal Logic Programs. Cambr. Univ. Press, Cambridge (1986)
10. de Roever, W.P., de Boer, F., Hannemann, U., Hooman, J., Lakhnech, Y., Poel, M., Zwiers, J.: Concurrency Verification: Introduction to Compositional and Noncompositional Methods. Cambridge Tracts in Theoretical Computer Science, vol. 54. Cambridge University Press, Cambridge (2001)
11. Burstall, R.M.: Program proving as hand simulation with a little induction. Information Processing 74, 309–312 (1974)

12. Bäumler, S., Balser, M., Nafz, F., Reif, W., Schellhorn, G.: Interactive verification of concurrent systems using symbolic execution. AI Communications 23(2,3), 285–307 (2010)
13. Schellhorn, G., Tofan, B., Ernst, G., Reif, W.: Interleaved programs and rely-guarantee reasoning with ITL. In: Proc. of TIME. IEEE, CPS (to appear, 2011)
14. Bäumler, S., Schellhorn, G., Tofan, B., Reif, W.: Proving linearizability with temporal logic. In: Formal Aspects of Computing (FAC) (2009), appeared online first http://www.springerlink.com/content/7507m59834066h04/
15. Tofan, B., Bäumler, S., Schellhorn, G., Reif, W.: Temporal logic verification of lock-freedom. In: Bolduc, C., Desharnais, J., Ktari, B. (eds.) MPC 2010. LNCS, vol. 6120, pp. 377–396. Springer, Heidelberg (2010)
16. Jones, C.B.: Specification and design of (parallel) programs. In: Proceedings of IFIP 1983, pp. 321–332. North-Holland, Amsterdam (1983)
17. Doherty, S., Groves, L., Luchangco, V., Moir, M.: Formal verification of a practical lock-free queue algorithm. In: de Frutos-Escrig, D., Núñez, M. (eds.) FORTE 2004. LNCS, vol. 3235, pp. 97–114. Springer, Heidelberg (2004)
18. Fu, M., Li, Y., Feng, X., Shao, Z., Zhang, Y.: Reasoning about optimistic concurrency using a program logic for history. In: Gastin, P., Laroussinie, F. (eds.) CONCUR 2010. LNCS, vol. 6269, pp. 388–402. Springer, Heidelberg (2010)
19. Derrick, J., Schellhorn, G., Wehrheim, H.: Verifying linearisabilty with potential linearisation points. In: Proc. Formal Methods (to appear, 2011)

Ambiguity of Unary Symmetric Difference NFAs

Brink van der Merwe, Lynette van Zijl, and Jaco Geldenhuys*

Department of Computer Science
Stellenbosch University, Private Bag X1, 7602 Matieland, South Africa
{abvdm,jaco}@cs.sun.ac.za, lvzijl@sun.ac.za

Abstract. Okhotin [9] showed an exponential trade-off in the conversion from nondeterministic unary finite automata to unambiguous nondeterministic unary finite automata. In this paper, we consider the trade-off in the case of unary symmetric difference finite automata to finitely ambiguous unary symmetric difference finite automata. Surprisingly, the trade-off is linear in the number of states of the finite automaton. In particular, for every n-state unary nondeterministic symmetric difference finite automaton, there is an equivalent finitely ambiguous n-state unary symmetric difference nondeterministic finite automaton. We also note other relevant ambiguity issues in the unary case, such as the ambiguity of k-deterministic finite automata.

Keywords: nondeterminism, ambiguity.

1 Introduction

Symmetric difference nondeterministic finite automata ($\oplus$-NFAs) are well-suited to the investigation of periodic or cyclic behaviour in regular languages. The succinctness of $\oplus$-NFAs has been investigated in some detail [15], but little work has been done on the language-theoretic properties of $\oplus$-NFAs. In this work, we therefore consider the issue of the *ambiguity* of unary $\oplus$-NFAs.

The ambiguity of a nondeterministic finite automaton (NFA) M refers to the maximum number of different accepting paths of M for all the words in the language accepted by M. For example, if M has only one accepting path for any word, then M is unambiguous. Or, M may have no more than c accepting paths for any word (with c a constant), in which case M is finitely ambiguous. Similarly, M may be polynomially or exponentially ambiguous, if the number of accepting paths is at most polynomial or exponential in the number of letters in an accepted word. The ambiguity of NFAs has been extensively investigated (see for example [5,6,10]), and recently Okhotin [9] considered the difference between unary NFAs and NFAs with larger alphabets as far as ambiguity is concerned.

In previous work [17] we investigated the ambiguity of $\oplus$-NFAs (as opposed to the ambiguity of traditional NFAs). We showed the existence of families of $\oplus$-NFAs for each ambiguity class, and also considered the descriptional complexity of ambiguous $\oplus$-NFAs. In particular, we showed that for each ambiguity class,

---

* This research was supported by NRF grant #69872.

A. Cerone and P. Pihlajasaari (Eds.): ICTAC 2011, LNCS 6916, pp. 256–266, 2011.
© Springer-Verlag Berlin Heidelberg 2011

there exists an n-state binary $\oplus$-NFA for which the minimal equivalent DFA has $O(2^n)$ states. In this work, we specifically consider the ambiguity of *unary* $\oplus$-NFAs. Here, we are interested in the state trade-off between equivalent finitely ambiguous unary $\oplus$-NFAs and unary $\oplus$-NFAs falling in any other ambiguity class. Okhotin [9] showed, for traditional NFAs, an exponential trade-off between unary NFAs and unary unambiguous NFAs. Surprisingly, quite different results hold for $\oplus$-NFAs, and we shall show that for any unary n-state $\oplus$-NFA, there is an equivalent unary finitely ambiguous $\oplus$-NFA with n states.

The remainder of this article is organised as follows: Sect. 2 gives background and definitions, and specifically establishes the algebraic background required in the rest of the paper. In Sect. 3 we prove the state trade-off between unary $\oplus$-NFAs and unary finitely ambiguous $\oplus$-NFAs. The next section notes some related results, such as the ambiguity of k-deterministic finite automata. We conclude in Sect. 5.

2   Background

$\oplus$-NFAs were defined in [15], and Vuillemin and Gama give an overview of the mathematical basis for $\oplus$-NFAs [14]. We therefore only briefly summarize the necessary definitions and background. We assume that the reader has a basic knowledge of automata theory and formal languages, as for example in [12], and a background in linear algebra, as for example in [11]. Note that symmetric difference is used in the usual set theoretic sense: for any two sets A and B, the symmetric difference of A and B is defined as $A \oplus B = (A \cup B) \setminus (A \cap B)$. Also note that for n sets $A_1, \ldots, A_n$, the expression $A_1 \oplus \ldots \oplus A_n$ is equal to the set of elements appearing in an odd number of the sets $A_1, \ldots, A_n$.

2.1   Definition of $\oplus$-NFAs

Definition 1. *A $\oplus$-NFA M is a 5-tuple $M = (Q, \Sigma, \delta, Q_0, F)$, where Q is the finite non-empty set of states, Σ is the finite non-empty input alphabet, $Q_0 \subseteq Q$ is the set of start states, $F \subseteq Q$ is the set of final states and δ is the transition function such that $\delta : Q \times \Sigma \to 2^Q$.*   □

The transition function δ can be extended to $\delta : 2^Q \times \Sigma \to 2^Q$ by defining

$$\delta(A, a) = \bigoplus_{q \in A} \delta(q, a)$$

for any $a \in \Sigma$ and $A \in 2^Q$. The transition function of the $\oplus$-NFA can be extended to $\delta^* : 2^Q \times \Sigma^* \to 2^Q$ by defining $\delta^*(A, \epsilon) = A$ and $\delta^*(A, aw) = \delta^*(\delta(A, a), w)$ for any $a \in \Sigma$, $w \in \Sigma^*$ and $A \in 2^Q$.

Note that, if the size of the alphabet is one (that is, $|\Sigma| = 1$), then the $\oplus$-NFA is called a *unary* $\oplus$-NFA.

Definition 2. *Let M be a $\oplus$-NFA $M = (Q, \Sigma, \delta, Q_0, F)$, and let w be a word in Σ^*. Then M accepts w if and only if $|F \cap \delta(Q_0, w)| \bmod 2 \neq 0$.*   □

For any word $w = w_0 w_1 \ldots w_k \in \Sigma^*$ read by a $\oplus$-NFA M, there is at least one associated sequence of states $s_0, s_1, \ldots, s_{k+1}$ such that $\delta(s_i, w_i) = s_{i+1}$. Such a sequence of states is a *path* for the word w. All possible paths on the word w can be combined into an *execution tree* of M. A path in the execution tree is an *accepting path* if it ends in a final state. It is important to note that in the execution tree of a $\oplus$-NFA, if there is an even number of occurrences of a state s_i on level i, then those states cancel out under the symmetric difference operation, and those paths terminate. If an odd number of occurrences of a state s_i occurs on level i, then none of the s_i cancel out and all their paths remain in the execution tree.

In other words, a $\oplus$-NFA accepts a word w by parity — if there is an odd number of accepting paths for w in the execution tree, then w is accepted; else it is rejected. This parity acceptance is motivated by the algebraic foundations of $\oplus$-NFAs, where unary $\oplus$-NFAs correspond to pseudo-noise sequences [4].

Example 1. Let $M = (\{q_1, q_2, q_3\}, \{a\}, \delta, \{q_1\}, \{q_3\})$ be a $\oplus$-NFA where δ is given by

δ	a
q_1	$\{q_2\}$
q_2	$\{q_3\}$
q_3	$\{q_1, q_3\}$.

Figure 1 shows a graphical representation of M; note that there is no visual difference from a traditional NFA. To find the DFA M' equivalent to M, we apply the subset construction using the symmetric difference operation instead of union. The transition function δ' of M' is

δ'	a
$[\,q_1\,]$	$[\,q_2\,]$
$[\,q_2\,]$	$[\,q_3\,]$
$*\ [\,q_3\,]$	$[\,q_1, q_3\,]$
$*\ [\,q_1, q_3\,]$	$[\,q_1, q_2, q_3\,]$
$*\ [\,q_1, q_2, q_3\,]$	$[\,q_1, q_2\,]$
$[\,q_1, q_2\,]$	$[\,q_2, q_3\,]$
$*\ [\,q_2, q_3\,]$	$[\,q_1\,]$.

$\square$

Note that each accepting state is marked by a '$*$'.

It is easy to see that any unary $\oplus$-NFA is an autonomous linear machine (see [13,15] for a formal exposition). As such, one can encode the transition table of a unary $\oplus$-NFA M as a binary matrix $\mathbf{A}$:

$$a_{ji} = \begin{cases} 1 \text{ if } q_j \in \delta(q_i, a) \\ 0 \text{ otherwise,} \end{cases}$$

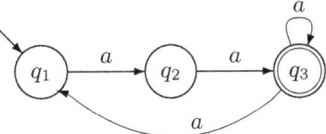

Fig. 1. The $\oplus$-NFA for Example 1

and successive matrix multiplications in the Galois field $GF(2)$ reflect the subset construction on M.

$\mathbf{A}$ is called the *characteristic matrix* of M, and $c(x) = \det(\mathbf{A} - x\mathbf{I})$ is known as its characteristic polynomial.

Similarly, we can encode any set of states $X \subseteq Q$ as an n-entry row vector $\boldsymbol{v}$ by defining

$$v_i = \begin{cases} 1 \text{ if } q_i \in X \\ 0 \text{ otherwise} . \end{cases}$$

Note that we place an arbitrary but fixed order on the elements of Q. We refer to $\boldsymbol{v}$ as the *vector encoding* of X, and to X as the *set encoding* of $\boldsymbol{v}$.

If $\boldsymbol{y}$ encodes the initial states of a $\oplus$-NFA M, and $\mathbf{A}$ is its characteristic matrix, then $\mathbf{A}\boldsymbol{y}^{\mathrm{T}}$ encodes the states reachable from the initial state after reading one letter, $\mathbf{A}^2\boldsymbol{y}^{\mathrm{T}}$ encodes the states reachable after two letters, and in general $\mathbf{A}^k\boldsymbol{y}^{\mathrm{T}}$ encodes the states reachable after k letters. If $\boldsymbol{z}$ encodes the final states of M, then standard linear algebra shows the following:

$$M \text{ accepts } a^k \text{ if and only if } \boldsymbol{z}\mathbf{A}^k\boldsymbol{y}^{\mathrm{T}} = 1.$$

Example 2. Consider the $\oplus$-NFA in Example 1. Its characteristic matrix is

$$\mathbf{A} = \begin{bmatrix} 0\,0\,1 \\ 1\,0\,0 \\ 0\,1\,1 \end{bmatrix}$$

and its characteristic polynomial is $c(x) = x^3 + x^2 + 1$. Interested readers may note that $c(x)$ is a primitive polynomial in $GF(2)$. If we encode the start state as a column vector $\boldsymbol{y}^T$, with only the first component of $\boldsymbol{y}$ equal to one, and compute $\mathbf{A}^k\boldsymbol{y}^T$, we end up with the k-th entry in the on-the-fly subset construction on M. For example, with the start state q_1 encoded as $\boldsymbol{y} = [\,1\,0\,0\,]$, we see that $\mathbf{A}^4$ is given by

$$\mathbf{A}^4 = \begin{bmatrix} 1\,1\,0 \\ 1\,1\,1 \\ 1\,0\,1 \end{bmatrix},$$

and hence $\mathbf{A}^4\boldsymbol{y}^T$ is given by $[\,1\,1\,1\,]$. This corresponds to the state $[\,q_1, q_2, q_3\,]$, which is reached after four applications of the subset construction on M. Similarly, $\mathbf{A}^6\boldsymbol{y}^T$ is given by $[\,0\,1\,1\,]$, which corresponds to $[\,q_2, q_3\,]$. $\qquad\square$

2.2   Analysis of $\oplus$-NFA Behaviour

In [15] we formally showed that the state behaviour of a unary $\oplus$-NFA is the same as that of a linear feedback shift register (LFSR). The similarity is intuitively straightforward, as an LFSR is a linear machine over $GF(2)$, and we can encode a unary $\oplus$-NFA as a linear machine over $GF(2)$ as shown above. This correspondence means that we can exploit the wealth of literature on LFSRs to analyse the behaviour of unary $\oplus$-NFAs, and in particular their cyclic behaviour (see, for example, [3] or [13]).

Because a unary $\oplus$-NFA is characterized by a matrix in $GF(2)$, one can perform a change of basis without changing the accepted language. It is precisely this observation that we use in the proof of the next theorem.

Theorem 1. *Let $M = (Q, \{a\}, \delta, Q_0, F)$ be a unary n-state $\oplus$-NFA that accepts a non-empty language L. Then for any non-empty subset of states $X \subseteq Q$ there exists unary $\oplus$-NFAs M' and M'', both accepting L, such that:*

1. $M' = (Q, \{a\}, \delta', X, F')$, *and*
2. $M'' = (Q, \{a\}, \delta'', Q_0'', X)$.

Proof. Both claims are based on the same principle; we only show the first. Let s, f, and x be the vector encodings of sets Q_0, F, and X, respectively, and let $\mathbf{A}$ be the characteristic matrix of M. Choose a non-singular matrix[1] $\mathbf{P}$ such that $x^T = \mathbf{P}s^T$. Note that Q_0 and F are non-empty sets, since L is non-empty, and thus s and f are non-zero. Let $y = f\mathbf{P}^{-1}$, and let $\mathbf{B} = \mathbf{P}\mathbf{A}\mathbf{P}^{-1}$. Let F' be the set encoding of y and define δ' by

$$q_i \in \delta'(q_j, a) \text{ if and only if } b_{ij} = 1.$$

Then

$$M' \text{ accepts } a^k$$
$$\Leftrightarrow y\mathbf{B}^k x^T = 1$$
$$\Leftrightarrow (f\mathbf{P}^{-1})(\mathbf{P}\mathbf{A}\mathbf{P}^{-1})^k(\mathbf{P}s^T) = 1$$
$$\Leftrightarrow f\mathbf{A}^k s^T = 1$$
$$\Leftrightarrow M \text{ accepts } a^k.$$

$\square$

In essence, the technique in Theorem 1 changes the basis of the characteristic matrix. This makes it possible to transform any unary $\oplus$-NFA into an equivalent automaton while controlling either the choice of start states, final states, or (nonsingular) characteristic matrix.

---

[1] Such a matrix $\mathbf{P}$ must exist. We can obtain $\mathbf{P}$ as the product $\mathbf{P_1}\mathbf{P_2}^{-1}$, where $\mathbf{P_1}$ and $\mathbf{P_2}$ are non-singular matrices obtained as follows: Denote by e_1 the vector with a 1 in the first component and 0's in all the other components. Let $\mathbf{P_1}$ and $\mathbf{P_2}$ be non-singular matrices such that $\mathbf{P_1}e_1^T = x^T$ and $\mathbf{P_2}e_1^T = s^T$. We construct for example $\mathbf{P_1}$ (and similarly $\mathbf{P_2}$) by setting the first column of $\mathbf{P_1}$ to be equal to x^T and then select the remaining columns in any way such that the column vectors of $\mathbf{P_1}$ are linearly independent.

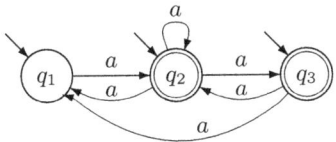

Fig. 2. The $\oplus$-NFA from Example 3

Example 3. Consider again the $\oplus$-NFA M in Example 1. To transform it to an automaton where all of the states are start states, we solve $\boldsymbol{x} = \mathbf{P}\boldsymbol{s}^{\mathrm{T}}$. We know from the definition of M that $\boldsymbol{s} = [1\ 0\ 0]$ and we want $\boldsymbol{x} = [1\ 1\ 1]$. We can take for example

$$\mathbf{P} = \begin{bmatrix} 1\ 0\ 0 \\ 1\ 1\ 0 \\ 1\ 1\ 1 \end{bmatrix} \quad \text{and} \quad \mathbf{P}^{-1} = \begin{bmatrix} 1\ 0\ 0 \\ 1\ 1\ 0 \\ 0\ 1\ 1 \end{bmatrix}$$

and therefore

$$\mathbf{B} = \mathbf{P}\mathbf{A}\mathbf{P}^{-1} = \begin{bmatrix} 0\ 1\ 1 \\ 1\ 1\ 1 \\ 0\ 1\ 0 \end{bmatrix}$$

and the vector encoding for the final states is $\boldsymbol{y} = \boldsymbol{f}\mathbf{P}^{-1} = [0\ 1\ 1]$. The resulting automaton is shown in Figure 2. One can also verify the fact that the language is not changed by the change in basis, by calculating the DFA corresponding to the new $\oplus$-NFA:

δ'	a
$[\,q_1, q_2, q_3\,]$	$[\,q_2, q_3\,]$
$[\,q_2, q_3\,]$	$[\,q_3\,]$
$*\ [\,q_3\,]$	$[\,q_1, q_2\,]$
$*\ [\,q_1, q_2\,]$	$[\,q_1, q_3\,]$
$*\ [\,q_1, q_3\,]$	$[\,q_1\,]$
$[\,q_1\,]$	$[\,q_2\,]$
$*\ [\,q_2\,]$	$[\,q_1, q_2, q_3\,].$

It is easy to check that this DFA is isomorphic to the DFA in Example 1.   □

2.3   Ambiguity

We briefly state the formal definitions for ambiguity.

Definition 3. Unambiguous: *An NFA or $\oplus$-NFA is said to be unambiguous if every word in the language is accepted with at most one accepting path.*

Definition 4. Finitely ambiguous: *An NFA or $\oplus$-NFA is said to be finitely ambiguous if every word in the language is accepted with at most k accepting paths, where k is a positive integer.*

Definition 5. Polynomially ambiguous: *An NFA or ⊕-NFA is said to be polynomially ambiguous if every word in the language is accepted with at most k accepting paths, where k is bound polynomially in the length of the input word.*

Definition 6. Exponentially ambiguous: *An NFA or ⊕-NFA is said to be exponentially ambiguous if every word in the language is accepted with at most k accepting paths, where k is bounded exponentially in the length of the input word.*

Ambiguity for a given NFA or ⊕-NFA can be visually demonstrated by drawing the execution tree of the corresponding automaton. Given an NFA or ⊕-NFA M, we assume that the root is on level 0 of the execution tree, and is a start state of M. Note that, if M has multiple start states, then one considers the forest of execution trees, where the root of each tree is one of the start states of M.

3 Ambiguity of Unary ⊕-NFAs

It is known that the conversion of a traditional n-state NFA to a DFA has an upper bound of $O(2^n)$ states, and this bound is tight [7,8]. This does not hold in the case of unary NFAs, where the bound is $g(n) + n^2$ states, where $g(n)$ is Landau's function [1]. In the case of unary n-state ⊕-NFAs, we recall a tight upper bound of $2^n - 1$ for the ⊕-NFA to DFA conversion [16].

Okhotin [9] showed that the $g(n) + n^2$ bound also holds for the unary NFA to unary unambiguous NFA trade-off. Surprisingly, the unary ⊕-NFA to unary finitely ambiguous ⊕-NFA trade-off is simply linear – any unary n-state ⊕-NFA has an equivalent n-state finitely ambiguous ⊕-NFA, as we show in detail below.

For any state in a ⊕-NFA, its *indegree* denotes the number of transitions entering the state in its graphical representation.

Theorem 2. *Any unary n-state ⊕-NFA such that each state has indegree at most two, is finitely ambiguous.*

Proof. Let N be any unary ⊕-NFA such that each state has indegree at most two. We have an execution tree associated with each initial state in N, but it is enough to show that there are finitely many accepting paths for a given word in each of the execution trees. Thus we may in fact assume that we have only one initial state in N and hence a single execution tree. First we show by induction that each state appears at most once on a given level in the execution tree. This is certainly true at the root of the tree where we have only the initial state. Assume the result for level i in the execution tree and consider level $i + 1$, and let q be any state in N. Since the indegree of q is at most two, precisely one of the following three statements hold:

– there is no transition from a state at level i to state q, and therefore state q is not present at level $i + 1$;
– there is a transition from a single state at level i to state q;

– there are transitions from precisely two states at level i to state q, and thus by definition of an $\oplus$-NFA, state q is not present at level $i + 1$.

We thus conclude that each state appears at most once on a given level in the execution tree. Since we therefore have only finitely many acceptance states at each level in the execution tree, we conclude that N is finitely ambiguous.   □

Theorem 3. *Let M be any unary $\oplus$-NFA. Then there exists a finitely ambiguous unary $\oplus$-NFA N, accepting the same language as M, and also with the same number of states as M.*

Proof. Let $\mathbf{A}$ be the characteristic matrix of M.

First recall from linear algebra that the companion matrix of the monic polynomial $p(x) = c_0 + c_1 x + \ldots + c_{n-1} x^{n-1} + x^n$ over $GF(2)$ is the square matrix

$$\mathbf{C}(p) = \begin{bmatrix} 0 & 0 & \ldots & 0 & c_0 \\ 1 & 0 & \ldots & 0 & c_1 \\ 0 & 1 & \ldots & 0 & c_2 \\ \vdots & \vdots & & \vdots & \vdots \\ 0 & 0 & \ldots & 1 & c_{n-1} \end{bmatrix}.$$

A classic result from linear algebra (see [11], Theorem 7.14), states that $\mathbf{A}$ has a rational canonical form with entries from $GF(2)$. More precisely, there exists an invertible matrix $\mathbf{Q}$ such that $\mathbf{B} = \mathbf{Q}^{-1}\mathbf{A}\mathbf{Q} = \operatorname{diag}[\mathbf{L}(f_1), \mathbf{L}(f_2), \ldots, \mathbf{L}(f_s)]$, where $\mathbf{L}(f_i)$ is the companion matrix for a monic polynomial f_i. By diag $[\mathbf{A_1}, \mathbf{A_2}, \ldots, \mathbf{A_s}]$, with the $\mathbf{A}_i$'s square matrices, we denote the matrix with the $\mathbf{A}_i$'s on the diagonal and all other entries equal to 0. In our context, the important property of the matrix $\operatorname{diag}[\mathbf{L}(f_1), \mathbf{L}(f_2), \ldots, \mathbf{L}(f_s)]$ is that the indegree of each state of a $\oplus$-NFA N, with characteristic matrix $\operatorname{diag}[\mathbf{L}(f_1), \mathbf{L}(f_2), \ldots, \mathbf{L}(f_s)]$, must be at most two. One can see this by noting that we have at most two non-zero entries in each row of $\operatorname{diag}[\mathbf{L}(f_1), \mathbf{L}(f_2), \ldots, \mathbf{L}(f_s)]$. We thus apply a change of basis (by using $\mathbf{Q}$) to $\mathbf{A}$ to obtain the characteristic matrix $\mathbf{B}$ of a $\oplus$-NFA N, and also to the initial and accepting vectors of M to obtain the initial and accepting vectors for N. Since a change of basis preserves the language accepted by a $\oplus$-NFA, M and N accept the same language. Note that M and N will also have the same number of states, and from the previous result we have that N is finitely ambiguous.   □

4   Other Ambiguity Results

There are a number of other results that follow from Theorem 2 in the previous section, in particular for the complement of a language, and for k-deterministic $\oplus$-NFAs.

We note that for any n-state unary $\oplus$-NFA M which accepts a language L, it is possible to construct an $n + 1$-state unary $\oplus$-NFA M' such that M' accepts the complement $\overline{L}$. This is in contrast to traditional unary NFAs [9], where the state complexity of complementation for unambiguous unary finite automata lies between the bounds $\frac{1}{42}n\sqrt{n}$ (for $n \geq 867$) and $e^{\Theta(\sqrt[3]{n \ln^2 n})}$.

Theorem 4. *Let M be a unary $\oplus$-NFA accepting the language L. Then there is an $n+1$-state unary $\oplus$-NFA M' such that M' accepts $\overline{L}$.*

Proof. By construction. Let $M = (Q, \{a\}, \delta, Q_0, F)$ such that $Q = \{q_1, \ldots, q_n\}$. We introduce a new state $q_0 \notin Q$. Define $M' = (Q \cup \{q_0\}, \{a\}, \delta', Q_0 \cup \{q_0\}, F \cup \{q_0\})$, where $\delta'(q_i, a) = \delta(q_i, a)$ when $i > 0$ and $\delta'(q_0, a) = \{q_0\}$. The DFA equivalent to M' is isomorphic to that of M, and during the subset construction the subsets are identical, except that q_0 is added to every single subset. The execution of M' is identical to that of M, except that an independent linear branch consisting of q_0 states is added "on the side".

Suppose that M accepts the word $w = a^k$. This means that there is an odd number of final states on level k of M's execution tree. On the other hand, in M''s execution tree there is one extra state (q_0) on level k, which therefore contains an even number of final states. Hence M' does not accept w.

The same argument shows that if M does not accept the word $w = a^m$, then M' *does* accept w. Hence M' accepts the language $\overline{L}$.   □

Theorem 5. *Assume the language L is accepted by an n-state unary finitely ambiguous $\oplus$-NFA M. Then there is an $n+1$-state unary $\oplus$-NFA M' that accepts $\overline{L}$.*

Proof. Directly from Theorem 2.   □

We now consider the ambiguity of k-deterministic unary $\oplus$-FAs. A k-deterministic FA (k-DFA) or $\oplus$-FA (k-$\oplus$-DFA) is a deterministic finite automaton, except that it has multiple initial states. Hence the only nondeterminism in a k-DFA occurs in its multiple initial states.

Definition 7. *A k-DFA M is a 5-tuple $M = (Q, \Sigma, \delta, Q_0, F)$, where Q is the finite non-empty set of states, Σ is the finite non-empty input alphabet, $Q_0 \subseteq Q$ is the set of start states, $F \subseteq Q$ is the set of final states and δ is the transition function such that $\delta : Q \times \Sigma \to Q$.*   □

Note that, as before, the difference between a traditional k-DFA and a k-$\oplus$-DFA lies in the application of the subset construction to get the equivalent DFA (without multiple initial states).

It is to be expected that a unary k-DFA should be either unambiguous or finitely ambiguous, and this is indeed the case both for the traditional k-DFA and the k-$\oplus$-DFA:

Theorem 6. *Any unary k-DFA or k-$\oplus$-DFA is finitely ambiguous, with the constant for the finite ambiguity no more than $|Q_0|$.*

Proof. The multiple initial states lead to a forest of disconnected execution trees, such that each tree is a single deterministic branch. In the case of k-DFAs the ambiguity is determined by the number of possible final states on each level, which is bounded below by zero and above by $|Q_0|$. Note that the number of trees stay constant. Hence, the k-DFA is finitely ambiguous.

In the case of k-$\oplus$-DFAs, the number of deterministic trees in the forest of disconnected execution trees cannot be more than $|Q_0|$, but may become less if an even number of identical states occur on the same level. The result holds by the same argument as above.   □

It is interesting to note, however, that there exists a family $\{M_n\}_{n \geq 2}$ of k-DFAs that are finitely ambiguous when considered as k-DFAs, but are unambiguous when considered as k-$\oplus$-DFAs.

Theorem 7. *There exists a family $\{M_n\}_{n \geq 2}$ of unary k-DFAs that are finitely ambiguous when considered as k-DFAs, but are unambiguous when considered as k-$\oplus$-DFAs.*

Proof. By construction. Let $M_n = (Q, \{a\}, \delta, Q_0, F)$ be defined by $Q = \{q_1, \ldots, q_{n-1}\}$, $Q_0 = Q$, $F = \{q_{n-1}\}$ and $\delta(q_i, a) = q_{i+1}$ for $1 \leq i < n - 1$, and $\delta(q_{n-1}, a) = q_{n-2}$.

Consider first the k-DFA case. The forest of execution trees contains $n = |Q_0|$ disconnected trees with no branches. Hence, on any level, there are exactly n states. The transition function ensures that each tree has the form $q_i \rightarrow q_{i+1} \rightarrow \cdots q_{n-2} \rightarrow q_{n-1} \rightarrow q_{n-2} \rightarrow q_{n-1} \ldots$. In other words, each tree consists of a single branch with consecutive states, until the last two states alternate indefinitely. Now, since all the elements in Q_0 are distinct, the trees all reach the state q_{n-1} within $n - 1$ steps. Hence, from step n onwards, there are at most $|Q_0|$ final states at any level, and hence the k-DFA is finitely ambiguous.

In the case of the k-$\oplus$-DFA, we note that on level one of the execution tree, there are n distinct states $\{q_1, q_2, \ldots, q_{n-1}\}$, and hence one final state. On level two, states q_{n-3} and q_{n-1} both result in state q_{n-2}, and symmetric difference causes the trees with state q_{n-2} to terminate. This process continues with the other branches, until only one tree remains which alternates between states q_{n-1} and q_{n-2}, or which ends in an empty set of states. Hence, the k-$\oplus$-DFA is unambiguous.   □

5   Conclusion and Future Work

We showed that, for any n-state unary $\oplus$-NFA, there is an equivalent n-state unary $\oplus$-NFA which is finitely ambiguous. This implies that, for unary regular languages, there are no languages which are strictly polynomially or strictly exponentially ambiguous with $\oplus$-NFAs. This result also holds for traditional unary NFAs, and a further avenue of investigation is to determine whether any kind of unary NFA (such as a $\cap$-NFA or XNOR-NFA) must be at most finitely ambiguous.

It also remains to investigate ambiguity issues in more detail for non-unary languages.

References

1. Chrobak, M.: Finite automata and unary languages. Theoretical Computer Science 47(3), 149–158 (1986), erratum appeared as [2]
2. Chrobak, M.: Errata on "Finite automata and unary languages". Theoretical Computer Science 302(1-3), 497–498 (2003)
3. Dornhoff, L., Hohn, F.: Applied Modern Algebra. Macmillan Publishing Company, Basingstoke (1978)
4. Goresky, M., Klapper, A.: Pseudonoise sequences based on algebraic feedback shift registers. IEEE Transactions on Information Theory 52(4), 1649–1662 (2006)
5. Leung, H.: Separating exponentially ambiguous finite automata from polynomially ambiguous finite automata. SIAM Journal of Computing 27(4), 1073–1082 (1998)
6. Leung, H.: Descriptional complexity of NFA of different ambiguity. International Journal of Foundations of Computer Science 16(5), 975–984 (2005)
7. Meyer, A.R., Fischer, M.J.: Economy of description by automata, grammars, and formal systems. In: Proceedings of the 12 Annual IEEE Symposium on Switching and Automata Theory, pp. 188–191 (October 1971)
8. Moore, F.R.: On the bounds for state-set size in the proofs of equivalence between deterministic, nondeterministic and two-way finite automata by deterministic automata. IEEE Transactions on Computing C-20(10), 1211–1219 (1971)
9. Okhotin, A.: Unambiguous finite automata over a unary alphabet. In: Hliněný, P., Kučera, A. (eds.) MFCS 2010. LNCS, vol. 6281, pp. 556–567. Springer, Heidelberg (2010)
10. Ravikumar, B., Ibarra, O.H.: Relating the type of ambiguity of finite automata to the succinctness of their representation. SIAM Journal of Computing 18(6), 1263–1282 (1989)
11. Roman, S.: Advanced Linear Algebra. Springer, Heidelberg (1992)
12. Sipser, M.: Introduction to the Theory of Computation. International Thomson Publishing (1996)
13. Stone, H.: Discrete Mathematical Structures. Science Research Associates (1973)
14. Vuillemin, J., Gama, N.: Efficient equivalence and minimization for nondeterministic XOR automata. Tech. rep., INRIA (December 2009)
15. van Zijl, L.: Generalized Nondeterminism and the Succinct Representation of Regular Languages. Ph.D. thesis, Stellenbosch University (November 1997)
16. van Zijl, L.: Magic numbers for symmetric difference NFAs. International Journal of Foundations of Computer Science 16(5), 1027–1038 (2005)
17. van Zijl, L., Geldenhuys, J.: Descriptional complexity of ambiguity in symmetric difference NFAs. Journal of Universal Computer Science (accepted for publication, 2011)

Author Index

GPSR Compliance

The European Union's (EU) General Product Safety Regulation (GPSR) is a set of rules that requires consumer products to be safe and our obligations to ensure this.

If you have any concerns about our products, you can contact us on ProductSafety@springernature.com

In case Publisher is established outside the EU, the EU authorized representative is:

Springer Nature Customer Service Center GmbH
Europaplatz 3
69115 Heidelberg, Germany

Batch number: 09504227

Printed by Printforce, the Netherlands